Global Warming and Other Eco-Myths

COMPETITIVE ENTERPRISE INSTITUTE
RONALD BAILEY, EDITOR

Global Warming and Other Eco-Myths

*How the Environmental Movement
Uses False Science to Scare Us to Death*

FORUM
An Imprint of Prima Publishing

Published by Prima Publishing, Roseville, California. Member of the Crown Publishing Group, a division of Random House, Inc., New York.

FORUM and colophon are trademarks of Random House, Inc. PRIMA PUBLISHING and colophon are trademarks of Random House, Inc., registered with the United States Patent and Trademark Office.

Library of Congress Cataloging-in-Publication Data
Global warming and other eco-myths : how the environmental movement uses false science to scare us to death / edited by Ronald Bailey
    p.   cm.
Includes bibliographical references and index.
ISBN 0-7615-3660-4
1. Deep ecology. 2. Environmentalism I. Bailey, Ronald.
GE195 .G58   2002
363.7—dc21   2002066284

02 03 04 05 06 QQ 10 9 8 7 6 5 4 3 2
Printed in the United States of America

First Edition

Visit us online at www.primapublishing.com

CONTENTS

FIGURES AND TABLES

CONTRIBUTORS

Jonathan H. Adler is an assistant professor of law at the Case Western Reserve University School of Law where he teaches environmental and constitutional law. Prior to joining the faculty at Case Western, Professor Adler clerked for the Honorable David B. Sentelle on the U.S. Court of Appeals for the District of Columbia Circuit. From 1991 to 2000, Prof. Adler worked at the Competitive Enterprise Institute, a free market research and advocacy group in Washington, D.C., where he directed CEI's environmental studies program. Prof. Adler is the author or editor of three books on environmental policy, including *Environmentalism at the Crossroads*, and his articles on environmental and regulatory policy have appeared in numerous publications from *Environmental Law* and *Supreme Court Economic Review* to the *Wall Street Journal* and *Washington Post*. He holds B.A. magna cum laude from Yale University and a J.D. summa cum laude from the George Mason University School of Law.

Ronald Bailey is science correspondent for *Reason*, a national monthly magazine on politics and culture. He writes a weekly online column dealing with science and technology policy for www.reason .com. Previously, he produced several weekly national public television series including *Think Tank* and *TechnoPolitics*, as well as several documentaries for PBS television and ABC News. Mr. Bailey was the 1993 Warren T. Brookes Fellow in Environmental Journalism at the Competitive Enterprise Institute. He was a staff writer for *Forbes* magazine (1987 to 1990) covering economic, scientific, and business topics. His articles and reviews have appeared in the *Wall Street Journal*, the *Washington Post*, *Commentary*, the *New York Times Book*

Review, The Public Interest, Smithsonian, National Review, Forbes, and *Reader's Digest.* He has lectured at numerous universities including Harvard University, Yale University, Morehouse University, the Massachusetts Institute of Technology, Rutgers University, the University of Virginia, McGill University, University of Alaska, and the Université de Québec. He is a member of the Society of Environmental Journalists and the American Society for Bioethics and Humanities. He is also an adjunct scholar at the Competitive Enterprise Institute and the Cato Institute. He edited *Earth Report 2000: Revisiting the True State of the Planet* (McGraw Hill, 1999), and is the author of *ECOSCAM: The False Prophets of Ecological Apocalypse* (St. Martin's Press, 1993). In 1995, he edited *The True State of the Planet* (The Free Press). He is the editor of this volume.

Dr. Norman E. Borlaug was awarded the Nobel Peace Prize in 1970 for launching the "Green Revolution" that dramatically raised agricultural productivity and saved millions of poor people around the world from famine. He now leads the Sasakawa-Global 2000 agriculture program, a joint venture between the Sasakawa Africa Association and The Carter Center's Global 2000 program. The Sasakawa-Global 2000 program works with more than 4,000,000 small-scale farmers in eleven sub-Saharan African countries. Now 88 years old, Dr. Borlaug was awarded his doctorate in plant pathology in 1942 by the University of Minnesota. He served at the Rockefeller Foundation as the scientist in charge of wheat improvement under the Cooperative Mexican Agricultural Program. With the establishment of the International Maize and Wheat Improvement Center (CIMMYT) in Mexico in 1964, he assumed leadership of the Wheat Program, a position he held until his official retirement in 1979. Since 1984, Dr. Borlaug has served at Texas A&M University as Distinguished Professor of International Agriculture.

Dr. John Christy received his Ph.D. in Climate Dynamics in 1987 from the University of Illinois. For the past two decades, he has investigated various aspects of the globe's climate as Professor of Atmospheric Science at the University of Alabama in Huntsville. He is also Alabama's State Climatologist and Director of the Earth System Science Center at UAH. He and Dr. Roy Spencer (also UAH) combined their talents to produce a satellite-based set of global temperature products that accurately depict temperature variations since 1979, earning the NASA Medal for Exceptional Scientific Achievement and a Special Award by the American Meteorological Society. Dr. Christy served as a contributor (1992, 1996) and lead author (2001) of the United Nations' Intergovernmental Panel on Climate Change assessments. He has appeared before several congressional committees to offer testimony on climate variability and change, and has been a member of National Research Council panels dealing with climate. Prior to his scientific career, Christy taught physics and chemistry as a missionary in Kenya.

Gregory Conko is Director of Food Safety Policy with the Competitive Enterprise Institute in Washington, D.C., where he specializes in issues of food and pharmaceutical drug safety regulation, and on the general treatment of health risks in public policy. He is also the Vice President and a co-founder of the AgBioWorld Foundation, a non-profit organization that provides information to teachers, journalists, policymakers, and the general public about developments in plant science, biotechnology, and sustainable agriculture. Mr. Conko frequently participates in international meetings on food safety and trade as a credentialed Non-Governmental Organization representative. His writings have appeared in journals, newspapers, and magazines, and he co-authored the chapter on appropriate regulation of genetically-engineered crops in the California Council on Science and Technology's January 2002 *Preliminary Report on the Benefits and Risks of Food Biotechnology*. Prior to joining CEI, Mr. Conko was a Research Associate with the Capital Research Center. He holds a bachelor's degree in Political Science and History from the American University.

Dr. Nicholas Eberstadt is the Henry Wendt Chair in Political Economy at AEI and is a member of Harvard University's Center for Population and Development Studies. He is also on the Board of Advisers of the National Bureau of Asian Research and the Statistical Assessment Service and is a member of the Environmental Literacy Council. He frequently serves as a consultant for the U.S. Census Bureau and other government organizations on such topics as demography, international development, and East Asian security. Mr.

Eberstadt has published over two hundred studies and articles in scholarly and popular journals, including *Foreign Affairs*, the *New York Review of Books*, *Commentary*, the *New Republic*, the *New York Times*, and the *Wall Street Journal*. His books include *Prosperous Paupers and Other Population Problems*, *The End of North Korea*, *The Tyranny of Numbers: Mismeasurement and Misrule*, *Korea Approaches Reunification*, and most recently, *Korea's Future and the Great Powers*.

Rakhi Gupta is a programme officer in Environment Management Capacity Building, a joint collaboration of World Bank and the Government of India. Prior to this, she has worked as a programme officer in Sustainable Development Networking Programme (India), a program funded jointly by United Nations Development Programme (UNDP) and International Development Research Centre (IDRC), and Canada, and implemented by Ministry of Environment and Forests (MoEF) India. She has also worked as a consultant with Environmental Resources Management (ERM) India in the Natural Resources Management and Social Development Group. She attained her postgraduate degree in Town and Country Planning from School of Planning and Architecture, New Delhi. Before joining ERM, as a program officer with a leading NGO, Asian Centre for Organisation, Research and Development (ACORD), she was responsible for the organization's projects on municipal solid waste management, low-cost sanitation, and safe drinking water use and research. She has also worked as a project scientist with the Centre for Atmospheric Sciences, Indian Institute of Technology (IIT), New Delhi. She has worked on community projects dealing with solid waste management strategies and sanitation services, and also need assessment for micro enterprise development, etc. She has research experience in policy analysis, especially in watershed management, privatization of water supplies, regional environmental profiling, and eco-labeling, etc.

John Jennrich is a fellow of the Institute for Energy Research, a nonprofit organization specializing in market-oriented approaches to energy and energy/environmental public policy issues. Jennrich has long specialized in reporting and analyzing energy issues. He has been editor of *Natural Gas Week* and *Natural Gas Week International*, two newsletters that he founded, and *The Oil Daily*. He was Washington editor of *Oil & Gas Journal*. He also was a senior editor for *Nation's Business* magazine and he served as vice president of corporate communications at Columbia Energy Group, a Fortune 500 company. He was the first journalist covering any subject to address scientists at Los Alamos National Laboratory. He also received the 1998 Award for Excellence in Written Journalism from the International Association for Energy Economics. Jennrich has a master's degree in journalism and a bachelor's degree in political science (minor in international affairs), both from the University of North Carolina at Chapel Hill. Jennrich also is a member of the National Press Club, International Association for Energy Economics, Capital Area Energy Association, and Washington Independent Writers.

Angela Logomasini is Director of Risk and Environmental Policy at the Competitive Enterprise Institute (CEI) where she conducts research and analysis on environmental regulatory issues. Logomasini is co-editor of CEI's book, *The Environmental Source*, and her articles have been published in the *Wall Street Journal*, the *New York Post*, the *Washington Times*, and other publications. Before joining CEI, she served as Legislative Assistant to Senator Sam Brownback (1996 to 1998), as Environmental Editor for the Research Institute of America (1994 to 1996), and as Director of Solid Waste Policy and as a policy analyst for Citizens for a Sound Economy Foundation (1989 to 1994). Logomasini earned a master's degree in Politics from the Catholic University of America, and she is working toward a Ph.D. in American Government from Catholic University.

Barun S. Mitra is a writer and commentator on public policy with a special interest in development, environment, trade, and technology related issues. He has been published in a wide range of national and international newspapers and magazines such as *The Economic Times*, and the *Wall Street Journal*. He has also contributed essays for books published by Hoover Institution at Stanford University and others. He is one of the founders of the Liberty Institute, a nonprofit, independent public policy research and educational organization. He edited a volume, *Population: The Ultimate Resource*, published by Liberty Institute, which was awarded the Sir Anthony Fisher Memorial

International Prize 2001, for the best book from a new think tank. He has written widely on environment, development, trade, and technology related issues. His current primary interest is the informal sector and spontaneous development of the institutions of the market among large segments of populations who have little access to the formal institutions of society. He is also working on a range of environmental issues looking at ways of harnessing the power of the market to improve environmental quality. He is also exploring the relationship between democracy in the political domain and the market in the economic domain.

Stephen Moore is a senior fellow in economics at the Cato Institute. He is formerly an economic analyst with the Heritage Foundation. He has also served as senior economist at the Joint Economic Committee of the United States Congress. He is the author of three books: *It's Getting Better All the Time: 100 Greatest Trends of the Last 100 Years* (with Julian Simon), *Still an Open Door? The Future of U.S. Immigration Policy* (with Vernon Briggs), and *Government: America's Number One Growth Industry*. Mr. Moore has a B.A. from the University of Illinois and an M.A. in economics from George Mason University.

C. S. Prakash is a professor in Plant Molecular Genetics and Director of the Center for Plant Biotechnology Research at Tuskegee University in Alabama. He is also the President and a co-founder of the AgBioWorld Foundation, a non-profit organization that provides information to teachers, journalists, policy makers, and the general public about developments in plant science, biotechnology, and sustainable agriculture. From 1999 to 2001, Dr. Prakash served on the U.S. Department of Agriculture's Agricultural Biotechnology Advisory Committee, and he currently serves on the Advisory Committee for the Department of Biotechnology of the Government of India. He also serves on the International Society for Horticultural Science's Commission on Biotechnology, on the Society for In Vitro Biology's ad-hoc committee on GMOs, and on the American Society of Plant Physiologists' Minority Affairs Committee. Dr. Prakash holds a bachelor's degree in agriculture and a master's degree in genetics from the University of Agricultural Sciences in Bangalore, India. He earned his Ph.D. in forestry/genetics from the Australian National

University, in Canberra. Dr. Prakash's research group at Tuskegee pioneered the development of transgenic sweet-potato plants, identification of DNA polymorphisms in peanut plants, and the development of a genetic map of cultivated peanut. They have recently enhanced the protein content of sweet-potato several-fold through genetic modification. Prakash has received funding for his research from the United States Department of Agriculture, National Science Foundation, National Aeronautics and Space Administration, Agency for International Development, and UNESCO. He has more than fifty scientific publications in refereed journals and has presented more than 100 papers at meetings.

David W. Riggs, most recently served as Director of Land and Natural Resource Policy at the Competitive Enterprise Institute. Currently, he is teaching economics at George Mason University. Prior to joining CEI, Dr. Riggs was senior fellow for economic and environmental studies at Center of the American Experiment, a state-based public policy think tank in Minneapolis, Minnesota. From 1995 to 1997, he held a joint appointment in the Texas A & M University System, where he worked as an economist for a state-level public agency and taught economics at Tarleton State University. He earned a B.A. at the University of North Carolina at Wilmington, and a Ph.D. in Applied Economics at Clemson University. Dr. Riggs has numerous published articles in professional journals, edited volumes, and newspaper op-eds.

Fred L. Smith, Jr. is the Founder and President of the Competitive Enterprise Institute (CEI), a public interest group dedicated to the principles of free enterprise and limited government activity in a wide range of economic and environmental public policy issues. Based in Washington, D.C., CEI works to educate and inform policy makers, journalists, and other opinion leaders on market-based alternatives to regulatory initiatives, ranging from antitrust and insurance to energy and environmental protection, and engages in public interest litigation to protect property rights and economic liberty. Before founding CEI, Mr. Smith served as the Director of Government Relations for the Council for a Competitive Economy, as a senior economist for Association of American Railroads, and for five years as a

Senior Policy Analyst at the Environmental Protection Agency. Mr. Smith has a degree in Mathematics and Political Science from Tulane University where he earned the Arts and Sciences Medal. He has also done graduate work at Harvard, SUNY at Buffalo, and the University of Pennsylvania. Mr. Smith is co-editor (with Michael Greve) of the book, *Environmental Politics: Public Costs, Private Rewards*, and has contributed chapters to over one dozen books, including *The True State of the Planet*, *Market Liberalism: A Paradigm for the 21st Century* and *Assessing the Reagan Years*.

INTRODUCTION:
THE RISE AND EVENTUAL
FALL OF IDEOLOGICAL
ENVIRONMENTALISM

———— ❖ ————

"YOU CANNOT GO to any corner of the globe and not find some degree of environmental awareness and some amount of environmental politics," declared Christopher Flavin, now head of the Worldwatch Institute, at the Earth Summit in Rio de Janeiro, 10 years ago. Flavin added that with socialism in disrepute, environmentalism is now the "most powerful political ideal today."

The ideological environmentalism that Flavin is talking about is far different from the pragmatic everyday kind of environmentalism that most of us favor; for example, being thrifty with resources, lowering air and water pollutants, and conserving wildlife. Ideological environmentalism embodies a sweeping agenda aimed at radically transforming how we live and work.

Since the Earth Summit in Rio, political environmentalism has grown ever more powerful. Green Party representatives sit in the world's parliaments. International environmental treaties like the Kyoto Protocol (to control projected man-made global warming), and the Biosafety Protocol (to regulate international trade in genetically enhanced crops) have been negotiated and adopted.

But there is a hidden crisis growing in the heart of ideological environmentalism. Key predictions made by environmentalist ideologues about the future state of the Earth and humanity are simply not coming true.

And this is critical because, as Robert Paehlke wrote in his book, *Environmentalism and the Future of Progressive Politics*, "Environmentalism is the first ideology to be deeply rooted in the natural sciences. Scientific findings do not themselves lead to a particular set of political conclusions, but they are essential to this ideology in a way that they are not to any other."[1]

At its modern founding, ideological environmentalists made sweeping claims about the impending fate of humanity and the Earth. One of the most important canonical works of environmentalist ideology is Rachel Carson's 1962 *Silent Spring. Time* called it "the cornerstone of the new environmentalism," and former Vice President Al Gore declared, "Without this book, the environmental movement might have been long delayed or never have developed at all." Carson predicted that modern synthetic chemicals, especially pesticides, would cause epidemics of cancer and kill off massive quantities of wildlife. Another canonical work is Stanford University biologist Paul Ehrlich's infamous *The Population Bomb.* In 1968, Ehrlich confidently predicted that "[t]he battle to feed all of humanity is over. In the 1970's the world will undergo famines—hundreds of millions of people are going to starve to death in spite of any crash programs embarked upon now." A third canonical book, *The Limits to Growth* report to the Club of Rome, was published in 1972. *The Limits to Growth* incorporated the dogma of imminent depletion of natural resources to concerns about growing population and rising pollution. Each of these books was a bestseller.

Thirty years later, the influence of these books remains strong. "*The Limits to Growth* is but one in a long series of books that have disturbed industrial society," declared Donella Meadows, a member of the original *The Limits to Growth* team, at the 1988 Cassandra Conference organized by Paul Ehrlich and John Holdren. Meadows went on to list "others in this tradition" including, of course, *Silent Spring,* by Rachel Carson; *The Population Bomb,* by Paul Ehrlich; *Small Is Beautiful,* by E. F. Schumacher; and *The Global 2000 Report to the President,* edited by Gerald O. Barney. Meadows stated that her fellow participants in the Cassandra Conference still "treasure and are sustained by all of them, quote from them, assign them to students. Each book in some way engenders another."

Indeed, these books together form a canon that continues to sustain ideological environmentalism to this day. As recently as the summer of 2001, Earth First! founder and environmental activist David Foreman was defending Ehrlich's *The Population Bomb* as being "misunderstood." The activist group Pesticide Action Network continues to claim that synthetic chemicals are dramatically increasing cancer rates in the tradition of *Silent Spring*. And Princeton University professor Jeffrey Deffeyes declared last year in his book *Hubbert's Peak: The Impending World Oil Shortage* that the world will face another "oil crisis" later in this decade.

Each of the original manifestos and the ones that followed were by no means dispassionate discussions of the results of scientific investigations but instead were chiefly calls to action: Ban synthetic chemicals, coercively limit births, and cut economic growth. The founders of ideological environmentalism justified these political goals by claiming that scientific findings demanded that they be adopted. So if their science is wrong, then so, too, are their policies.

Like all ideologies, political environmentalism consists of two parts: a diagnosis and a cure. The environmentalist diagnosis of the problems facing humanity is that modern societies are destroying the Earth and thus imperiling humanity. The cure they recommend is a series of sweeping policies that would radically reshape how the world works. "[W]e must make the rescue of the environment the central organizing principle for civilization," declared Gore in his own manifesto, *Earth in the Balance*.[2] The political message at the core of ideological environmentalism was then and is now "Do what I say or the world will come to an end."

But the fact is that the original, enduring claims that first captured the attention of the public and policy makers have not turned out to be true. Science and economics simply have not backed up the predictions of ideological environmentalism.

For example, fears of global famines caused by "overpopulation" are receding. The growth in human numbers is decreasing. The United Nations and demographers expect that human population growth is likely to track low projections and never exceed 10 billion if current trends continue. In fact, human population may reach a bit over 8 billion or so by 2050 and begin declining. And food grows ever cheaper and more available. Also, despite the introduction of thousands of new synthetic chemicals, age-adjusted cancer rates are in fact falling. Indeed, synthetic chemicals have not killed off thousands of species, including those pests at which pesticides are specifically aimed. And the world is not running out of any important nonrenewable fuel or mineral resources. Even the alarmist Worldwatch Institute's *Vital Signs 2001* report acknowledges that "nonfuel commodities now fetch only about 46 percent as much as in the mid-1970s." Indeed, the editors note that "[f]ood and fertilizer prices are about one-fourth their 1974 peak" and that metals are "at half their 1974 peak." Even the price of crude oil, which has risen lately, "nevertheless remains at about half the zenith reached in 1980." Overall, nonfuel commodities cost only a third of what they did in 1900.[3] As we all know, falling prices generally indicate lessening, not greater, scarcity.

"Ecology is now a political category, like socialism or conservatism," concluded historian Anna Bramwell in her book *Ecology in the 20th Century: A History.* She further noted that ideological environmentalism "has not developed from observation or prediction about human societies, but required an ethic which saw man and animal as comparable before ecologists could extend their observations to human society. This is crucial to the political implications of ecologism."[4]

Why is this crucial? Because ultimately, ideological environmentalists view human societies as merely elaborate and ultimately fragile superstructures tottering on a foundation of population and evolutionary biology. Frolic as we will with our complicated technologies and social institutions, biology and nature will not be denied. Essentially, environmentalists simplemindedly apply concepts from zoology and biology to human societies to create a theory of political ecology.

But this intellectual strategy of simplistically extending insights from population biology to human societies has failed. Not a single major prediction of ideological environmentalism has come true— no global famines, no cancer epidemics, and no resource depletion crisis. Environmentalist ideologues have been proven wrong because they fail to understand that the economic processes in which humans engage are radically different from the ecological processes that govern other creatures. Human beings not only consume given resources but also make new resources by using their fertile minds. Economic growth and increases in human well-being are not fueled by simply using up resources the way a herd of zebra would do, but by creating new recipes to use the limited resources available in ever more effective ways. Coal, tin, freshwater, forests, and so forth may all be limited, but the ideas for extending and improving their uses are not.

"Every generation has perceived the limits to growth that finite resources and undesirable side effects would pose if no new recipes or ideas were discovered," explains Stanford University economist Paul Romer. "And every generation has underestimated the potential for finding new recipes and ideas. We consistently fail to grasp how many ideas remain to be discovered. The difficulty is the same one we have with compounding. Possibilities do not add up. They multiply."[5]

In other words, we make ourselves better off not by increasing the amount of stuff on planet Earth—which is, of course, fixed— but by rearranging the stuff we have available so that it provides us with more of what we want: food, clothing, shelter, and entertainment. As we become more clever about rearranging material, the more goods and services we can get from relatively less stuff. Even former Vice President Gore acknowledged this fact at the 1999 annual meeting of the American Association for the Advancement of Science, when he declared, "Throughout our economy, skills, intelligence, and creativity are replacing mass and money—which is why, in the past 50 years, the

> Not a single major prediction of ideological environmentalism has come true—no global famines, no cancer epidemics, and no resource depletion crisis.

value of our economy has tripled, while the physical weight of our economy as a whole has barely increased at all."

By using better and better recipes, humanity has avoided the Malthusian traps of famine and depleted resources predicted by ideological environmentalists while, at the same time, making the world safer, more comfortable, and more pleasant for both larger numbers of people as well as for a larger proportion of the world's people. We cannot deplete the supply of ideas, designs, and recipes. They are immaterial and essentially limitless. And as humanity discovers new ideas and recipes, the opportunities for protecting and improving the natural world will also grow.

So at the moment of its ascendancy, it is environmentalism, not modern civilization, that is tottering. As more critics—including epidemiologists, demographers, toxicologists, climatologists, and economists like those featured in this volume—point ever more insistently at the yawning gap between claims of political environmentalism and scientific and economic reality, green ideologues are becoming ever more frantic to deny the growing contradictions.

Flavin is correct—environmentalism now stands as the only global ideological competitor to liberal democratic capitalism. Environmentalism is the latest totalizing ideology that has arisen in the West during the past two centuries. Like communism before it, ideological environmentalism wants to claim the mantle of objective science to justify its political programs because in the post-Enlightenment world, science is the final arbiter of what is objectively true or not. However, as the communists discovered, the failure of one's ideology to correspond to reality is ultimately fatal.

CHAPTER ONE

THE GLOBAL WARMING FIASCO

John R. Christy

ECO-MYTHS DEBUNKED

- *No global climate disaster is looming. Humans are causing an increase in carbon dioxide and other greenhouse gases, which will likely cause a very slow rise in global temperatures with which we can easily cope.*
- *The types of damaging weather people worry about, including hurricanes, tornadoes, floods, and droughts, are not increasing in number or severity.*
- *Barring another ice age, sea level will rise naturally and slowly for centuries to come.*
- *There have always been changes in the background climate, such as the recent warming of the global average temperature. Since 1979, the global temperature trend is a modest +0.06°C increase per decade through March 2002. Note that this increase is only one-third the rate measured by thermometers scattered unevenly across the globe.*
- *Carbon dioxide (CO_2) is the lifeblood of the planet, not a pollutant.*
- *Model projections of climate and weather are scientifically crude at best and should not be used as pretexts for imposing a global energy policy.*
- *Access to affordable energy enhances human life and is especially important to improving the lives of the poorest of Earth's inhabitants.*

THE MOST ACCURATE characterization of the current international discussion about climate change (or global warming) appeared in the *Times* of London. The science of "climatology," the *Times* notes, has become "calamitology."[1]

Readers, viewers, listeners, and Web surfers of climate change news are now relentlessly assaulted by that which alarms rather than that which educates. Three recent examples from sources no less than the *New York Times*, the *Washington Post*, and *Time* magazine demonstrate how politicized, misinformed, and distorted this issue has become. Beginning with the *New York Times*:

The North Pole is Melting . . . the last time scientists can be certain that the Pole was awash in water was more than 50 million years ago.[2]

The *New York Times* based its story on a report from Harvard's James J. McCarthy, professor of oceanography and cochair of Working Group II ("Adaptation and Impacts of Climate Change") of the United Nations (UN) Intergovernmental Panel on Climate Change (IPCC). He was a tourist on a Russian icebreaker and saw a patch of open water at the pole. Knowing little about natural variations of water and ice distributions at the pole, an alarmed McCarthy contacted the *New York Times*. McCarthy and the *Times* simply leapt to the conclusion that open water at the North Pole must be caused by human-induced climate change.

During the next eight days, numerous eyewitness accounts and photographic evidence of open water at the Pole in past years were sent to the *Times*. Finally relenting, the *Times* admitted in a story, buried deep in the paper, "Those reports [of open water] are not as surprising as suggested [earlier] in the *New York Times*."[3] And . . . sorry for the confusion.

> The *Times* simply leapt to the conclusion that open water at the North Pole must be caused by human-induced climate change.

Similarly, the *Washington Post* announced in July 2001 that Peruvian glaciers were rapidly retreating because of global warming. Their expert? . . . Benjamin Morales, "the dean of Peru's glaciologists." Morales said, "'The temperature was rising very slowly until 1980, and then'—he swept his arm up at a steep angle."[4] However, had Morales looked at the climate records of surface temperature or satellite-measured air temperatures (at elevations where glaciers reside), he would have discovered that since 1979 Peru has been experiencing a cooling trend. The temperature in Peru has not swept upward since 1980, but climatology was swept out the door. Morales's views were not constrained by real data and therefore made perfect material for a front-page story on climate change.

Finally, *Time* magazine, in a cover story in April 2001,[5] declared that the Antarctica summer "melt season has increased up to three weeks in 20 years." Adélie penguins were suffering (of course, there was an accompanying photo of the adorable creatures, wings extended as if asking for help, when in fact they were sunning themselves in the frigid air). *Time* must have been thinking of temperatures at one tiny spot on this icebound continent. The data show that for the whole of Antarctica, the summer melt season is actually *decreasing* because the average surface temperature there has *declined* in the past 30 years. And new evidence suggests the ice cap is actually thickening after 10,000 years of thinning—a surprising result that contradicts the catastrophists' expectations.[6]

Were readers alarmed or educated by these stories? Clearly, the media are not innocent bystanders in the climate change debate. Alarmism sells the product. A drought here, a flood there, a blizzard here, a warm day there—such normal weather events are seized upon by enterprising reporters as evidence for a changing climate caused by human industrialization. As *Time* stated in the same April 2001 story, "Temperatures sizzled from Kansas to New England last May [2000], surprising residents . . . with an unusually early heat wave." This was supposedly further evidence of a catastrophic global warming problem.

These words, published in the spring of 2001, were misleading. Were *Time*'s readers told that after that warm spell in May, the summer in New England and the Great Lakes was especially cool? Did *Time* mention that for the nation as a whole, the combined months of the following November and December 2000 were the coldest in 106 years of record keeping? *Time* overlooked the climatological facts in favor of their own version of "calamitology."[7] This journalistic travesty did not stop with peddling misleading catastrophism, but, as one of *Time*'s reporters told me, "the tone of the package . . . is decidedly alarmist and aimed at bringing pressure to bear on the Bush administration." *Time* was no longer a newsmagazine in my view.

The science of climate deals with quantities we can measure in the natural world. Evidence for global warming, however, is often presented as the latest disaster-by-anecdote. And when characterizing the future, journalists employ these most useful words as their insurance policy—"seem," "if," "might," and "could"—before launching into a brutalizing description of the latest disaster and its potential for getting worse. (Anything *might* happen.) Rarely are *numbers*, which can be assessed objectively, reported in such stories. All science, as Massachusetts Institute of Technology (MIT) professor Richard Lindzen notes, echoing Lord Kelvin, is numbers.

GLOBAL TEMPERATURES

WHEN PEOPLE MENTION global warming in a rudimentary scientific context, they probably have in mind a graph of the temperature of the planet rising over the past 100 years or so (Figure 1.1). In fact, the surface of the globe has never been completely monitored so that a true global average temperature could be determined. What has been done is to take whatever

A drought here, a flood there, a blizzard here, a warm day there—such normal weather events are seized upon by enterprising reporters as evidence for a changing climate caused by human industrialization.

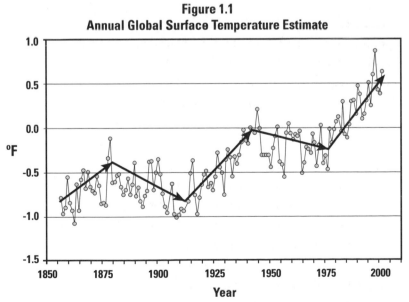

Figure 1.1
Annual Global Surface Temperature Estimate

Source: Derived from U.S. (NOAA/NCDC, NASA/GISS) and U.K. (The Met Office, U.E. Anglia) datasets.

measurements are available and to estimate from those what the global average might be.

Most of these instrumental reconstructions of surface temperature begin in the mid-19th century when, in the view of many scientists, enough scattered thermometer readings were taken to attempt the global estimates. Actual coverage, however, was a small fraction of the globe in the early decades shown in Figure 1.1, with much of the oceanic regions (especially in the Southern Hemisphere) and large continents like Antarctica, Africa, and South America almost completely void of any readings at all.

Through time, the coverage increased, though even today large portions of the oceans and continents are not directly monitored at the surface. The global estimates from different government organizations have been averaged in Figure 1.1, though all show the same year-to-year features, which should not be surprising since all use virtually identical sources of data.

Dealing with global warming in a scientific way means looking at numbers. The general pattern of surface temperature change since the mid-19th century shows that the Earth has experienced changes in roughly five segments:

warming to 1878 (+0.31°F over 22 years)
cooling to about 1911 (-0.43°F in 34 years)
noticeable warming to 1944 (+0.86°F in 34 years)
slight cooling to 1976 (-0.13°F in 33 years)
noticeable warming to the present (+0.77°F in 25 years)

Though the increase between 1911 and 1944 is greater than that of the most recent quarter century and too early to be related to human causes, the *rate* of warming of the last 25 years is slightly larger, and hence, something about which one can be alarmed if one is so inclined. The coldest year of record is difficult to determine, because of poor coverage (thus large error) when it occurred, but it appears to be a near tie between 1862 and the years 1907 to 1909. The warmest year, 1998, easily stands out above the rest.

Cruder estimates of the global temperature have been developed using proxy data (tree rings, corals, ice cores, etc.) that extend backward much farther in time. A common feature of these non-instrumental reconstructions is that the 19th century appears as the coldest or near coldest period of the last 1,000 years. From a period of relative warmth around A.D. 1000, these records show an unsteady cooling to the 19th century and then the unsteady rise described earlier. The period of coolness in the 15th to the 19th century is often called the Little Ice Age, being especially noticeable in Europe where historical documentation supports the proxy data. Thus the natural cooling of the Earth to the 19th century is a well-known feature.

In an effort to make sense of the tremendous complexity of the climate system, the UN instituted the Intergovernmental Panel on Climate Change. The IPCC reports are written by a selection of (mostly) government-nominated scientists whose backgrounds vary from the most accomplished scientists to relatively unknown bureaucrats. The latest IPCC document on the science of climate was released in August 2001 on which 122 lead authors, spread out amongst 14 chapters, worked for three years to provide an assessment of as much information as possible. Most lead authors had nothing to do with chapters other than their own. Several hundred reviewers provided comments but in no way could they be considered intimate with the final product, nor was their approval solicited. Statements by ideological environmentalists that thousands of IPCC scientists agree on anything is simply untrue and misrepresents the process. None of the 122 lead authors had the opportunity to place a stamp of approval on every statement. Simply put, most of us had nothing to do with most of the report.[8] Though drafted by a small group of IPCC scientists, the brief account of the main points used by the media and called the Summary for Policymakers, was actually edited and approved by a political body.

Given this bit of background, it is somewhat of an overstatement when the IPCC 2001 says that "the increase in [Northern Hemisphere] temperature in the 20th century is likely to have been the largest of any century during the past 1,000 years." One should be aware that the past century represents the *only* period of extended warming to have occurred in the previous 1,000 years, which were generally dominated by a cooling trend.

Has human activity been responsible for some of the last century's temperature rise? The IPCC 2001 claims the following:

> *There is new and stronger evidence that most of the warming observed over the past 50 years is attributable to human factors.*

Note carefully what the preceding IPCC quote actually says. The evidence is "new and stronger." But is this evidence truly "convincing" or "beyond doubt" or "stronger than a DNA test?" The evidence is described only as "new and stronger" and hides the fact that uncertainties and inconsistencies are not only still present but in some cases growing.

Let us look at some of this evidence. As a starting point, Figure 1.1 indicates the surface temperature warmed over the past 50 years by +0.8°F. Accepting, for the moment, the IPCC comment that "most of the warming" is due to human factors, we are therefore responsible for a temperature increase of about 0.5°F through the enhancement of the Earth's greenhouse effect. This enhanced greenhouse effect is believed to be caused by human progress and development.

CARBON DIOXIDE (CO_2) AND THE GREENHOUSE EFFECT

To UNDERSTAND THE greenhouse effect, it is important to understand a little about the way energy is transferred from the ultimate source, the Sun, to and within the Earth system. The processes involved are quite complex; but for our purposes here, we will consider only a few main points.

Of the Sun's energy arriving at the top of the atmosphere, about one-third is reflected back to space by clouds (among other things), about one-sixth is directly absorbed in the atmosphere, and the remaining half is absorbed into the Earth's surface. Because the Earth and the atmosphere do not continually heat up, we know that the incoming solar energy is somehow returned back to space, to maintain a balance between incoming and outgoing energy. (If more energy were absorbed than released, the temperature would be consistently increasing until the Earth was much hotter.)

The Earth's surface expels or emits a major portion of the energy absorbed from sunlight by invisible waves known as *thermal* or *infrared radiation*. Though you cannot see this type of energy, this is the same energy you feel when standing near a campfire. Thus, for every unit of solar energy absorbed in the Earth's surface, a unit of energy, much in the form of thermal radiation, is emitted to the atmosphere above to maintain the balance. (Additional energy is extracted from the surface by the evaporation of water and the transfer to energy to the atmosphere by direct contact.)

Water vapor, clouds, and CO_2 act like a blanket and keep the surface warmer than would otherwise be the case if the thermal energy could escape directly through the air to space.

The atmosphere is mostly transparent to incoming solar energy since, for example, you can look up and see the Sun from the ground on a clear day without any trouble. However, some constituents of the atmosphere—for example, water vapor, cloud droplets, and CO_2—absorb thermal radiation that is sent up from the Earth's surface. This means that water vapor, clouds, and CO_2 intercept and absorb the radiation and then warm the surrounding air as a result, which reemits the energy in all directions, including back to the surface. They act like a blanket and keep the surface warmer than would otherwise be the case if the thermal energy could escape directly through the air to space.

The greenhouse process is illustrated in the climate differences of, for example, Arizona and Alabama in the summer. In both places, the Sun's energy heats the surface to very high temperatures during the day. After sundown, this stored-up energy is released from the ground to the atmosphere above. In the dry desert air, the surface temperature falls rapidly as the thermal radiation escapes to space. Typically in Alabama, however, this heat is prevented from taking a direct path to space by the abundant water vapor molecules in the air (i.e., high humidity). This heat energy is absorbed and reemitted by these molecules, keeping the surface warmer than would be the case in the desert. In simplified terms, Alabama typically has a summer greenhouse blanket, while Arizona does not.

This is the natural greenhouse effect. Without it, the surface of the Earth would be about 60°F colder than it is—and virtually lifeless. Recalling the global warming statement of the IPCC 2001 mentioned earlier, we are told that the influence of the greenhouse effect is now 60.5°F, the extra half degree thought to originate from human factors.[9]

Carbon dioxide is increasing in the atmosphere due to human activity and therefore contributes to an "enhanced" greenhouse effect (i.e., the potential excess above the 60°F "natural" greenhouse effect). When we burn any type of carbon-based fuel (coal, gasoline, natural gas, wood, etc.), heat (energy) is released and CO_2 is created. In the last 200 years, the atmospheric concentration of CO_2 has risen more than 30 percent, from 280 to 370 parts per million, and is still rising as we humans, to our considerable benefit, burn more and more carbon fuels every day for transportation and energy.[10] In addition, the removal and burning of forests (mainly in impoverished countries), which generally absorb CO_2 from the atmosphere, also contribute to its increasing atmospheric accumulation.

The net yearly increase in atmospheric CO_2 (due to humans) as measured in terms of carbon mass is 3.2 petagrams (1 petagram equals 1 billion metric tons) of carbon (PgC). The amount now in the atmosphere is up to about 730 PgC. Each year the nonhuman world (forests, oceans, etc.) releases about 210 PgC to the atmosphere but in turn absorbs about 213 PgC. What this means is that human activity actually produces about 6.3 PgC each year, because the natural world is pulling about 3 more PgC out than it is putting in. There is very strong evidence to show that the plant world (which includes agricultural production) is thriving as a result of this additional CO_2 and is helping to remove half of the portion humans are producing.

Is increasing CO_2 a harmful pollutant? The answer is absolutely no. In simple terms, CO_2 is the lifeblood of the planet. The green world we see around us would disappear if not for atmospheric CO_2. Plant life largely evolved at a time when the atmospheric CO_2 concentration was many times what it is today. We are, from the plants' point of view, putting more of their food into the air, and they are gobbling it up. If plants (and animals that like plants) could vote to offer awards, producers of CO_2 would win in a landslide. So the increasing concentration of CO_2 does not pose a toxic risk to the planet. Efforts to designate CO_2 a pollutant by the U.S. government have not considered the plants' point of view.

The danger being attached to increasing CO_2, as indicated earlier, arises from another area of science—climate. It has been proposed that CO_2 increases could cause climate change (or global warming) of a magnitude beyond what naturally occurs, which would force costly adaptation for humans and/or significant ecological stress. For example, enhanced sea level rise and/or reduced rainfall would be two possible effects likely to be costly to those regions so affected. Of course, any climate change, human related or not, to which adaptation is necessary would cost something. Considering that our planet's life system has experienced multimillennial periods of both warmer and colder weather, successful adaptation is the defining characteristic of every living plant and creature in our world today.

The critical scientific point for the issue at hand is the idea that any increase in one of these greenhouse gases, such as water vapor or CO_2, will theoretically lead to a further warming of the surface temperature, all things being equal. With the current natural greenhouse effect at 60°F, would an increase to, say, 63, 65, or 68°F cause problems for people and ecosystems? If we estimate that the added human impact is +0.5°F over the past 50 years, does this mean the total effect will be another 1°F (or 61.5°F) by 2100? Will other factors enter into the system and magnify the human CO_2 effect to, say, 63 or 68°F? Or will counterbalancing factors come into play and mitigate the rise? Definitive answers are not to be found because the future projections (theory) are based on elementary prescriptions of complicated processes.

THEORY

The theory that says the temperature of a gas will increase when concentrations of greenhouse gases are increased is well established by laboratory tests. Whenever a volume of air is exposed to heat radiation and reaches a constant temperature, the temperature will always increase further if a greenhouse gas is then added. There is no dispute of this result, which supports the global warming theory. If the real atmosphere were like the laboratory container, and given the present increase of greenhouse gases, we would expect that by 2100 the global greenhouse effect would rise from 60 to 62°F.

The difficulty for greenhouse alarmists is that the Earth system is not a simple volume of air in the laboratory container. The Earth has innumerable ways and means to process and eject (or store) extra energy that otherwise might tend to dissipate (or accumulate in) the system. Finding out exactly how the increasing CO_2 will affect climate is a vastly complex problem, requiring the discovery and testing of many theories, and is by no means a solved problem. The answers are hampered by our inability to measure what has gone on with the climate and our ignorance about the major and minor factors that influence the climate. To know the present and past, we sift through weather observations of all kinds, as described earlier. In an attempt to anticipate the future, researchers employ computer climate models based on theories of how they think the real world functions.

> The difficulty for greenhouse alarmists is that the Earth system is not a simple volume of air in the laboratory container.

Climate models may be thought of as very long and complicated lists of rules that generally follow this formula: If X happens this much, then Y will happen that much. Major controversies regarding the climate change issue deal with whether climate models have all of the rules that are necessary for predicting the future and whether the rules are even correct. A very slight error in a single rule and the final answer may be seriously wrong.

For example, certain types of clouds act to cool the Earth's surface, while other types act to warm it. At this time, we do not know for certain, from observations or from climate models, whether either type of cloud might become more or less prevalent with increasing

CO_2. In other words, clouds are extremely difficult to observe quantitatively (i.e., with numbers), and the rules (theories) about clouds in models are only very simple approximations that have many problems.

In the air-filled container used in the laboratory experiment described earlier, suppose we began as before, except this time an insulating blanket covered part of the container initially, preventing some of the internal heat from escaping. As greenhouse gases are increased in this experiment, we now proportionally remove the insulating blanket on the container. This would allow some of the newly trapped heat to escape even though CO_2 was increasing. As the greenhouse gas tries to warm the air in the container, removing the blanket would reduce the quantity of accumulated heat available for warming. The net result is that the container warms to a level less than would be the initial experiment in which the only change was CO_2 increases. This blanket-removal idea during an increase in CO_2 is called a *negative feedback.*

Several climate models use sets of rules (theories) which produce the result that as the temperature rises from CO_2 increases (i.e., X happens), the warming effect of clouds (and associated humidity) will also increase (i.e., Y happens). These rules therefore lead the model to produce a climate that is much warmer than would be the case if the temperature increase were due to CO_2 alone. In the laboratory experiment described earlier, this would be analogous to a third experiment in which an insulating blanket were *added* as CO_2 increased (i.e., a *positive feedback*).

In the models, this enhanced blanket effect is created by additional water vapor (a greenhouse gas) and greater amounts of the type of clouds that warm the Earth. These positive feedbacks, when applied over a forecast of the next 100 years, produce a total greenhouse effect of about 63 to 70°F versus the natural effect of 60°F and the enhanced CO_2-only effect of 62°F. In other words, the global average surface temperature would increase 3 to 10°F over what it is now if these feedbacks (rules) are correctly modeled. (Note: The large range of model possibilities, 3 to 10°F, should give the reader an idea that even the current models and theories have significant differences among them.[11])

Again, science is numbers. Some recent observational research by MIT climatologist Richard Lindzen and colleagues used satellites to measure the expanse of clouds in association with surface temperatures. As surface temperatures increased over the ocean, they discovered that the type of clouds that warm the Earth tend to diminish in size. Their work was published in the highly regarded *Bulletin of the American Meteorological Society.*

> *The calculations show that such a change in the Tropics could lead to a negative feedback in the global climate . . . , which, if correct, would more than cancel all of the positive feedbacks in the more sensitive current climate models.*[12]

Their result strongly suggests that the clouds that warm the Earth will *decrease* as CO_2 increases and thus work like the second experiment described earlier, where the blanket is removed. In other words, as CO_2 increases, the clouds that have a blanket effect will decrease in coverage, allowing more heat to escape to space and reducing the warming potential. Thus, the effect of clouds in a climate with more CO_2 may be to lessen rather than magnify the relatively small warming of CO_2 alone. This observational evidence suggests that at least some of the typical climate model's positive feedback rules should be changed to negative feedback rules; otherwise, the future temperature of the planet will be considerably overstated.

In fact, several studies published in *Science* reported that the Earth evidently has increased its rate of energy loss over the last 22 years by 4 watts per meter squared (W/m^2), while during the same period, the amount absorbed from the sun increased by only 1 to 2 watts per meter squared (W/m^2).[13] Apparently, the Earth has a mechanism that allows the atmosphere to shed more heat than is absorbed over decadal time scales. This appears to be consistent with the "iris effect" hypothesized by Lindzen in which clouds act to allow more heat to escape whenever there is an increase in the surface temperature of the ocean. However, this is not the interpretation as viewed by the studies' authors who believe the "iris effect" does not exist. This is one of many controversies that will take time to resolve. However, the team led by Bruce Wielicki could not escape noting what they found regarding climate model comparisons.

We conclude that the [observed] large decadal variability of the LW [Earth's heat loss] and SW [Earth's heat gain from sun] radiative fluxes . . . appear to be caused by changes in both the annual average and seasonal tropical cloudiness. In general, these changes are not well predicted by current climate models. . . . Indeed, the current assessments of global climate change have found clouds to be one of the weakest components of climate models. This leads to a threefold uncertainty in the predictions of the possible global warming over the next century.[14]

This is a controversial area of climate research and unlikely to be resolved anytime soon.[15]

Keep firmly in mind that models can't prove anything. Even when a model generates values that look like those shown in Figure 1.1, appearing to match the past 150 years, one must remember that modelers have had 20 years of practice to make the match look good. Is such model agreement due to fundamentally correct science or to lots of practice with altering (or tuning) the sets of rules in a situation where one knows what the answer should be ahead of time?

One way to check this is to compare model results with another basic quantity to which modelers have not had the opportunity to tune. Comparing models' bulk temperature of the atmosphere with real observations indicates there are still serious questions about how heat is moved around in the model atmospheres. Heat transport properties are absolutely crucial in the long simulations of century-scale climate. If the model rules allow just the slightest amount of excess heat to accumulate over a century, the temperature rise will be spuriously exaggerated.

> Is such model agreement due to fundamentally correct science or to lots of practice with altering (or tuning) the sets of rules in a situation where one knows what the answer should be ahead of time?

BULK ATMOSPHERIC TEMPERATURES

The discussion thus far has dealt with the temperature of the Earth near the surface. (This is obviously important because we humans live and work on the surface.) The theory of the enhanced CO_2 greenhouse effect, as embodied in the complicated—but not complete nor necessarily correct—list of rules in climate models, states that the air near the surface should warm up over the next century. As noted earlier, the models project that only about one-third of the warming (about 2°F) is due directly to CO_2 and the rest (1 to 8°F) to positive feedbacks generated by the models themselves.

These same models also project that the deep layer of air from the surface to about 5 miles altitude will warm at least as rapidly as the surface air. Since 1979, the National Oceanic and Atmospheric Administration's TIROS-N satellites have carried instruments called Microwave Sounding Units (MSUs), which are able to determine the temperature of this layer to a high level of precision. What is especially valuable about satellites is the daily, full global coverage they provide. In other words, we do not have to estimate temperatures anywhere because there are now direct measurements everywhere, be it in the middle of the South Pacific Ocean or the uninhabited rain forests of Brazil. Satellite data in their raw form are not perfect and require adjustments to account for changes or drifts in the spacecraft orbital parameters. Even after these adjustments, there is still some level of uncertainty in the long-term trends, but a level small enough to be useful for climate studies.

An important situation exists for the satellite data—the opportunity for independent validation. Hundreds of locations around the world release instrumented helium balloons that monitor the temperature of the column of air through which they rise. These data are radioed back to ground stations so that the temperature of a bulk layer can be accurately determined for each of these locations. In this way, the satellite and balloon temperatures may be directly compared. The agreement between these two independent means of calculating the deep-layer temperature confirms the lack of warming in the atmosphere over the past 23 years—the very years the surface has warmed supposedly most rapidly.

In December 2001, compilers of global surface temperatures announced that the year 2001 was hot, the second warmest since records were first kept. Many stories linked this to global warming. However, after processing the satellite data, my colleague Roy Spencer and I found that the true bulk of the atmosphere experienced a tiny +0.06°C departure from average, making 2001 quite unremarkable as only the ninth warmest in the 23 years of record keeping. (Figure 1.2) Unremarkable means unnewsworthy, and none of the wire services, to our knowledge, bothered to report this to the public. And since 1979, the global temperature trend is a modest +0.06°C increase per decade through March 2002. Note that that increase is only one-third the rate measured by thermometers scattered unevenly across the globe.

So these satellite data show that globally, there has been little trend at all in the temperature of the bulk of the atmosphere since 1979 (Figure 1.3) One interesting feature of the deep-layer atmosphere is

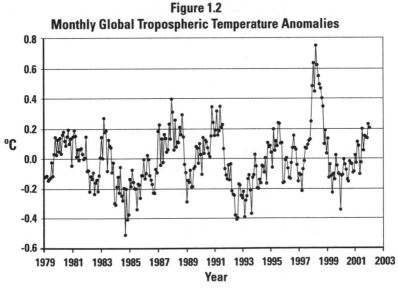

Figure 1.2
Monthly Global Tropospheric Temperature Anomalies

Source: Christy, et al., *Journal of Atmospheric and Oceanic Technology,* 2000

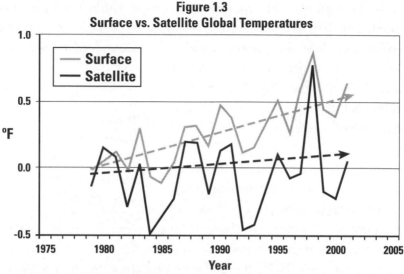

Figure 1.3
Surface vs. Satellite Global Temperatures

Source: John R. Christy and Roy W. Spencer, University of Alabama in Huntsville.

that because it is a freely moving, low-density gaseous fluid, it tends to respond rather quickly and obviously to forces acting upon it. The chart shows how the global atmosphere warms up during El Niños, or the warming of the tropical Pacific waters (e.g., 1998), and cools following large volcanic eruptions (e.g., 1991).

The IPCC, in summarizing the results of several model studies, states that:

> *models generally predict an enhanced rate of warming in the mid- to upper troposphere over that at the surface.*[16]

The fact that there has been no obvious deep-layer warming in the past 23 years, as indicated by bulk temperature data, is a curious result that has confused people studying the global warming issue. If the surface is warming because of human impact, why is the atmosphere not warming? One must question whether the way climate model rules force the bulk of the atmosphere to retain heat energy and warm up are correct because empirical data from the satellites and weather balloons show this is not the case.

This inconsistency was noted in a National Academy of Sciences (NAS) report requested by U.S. President George W. Bush in 2001 to answer several questions about climate change. The NAS report describes several of the uncertainties of global warming, including the surface/atmosphere issue.

The finding that the surface and troposphere temperature trends have been as different as observed over intervals as long as a decade or two is difficult to reconcile with our current understanding of the processes that control the vertical distribution of temperature in the atmosphere.[17]

Other uncertainties are discussed, such as the magnitude and sign of feedbacks related to water vapor and clouds mentioned earlier, how the ocean absorbs and transports heat, and whether the aerosols in the air really do what models now claim they do. The NAS report indicates there is no answer to the question of what constitutes dangerous CO_2 levels and sums up the issue of climate models and natural variability with this statement:

Because of the large and still uncertain level of natural variability inherent in the climate record and the uncertainties in the time histories of the various forcing agents (and particularly aerosols), a causal linkage between the buildup of greenhouse gases in the atmosphere and the observed climate changes during the 20th century cannot be unequivocally established. The fact that the magnitude of the observed warming is large in comparison to natural variability as simulated in climate models is suggestive of such a linkage, but it does not constitute proof of one because the model simulations could be deficient in natural variability on the decadal to century time scale.[18]

These observations and uncertainties notwithstanding, the IPCC's statement assumes there is a consensus among scientists (I do not know how this statement was developed) that more than half of the warming of the past 50 years is due to human-caused increases in greenhouse gases. As we saw in Figure 1.1, the warming of the last

50 years occurred only in the last 25. Thus the statement implies that the surface warming of the last 25 years is mostly greenhouse related. But the models, which reproduce rapid *surface* warming in the past 25 years, erroneously show a large warming in the bulk of the atmosphere, which as we've seen is not observed. This error leads many climatologists to believe that the models are still in such infancy given their current sets of rules that they should be viewed with considerable skepticism regarding predictions of climate over the next century.

Given this relatively major inconsistency between models and observations, it is reasonable to conclude that climate models simply do not provide us with the kind of information we need for making policy decisions yet.

IS THE CLIMATE CHANGING?

THIS IS THE easiest question of all to answer. The background climate of Earth has always changed and will continue to change. There have never been two centuries or even two decades exactly alike in the 4+ billion-year history of the planet. The 21st century's climate will be different from that of the 20th, as the 20th was different from that of the 19th, and all others before. The factors that influence climate are too numerous to even document, much less understand from our present level of ignorance. From the massive doses of solar radiation striking the planet to the chemical activities of microbes that affect the air's chemistry, the uncertainties about impacts are profound. With so many fluctuating factors acting in their own way on the system, the climate changes. The notion that climate *should* be stationary (i.e., our weather should stay the way we think it should be) does not come from science.

The alarmist media reports described in the introduction become the source of downstream hysteria promoted by those with extreme environmental agendas. Such pronouncements by ideological environmentalists that the globe's weather is worsening are actually false. Even the IPCC states clearly that, after looking at real data (i.e., numbers):

the intensity and frequency of tropical and extra-tropical cyclones and severe local storms show no clear trends in the last half of the 20th century.[19]

This is "climatespeak" for stating that no changes in hurricanes, thunderstorms, hail, floods, tornadoes, and the like have been observed. Thus the kind of severe weather people really care about shows normal natural variability but no significant long-term trend.

So we see that the global temperature (surface, at least) has risen in the past 25 years but that the rest of the atmosphere is not changing in a way that points to human activity as the cause. Fundamentally, this suggests climate models have serious problems with expressing the impacts of increased greenhouse gases on climate. We also note that disastrous weather is not increasing or decreasing and that the plant world (along with food production) is definitely enjoying rising levels of CO_2. There are two significant issues related to climate change—sea level rise and increased droughts—that are important to consider.

> The notion that climate *should* be stationary (i.e., our weather should stay the way we think it should be) does not come from science.

SEA LEVEL RISE

SEA LEVEL RISE is a serious concern because many human settlements live at the margin of low coastal plains and islands so that small changes could have significant consequences. Sea level, however, should not be thought of as being constant. Science is clear that, just as with climate, there is no law that states sea level should remain stationary. During the last major ice age, 25,000 years ago, the sea level was more than 300 feet lower than today, so a considerable amount of rise has already occurred naturally. In the past 6,000 years, the sea rose about 2 inches per century, but the rate increased about 1,850 to 6 inches per century, a rate change occurring before humans could have had any influence. Sea level changes naturally.

Over the time period shown in Figure 1.1, the total rise in average sea level has been about 9 inches. Individual coastlines have wide variations in the rise (or fall) because local changes in sea level depend on many factors, including rising or subsiding coastal land. This 6-inch-per-century rate has remained steady since 1850 and has not accelerated.

Two main factors are likely causing average sea level to rise: (1) the thermal expansion of the ocean as it warms from the cold 15th to 19th centuries and (2) the melting (or nongrowth) of many glaciers. Other smaller factors, which are directly related to human development, are (1) enhanced deposition of silt in the ocean from eroded farmlands or deforested mountains, (2) subsiding land from well water, oil, and natural gas drilling, (3) runoff of water pumped from underground wells, and (4), a negative factor, large reservoirs that keep water from flowing to the sea. These and other factors make the calculation of the global average change in sea level a very complicated problem. The present rate of sea level increase noted in the IPCC 2001 as 6 ± 4 inches per century acknowledges these uncertainties.[20]

We know from relatively recent geological periods of warmth (e.g., 130,000 years ago) that sea level has been even higher than it is today. We would expect, therefore, in the absence of a return to an ice age, that there should be more sea level creep in the future even without a contribution from extra greenhouse gas warming and plan accordingly. Sea level, like climate, is always changing.

In early 2002, a large section of the Larsen Ice Shelf (Larsen B) on the Antarctic Peninsula disintegrated into the adjacent Weddell Sea. The size, 1,250 square miles by 650 feet thick, made it easily visible by satellites, which quickly provided the all-important video for the evening news broadcasts. Was this evidence of the global warming catastrophe in which Antarctica melts and floods our coastal cities? The Antarctic continent, of which the peninsula is only a tiny portion, is a giant complex system of interlocking ice caps and glacial "rivers" of ice that constantly flow into the surrounding oceans. When the continent is viewed as a whole, surprising results (at least to global warming alarmists) appear: The temperature of the continent has actually declined over the past 30 years, major portions of the West Antarctic ice cap are thickening, and the extent of the sea ice around the continent has actually expanded since 1980. In fact, hundreds of thousands of penguin chicks died during the most recent Antarctic summer (2001–02) because the sea ice was too extensive for parents to reach the sea from their nesting grounds and return in time with food.[21] Yes, the local temperature of the peninsula has risen in the past 50 years, but this small area does not serve to inform us of the much bigger Antarctic picture. And the melting of Larsen B has no impact on global sea level since the ice shelf was already floating on the water.

REAL DROUGHTS

WEATHER INSTRUMENTS HAVE covered most of the United States since the end of the 19th century. One measure of weather that is critical to our economy and thus our well-being is the occurrence of droughts and wet spells. The National Climatic Data Center keeps track of such quantities (Figure 1.4) In the past 100+ years we have had some significant droughts—everyone knows of the 1930's Dust Bowl—and major wet spells, but there is no obvious trend in either direction.

Figure 1.4
U.S. Percentage Area Wet or Dry, January 1900–February 2001

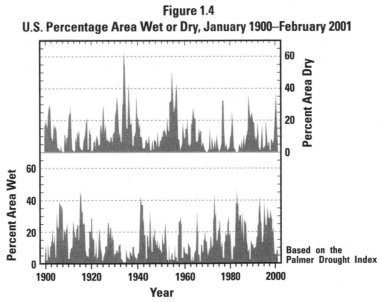

Source: National Climatic Data Center/NESDIS/NOAA.

Using proxy records of the central and western United States, researchers have uncovered a disturbing finding. Our country has experienced multidecadal droughts that completely overwhelm the effect of the 1930's experience. The five most significant droughts in the past 2,000 years all occurred prior to 1600. The Sand Hills of Nebraska, now covered with a layer of prairie foliage, were literally desert sand dunes during such droughts. This tells us that our nation should be aware that significant disruption is possible due to the natural variations of climate. However, it is a foregone conclusion that if a significant drought strikes the United States in the next few years, it will be blamed on CO_2 increases. A fear many of us have is that if this occurs, the country would likely adopt a knee-jerk remedy of limiting energy use at the very moment energy would be most critically needed to alleviate drought problems. The science (i.e., the numbers) tells us major droughts are likely to occur naturally as a matter of course.

LIMITING ENERGY USE

IT IS COMMON today to hear pleas that we should reduce carbon-based energy production so that we might "save the planet." This notion is embodied most obviously in the Kyoto Protocol, adopted in 1997 by representatives of most of the world's industrialized governments. As of this writing, few nations have legally adopted the treaty, and the United States has opted out, thus drawing high-level criticism from, it seems, everyone. The basic goal of Kyoto is to require the most-developed nations to reduce their CO_2 emissions by 5.2 percent compared with 1990 levels by about 2010, although changes agreed to in Bonn in July 2001 allow that number to slip to only 1.8 percent. No limits were imposed on countries deemed "developing." (Aren't all countries developing?) The U.S. share was to amount to a 7 percent reduction.

Among the many problems with Kyoto is one demonstrated by a very simple scientific result. (Science, recall, deals with numbers.) Because of the healthy economic expansion of the 1990s, as of this writing, virtually no country is on track to meet their Kyoto target.

Those few countries close to meeting their goals may actually do so because of unique circumstances tied to the peculiar base year of 1990 in which other countries cannot share (e.g., England's switch from government-controlled coal-based energy production to North Sea natural gas, and Germany's acquisition and elimination of the massively inefficient communist East German energy infrastructure). If a true level playing field were proposed (i.e., identifying the base year as 2000 instead of 1990), England and Germany would hypocritically cry foul as they would lose their unique advantages.

However, suppose all of these countries found some way, certainly with considerable economic hardship, to meet the goals of Kyoto. The science (from models, admittedly) indicates that the net impact on global temperatures over the next 100 years would be at most an almost undetectable 0.2°F. Global temperatures can change that much from month to month. Will democratically accountable governments truly subject their constituents to economic pain for a result that is this minuscule? Such a move appears scientifically, economically, and politically untenable. Americans in particular believe we should "get what we pay for," and paying 1 to 3 percent of our personal wealth every year for a non-result is literally unsustainable.[22]

A common criticism of the United States is that our country produces about 25 percent of the world's CO_2, therefore we are the biggest part of the "problem." Without much effort, one may see straight through this claim. Yes, the United States is a large emitter of CO_2. However, with that CO_2, the United States produces 31 percent of what the world wants, and the type of things the world desperately needs that no one else provides. Consider food production, medical advances, technology in all areas, and even global defense-of-freedom capabilities. Do these fundamental CO_2-based "products," which benefit the world, not deserve recognition and even applause?

Add to the problems of Kyoto the thorny notions of sovereignty and self-determination. Will the United States surrender any of its sovereignty to an international treaty developed largely by unelected bureaucrats for at best a minuscule result based on uncertain theories? The governments of the geographically small European countries

(Canada and Australia are not nearly so strident) appear to believe they should have some control over American prosperity because ours is based on market-based access to energy. The developing (i.e., poorer) countries have no sacrifice at all to pay, so they would gladly agree to inhibit the productive power of the U.S. economy in the hopes more jobs would be transferred to them. What they are likely to experience, however, is further economic decline if the bountiful, job-producing, wealth-enhancing, technology-leading U.S. economy takes a downturn.

> The governments of the geographically small European countries appear to believe they should have some control over American prosperity because ours is based on market-based access to energy.

European governments (among many) deny ready access to energy through high taxes, which are needed to support their large, expensive social programs. During the summer of 2000, several groups in England and France took exception to these energy taxes and supported widespread protests. Gasoline costs the same to produce and deliver in the United States as it does in England. The price difference of $4 per gallon there versus $1.50 here is due entirely to taxation. It seemed to me, a visiting scientist in England that summer, the protesting taxi, truck, and automobile drivers were in effect protesting the idea of "taxation without representation."

WHAT DO WE KNOW TO DO?

THIS DISCUSSION OF global warming has been wide-ranging, yet in reality has been quite limited. What does the best information today tell us? Here are some fundamental points to consider:

> The types of bad weather people really care about are not changing enough to notice. Winters seem to be getting a little warmer in some of the coldest places. Sea level is creeping upward on average at less than an inch per decade.

The plant world, and by extension all of life, thrives on enhanced CO_2.

People are clever and, at least those who live with a good measure of personal freedom, are able to create better and better resources for themselves. Consider the following:

- In just 30 years, people in the United States have reduced the energy required to produce one unit of gross domestic product (GDP) by almost half.
- Though the world's population has quadrupled in the past century, the number of food calories available *per person* has actually increased.
- Americans grow corn in climates from Alabama to North Dakota.

Affordable energy produces longer and better lives, in the form of better health, wealth, and security.

Carbon-based energy is inexpensive but is not free. Clever people will develop cheaper ways to create energy with less carbon. Wealthy countries can afford to search for these new sources of energy. The next innovation will come from inventors who want to be rich or famous or accomplished, not by decrees from legislative bodies.

Limiting carbon-based energy production to levels adopted in the Kyoto Protocol will make an imperceptible difference in global temperature and an undetectable difference in local weather. If achieved, it would reduce the standard of living for millions—and by extension, billions—of people. The poorest are the most vulnerable to such edicts made by proponents of such efforts at centralized planning.

Given what has been presented, what should we expect and what should we hope for?

One should expect a rise in the global average temperature of an amount to which regional adaptation is entirely feasible. Local weather will not become something out of the ordinary. One should expect to see an increase in natural and agricultural plant productivity. We can anticipate better efficiencies of carbon-based energy and new sources of non-carbon energy.

One should hope that governments would encourage research into new technologies that, when proven, will be naturally adopted by the marketplace. One should also hope that governments would not issue decrees in which energy is rationed, thereby reducing the standard of living. And one should hope that, with accessible energy, the real environmental problems of water pollution and habitat loss, particularly in the poor developing countries, will be addressed. And finally, one can only dream that the world will continue on a path that eliminates that which has proven to be the most dangerous threat to human life—governments and bureaucracies that have no democratic accountability.

CHAPTER TWO

FEEDING A WORLD OF 10 BILLION PEOPLE: THE MIRACLE AHEAD

Norman E. Borlaug

ECO-MYTHS DEBUNKED

- *Contrary to the predictions of many environmentalist ideologues, world food supplies have more than tripled in the past 30 years, staying well ahead of world population growth. Global food supplies, if equitably distributed, could provide an adequate diet for 700 million more people than there are living in the world today.*
- *Had the global cereal yields of 1950 still prevailed in 1999, humanity would have needed nearly 1.8 billion hectares of land of the same quality—instead of the 600 million that were used—to equal the current global harvest.*
- *To feed the world's growing population a better diet, it is likely that an additional 1 billion tons of grain will be needed annually by 2025. Most of this increase must be supplied from lands already in production, through yield improvements.*
- *Organic agriculture is incapable of feeding the world's current population, much less providing for future population growth.*
- *Scientific breakthroughs, particularly in agricultural biotechnology, will likely permit another 50 percent increase in yields over the next 35 years if their development is not hindered by antiscience activism.*
- *While challenging, the prospects are good that the world's farmers will be able to provide a better diet at lower prices to more people in the future.*

I AM NOW in my 58th year of continuous involvement in food production programs in developing nations. During this period, I have seen much progress in increasing the yields and production of various crops, especially the cereals, in many food-deficit countries. Clearly, the research that backstopped this progress has produced huge returns. Yet despite a more than tripling in the world food supply during the past three decades, the so-called Green Revolution in cereal production has not solved the problem of chronic undernutrition for hundreds of millions of poverty-stricken people around the world, who are unable to purchase the food they need, despite abundance in world markets, due to unemployment or underemployment. Still, the world's food situation has improved markedly.

Thirty years ago there were many who claimed that global famine was unavoidable. For example, in 1968 biologist Paul Ehrlich predicted in *The Population Bomb,* "The battle to feed all of humanity is over. In the 1970s the world will undergo famines—hundreds of millions of people are going to starve to death in spite of any crash programs embarked upon now."[1] In 1967, Lester Brown, who later founded the environmentalist think tank the Worldwatch Institute, declared, "The trend in grain stocks indicates clearly that 1961 marked a worldwide turning point . . . food consumption moved ahead of food production."[2] Brown, too, saw famine looming. But fortunately they were wrong. They merely extrapolated trends without taking into account how the hard work of farmers, combined with breakthroughs developed by researchers, would dramatically boost world food supplies.

Sometime during the 21st century, world population will reach—and hopefully stabilize at—9 to 10 billion people. This event is likely to occur sometime around 2050. To give you some idea of the population increase that the world experienced during the 20th century, when I was born in 1914, there were only about 1.6 billion mouths to feed; in 2002 we will number some 6.1 billion. While global population growth rates have slowed over the past 20 years—and are actually negative in some industrialized countries—absolute population increases are still on the order of 75 to 80 million per year.

It must also be acknowledged that in many of the more productive areas—especially the irrigated areas located in warm climates—there are problems of soil erosion and declining water quality, which if left unchecked can lead to the permanent loss of prime agricultural land. In most cases, we shall see, the root cause of this environmental degradation has been mistaken economic policy—such as mistaken pricing policies and poor engineering design—not modern, science-based technology.

The invention of agriculture, some 10,000 to 12,000 years ago, heralded the dawn of civilization. It began with rainfed, hand-hoed agriculture, which evolved into an animal-powered, scratch-tooled agriculture, and finally into an irrigated agriculture along the Euphrates and Tigris Rivers, that for the first time allowed humankind to produce food surpluses. This permitted the establishment of permanent settlements and urban societies, which, in turn, engendered culture, science, and technology. The rise and fall of ancient civilizations in the Middle East and Mesoamerica were directly tied to agricultural successes and failures, and it behooves us to remember that this axiom remains valid today.

Poets—and city folk—love to romanticize agriculture, portraying it as some sort of idyllic state of harmony between humankind and nature. How far this is from the truth! Ever since Neolithic man—or more probably woman—domesticated the major crop and animal species some 10 to 12 millennia ago, agriculture has been a struggle between the forces of natural biodiversity and the need to produce food using increasingly intensive production systems. Thanks to advances in science during the past century, food production has kept ahead of population growth and, in general, has become more reliable. But with global population likely to continue substantially over the next 50 years, meeting future food demand will be a challenging task.

> The rise and fall of ancient civilizations in the Middle East and Mesoamerica were directly tied to agricultural successes and failures, and it behooves us to remember that this axiom remains valid today.

DAWN OF MODERN AGRICULTURE

SCIENCE-BASED AGRICULTURE IS really a 20th-century invention. Until the 19th century, crop improvement was in the hands of farmers, and food production grew largely by expanding the cultivated land area. As sons and daughters of farm families married and formed new families, they opened new land to cultivation. Improvements in farm machinery expanded the area that could be cultivated by one family. Machinery made possible better seedbed preparation, moisture utilization, and improved planting practices and weed control, resulting in modest increases in yield per hectare.

By the mid-1800s, German scientist Justus von Leibig and French scientist Jean-Baptiste Boussingault had laid down important theoretical foundations in soil chemistry and crop agronomy. Sir John Bennet Lawes produced superphosphate in England in 1842, and shipments of Chilean nitrates (nitrogen) began arriving in quantities to European and North American ports in the 1840s. However, the use of organic fertilizers (animal manure, crop residues, green manure crops) remained dominant into the early 1900s.

Groundwork for more sophisticated genetic crop improvement was laid by Charles Darwin in his writings on the variation of species (published in 1859) and by Gregor Mendel through his discovery of the laws of genetic inheritance (reported in 1865). Darwin's book immediately generated a great deal of interest, discussion, and controversy. Mendel's work was largely ignored for 35 years. The rediscovery of Mendel's work in 1900 provoked tremendous scientific interest and research in plant genetics.

The first decade of the 20th century brought a fundamental scientific breakthrough, which was followed by the rapid commercialization of the breakthrough. In 1909, Fritz Haber (1918 Nobel laureate in chemistry) demonstrated the synthesis of ammonia from its elements. In 1913, the company BASF, thanks to the innovative technologies devised by Carl Bosch, began operation of the world's first ammonia plant. Fertilizer industry growth was first delayed by World War I (ammonia was used to produce nitrate for explosives), then by the great economic depression of the 1930s, and then by the demand for explosives during World War II. However, after World War II, inexpensive nitrogen fertilizer became increasingly available and contributed greatly to boosting crop yields and production.

It is only over the past 50 years that the application of low-cost nitrogen derived from synthetic ammonia has become an indispensable component of modern agricultural production. Today nearly 80 million nutrient metric tons of synthetic nitrogen are consumed annually. To provide this amount of nitrogen from cattle manure, for example, the world cattle population would have to increase from roughly 1 billion to some 7 to 8 billion head, clearly not a viable alternative in today's land-short world. Put another way, without the Haber-Bosch process of synthesizing ammonia another way, only about 60 percent of the world's population could be fed.[3]

By the 1930s, much of the scientific knowledge needed for high-yield agricultural production was available in the United States. However, widespread adoption was delayed by the great economic depression of the 1930s, which paralyzed the world agricultural economy. It was not until World War II brought a much greater demand for food to support the Allied war effort that the new research findings began to be applied widely, first in the United States and later in many other countries.

Maize (corn) cultivation led the modernization process. In 1940, U.S. farmers produced 56 million tons of maize on roughly 31 million hectares, with an average yield of 1.8 tons/hectares. In 1999, U.S. farmers produced 240 million tons of maize on roughly 29 million hectares, with an average yield of 8.4 tons/hectares. This more than fourfold yield increase, grown on a smaller land area, is the impact of modern hybrid seed-fertilizer-weed control technology!

I often ask the critics of modern agricultural technology what the world would have been like without the technological advances that have occurred, largely during the past 50 years. For those whose main concern is protecting the environment, let's look at the positive impact that the application of science-based technology has had on land use.

> I often ask the critics of modern agricultural technology what the world would have been like without the technological advances that have occurred, largely during the past 50 years.

Had the global cereal yields of 1950 still prevailed in 1999, we would have needed nearly 1.8 billion hectares of land of the same quality—instead of the 600 million that was used—to equal the current global harvest (Figure 2.1). Obviously, such a surplus of land was not available, and certainly not in populous Asia. Moreover, if more environmentally fragile land had been brought into agricultural production, think of the impact on soil erosion, loss of forests and grasslands, biodiversity and extinction of wildlife species that would have ensued.

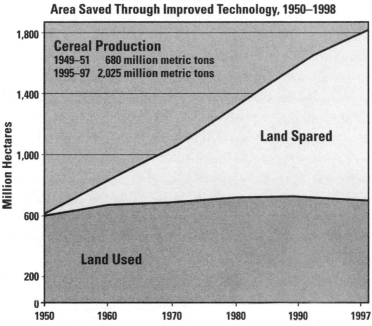

Figure 2.1
World Cereal Production—
Area Saved Through Improved Technology, 1950–1998

GREEN REVOLUTION

THE BREAKTHROUGH IN wheat and rice production in Asia in the mid-1960s, which came to be known as the Green Revolution, symbolized the process of using agricultural science to develop modern techniques for the Third World. It began in Mexico with the "quiet" wheat revolution in the late 1950s. During the 1960s and 1970s, India, Pakistan, and the Philippines received world attention for their agricultural progress. Since 1980 China has been the greatest success story. Home to one-fifth of the world's people, China today is the world's biggest food producer. With each successive year, its cereal crop yields approach that of the United States.

The adoption of modern production technology explains the tremendous increase in food production in the developing countries of Asia, stretching from Turkey in West Asia to the Pacific rim of East and Southeast Asia. Over the past 40 years, Asia's irrigated area has more than doubled to 176 million hectares; fertilizer consumption has increased more than 30-fold and now stands at about 70 million metric tons of nutrients; and tractors in use have increased from 200,000 to 4.6 million (Table 2.1).

The impact of improved technology in cereal production has been tremendous (Table 2.2). Increases in wheat production have been the most spectacular, increasing more than fivefold over the past 40 years. Rice production has increased 235 million metric tons in developing Asia, and maize production in China has increased nearly sixfold.

In 1961, developing Asia had an estimated population of 1.6 billion people. By 2000 the population had swelled to 3.5 billion people. While serious problems continue to exist in food distribution, especially in the countries of South Asia, the nutritional levels for most of the nearly 2 billion additional people in developing Asia have improved. What would have been the food situation had there not been a Green Revolution? For me the consequences are too terrible to even imagine.

OUR WORLD FOOD SUPPLY

IN 1998, GLOBAL food production of all types stood at 5.03 billion metric tons of gross tonnage and 2.48 billion tons of edible dry matter (Table 2.3). Of this total, 99 percent was produced on the land— only about 1 percent came from the oceans and inland waters.

Plant products constituted 92 percent of the human diet, with about 30 crop species providing most of the world's calories and pro-

Table 2.1.   Changes in Factors of Production in Developing Asia

| | Modern Varieties | | Fertilizer Nutrients | | |
	Wheat Million ha/%	Rice Total Area	Irrigation Million ha	Consumption Million metric tons	Tractors Millions
1961	0/0%	0/0%	87	2	0.2
1970	14/20%	15/20%	106	10	0.5
1980	39/49%	55/43%	129	29	2.0
1990	60/70%	85/65%	158	54	3.4
1998	70/84%	100/74%	176	70	4.6

Source: FAO AGROSTAT (April 2000); IRRI and CIMMYT Impact Data.

Table 2.2.   Growth in Cereal Production in Developing Asia

	1961	1970	1980	1990	2000	% Increase
		(million metric tons)				1961–2000
South Asia*						
Rice, Milled	49	58	74	100	121	+147
Wheat	15	28	44	66	100	+567
China						
Maize	18	33	63	97	106	+489
Rice, Milled	38	76	96	128	127	+234
Wheat	14	29	55	98	100	+614
Total Developing Asia**						
Rice, Milled	122	183	233	311	357	+193
Wheat	44	51	128	202	232	+427

*South Asia region includes Bangladesh, Bhutan, India, Nepal, Pakistan, and Sri Lanka.
**Developing Asia region includes all developing countries, from Turkey in West Asia to China in East Asia.
Source: FAOSTAT (November 2001).

tein, including eight species of cereals, which collectively accounted for 70 percent of the world food supply. Animal products, constituting 8 percent of the world's diet, also come indirectly from plants. Fish, while an important source of protein (7 percent), only accounted for 1 percent of the world's calories.

Table 2.3.   World Food Supply, 1998

Commodity	Production, Million Metric Tons		
	Gross Tonnage	Edible Matter*	Dry Protein*
Cereals	**2,072**	**1,725**	**172**
Maize	613	539	56
Wheat	589	519	61
Rice	577	391	33
Barley	139	122	12
Sorghum/Millet	89	80	7
Roots & Tubers	**652**	**174**	**11**
Potato	299	65	8
Sweet Potato	139	42	2
Cassava	162	60	1
Legumes, Oilseeds, & Oil Nuts	**162**	**110**	**38**
Sugarcane & Sugar Beets**	**152**	**152**	**0**
Vegetables & Melons	**615**	**72**	**6**
Fruits	**430**	**59**	**3**
Animal Products	**951**	**188**	**83**
Milk, Meat, & Eggs	830	157	63
Fish	121	31	2
All Food	**5,034**	**2,480**	**313**

*At zero moisture content, excluding inedible hulls and shells.
**Sugar content only.
Source: FAOSTAT (1999).

Had the world's food supply been distributed evenly, it would have provided an adequate diet in 1998 (2,350 calories, principally from grain) for 6.8 billion people—about 900 million more than the actual population in that year. However, had people in Third World countries attempted to consume a diet based on high-intake animal products—as in the United States, Canada, or European Union countries—only about half of the world population could be fed.

These statistics point out two key problems. The first is the complex task of producing sufficient quantities of the desired foods to satisfy needs, and to accomplish this Herculean feat in environmentally and economically sustainable ways. The second task, equally or even more daunting, is to distribute food equitably. Poverty is the main impediment to equitable food distribution, which, in turn, is made more severe by rapid population growth.

PROJECTED WORLD FOOD DEMAND

THE UNITED NATION's medium projection is for world population to reach about 7.9 billion by 2025, before hopefully stabilizing at about 9 to 10 billion toward the end of the 21st century.[4] At least in the foreseeable future, plants—and especially the cereals—will continue to supply much of our increased food demand, both for direct human consumption and as livestock feed to satisfy the rapidly growing demand for meat in the newly industrializing countries. It is likely that an additional 1 billion metric tons of grain will be needed annually by 2025. Most of this increase must be supplied from lands already in production, through yield improvements. Using these estimates, I have come up with projections on future cereal demand and the requisite yields needed by the year 2025 (Table 2.4).

Population growth, urbanization, and rising incomes are fueling a massive increase in the demand for animal products.[5] By 2020, people in developing countries are likely to consume 100 million metric tons more meat and 223 million metric tons more milk than they did in 1993 (Table 2.5). The demand for poultry will increase the most. By 2020, China will become the world's largest meat producer, and India has already become the world's largest milk producer.

Table 2.4. Current and Projected World Cereal Production and Demand
(million metric tons) and Yield Requirements (t/ha)

	Actual Production 1990	Actual Production 1999	Projected Demand 2025	Yield t/ha Actual 1990	Yield t/ha Actual 1999	Yield t/ha Required 2025
Wheat	592	585	900	2.6	2.7	3.8
Rice, Paddy	528	607	900	2.4	3.1	4.3
Maize	483	605	1,000	3.7	4.1	5.9
Barley	178	127	140	2.4	2.7	2.9
Sorghum/Millet	87	86	100	1.1	1.1	1.6
All Cereals	1,953	2,074	3,100	2.5	2.9	4.1

Source: *FAO Production Yearbook* and author's estimates.

Table 2.5. Actual and Projected Meat Consumption by Region

Region	Total Meat Consumption (million metric tons) 1983	Total Meat Consumption (million metric tons) 1993	Total Meat Consumption (million metric tons) 2020
China	16	38	85
Other East Asia	1	3	8
India	3	4	8
Other South Asia	1	2	5
Southeast Asia	4	7	16
Latin America	15	21	39
West Asia/North Africa	5	6	15
Sub-Saharan Africa	4	5	12
Developing World	50	87	188
Industrialized World	88	97	115
World	139	184	303

Source: IFPRI (2001).

Globally, the livestock subsector will become increasingly important within agriculture. However, increases in the supply of livestock
products are coming primarily from industrial production. This is
because of the undeveloped state of traditional smallholder livestock
systems. Yet with appropriate policies that encourage improvements
in animal health and nutrition, the rewards of a rapidly growing livestock sector could benefit the smallholder producer.

RAISING YIELDS ON EXISTING
AGRICULTURAL LANDS

WHILE SOMEWHAT OF an oversimplifying assumption, since there
are still some vast areas to bring into production in South America

and Africa, much of the projected increases in food supply will have to come from land currently in production. To meet the projected food demands, therefore, the average yield of all cereals must be increased by 65 percent between 1990 and 2025. Fortunately, there are many improved agricultural technologies—already available or well advanced in the research pipeline—that can be employed in future years to raise crop yields, especially in the low-income food deficit countries where most of the hunger and poverty exist.

Yield gains in China and industrialized North America and western Europe will be much harder to achieve, since they are already at very high levels. Still, I am hopeful that scientific breakthroughs, particularly from genetic engineering, will permit another 50 percent increase in yields over the next 35 years. Even without using advances in plant biotechnology, yields can still be increased by 50 to 70 percent in much of the Indian subcontinent, Latin America, the former Soviet Union, and eastern Europe, and by 100 to 150 percent in much of sub-Saharan Africa, providing political stability is maintained, bureaucracies that destroy entrepreneurial initiative are reined in, and their researchers and extension workers devote more energy to putting science and technology to work at the farm level.

THE WORRYING AFRICAN SITUATION

THE MOST FRIGHTENING prospect for food insecurity is found in sub-Saharan Africa, where the number of chronically undernourished could rise to several hundred million people if current trends of declining per capita production are not reversed. Sub-Saharan Africa's increasing population pressures and extreme poverty, the presence of many human diseases (e.g., malaria, tuberculosis, river blindness, trypanosomiasis, guinea worm, AIDS, etc.), poor soils and uncertain rainfall, changing ownership patterns for land and cattle, inadequacies of education and public health systems, poorly developed physical infrastructure, and weaknesses in research and technology delivery systems will all make the task of agricultural development very difficult.

Despite these formidable challenges, many of the elements that worked in Asia and Latin America during the 1960s and 1970s will also work to bring a Green Revolution to sub-Saharan Africa. An effective system to deliver modern inputs—seeds, fertilizers, crop protection chemicals—and to market output must be established. If this is done, Africa can make great strides toward improving the nutritional and economic well-being of the downtrodden African farmer, who constitutes more than 70 percent of the population in most countries.

Since 1986, I have been involved in food crop production technology transfer projects in sub-Saharan Africa, spearheaded by the Nippon Foundation and its former chairman, the late Mr. Ryoichi Sasakawa, and enthusiastically supported by former U.S. President Jimmy Carter. Our joint program is known as Sasakawa-Global 2000 and currently operates in 10 African countries: Burkina Faso, Ethiopia, Ghana, Guinea, Malawi, Mali, Mozambique, Nigeria, Tanzania, and Uganda. Previously, we operated similar projects in Benin, Eritrea, Togo, Sudan, and Zambia.

The most frightening prospect for food insecurity is found in sub-Saharan Africa, where the number of chronically undernourished could rise to several hundred million people if current trends of declining per capita production are not reversed.

Dynamic field-testing and demonstration programs for the major food crops form the core of these projects. Although improved technology developed by national and international research organizations had been available for more than a decade, for various reasons it was not being adequately disseminated among farmers. Working in concert with national extension services during the past 15 years, more than 1 million demonstration plots (usually from 0.25 to 0.5 hectares) have been grown by small-scale farmers. Most of these plots have been concerned with demonstrating improved basic food crops production technology for maize, sorghum, wheat, cassava, and grain legumes. The packages of recommended production technology include (1) the use of the best available commercial varieties or hybrids, (2) proper land preparation and seeding dates and rates to achieve good stand establishment, (3) proper application of the appropriate fertilizers, including green manure and animal dung, when available, (4) timely weed control and, when needed, crop protection chemicals, and (5) moisture conservation and/or better water use, if under irrigation.

Virtually without exception, the yields obtained by participating farmers on these demonstration plots are typically two to three times higher than the control plots employing traditional methods. Only rarely have plot yields failed to double that of the control. Hundreds of field days attended by tens of thousands of farmers have been organized to demonstrate and explain the components of the production package. In project areas, farmers' enthusiasm is high and political leaders are now taking much interest in the program. From our experiences over the past decade, I am convinced that if there is political stability and if effective input supply and output marketing systems are developed, including a viable agricultural credit system, the nations of sub-Saharan Africa can make great strides in improving the nutritional and economic well-being of their desperately poor populations.

BRINGING NEW LANDS INTO PRODUCTION— THE REMAINING FRONTIERS

MOST OF THE opportunities for opening new agricultural land to cultivation have already been exploited (Table 2.6). This is certainly true for densely populated Asia and Europe. Only in sub-Saharan Africa and South America do large unexploited tracts exist, and only some of this land should eventually come into agricultural production. But in populous Asia, home to half of the world's people, there is very little uncultivated land left to bring under the plow. Apparently, in West Asia there are already some 21 million hectares being cultivated that shouldn't be. Most likely, such lands are either too arid or, because of topography, are so vulnerable to erosion that they should be removed from cultivation.

One of the last major land frontiers are the vast acid-soils areas found in the Brazilian *cerrado* and llanos of Colombia and Venezuela, central and southern Africa, and Indonesia. Historically, bringing these unexploited potentially arable lands into agricultural production posed what were thought to be insurmountable challenges. But

Table 2.6. Potential Cropland in the Less-Developed Countries

	Africa	West Asia	South/Southeast Asia	East Asia	South America	Central America	Total
			Million ha				
Potentially Cultivated	789	48	297	127	819	75	2,155
Presently Cultivated	168	69	274	113	124	36	784
Uncultivated	621	0	23	14	695	39	1,392

Source: Calculated from Buringh and Dudal (1987) Table 2.6, p. 22, World Bank.

thanks to the determination of interdisciplinary teams in Brazil and international research centers, the prospects of making many acid-soil savanna areas into productive agricultural areas has become a viable reality.

Let's look briefly at the Brazilian *cerrado*. The central block, with 175 million hectares in one contiguous area, forms the bulk of the savanna lands. Approximately 112 million hectares of this block are considered potentially arable. Most of the remainder has potential value for forest plantations and improved pastures for animal production. The soils of this area are mostly various types of deep loam to clay-loam latosols (oxisols, ultisols), with good physical properties but highly leached of nutrients by Mother Nature in geologic time, long before humankind appeared on the planet. These soils are strongly acidic and have toxic levels of soluble aluminum, with most of the phosphate fixed and unavailable.

In precolonial times, the area was sparsely inhabited by a number of Amerindian tribes dependent on a culture based on hunting and gathering of wild plants. During the colonial period, and continuing from independence up until about 35 years ago, the *cerrado* was considered to be essentially worthless for agriculture (except for the strips of alluvial soils along the margins of streams, which were less acidic and where there had been an accumulation of nutrients). The natural savanna/brush flora of poor digestibility and nutritive quality—resulting in low carrying capacity—was utilized for extensive cattle production.

Through a slow, painful process over the past 50 years, involving some outstanding scientists, bits and pieces of research information and new types of crop varieties have been assembled; only during the past 20 years have these "pieces" been put together into viable technologies that are now being applied by pioneering farmers. By the end of the 1980s, Brazil's national research corporation, EMBRAPA, and several international agricultural research centers (especially CIMMYT and CIAT) had developed a third generation of crop varieties combining tolerance to aluminum toxicity with high yield, better resistance to major diseases, and better agronomic type. These included rice, maize, soybeans, wheat, and several species of pasture grasses, including the panicums, pangola, and brachiaria. Triticale is an interesting man-made cereal that has a very high level of aluminum tolerance, although it has not been utilized much yet either for forage or for grain production.

Improved crop management systems were also developed, built around liming, fertilizer to restore nutrients, crop rotations, and minimum tillage that leave crop residues on the surface to facilitate moisture penetration and reduce runoff and erosion. However, with conservation tillage coming into widespread use, it will be absolutely necessary to work out better crop rotations to minimize the crop diseases that are transmitted by plant crop residues left on the surface from previous seasons.

In 1990, roughly 10 million hectares of rainfed crops were grown in the *cerrado*, with an average yield of 2 tons/hectares and a total production of 20 million tons (Table 2.7). The irrigated area is still relatively small with an average yield of 3 tons/hectares and a total production of 900,000 tons. There are also 35 million hectares of improved pasture supporting an annual meat production of 1.7 million tons.

The *cerrado* area, using improved technology, has expanded greatly over the past five years. If it continues to spread, farmers

Table 2.7.   Production of Cereals and Meat in the *Cerrado* in 1990

Land Use	Area (million ha)	Productivity (t/ha per year)	Production (million t)
Crops (Rainfed)	10.0	2.0	20.0
Crops (Irrigated)	0.3	3.0	0.9
Meat (Pasture)	35.0	0.05	1.7
Total	45.3	5.05	22.6

Source: *Prospects for the Rational Use of the Brazilian Cerrado for Food Production* by Dr. Jamil Macedo, CPAC, EMBRAPA (1995).

Table 2.8. Potential Food Production if Available Technology Is Adopted on *Cerrado* Area Already in Production

Land Use	Area (10⁶ ha)	Productivity (t/ha per year)	Production (10⁶ t)
Crops (Rainfed)	20.0	3.2	64
Crops (Irrigated)	5.0	6.0	30
Meat (Pasture)	20.0	0.2	4
Total	**45.0**	**9.4**	**98**

Source: *Prospects for the Rational Use of the Brazilian Cerrado for Food Production* by Dr. Jamil Macedo, CPAC, EMBRAPA (1995).

could attain 3.2 tons/hectares in rainfed crops and 64 million tons of production. If the irrigation potential is developed, which can add another 30 million tons of food production, it is likely that by 2010 food production in the *cerrado* will have increased to 98 million tons—or a fourfold increase over 1990 (Table 2.8).

INCREASING EFFICIENCY OF WATER USE

ALTHOUGH WATER COVERS about 70 percent of the Earth's surface, only about 2.5 percent is freshwater, and most of this is frozen in the ice caps of Antarctica and Greenland, in soil moisture, or in deep aquifers not readily accessible for human use. Indeed, less than 1 percent of the world's freshwater—that found in lakes, rivers, reservoirs, and underground aquifers shallow enough to be tapped economically—is readily available for direct human use.[6] Irrigated agriculture—which accounts for 70 percent of global water withdrawals—covers some 17 percent of cultivated land (about 275 million hectares) yet accounts for nearly 40 percent of world food production.

The rapid expansion in world irrigation and in urban and industrial water uses has led to growing shortages. The UN's Comprehensive Assessment of the Freshwater Resources of the World estimates that "about one-third of the world's population lives in countries that are experiencing moderate-to-high water stress, resulting from increasing demands from a growing population and human activity. By the year 2025, as much as two-thirds of the world's population could be under stress conditions."[7]

In many of the irrigation schemes, especially in developing Asia, proper investments were not made originally in drainage systems to prevent water tables from rising too high and to flush salts that rise to the surface back down through the soil profile. We all know the consequences—serious salinization of many irrigated soils, especially in drier areas, and waterlogging of irrigated soils in the more humid areas. In particular, many Asian irrigation schemes—which account for nearly two-thirds of the total global irrigated area—are seriously affected by both problems. The result is that most of the funds going into irrigation end up being used for stopgap maintenance expenditures for poorly designed systems rather than for new irrigation projects. In future irrigation schemes, water drainage and removal systems should be designed properly from the start of the project. Unfortunately, proper designs are often costly and will result in a poor return on investment, raising the question of how much a country will be willing to spend on new irrigation development.

There are many technologies for improving the efficiency of water use. Wastewater can be treated and used for irrigation. This could be an especially important source of water for peri-urban agriculture, which is growing rapidly around many of the world's megacities. Water can be delivered much more efficiently to the plants and in ways to avoid soil waterlogging and salinization. Changing to new crops requiring less water (and/or new improved varieties), together with more efficient crop sequencing and timely planting, can achieve significant savings in water use.

Proven technologies, such as drip irrigation, which saves water and reduces soil salinity, are suitable for much larger areas than they are currently being used for. Various new precision irrigation systems are also on the horizon, which will supply water to plants only when they need it. There is also a range of improved small-scale and supplemental irrigation systems to increase the productivity of rainfed areas, offering much promise for smallholder farmers.

Clearly, we need to rethink our attitudes about water and move away from thinking of it as nearly a free good and a God-given right.

> In the new Blue Revolution, water-use productivity must be wedded to land-use productivity. New science and technology must lead the way.

Pricing water delivery closer to its real cost is a necessary step to improving use efficiency. Farmers and irrigation officials (and urban consumers) will need incentives to save water. Moreover, management of water distribution networks, except for the primary canals, should be decentralized and turned over to the farmers.

In order to expand food production for a growing world population within the parameters of likely water availability, the inevitable conclusion is that humankind in the 21st century will need to bring about a Blue Revolution to complement the so-called Green Revolution of the 20th century. In the new Blue Revolution, water-use productivity must be wedded to land-use productivity. New science and technology must lead the way.

IMPROVING CROP MANAGEMENT

CROP PRODUCTIVITY DEPENDS both on the yield potential of the varieties and the crop management employed to enhance input and output efficiency. Productivity gains can be made all along the line—in tillage, water use, fertilization, weed and pest control, and harvesting.

An outstanding example of new Green/Blue Revolution technology in irrigated wheat production is the bed planting system, which has multiple advantages over conventional planting systems. Plant height and lodging are reduced, leading to 5 to 10 percent increases in yields and better grain quality. Water use is reduced 20 to 25 percent, a spectacular savings, and input efficiency (fertilizers and herbicides) is also greatly improved by 30 percent. This technology has already been adopted in northwest Mexico and is growing in acceptance in other countries, including Pakistan, India, and China.

Conservation tillage (no tillage, minimum tillage) is another soil and water management technology that is spreading rapidly in many parts of the world. The Monsanto Company has estimated that farmers used conservation tillage practices on 95 million hectares in the year 2000. By reducing and/or eliminating the tillage operations, turnaround time on lands that are double- and triple-cropped annually can be significantly reduced, especially rotations like rice/wheat and cotton/wheat. This leads to higher production and to lower production costs. Conservation tillage also controls weed populations and greatly reduces the time that small-scale farm families must devote to this backbreaking work. Finally, the mulch left on the ground reduces soil erosion, increases moisture conservation, and builds up the organic matter in the soil—all very important factors in natural resource conservation. Conservation tillage does, however, require modification in crop rotations to avoid the buildup of diseases and insects that find a favorable environment in the crop residues for survival and multiplication.

DEVELOPING NEW CROP VARIETIES

AGRICULTURAL RESEARCHERS AND farmers worldwide face the challenge during the next 20 years of developing and applying technology that can increase the global cereal yields by 50 to 75 percent, and to do so in ways that are economically and environmentally sustainable. Much of the yield gains will come from applying technology already "on the shelf" but yet to be fully utilized. But there will also be new research breakthroughs from biotechnology, especially in plant breeding to improve yield stability and, hopefully, for maximum genetic yield potential.

Continued genetic improvement of food crops—using both conventional as well as biotechnology research tools—is needed to shift the yield frontier higher and to increase stability of yield. While biotechnology research tools offer much promise, it is also important to recognize that conventional plant-breeding methods are continuing to make significant contributions to improved food production and enhanced nutrition. In rice and wheat, three distinct but interrelated strategies are being pursued to increase genetic maximum yield potential: changes in plant architecture, hybridization, and wider genetic resource utilization.[8] Significant progress has been made in all three areas, although widespread impact on farmers' fields is still probably 10 to 12 years away. The International Rice Research Institute (IRRI) claims that the new "super rice" plant type, in association with direct seeding, could increase rice yield potential by 20 to 25 percent.[9]

In wheat, new plants with architecture similar to the "super rices" (larger heads, more grains, fewer tillers) could lead to an increase in yield potential of 10 to 15 percent.[10] Introducing genes from related wild species into cultivated wheat can introduce important sources of resistance for several biotic and abiotic stresses and perhaps for higher yield potential as well, especially if the transgenic wheats are used as parent material in the production of hybrid wheats.[11]

The success of hybrid rice in China (now covering more than 50 percent of the irrigated area) has led to a renewed interest in hybrid wheat, when most research had been discontinued for various reasons, mainly low hybrid vigor and high seed production costs. However, recent improvements in chemical hybridization agents, advances in biotechnology, and the emergence of the new wheat plant type have made an assessment of hybrids worthwhile. With better hybrid vigor and increased grain filling, the yield frontier of the new wheat genotypes could be 25 to 30 percent above the current germplasm base. In addition, hybrid triticale offers the promise of higher yield potential than wheat for some areas and uses.

Maize production has really begun to take off in many Asian countries, especially China. It now has the highest average yield of all the cereals in Asia, with much of the genetic yield potential yet to be exploited. Moreover, recent developments in high-yielding quality protein maize (QPM) varieties and hybrids using conventional plant-breeding methods stand to improve the nutritional quality of the grain without sacrificing yields. This research achievement offers important nutritional benefits for livestock and humans. With biotechnology tools, it is likely that we will see further nutritional quality enhancements in the cereals in years to come.

The recent development, by researchers at Purdue University in the United States, of high-yielding sorghum varieties and hybrids with resistance to the heretofore-uncontrollable parasitic witchweed of the *Striga* genus is an important research breakthrough that should benefit many areas of Asia and Africa.

There is growing evidence that genetic variation exists within most cereal crop species for developing genotypes that are more efficient in the use of nitrogen, phosphorus, and other plant nutrients than are currently available in the best varieties and hybrids. In addition, there is good evidence that further heat and drought tolerance can be built into high-yielding crop varieties.

WHAT CAN WE EXPECT FROM BIOTECHNOLOGY?

CONVENTIONAL BREEDING HAS produced a vast number of varieties and hybrids that have contributed immensely to higher grain yield, stability of harvests, and farm income over the past seven decades. Surprisingly, however, there have been no major breakthroughs in the maximum genetic yield potential of the high-yielding semidwarf wheat and rice varieties commercially being grown since those that served to launch the so-called Green Revolution of the 1960s and 1970s. Of course, there have been important improvements in resistance to diseases and insects and in tolerance to a range of abiotic stresses, especially soil toxicities. But we must also find new and appropriate technology to raise genetic yield potential to higher levels if we are to cope with the food production challenges before us.

Until recently, it has been generally assumed that the genetic yield potential in plants (and animals) is controlled by a large number of genes, each with small additive effects. However, the work of recent years shows that there may also be a few genes that are sort of "master genes" that affect the interaction, either directly or indirectly, of several physiological processes that influence yield. For example, the genes for the growth hormones bovine somatotropin (BST) and pork somatotropin (PST) are apparently such master genes. They not only affect the total production of milk or meat but also the efficiency of production per unit of feed intake. It now appears that the dwarfing genes Rht1 and Rht2, used to develop the high-yielding Mexican wheats that launched the Green Revolution, also acted as master genes, for at the same time that they reduced plant height and improved standability, they also increased tillering and the number of fertile florets and the number of grains per spike (harvest index). Biotechnology may be a new window through which to search for new master genes for high yield potential by eliminating the confounding effects of other genes.

In the last 20 years, biotechnology based on recombinant DNA has developed invaluable new scientific methodologies and products in food and agriculture. This journey deeper into the genome is the continuation of our progressive understanding of the workings of nature. Recombinant DNA methods have enabled breeders to select and transfer single genes, reducing the time needed in conventional breeding to eliminate undesirable genes, but have also allowed breeders to access useful genes from other taxonomic groups—distinct genera, families, orders, or kingdoms.

Biotechnology, to date, has had the greatest impact in medicine and public health. However, there are a number of fascinating developments now entering commercial applications in agriculture. In animal biotechnology, we have BST, now widely used to increase milk production. Transgenic varieties and hybrids of cotton, maize, and potatoes, containing genes from *Bacillus thuringiensis*, which effectively control a number of serious insect pests, are now being successfully introduced commercially in the United States. The use of such varieties will greatly reduce the need for insecticide sprays and dusts. Considerable progress also has been made in the development of transgenic plants of cotton, maize, oilseed rape, soybeans, sugar beet, and wheat, with tolerance to selected herbicides. This can lead to a reduction in overall herbicide use through applying much more specific dosages and interventions.

Despite the formidable opposition by many ideological environmentalists to transgenic crops, commercial adoption by farmers of the new varieties has been one of the most rapid cases of technology diffusion in the history of agriculture. Between 1996 and 2001, the area planted commercially to transgenic crops has increased 30-fold (Table 2.9).

The International Service for the Acquisition of Agri-biotech Applications (ISAAA) reports that in 2001, 52.6 million hectares were planted to transgenic crops in 13 countries and grown by 5.5 million farmers, compared to only 1.7 million hectares in 1996.[12]

Table 2.9.   Transgenic Crop Coverage, 2001

Area	Million ha	Crops	Million ha
United States	35.7	Soybeans	33.3
Argentina	11.8	Maize	9.8
Canada	3.2	Cotton	6.8
China	1.5	Canola	2.7
Others	0.4		
Total	52.6	Total	52.6

Source: Clive James, ISAAA Brief #24 (2002).

During this period, herbicide tolerance has been the dominant trait, accounting for 77 percent of the area. One quarter of the global transgenic crop area is now found in developing countries, with the highest year-on-year percentage growth occurring in China between 2000 and 2001, where the cotton area planted with genetically modified varieties containing the pest resistance genes derived from the *Bacillus thuringiensis* (Bt) microbe tripled from 0.5 to 1.5 million hectares.

There are several future breakthroughs that genetic engineering could bring to the cereals that could result in enormous benefits, and especially to the poor producer and consumer. One deals with disease resistance and two others with grain quality. Among all the cereals, rice is unique in its immunity to the rusts (*Puccinia* species). All the other cereals—wheat, maize, sorghum, barley, oats, and rye—are attacked by two to three species of rusts, often resulting in disastrous epidemics and crop failures. Enormous scientific effort over the past 80 years has been devoted to breeding wheat varieties for resistance to stem, leaf, and yellow rust species. After many years of intense crossing and selecting, and multilocation international testing, a good, stable, but poorly understood type of resistance to stem rust was identified in 1952 that remains effective worldwide to the present. However, no such success has been obtained with resistance to leaf or yellow rust, where genetic resistance in any particular variety has been short-lived (three to seven years). Imagine the benefits to humankind if the genes for rust immunity in rice could be transferred to wheat, barley, oats, maize, millet, and sorghum. Finally, the world could be free of the scourge of the rusts, which have led to so many famines over human history.

On another front, bread wheat has superior dough for making leavened bread and other bakery products due to the presence of two proteins, gliadin and glutenin. No other cereals have this combination. Imagine if the genes for these proteins could be identified and transferred to the other cereals, especially rice and maize, so that they, too, could make good-quality leavened bread. This would help many countries, and especially the developing countries in the tropics, where bread wheat flour is often the single largest food import.

Finally, it is also important to mention the growing potential of science to improve the nutritional quality of our food supply. The development, using conventional plant-breeding methods of high-lysine, high-tryptophan QPM varieties and hybrids, took some two decades of painstaking research work. In the future, through biotechnology, we should be able to achieve further nutritional quality enhancements in the cereals and other foods at a much faster rate. The transfer of genes to increase the quantity of vitamin A, iron, and other micronutrients contained in rice can potentially bring significant benefits for millions of people with deficiencies of vitamin A and iron, causes of blindness and anemia, respectively.

> Imagine the benefits to humankind if the genes for rust immunity in rice could be transferred to wheat, barley, oats, maize, millet, and sorghum. Finally, the world could be free of the scourge of the rusts, which have led to so many famines over human history.

Beyond the food, feed, and fiber production benefits that can be forthcoming through biotech products, the possibility that plants can actually be used to vaccinate people against diseases, simply by growing and eating them, offers tremendous possibilities in poor countries.[13] This line of research and development should be pursued aggressively and probably through private-public partnerships, since traditional vaccination programs are costly and difficult to execute.

To date, there is no reliable scientific information to substantiate that transgenic crops are inherently hazardous. Recombinant DNA has been used for 25 years in pharmaceuticals, with no documented cases of harm attributed to the genetic modification process. So far, this is also the case in genetically modified foods. The seed industry has been doing a good job in ensuring that its transgenic crop varieties are safe to plant and that the food they produce is safe to eat.

The transgenic crops released so far generally reduce production costs per unit of output and thus, in theory, are especially appropriate to the developing world, where more than half the population is still engaged in agriculture and where cost-reducing, yield-increasing technologies are the key to poverty reduction. In South Africa, for example, smallholders in the Makhathini Flats area who have adopted Bt cotton have increased their yields by an average of 26 percent, reduced insecticide applications from seven sprays to one, and increased their income by $165 per hectare.[14] Since the biotechnology is packed into the seed, transgenic crops can help to simplify input delivery, often a major bottleneck in reaching smallholder farmers.

However, one major concern is how resource-poor farmers will gain access to the products of biotechnology research. What will be the position of the transnational agribusinesses toward this enormous section of humanity, many of whom still live at the margin of the commercial market economy? This issue goes far beyond economics; it is also a matter for serious ethical reflection and debate. Fundamentally, the issue is whether small-scale farmers of the developing world also have a right to share the benefits of biotechnology. If the answer is yes, then what is the role of international and national governments to ensure that this right is met? I believe we must give this matter very serious thought.

There is an urgent need for developing nations to put into place legal frameworks to facilitate the development, testing, and use of transgenic crops while protecting people and the natural environment. In this legal process, the intellectual property rights of private companies should be safeguarded to ensure fair returns to past investments and to encourage greater investments in the future. In addition, frameworks should not be overly bureaucratic nor should they have unreasonable risk-aversion expectations. Indeed, we believe that the seed industry itself should be given primary responsibility for ensuring the safety of its products.

Although the majority of agricultural scientists anticipate great benefits from biotechnology in the coming decades, new forms of public-private collaboration should be pursued to ensure that all farmers and consumers worldwide have the opportunity to benefit from this new genetic revolution. In particular, public biotechnology research will be needed to balance—and complement—private sector research investments. This is true both for the industrialized countries as well as the developing world.

I am pleased to see that private biotechnology companies are showing considerable willingness to form such partnerships. Monsanto has been a leader in establishing developing country initiatives in agricultural product and technology cooperation; Syngenta is doing likewise, building partnerships with national and international agricultural research centers to address production problems in Africa and elsewhere. The Donald Danforth Plant Science Center in St. Louis, Missouri—cofounded in 1998 by Monsanto and a consortium of universities, public research institutes, and private foundations—is an especially exciting development, given the strong developing country orientation in its research agenda and training programs.

CAN AGRICULTURAL SCIENCE STAY AHEAD OF WORLD POPULATION?

SO FAR, AGRICULTURAL research and production advances—and the efforts of the world's farmers and ranchers—have kept food production ahead of aggregate world population changes. However, the efforts of those on the food-production front are a holding operation that is providing the time needed for economic growth and improvements in education, medicine, and family planning to stabilize the world's population.

There is a crying need today for creative pragmatism in research and extension organizations in many parts of the developing world. In particular, we need more venturesome young scientists willing to dedicate their lives to helping to solve the production problems facing several billion small-scale farmers. In seeking to push forward the frontiers of scientific knowledge, some researchers lose sight of the most pressing concerns of farmers and cease to develop products that extension workers can promote successfully. For the developing countries, impact on farmers' fields should be the primary measure by which to judge the value of this research work, rather than by a flood of publications that often serve to enhance the position of the scientist but do little to alleviate hunger.

STANDING UP TO THE ANTISCIENCE CROWD

SCIENCE AND TECHNOLOGY are under growing attack in the affluent nations where misinformed ideological environmentalists claim that the consumer is being poisoned out of existence by the current high-yielding systems of agricultural production. While I contend this isn't so, I ask myself how it is that so many people believe to the contrary.

First, there seems to be a growing fear of science, per se, as the pace of technological change increases. The late British physicist and philosopher-writer C. P. Snow first wrote about the split between scientists and humanists in his little book, *The Two Cultures*, published in 1962. It wasn't that the two groups necessarily disliked each other; rather, they just didn't know how to talk to each other. The rift has continued to grow since then. The breaking of the atom and the prospects of a nuclear holocaust added to people's fear and drove a bigger wedge between the scientist and the layperson. The world was becoming increasingly unnatural, and science, technology, and industry were seen as the culprits. Rachel Carson's 1962 book, *Silent Spring*—which reported that poisons were everywhere, killing the birds first and then us—struck a very sensitive nerve.

Of course, this perception was not totally unfounded. As Otto Bettmann's book published in 1974 (*The Good Old Days: They Were Terrible*) about environmental quality in America (and the United Kingdom and other industrialized nations) in the late 19th and early 20th centuries graphically pointed out, we were poisoning ourselves. By the mid-20th century, air and water quality had been seriously damaged through wasteful industrial production systems that pushed effluents often literally into "our own backyards."

Over the past 35 years, we have seen dramatic improvements in air and water quality, wildlife protections, the disposal of wastes, and the protection of soils. In almost every environmental category, far more progress has been made than most commentators in the media are willing to admit. Why? I believe that it's because "apocalypse sells."

Sadly, all too many scientists, many of whom should (and do) know better, have jumped on the environmentalist bandwagon in search of research funds. When scientists align themselves with anti-science political movements, like Jeremy Rifkin's antibiotechnology crowd, what are we to think? When scientists lend their names and credibility to unscientific propositions, what are we to think? Is it any wonder that science is losing its constituency? We must be on guard against politically opportunistic, charlatan scientists like T. D. Lysenko, whose pseudoscience in agriculture and vicious persecution of anyone who disagreed with him contributed greatly to the collapse of the former Soviet Union.

However, in sharp contrast to the rich countries—where most remaining environmental problems are urban, industrial, and a consequence of high incomes—the critical environmental problems in most of the low-income developing countries remain rural, agricultural, and poverty-based. More than half of the world's poorest people live on lands that are environmentally fragile and rely on natural resources over which they have little legal control. Land-hungry farmers resort to cultivating unsuitable areas, such as erosion-prone hillsides, semiarid areas where soil degradation is rapid, and tropical forests, where crop yields on cleared fields drop sharply after just a few years.

Professor Robert Paarlberg from Wellesley College and Harvard University has sounded the alarm about the consequences of the debilitating debate between agriculturalists and environmentalists about what constitutes so-called sustainable agriculture in the developing countries. This debate has confused—if not paralyzed—policy makers in the international donor community who, afraid of antagonizing powerful environmentalist lobbying groups, have turned away from supporting science-based agricultural modernization projects so urgently needed in sub-Saharan Africa and parts of Latin America and Asia. The result has been increasing misery in smallholder agriculture and accelerating environmental degradation. This policy deadlock must be broken. In doing so, we cannot lose sight of the enormous job before us to feed 10 billion people.

Certainly, we must be environmentally responsible in our efforts to produce ever-greater quantities of food to feed our growing population. But we must also face up to the fact that we cannot turn back the clock and use technologies that were adequate to a much smaller world population. We must also recognize the vastly different circumstances faced by farmers in different parts of the Third World and assume different policy postures. For example, in Europe or the U.S. Corn Belt, the typical application of 300 to 400 kilograms of fertilizer nutrients per hectare of arable land might cause some environmental problems due to runoff or leaching. But surely, increasing fertilizer use on food crops in sub-Saharan Africa from about 5 kilograms of nutrients per hectare of arable land to 30 to 40 kilograms is not an environmental problem but rather central to Africa's environmental solution.

> We must face up to the fact that we cannot turn back the clock and use technologies that were adequate to a much smaller world population.

CONCLUSION

AT THE CLOSURE of the Earth Summit in 1992 in Rio de Janeiro, 425 members of the scientific and intellectual community presented to the heads of state and government what is now being called the Heidelberg Appeal. Since then, some 3,000 scientists have signed this document, including myself. Permit me to quote the last paragraph of the appeal:

> *The greatest evils which stalk our Earth are ignorance and oppression, and not science, technology, and industry, whose instruments, when adequately managed, are indispensable tools of a future shaped by Humanity, by itself and for itself, in overcoming major problems like overpopulation, starvation, and worldwide diseases.*

Thirty-two years ago, in my acceptance speech for the Nobel Peace Prize, I said that the Green Revolution had won a temporary success in man's war against hunger, which, if fully implemented, could provide sufficient food for humankind through the end of the 20th century. But I warned that unless human population growth eventually stopped, the success of the Green Revolution would only be ephemeral.

I now say that the world has the technology—either available or well advanced in the research pipeline—to feed a population of 10 billion people. The more pertinent question today is whether farmers and ranchers will be permitted to use this new technology. Extremists in the environmental movement from the rich nations seem to be doing everything they can to stop scientific progress in its tracks. Small, but vociferous and highly effective and well-funded, antiscience and technology groups are slowing the application of new technology, whether it be developed from biotechnology or more conventional methods of agricultural science. I am particularly alarmed by those who seek to deny small-scale farmers in the developing countries—and especially those in sub-Saharan Africa—access to the improved seeds, fertilizers, and crop protection chemicals that have allowed the affluent nations the luxury of plentiful and inexpensive foodstuffs, which, in turn, has accelerated their economic development.

While the affluent nations can certainly afford to pay more for food produced by the so-called organic methods, the 1 billion chronically undernourished people of the low-income, food-deficit nations cannot. As the archaeologist Richard Leakey likes to remind his environmental supporters, "You have to have at least one square meal a day to be a conservationist."

Hunger still stalks far too many people today. However, expanding the reach of current crop technologies to areas of the globe passed by the Green Revolution combined with foreseeable improvements in crop productivity will make it possible to provide a better diet at lower prices to more people in the future. The prospect for feeding a world population of 10 billion, while challenging, is bright.

CHAPTER THREE

POPULATION, RESOURCES, AND THE QUEST TO "STABILIZE HUMAN POPULATION": MYTHS AND REALITIES

Nicholas Eberstadt

ECO-MYTHS DEBUNKED

- *World population rose from 1.6 billion in 1900 to more than 6 billion today.*
- *Between 1960 and 2000, global fertility levels dropped by almost half, from a total fertility rate (births per woman per lifetime) of around 5 in 1960 to 65 to one of about 2.7 in 1995 to 2000.*
- *Rapid population growth occurred in the 20th century because of rapidly falling death rates, not rising birth rates. People had not suddenly started breeding like rabbits; instead, they stopped dying like flies.*
- *The end of population growth may be in sight. Forthcoming United Nations Population Division projections are expected to depict global population as peaking at about 7.5 billion in 2050 and declining thereafter.*
- *"Overpopulation" has no clear scientific or demographic meaning. The problems commonly associated with the term (hungry people, squalid living conditions) are more properly understood as issues of human poverty.*

THE IMPERATIVE OF "STABILIZING WORLD POPULATION": A WIDELY ACCEPTED NOTION

A DEMOGRAPHIC SPECTER is haunting authoritative and influential circles in both the United States and the international community. This specter is the supposed imperative to "stabilize human population".

The quest to stabilize human population (or to stabilize world population, or sometimes just to stabilize population) is currently affirmed by the World Bank and many other multilateral and bilateral aid organizations within the international development community. That objective is likewise praised by the United Nations' current secretary-general, Kofi Annan, and is now embraced by a panoply of subsidiary institutions within the UN family, including the United Nations Environmental Programme (UNEP), and the United Nations Children's Fund (UNICEF), and the United Nations Population Fund (UNFPA), which explicitly declares its mission to be the promotion of the "universally accepted aim of stabilizing world population."[1]

Closer to home, the goal of stabilizing human population is championed by a broad network of population and environmental activist groups, including most prominently Planned Parenthood and the Sierra Club (the latter of which has established stabilizing world population as the fourth goal of its 21st-century agenda[2]). The objective, however, is not merely proclaimed by an activist fringe; to the contrary, it is broadly shared by many elements of what might be called the American establishment. Stabilizing world population, for example, is now a programmatic effort for most of the prestigious multibillion-dollar American philanthropic organizations that commit their resources to international population activities, a list including, but not limited to, the Ford Foundation, the Hewlett Foundation, the MacArthur Foundation, the Packard Foundation, and the Rockefeller Foundation. Further, stabilizing world population is a prospect welcomed and financially supported by many of America's most prominent and successful captains of industry, among them self-made multibillionaires Ted Turner, Warren Buffet, and Bill Gates. The propriety—or necessity—of stabilizing global population has been expounded by a wide array of respected writers, spokespersons, and commentators in the U.S. and international media. Politically, the goal of stabilizing world population has been approved by the U.S. State Department and USAID (America's foreign aid apparatus) for fully a generation. The quest to stabilize world population, in fact, is championed in the United States by political figures who are both influential and widely popular. One of America's most passionate and outspoken exponents of world population stabilization, former Vice President Al Gore, very nearly won the presidency in the closely contested 2000 election.

> The banner itself is somewhat misleading, for advocates of stabilizing population are in fact not concerned with *stabilizing* human numbers.

What, exactly, does "stabilizing human population" actually mean? Though the objective is widely championed today, the banner itself is somewhat misleading, for advocates of stabilizing population are in fact not concerned with *stabilizing* human numbers. If they were, one would expect champions of population stabilization to turn their attention to the outlook for Europe and Japan, where populations are currently projected to drop significantly over the next half century.[3] On a more immediate front, human numbers have entered into an abrupt and as yet unchecked decline in the Russian Federation over just the past decade. In 1999 alone, that country suffered almost 1 million more deaths than births.[4] Yet supporters of population stabilization have agitated for coordinated measures to lower Russia's death rate, raise its birth rate, and stanch its ongoing demographic losses.

The reason for such seemingly curious insouciance about demographic decline by self-avowed population stabilizers is that their chosen standard does not quite describe their true quest. For exponents of stabilizing human population do not simply look for population stabilization, but rather, as a former UNFPA executive director framed the goal, they strive "for stabilization of world population at the lowest possible level, within the shortest period of time."[5]

Upon inspection it is apparent that "stabilizing human population" is really code language, a new name for an old and familiar project. Today's call for stabilizing human population is actually a rallying cry for antinatalism, a fervently held dogma of ideological environmentalism. After all, its envisioned means of achieving stabilization is through limiting the prevalence and reducing the level of childbearing around the world, especially in the Third World—implementing policies to reduce births, and thereby depressing fertility in various venues around the globe (and particularly where fertility levels are deemed to be unacceptably high).

Whether they realize it or not, advocates of world population stabilization are devotees of an ideology, not followers of facts.

The ongoing antinatal population crusade by ideological environmentalists couches its arguments in the language of social science and invokes the findings of science to bolster its authority, but it cannot withstand the process of empirical review that lies at the heart of the rational scientific method. Whether they realize it or not, advocates of world population stabilization are devotees of an ideology, not followers of facts.

THE PREMISES OF WORLD POPULATION STABILIZATION

REDUCED TO ITS essence, the case for action to stabilize world population rests upon four specific premises.

The first quite simply holds that we are manifestly in the midst of a world population crisis—a crisis defined by rapid population growth, which in turn is exacerbating overpopulation. Former Vice President Gore nicely illustrated this tenet in his bestselling book, *Earth in the Balance,* and elsewhere, when he stated that in today's global population trends "the absolute numbers are staggering"[6] and that "we can't acquiesce in the continuation of a situation that adds another . . . China's worth of people every decade."[7]

The second premise underpinning the population stabilization project is that current rates of world population growth are not only unsustainable over the long-term, but they also have direct and immediate adverse repercussions upon living standards, resource availability, and even political stability today. In the estimate of the Planned Parenthood Federation of America, for example, "Slowing population growth helps poorer countries develop politically and economically."[8] Gore is more vivid. He maintains that "Population is pushing many countries over an economic cliff as their resources are stripped away and the cycle of poverty and environmental destruction accelerates"[9] and that "societies cannot maintain stability with [that] kind of rapid, unsustainable [demographic] growth"[10] that is being registered in many regions of the world; pointing to such strife-rent spots as Somalia, Rwanda, and the former Yugoslavia, Gore claims that "you can look at the contribution of rapid destabilizing population growth."[11]

The third premise implicit in the agenda of stabilizing human population is that reduced birth rates constitute the solution to the population problems adduced by premises one and two. The fourth and final premise bolstering this agenda is the presumption that well-placed decision makers can effectively and expeditiously engineer the desired changes in worldwide population patterns through deliberate policy interventions. Once again, Gore may have represented this presumption best. In his words, "We know how to stabilize world population"[12] because "population specialists now know with a high degree of confidence what factors dramatically reduce birth rates."[13]

However, all of these premises are highly problematic. None of them are self-evidently true. And to the extent that any of these separate premises are testable, it would appear that they are demonstrably false.

OVERPOPULATION: A PROBLEM MISDEFINED

Consider the first premise: that the world faces a crisis of being burdened by simply too many people. If that premise is offered as an aesthetic judgment, it is irrefutable. (By their very nature, subjective opinions are not falsifiable.) But how does it fare if treated as a testable proposition?

Gore writes that an "overcrowded world is inevitably a polluted one"[14]—a verdict that many of those worried about world population growth would accept without reservation. But overcrowding is not as easily established as some might suppose.

Population density, for example, might seem to be a reasonable criterion for overcrowding. By that criterion, Haiti, India, and Rwanda (each with more than six times the world's average population density) would surely qualify as overcrowded, and Bangladesh—with almost 20 times the inhabited globe's average density—would be manifestly overcrowded. By that same criterion, however, Belgium (1998 population density per square kilometer: 335) would be distinctly more overcrowded than Rwanda (1998 population density per square kilometer: 272). Similarly, the Netherlands would be more overcrowded than Haiti, Bermuda would be more overcrowded than Bangladesh, and oil-rich Bahrain would be three times as overcrowded as India. But the most overcrowded country in the world would be Monaco. With a dire 32,894 persons per square kilometer in 1998, it suffers a population density almost 40 times that of Bangladesh, and more than 700 times the world average.[15] Yet as we all know, population activists do not agitate themselves about the overcrowding problem in Monaco—or in Bermuda or in Bahrain.

Moreover, it is hardly self-evident that there is any association at the international level between population density and economic performance. Figures 3.1 through 3.4 make the point. (They are specifically drawn from data compiled by the World Bank in its compendium of *World Development Indicators;* other databases, however, could be used to much the same effect.)

As Figures 3.1 and 3.2 attest, there was no discernable international relationship between overall national population density and a country's per capita GDP in the year 1999, regardless of whether one measured per capita output on an exchange rate basis or in terms of purchasing power parity (i.e., international dollars). The same holds true for the density of population with respect to arable land: By the data in Figures 3.3 and 3.4, it is impossible to distinguish any meaningful association—positive or negative—between a country's per capita output level and the number of people supported by each local hectare of farm- or pasture-land. Surprising as it may sound to those convinced that the world is beset by overpopulation, the fact is that in our era, population density provides us with no information whatsoever

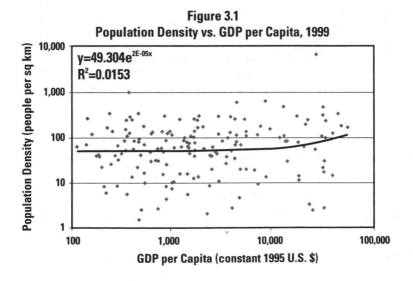

Figure 3.1
Population Density vs. GDP per Capita, 1999

$y=49.304e^{2E\text{-}05x}$
$R^2=0.0153$

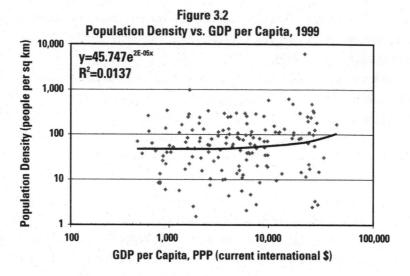

Figure 3.2
Population Density vs. GDP per Capita, 1999

$y = 45.747e^{2E-05x}$
$R^2 = 0.0137$

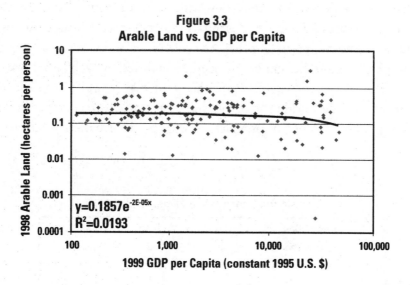

Figure 3.3
Arable Land vs. GDP per Capita

$y = 0.1857e^{-2E-05x}$
$R^2 = 0.0193$

for predicting a country's level of economic development or economic performance.

Do other simple demographic measures provide a better reading of the population problem that so many take to be so very obvious today? Perhaps we might look at rates of population growth. In the 1990s, sub-Saharan Africa was estimated to have the world's very

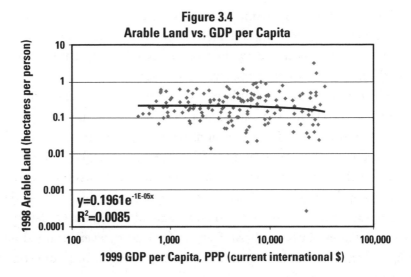

Figure 3.4
Arable Land vs. GDP per Capita

highest rate of population growth—the United Nations Population Division (UNPD) put its pace at more than 2.5 percent a year for the period 1995 to 2000[16]—and sub-Saharan Africa is clearly a most troubled area these days. However, if we look back in history, we will discover that the United States had an even higher rate of population growth at the end of the 18th century. In the decade 1790 to 1800, in fact, the U.S. pace of population growth was 3 percent a year.[17] Some today may believe that sub-Saharan Africa has too many people—but would they say the same about early frontier America?

Fertility rates are hardly more illuminating. In *Earth in the Balance,* Gore expressly mentions Egypt, Kenya, and Nigeria as candidates for places with too many people (either today or in the decades immediately ahead).[18] All three countries are thought to experience fertility levels above the current world average. According to the latest (May 2000) projections by the U.S. Census Bureau, in 1998 the total fertility rate (births per woman per lifetime under prevailing childbearing schedules) for the world as a whole was about 2.8, as against 3.4 in Egypt, 4.4 in Kenya, and 5.8 in Nigeria.[19] But once again, fertility levels were far higher in the United States in the early years of the Republic than in any of these places today. Around 1800, according to estimates by the demographer Michael Haines, the total fertility rate for white Americans was just over *seven* births per woman per lifetime[20]—yet Thomas Jefferson's America is not today widely regarded as a society in the throes of a population crisis. Clearly, fertility rates by themselves tell us very little.

We could continue combing for demographic measures that might help to clarify the nature and pinpoint the epicenters of the population crisis that Gore envisions. But as our exercise should already indicate, that would be a fruitless task. Additional demographic criteria will confront the same problem of obvious misidentification of presumptive regions suffering from too many people because demographic criteria cannot by themselves unambiguously describe overpopulation. This is a basic fact, recognized by every trained demographer. And that basic fact raises correspondingly basic questions about the concept of overpopulation.

The alleged population crisis that advocates of world population stabilization wish to resolve is impossible to define in demographic terms because it is a problem that has been misdefined. In most minds, the notions of overpopulation, overcrowding, or too many people are associated with images of hungry children, unchecked disease, squalid living conditions, and awful slums. Those problems, sad to say, are all too real in the contemporary world. But the proper name for those conditions is *human poverty*. And the correspondence between human poverty and demographic trends, as we shall see in a moment, is by no means as causal and clear-cut as some would suppose.

> The correspondence between human poverty and demographic trends is by no means as causal and clear-cut as some would suppose.

If we are to make inroads against the problems confronting humanity, it is important that we begin by calling those problems by their proper names. The problem of global poverty, in and of itself, cannot in an empirical sense be defined as a world population crisis—unless one means it is a crisis that so many people today should be suffering from poverty. But it is a fundamental lapse in logic to assume that poverty is a population problem simply because it is manifest today in large numbers of human beings. The proper name for that logical error is the *fallacy of composition*.

POPULATION GROWTH, DEVELOPMENT, AND POLITICAL STABILITY

Let us now consider the second premise of world population stabilization: that rapid population growth and high fertility levels cause or exacerbate poverty, resource scarcity, and political instability. If we wish to treat this premise as an empirically testable proposition (rather than an unchallengeable tenet of faith), we will recognize immediately the complexity of the processes we propose to observe. The relationships between population change and economic or political change encompass an extraordinarily broad and complicated set of interactions with an array of multidirectional influences and consequential second-, third-, and even higher-order impacts.

Describing these interactions comprehensively and accurately is a tremendous and subtle challenge. And researchers who have approached this challenge with care and objectivity typically have described the economic impact of demographic changes in nuanced and qualified terms. Typical of such work are the findings of econometrician Dennis Ahlburg, who concludes that "it is not clear whether population growth causes poverty in the long run or not, [although] high fertility leading to rapidly growing population will increase the number of people in poverty in the short run."[21] Development economist Robert Cassen accurately describes the state of current research when he notes "the issue of whether per capita economic growth is reduced by population growth remains unsettled. Attempts to demonstrate such an effect empirically have produced no significant and reliable results."[22]

Even so, we need not rely upon the judgments of experts, or attempt to replicate their efforts at model building, to appreciate the flaws inherent in this premise.

We can begin by recalling the reason for the 20th century's population explosion. Between 1900 and 2000, human numbers almost quadrupled, leaping from about 1.6 billion to more than 6 billion[23]—in pace or magnitude, nothing like that surge had ever previously taken place. But why exactly did we experience a world population explosion in the 20th century? It was not because people suddenly started breeding like rabbits—rather, it was because they finally stopped dying like flies.

Between 1900 and the end of the 20th century, the human life span likely doubled, from a planetary life expectancy at birth of perhaps 30 years[24] to one of more than 60 years.[25] By this measure, the overwhelming preponderance of the health progress in all of human history took place during the past 100 years.

Over the past half century, worldwide progress in reducing death rates has been especially dramatic. Tables 3.1 and 3.2 underscore this important fact. Between the early 1950s and the late 1990s, according to estimates by the United Nations Population Division (UNPD—not to be confused with UNFPA), the planetary expectation of life at birth jumped by almost 19 years, or two-fifths, from under 47 years to 65 years. For the low-income regions, the leap was even more dramatic. Taken together, average life expectancy in these areas surged up by well over two decades, a rise of more than 50 percent. Even troubled sub-Saharan Africa—despite its protracted postindependence-era political and economic turmoil and the advent of a catastrophic HIV/AIDS epidemic—is thought to have enjoyed an increase in local life expectancy of nearly a third. (Practically the only countries to register no appreciable improvements in life expectancy over this period were the handful of European territories within what was once

Table 3.1.   Estimated Life Expectancy at Birth (Both Sexes)

	1950–1955	1995–2000	Absolute Change (years)	% Change
Developed Countries	66.2	74.9	8.7	13%
Developing Countries	41.0	62.9	21.9	53%
Latin America and Caribbean	51.4	69.3	17.9	35%
Asia	41.3	65.8	24.4	59%
Sub-Saharan Africa	36.7	48.6	11.9	32%
Memorandum Items:				
Russia	64.6	66.1	1.5	2%

Source: UN World Population Prospects, 2000 Revision.

**Table 3.2.   Estimated Infant Mortality (Both Sexes)
(Deaths per 1,000 Live Births)**

	1950–1955	1995–2000	Absolute Change (years)	% Change
Developed Countries	59.1	8.3	-50.8	-86%
Developing Countries	180.2	65.3	-114.9	-64%
Latin America and Caribbean	126.2	35.6	-90.6	-72%
Asia	182.4	59.3	-123.1	-67%
Sub-Saharan Africa	178.7	97.0	-81.7	-46%
Memorandum Items:				
Russia	97.5	16.7	-80.7	-83%

Source: UN World Population Prospects, 2000 Revision.

the Soviet Union; in the Russian Federation in particular, gains over these four and a half decades were almost negligible.)

Among the most important proximate reasons for the global surge in life expectancy was the worldwide drop in infant mortality rates. In the early 1950s, according again to UNPD estimates, 167 out of every 1,000 children born around the world did not survive their first year of life; by the late 1990s, that toll was down to 60 per 1,000. In developed countries, infant mortality is thought to have fallen by five-sixths during those decades and by almost two-thirds in the collectivity of developing countries. Even in troubled regions, great advances in infant survival were achieved; in sub-Saharan Africa, for example, the infant mortality rate is thought to have declined by nearly half, and Russia's infant mortality rate probably fell by more than 80 percent

This radical drop in mortality is entirely responsible for the increase in human numbers over the course of the 20th century; the population explosion, in other words, was really a health explosion.

Now with respect to economic development, the implications of a health explosion—of *any* health explosion—are, on their face, hardly negative. Quite the contrary: A healthier population is clearly going to be a population with greater productive potential. Healthier people are able to learn better, work harder, and engage in gainful employment longer and contribute more to economic activity than unhealthy, short-lived counterparts. Whether that potential actually translates into tangible economic results will naturally depend on other factors, such as social and legal institutions or the business and policy climate. Nevertheless, the health explosion that propelled the 20th century's population explosion was an economically auspicious phenomenon rather than a troubling trend.

All other things being equal, one would have expected the health explosion to contribute to the acceleration of economic growth, the increase of incomes, and the spread of wealth. And as it happens, the 20th century witnessed not only a population explosion and a health explosion but also a prosperity explosion. Estimates by the economic historian Angus Maddison, who has produced perhaps the most authoritative reconstruction of long-term global economic trends presently available, demonstrate this.[26] (See Figure 3.5.)

Between 1900 and 1998, by Maddison's reckoning, global GDP per capita (in internationally adjusted 1990 dollars) more than quadrupled. Gains in productivity were globally uneven. In both relative and absolute terms, today's OECD states enjoyed disproportionate improvements. Nonetheless, every region of the planet became richer. Africa's economic performance, according to Maddison, was the most dismal of any major global region over the course of the 20th

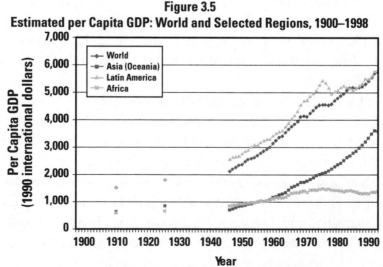

Figure 3.5
Estimated per Capita GDP: World and Selected Regions, 1900–1998

Sources: Angus Maddison. *Monitoring the World Economy 1820–1992* (OECD 1995). Angus Maddison. *The World Economy: A Millennial Perspective* (OECD 2001).

century. Yet even there, per capita GDP was approximated to be more than two and a half times higher in 1998 than it had been in 1900.[27]

Suffice it then to say that the 20th century's population explosion did not forestall the most dramatic and widespread improvement in output, incomes, and living standards that humanity had ever experienced. Though severe poverty still endures in much of the world, there can be no doubt that its incidence has been markedly curtailed over the past 100 years, despite a near quadrupling of human numbers.

Maddison's estimates of global economic growth highlight another empirical problem with the second premise of the population stabilization project. With a near quadrupling of the human population over the course of the 20th century and a more than fourfold increase in human GDP per capita over those same years, global economic output has taken an absolutely amazing leap. Maddison's own figures suggest world GDP might have been more than 18 times higher in 1998 than it was in 1900. (See Figure 3.6.) But GDP is a measure of economic output—and for the world as a whole, economic output and economic demand must be identical. If the demand for goods and services has multiplied nearly 20-fold during the 20th century, humanity's demand for, and consumption of, natural resources

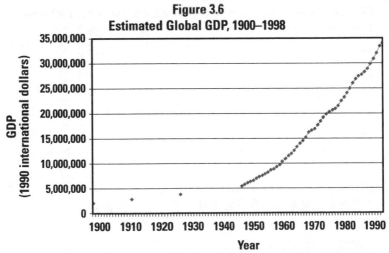

Figure 3.6
Estimated Global GDP, 1900–1998

Sources: Angus Maddison. *Monitoring the World Economy 1820–1992* (OECD 1995). Angus Maddison. *The World Economy: A Millennial Perspective* (OECD 2001).

has also rocketed upward. But despite humanity's tremendous new pressures on planetary resources, the relative prices of virtually all primary commodities have *fallen* over the course of the 20th century, and many of them, quite substantially.

Despite the tremendous expansion of the international grain trade over the past century, for example, the inflation-adjusted, dollar-denominated international price of each of the major cereals—corn, wheat, and rice—fell by more than 70 percent between 1900 and 1998.[28] (See Figure 3.7.) By the same token, the *Economist* magazine's industrials price index—a weighted composite for 14 internationally traded metals and nonfood agricultural commodities[29]—registered a decline in inflation-adjusted dollars of almost 80 percent between 1900 and 1999.[30] Perhaps the most comprehensive index of long-term real primary commodity prices was the one constructed by Enzo Grilli and Maw Cheng Yang.[31] (See Figure 3.8.) Their series encompassed 24 in-ternationally-traded nonfuel primary commodities, plus coal and oil. Their calculations extend from 1900 only up to 1986, but their results are nevertheless arresting. For that 86-year period, Grilli and Yang found that real prices of nonfuel primary commodities—renewable re-sources like cereals and nonrenewable resources such as metals—fell

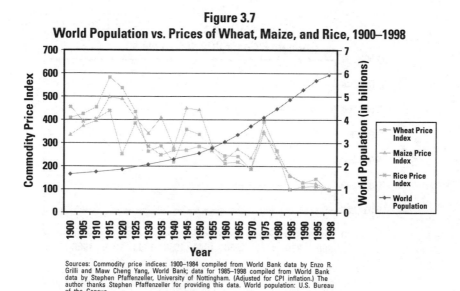

Figure 3.7
World Population vs. Prices of Wheat, Maize, and Rice, 1900–1998

Sources: Commodity price indices: 1900–1984 compiled from World Bank data by Enzo R. Grilli and Maw Cheng Yang, World Bank; data for 1985–1998 compiled from World Bank data by Stephen Pfaffenzeller, University of Nottingham. (Adjusted for CPI inflation.) The author thanks Stephen Pfaffenzeller for providing this data. World population: U.S. Bureau of the Census.

Figure 3.8
World GDP vs. Relative Primary Commodity Prices, 1900–1998

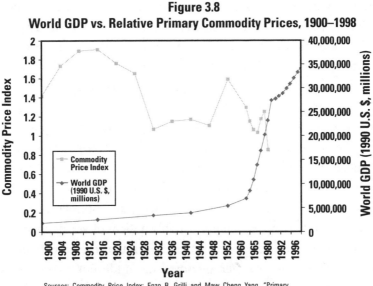

Sources: Commodity Price Index: Enzo R. Grilli and Maw Cheng Yang, "Primary Commodity Prices, Manufactured Goods Prices, and the Terms of Trade of Developing Countries: What the Long Run Shows" (*World Bank Economic Review* 2:1 (1988), pp. 1–47). World GDP: Angus Maddison, *The World Economy: A Millennial Perspective* (Paris: OECD, 2001).

substantially, trending downward by an average of 0.6 percent per year. When fuels were included in the series, the picture changed only slightly. With energy included in their primary commodity index, real overall prices still trended downward at a pace of 0.5 percent per annum. On that trajectory, real primary commodity prices would be expected to decline by nearly 40 percent over the course of a century.

> Falling prices indicate that the resources humanity makes use of grew *less scarce* over the course of the 20th century.

The paradox of exploding demand for resources and simultaneous pronounced declines in real resource prices will appear curious and compelling to any observer, but it should be especially arresting to the viewer who shares the essentially Malthusian sensibilities of ideological environmentalism. In the most fundamental sense, after all, price data are meant to convey information about scarcity—and by the sorts of information that they convey, they would seem to indicate that the resources humanity makes economic use of grew *less scarce* over the course of the 20th century. There are, to be sure, explanations for this paradox—but the stabilization project's second premise, which holds that population growth must result in resource scarcity, is hardly able to provide it.

The dilemma can be stated even more starkly: If the presumptions incorporated in that premise regarding the interplay between population growth, living standards, and resource scarcity were valid, the 20th century should not have occurred.

What about the supposed relationship between rapid population growth and political strife? The hypothesis that population growth could affect political stability is certainly worth entertaining. It is plausible, after all, to conjecture that instability is more of a risk for governments that do not cope well with change—and population growth, whatever else it may be, is also inescapably a form of social change.

The vision of the link between rapid population growth and political destabilization, however, is sometimes undercut by the very evidence adduced to support it. Take Gore's aforementioned attribution of the carnage in the former Yugoslavia in the early 1990s to rapid population growth. The problem with the argument is that the former Yugoslavia was characterized neither by especially rapid rates of population growth nor by particularly high levels of fertility.

Consider Bosnia and Herzegovina, which suffered war, horrific ethnic cleansing, and other atrocities in the early 1990s. Over the three decades before pandemonium erupted (i.e., 1961 to 91), Bosnia and Herzegovina recorded a population growth rate of about 1 percent a year—slower than the United States' 1.1 percent per annum rate over the same period and barely half the average worldwide pace of 1.9 percent during those years. Moreover, in 1991— on the eve of its descent into chaos— Bosnia's estimated total fertility rate was 1.7 births per woman per lifetime, well below the replacement level. Estimates by the UNPD suggest that Bosnia and Herzegovina's fertility levels had been below replacement throughout the 1980s as well. The situation is little different in the other fragments of the former Yugoslavia. Fertility levels and population

> It does not follow that the surest and soundest way of preventing political conflict is simply to prevent the existence of people in the first place.

growth rates were even lower than Bosnia's in Croatia and Slovenia and only marginally higher in Macedonia; Serbia's fertility level was slightly higher, but its rate of population growth was slightly lower.[32] (Today, incidentally, all the countries carved out of the former Yugoslavia report fertility levels far below the replacement.[33])

One can only wonder, if the former Yugoslavia is an example of a region rent by demographically driven political turmoil, exactly how low are population growth rates supposed to fall, and birth rates to sink, before a region is safe from this purported menace? It is perfectly true that political conflict cannot take place without human populations—but it does not follow that the surest and soundest way of preventing political conflict is simply to prevent the existence of people in the first place.

WORLD POPULATION STABILIZATION THROUGH SCIENTIFIC POPULATION POLICIES?

The third premise of world population stabilization—that birth rates must be lowered to alleviate the world population crisis and to mitigate the adverse economic, resource, and political consequences of rapid population growth—requires absolutely no substantiation if one is a true believer in the antinatalist dogma of ideological environmentalism. To the antinatalist way of thinking, the purposeful reduction of birth rates (and especially birth rates in poorer regions) is an incontestably worthy policy objective—for to this way of thinking, it is axiomatic that fewer births translates directly into benefits for present and future generations. For those who must be convinced that a problem exists before consenting in the public action proposed to redress it, that conclusion rests on the first two premises—and for the empirically inclined, as we have seen, those are shaky foundations indeed.

But even if we were convinced of the pressing need to take public action to lower worldwide birth rates, it would not necessarily follow that the desired result could be achieved, or achieved at an acceptable cost, or achieved voluntarily. Here lies the pivotal importance of the fourth premise of world population stabilization, for this tenet maintains that it is an established fact that population specialists know how international birth rates can be lowered, and that these specialists can consequently provide policy makers with reliable advice about the precise interventions that will bring about fertility declines.

But once again, the final premise underpinning the quest for stabilizing world population is badly flawed. The plain fact is that students of contemporary and historical childbearing patterns have *not* uncovered the magic formula that explains why fertility changes occurred in the past, much less identified the special levers that can determine how these trends will unfold in the future.

The trouble with the mission to identify universal and reliable determinants of fertility decline goes back literally to the origins of the phenomenon. Secular fertility decline—the sustained, long-term shift from big families to small ones—commenced for the first time in Europe, about 200 years ago. But it did not begin in England and Wales, then perhaps the most open, literate, and industrialized part of the Continent, if not the world. Instead, it began in France, a country then impoverished, overwhelmingly rural, predominantly illiterate— and, not to put too fine a point on it, Catholic. Clearly, the modernization model does not plausibly explain the advent of fertility decline in the modern world. And unfortunately, alternative models do not really fare much better. Reviewing the theories of fertility decline in western Europe and the evidence adduced to support them, the historian Charles Tilly wrote that "[t]he problem is that we have too many explanations which are plausible in general terms, which contradict each other to some degree and which fail to fit some significant part of the facts."[34] But what was true for western Europe at the onset of this process holds equally for the rest of the world today.

Al Gore's bestseller, *Earth in the Balance*, exemplifies the thinking of many current proponents of world population stabilization in describing the factors that he holds to be instrumental in achieving sustained fertility reductions:

High literacy rates and education levels *are important, especially for women; once they are empowered intellectually and socially they make decisions about the number of children they wish to have. Low infant mortality rates give parents a sense of confidence that even with a small family, some of their children will grow to maturity . . . and provide physical security when they are old. Nearly ubiquitous access to a variety of affordable birth control techniques gives parents the power to choose when and whether to have children.*[35] *[emphasis in original]*

Each of these three desiderata may qualify as a social objective in its own right, entirely irrespective of its influence on demographic trends. As purported determinants of fertility change, however, the explanatory and predictive properties of these three factors largely fail.

Data from the 2000/2001 edition of the World Bank's *World Development Report* underscore the problem.[36] According to the World Bank's figures, the adult illiteracy rate for both males and females was higher in 1998 in Mongolia than in Tanzania—but Tanzania's fertility level in 1998 was reportedly more than twice as high as Mongolia's (5.4 versus 2.5 births per woman). Tunisia and Rwanda were said to have almost identical rates of adult female illiteracy (42 percent versus 43 percent), yet Tunisia's fertility level is put at just over replacement (2.2) while Rwanda's is almost three times higher (6.2.). And although Bangladesh's female illiteracy rate is still placed at more than 70 percent, the country's fertility level is said to have fallen by almost half between 1980 and 1998. Iran's total fertility rates is said to have plummeted by a remarkable 60 percent, from 6.7 to 2.7, over those same 18 years. But presumably the Iranian revolution was not quite what Gore and other ideological environmentalists had in mind in arguing that intellectual and social empowerment of women would lead to smaller families.

Infant mortality provides scarcely more information about fertility levels or fertility change. By the UNPD's projections, for example, Jordan's infant mortality rate was about the same as Thailand's in the early 1990s. But where Thailand's fertility level at that time was below replacement, Jordan's was above 5 births per woman per lifetime. By the same token, although infant mortality rates were said to be almost identical in Bangladesh and Yemen in the late 1990s, Yemen's total fertility rate at that time was twice as high as Bangladesh's (7.6 versus 3.8)—and while fertility levels had dropped substantially in Bangladesh over the previous generation, movement in Yemen's fertility rate had yet to be detected.[37] Historically, the onset of sustained fertility decline in France took place during a period (1780 to 1820) when the country suffered an estimated average of almost 200 infant deaths for every 1,000 births.[38] No country in the contemporary world suffers from such a brutally high infant mortality rate, but a number of present-day countries with considerably lower infant mortality rates than prevailed in Napoleonic France apparently have yet to enter into fertility decline. Conversely, literally dozens of contemporary low-income countries with much more favorable infant and child survival schedules than prevailed in that bygone France have yet to report fertility levels as low as the four births per woman per lifetime estimated for French society around 1800.[39]

As for the relationship between fertility and the availability of modern contraceptives (or national programs to subsidize or encourage their use), inconvenient facts must once again be faced. To start with, the utilization rates for modern contraceptive methods are not an especially reliable indicator of a society's fertility level. In the early 1990s, among married women ages 15 to 49, Zimbabwe's rate of modern contraceptive utilization was three times as high as Romania's (42 percent versus 14 percent), yet Romania's total fertility rate was about 1.4 whereas Zimbabwe's was about 4.1. Syria's 1993 rate of modern contraceptive prevalence was likewise higher than Lithuania's rate for 1994 to 95 (29 percent versus 22 percent), yet total fertility rate was also three times the Lithuanian level (4.6 versus 1.5).[40] Further such examples abound.

> The independent influence of national population programs on national birth rates appears to be much more limited than enthusiasts are willing to recognize.

For another thing, the independent influence of national population programs on national birth rates appears to be much more limited than enthusiasts are willing to recognize. A comparison of Mexico and Brazil, Latin America's two most populous countries, illustrates the point. Since 1974, the Mexican government has sponsored a national family planning program expressly committed to reducing the country's rate of population growth. Brazil, by contrast, has never implemented a national family planning program. In the quarter century after the introduction of Mexico's national population program, Mexican fertility levels fell by an estimated 56 percent. In Brazil, during the same period, fertility is estimated to have declined by 54 percent—an almost identical proportion. And despite the absence of a national family planning program, Brazil's fertility levels today remain lower than Mexico's.[41]

In the final analysis, the single best international predictor of fertility levels turns out to *desired* fertility levels: the number of children that women say they would like to have.[42] Perhaps this should not be surprising. Parents tend to have strong opinions about important matters pertaining to their family; parents tend to act on the basis of those opinions; and even in poor developing countries, parents do not believe that babies are found under cabbages. The primacy of desired fertility explains why birth rates can be higher in regions where contraceptive utilization rates are also higher, for it is parents, not pills, that make the final choice about family size.

For advocates of stabilizing world population, the predominance of parental preferences in the determination of national and international birth rates poses an awkward dilemma. If parental preferences really rule, and a government sets official population targets for a truly voluntary family planning program, those targets are not likely to be it. Indeed, if parents are genuinely permitted to pursue the family size they personally desire, national population programs can only meet preestablished official demographic targets by complete and utter chance.

On the other hand, if a government sets population targets and wishes to stand a reasonable chance of achieving them, the mischievous independence of parental preferences means that wholly voluntary population programs cannot be relied upon. If states, rather than the parents, are to determine a society's preferred childbearing patterns, governments must be able to force parents to adhere to the officially approved parameters.

Thus, whether they recognize it or not, every advocate of antinatal population programs must make a fateful choice. They must either opt for voluntarism, in which case their population targets will be meaningless. Or else they must opt for attempting to meet their population targets, in which case they must embrace coercive measures. There is no third way.

PROSPECTS FOR WORLD POPULATION GROWTH IN THE 21ST CENTURY

ADVOCATES OF STABILIZING human population characteristically regard the phenomenon of natural increase as an inexorable and almost uncontrollable phenomenon. (The purportedly all-but-irrepressible nature of human population growth, in turn, helps to explain why ideological environmentalists view the process as inherently fraught with terrifying consequence.) Some of these advocates have warned that the human population will double, or more than double, over the course of the coming century unless the comprehensive program of population action that they prefer is rigorously implemented. Thus Alex Marshall, a spokesperson for the UNFPA, speaks ominously of a near doubling of global population in the next half century. Without "promised cash for family planning in developing countries," he reportedly explained, world population is likely to hit 11 billion—a prospect he likened to "looking over a cliff."[43] Likewise, Gore justifies his call for a Global Marshall Plan—the first of whose four points is stabilizing world population—with the assertion that experts "say the [world population] total could reach 14 billion or even higher before leveling off" at the end of the 21st century.[44]

As we have already seen, the grim and inescapable connection between population growth and mounting economic problems that is posited by today's antinatal doctrine is hardly faithful to the actual record of global demographic and economic development over the past century. But the apparent anxiety that some proponents of stabilizing world population experience in contemplating a future with 11 billion, 14 billion, or more human inhabitants of our planet may also be misplaced for a more prosaic reason: To judge by current trends, such levels may never be achieved.

To be sure, long-term population projections are extraordinarily problematic. No robust scientific basis exists for anticipating desired parental fertility in *any* locale, much less for the world as a whole, very far in advance. Since it is fertility levels that largely determine future population trajectories, this is more than an incidental inconvenience. The experience of the past four decades, however, is worth bearing in mind. Between the early 1960s and the late 1990s, global fertility levels are thought to have dropped by almost half, from a total fertility rate (TFR, or births per woman per lifetime) of around 5 in 1960 to 65 to one of about 2.7 in 1995 to 2000. Over that same period, the average TFR for developing countries is thought to have dropped fully by half, from 6 to roughly 3.[45] Although there is a well-known and general correspondence between increasing affluence and lower fertility, material progress alone does not account for this tremendous decline in birth rates in low-income countries. Equally important has been the largely overlooked fact that parents still caught in Third World poverty have been choosing to have ever-smaller families.

Figures 3.9 to 3.14 illustrate the point. They draw upon World Bank data on fertility levels, per capita income levels, and adult female illiteracy levels for almost 200 countries over the period 1960 to 99. In 1960, the international association between per capita GDP (calculated

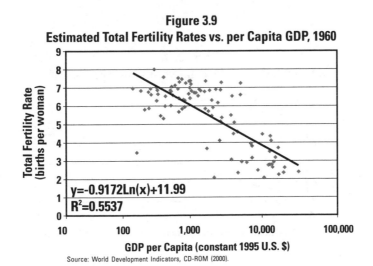

Figure 3.9
Estimated Total Fertility Rates vs. per Capita GDP, 1960

$y=-0.9172\text{Ln}(x)+11.99$
$R^2=0.5537$

GDP per Capita (constant 1995 U.S. $)

Source: World Development Indicators, CD-ROM (2000).

Figure 3.10
Estimated Total Fertility Rates vs. per Capita GDP, 1999

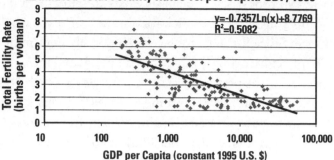

Source: World Development Indicators, CD-ROM (2000).

Figure 3.11
Estimated Total Fertility Rates vs. GDP per Capita: 1960 vs. 1999 Correlations

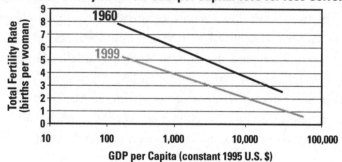

Source: World Development Indicators, CD-ROM (2000).

Figure 3.12
Estimated Total Fertility Rates vs. Illiteracy Rates, 1980

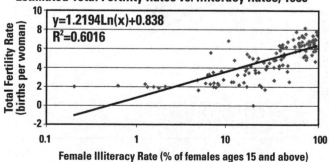

Source: World Development Indicators, CD-ROM (2000).

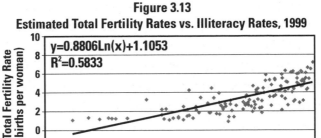

Figure 3.13
Estimated Total Fertility Rates vs. Illiteracy Rates, 1999

Source: World Development Indicators, CD-ROM (2000).

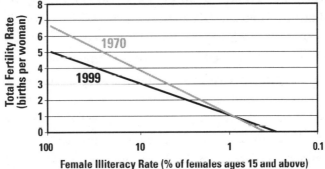

Figure 3.14
Estimated Total Fertility Rates vs. Illiteracy Rates: 1970 vs. 1999 Correlations

Source: World Development Indicators, CD-ROM (2000)

on the basis of exchange rates) and TFRs was relatively strong (although by no means mechanistic); the same was true in 1999. (See Figures 3.9 and 3.14.) But over the intervening four decades, the particulars of that association had shifted dramatically, and the income-fertility curves of 1960 and 1999 look quite different. (See Figure 3.11.) In 1960, a country with a per capita GDP of $100 (on exchange-rate basis) would have a TFR of more than 7. In 1999, a country with that same income level would have been predicted to have a TFR of about 5 to 2 births per woman per lifetime fewer. At any given income level, including even very low income levels, parents around the world have generally been opting for fewer children over the past four decades.

The World Bank does not offer estimates of illiteracy rates for women for 1960, but a comparison of the illiteracy-fertility situation in 1980 and 1999 is possible. (See Figures 3.12 through 3.14.) Once again, it appears that even in settings where female illiteracy levels happen to be very high, fertility levels are, in general, noticeably lower now than they would have been just two decades ago.

Few people would choose to be poor or illiterate. Yet poor and illiterate people have demonstrated, over the past generation and a half, that they, too, can make family planning choices—and they have increasingly chosen post-traditional fertility regimens. Quite clearly, neither low income levels nor the lack of education among young women constitutes the sort of structural barrier against fertility decline that many population activists have heretofore supposed.

Expert demographic opinion is today catching up with revealed reality. Thus in August 2001, a study in *Nature* by researchers with the International Institute for Applied Systems Analysis spoke of "the end of world population growth," contending that "there is around an 85 percent chance that the world's population will stop growing before the end of the century . . . [and] a 60 percent probability that the world's population will not exceed 10 billion people."[46] In March 2002, in a major shift from its previous practices, the UNPD announced that the 2002 revision of its *World Population Prospects* would presume subreplacement fertility levels for 80 percent of the world by the middle of the 21st century, hypothesizing further that "below replacement fertility will lead first to the slowing of population growth rates and then to slow reductions in the size of world population";[47] UNPD's director, Joseph Chamie, is quoted in London's *Sunday Times* as stating that the forthcoming UNPD projections will depict global population as peaking at about 7.5 billion in 2050 and declining thereafter.[48]

These latest population projections are, of course, based on the same fragile theoretical foundations as the earlier projections they supersede; there is no reason to accord them special and unparalleled authority. The simple fact of the matter, however, is that even poor people can choose to have small families and that increasing numbers of poor couples around the world are doing just that. If poor people in low-income countries reveal a preference for smaller families in the decades to come, world population totals will be distinctly lower than proponents of world population stabilization have heretofore imagined—and those lower totals would have been reached without the emergency worldwide population programs that many activists today advocate.

NATURAL RESOURCES, HUMAN RESOURCES, AND DEVELOPMENT

FORTUNATELY FOR OUR perennially troubled planet, humanity's population demographic and development prospects appear to be seriously misconstrued by the pessimistic doctrine of world population stabilization.

While the prevalence of poverty across the globe is unacceptably great today—and will continue to be so in the future (after all, what level of poverty should be acceptable?)—humanity has enjoyed unprecedented and extraordinary improvements in material living standards over the past century, and over the past few decades in particular. Those improvements are represented in the worldwide increases in life expectancy and per capita income levels that we have already reviewed.

The tremendous and continuing spread of health and prosperity around the planet betokens a powerful and historically new dynamic that antinatalists today only dimly apprehend. This is the shift on a global scale from the reliance on natural resources to the reliance on human resources as fuel for economic growth. The worldwide surge in health levels has not been an isolated phenomenon. To the contrary, it has been accompanied by, and is inextricably linked to, pervasive and dramatic (albeit highly uneven) increases in nutrition levels, literacy levels, and levels of general educational attainment. (See Figure 3.15 and Tables 3.3 and 3.4.) These interlocked trends speak to a profound and continuing worldwide augmentation of what some have called *human capital* and others term *human resources*—the human potential to generate a prosperity based upon knowledge, skills, organization, and other innately human capabilities.

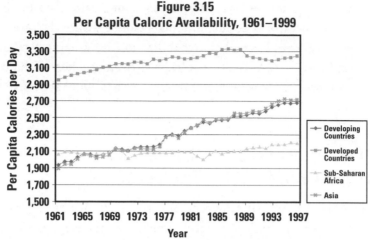

Figure 3.15
Per Capita Caloric Availability, 1961–1999

Source: Food and Agriculture Organization of the United Nations. http://www.apps.fao.org

In a physical sense, the natural resources of the planet are clearly finite and therefore limited. But the planet is now experiencing a monumental expansion of a different type of resource: human resources. Unlike natural resources, human resources are in practice always renewable and in theory entirely inexhaustible. Indeed, it is not at all self-evident that there are any natural limits to the buildup of such potentially productive human-based capabilities.

It is in ignoring these very human resources that so many contemporary surveyors of the global prospect have so signally misjudged the demographic and environmental constraints upon development today—and equally misjudged the possibilities for tomorrow.

Table 3.3.   Estimated Illiteracy Rate (Both Sexes, Ages 15 and Over)

	1970	1980	1990	1995	2000
World	37.0	30.6	24.8	22.7	20.6
Developed Countries	5.7	3.4	1.9	1.4	1.1
Developing Countries	51.9	41.8	32.6	29.5	26.3
Least Developed Countries	73.2	66.0	57.7	53.7	49.3
Latin America and Caribbean	26.1	20.3	14.9	13.3	11.7
Asia	49.1	39.4	30.5	27.7	24.9
Sub-Saharan Africa	71.6	61.7	50.7	45.2	39.7

Source: UNESCO Institute for Statistics. http://www.unescostat.unesco.org/en/stats/stats0.htm

Table 3.4. Estimated Educational Attainment by Sex
(Population Age 15 and Over)

		Average School Year		Gender Ration
		Females	Males	(Female/Male, %)
World	1960	4.31	4.98	86.7
	1970	4.74	5.59	84.7
	1980	5.42	6.43	84.3
	1990	5.93	6.94	85.5
	1995	5.94	6.95	85.4
	2000	6.13	7.19	85.3
All	1960	1.46	2.63	55.7
Developing	1970	1.94	3.38	57.2
Countries	1980	2.74	4.37	62.5
	1990	3.61	5.21	69.3
	1995	3.99	5.56	71.8
	2000	4.33	5.92	73.2
Middle East/	1960	0.83	1.63	51.0
North America	1970	1.39	2.75	50.5
	1980	2.41	4.15	58.0
	1990	3.57	5.17	69.1
	1995	4.21	5.74	73.3
	2000	4.69	6.17	76.0
Sub-Saharan	1960	1.34	2.17	61.8
Africa	1970	1.56	2.60	60.1
	1980	1.91	2.89	66.0
	1990	2.49	3.83	65.0
	1995	2.82	3.98	70.8
	2000	3.01	4.04	74.4
Latin America/	1960	3.24	3.36	96.3
Caribbean	1970	3.52	4.14	85.0
	1980	4.29	4.57	93.7
	1990	5.24	5.41	96.8
	1995	5.58	5.91	94.4
	2000	5.81	6.31	92.2

Source: Barro, Robert J. and Jong-Wha Lee, *International Data on Educational Attainment: Updates and Implications*, CID Working Paper No. 42, Harvard University (April 2000).

CHAPTER FOUR

A Century of Environmental Progress and Natural Resource Abundance

Stephen Moore

ECO-MYTHS DEBUNKED

- *Contrary to infamous doom and gloom reports of the 1960s and 1970s, including the Club of Rome's 1972* The Limits to Growth *and the Carter Administration's 1980* Global 2000 Report, *we are not running out of energy, food, or minerals. The data clearly show that natural resource scarcity—as measured by cost or price—has been decreasing rather than increasing in the long run for all raw materials, energy, and food with only temporary exceptions from time to time. That is, resources have become more abundant, not less so.[1]*

- *The water that we drink today is not just healthier, it is* substantially *healthier than it was 100 years ago, and the water is getting cleaner with every passing year. At least one of every five deaths prior to 1900 was attributable to contaminants in the drinking water. U.S. lakes and streams that were once threatened by pollution have been dramatically cleaned up over the past 30 years.[2]*

- *Air pollution levels are falling, not rising. Smog levels in major U.S. cities including Chicago, Houston, Los Angeles, Philadelphia, and Pittsburgh have declined steadily since the 1960s.[3] Lead levels in the air have fallen by an astonishing 90 percent over the past three decades.[4]*

- *We are by no means running out of trees or forests. Over the past 50 years, American landowners and private industry have been growing more trees than they have been cutting down.[5]*

THERE IS ALMOST certainly no other issue on which the general beliefs of most Americans and many others around the world about the state of affairs is so contrary to objective reality than in the area of the environment. Hundreds of millions of people around the world believe that, because of industrialization, population growth, and mass consumption, our air and our water are deteriorating and that our natural resources are being depleted. In a recent CNN/*USA Today* poll, when the American public was asked what would be some of the greatest problems that humankind will confront over the next 50 years, two of the top responses dealt with the environment. More than four of five said they feared "severe water pollution" and "severe air pollution."

This pervasive public pessimism about the state of the planet is undoubtedly reinforced by the incessant din of propaganda issued by activist organizations devoted to ideological environmentalism. Those claims are picked up by the media, which then bombards us with tales of impending shortages of electricity, oil, clean drinking water, farmland, forests, and food. Millions of people have been influenced by famous doomsday reports issued in the 1960s and 1970s, such as *The Limits to Growth* and *The Global 2000 Report to the President: Entering the 21st Century*, both of which predicted impending resource shortages, imminent global famines, and worsening environmental degradation due to increased population, consumption, and economic growth.

Hundreds of millions of people around the world believe that, because of industrialization, population growth, and mass consumption, our air and our water are deteriorating and that our natural resources are being depleted. They are wrong.

However, the basic trends of environmental conditions and natural resource availability over the past 100 years or so tell a very different story. Focusing on the United States as the most advanced modern economy, the trend data presented on the pages that follow deal with four areas of environmental concern: (1) air quality, (2) water quality, (3) energy, and (4) availability of natural resources.

In each of these areas, the basic data and trend lines generally indicate substantial improvement both in the near term and especially over the long run. That is to say, the data contradict the popular but discredited "limits to growth" model that is still taught in schools and receives such widespread attention from worldwide organizations and the national media.

What follows is an explanation for why these environmental improvements have occurred in recent times and why it is that these favorable trends toward a healthier environment and a more livable planet should show continued gains in the future. The trends of general improvement will undoubtedly strike many readers as counterintuitive. After all, with more people on the planet all the time, and a world of supposed finite resources, it would make sense that as we use more copper, tin, water, or oil, there must be less available for the future. However, in general, that is not so. And the underlying explanation behind this seeming paradox is that human beings are net resource creators, not net resource destroyers. The human intellect is the most valuable resource on this Earth, and thanks to our ingenuity, we are always finding new supplies and kinds of resources on the Earth. For example, thanks to leaps forward in technology, we can drill deeper into the Earth's crust to recover and use oil and other valuable resources. Technological advances allow us to find substitutes for resources that may genuinely be running low in supply. For instance, we now use satellite technology, the Internet, and fiberoptic cables for transmitting information rather than old-fashioned copper wiring.

Even the U.S. government now apparently recognizes the errors of its earlier judgments about resource and pollution trends. Reversing the forecasts of studies such as *The Global 2000 Report,* the Office of Technology Assessment has concluded that "[t]he nation's future has probably never been less constrained by the cost of natural resources."[6] In fact, thanks to improvements in technology and know-how, the last 100 years have been noteworthy for the very rapid reduction in resource scarcity.

It is also true that a wealthier society is a healthier one. Wealthier societies can afford to devote more resources to combating pollution. We now know that the greatest environmental catastrophes of this century were caused by socialist nations. The communists in the Soviet Union in the 1950s, 1960s, and 1970s were perhaps the greatest environmental villains in history. Prudent government regulation, such as basic public health measures, clean water laws, and air pollution abatement laws, are certainly necessary to protect the environment. But more important is a free market economy—one that protects property rights, produces wealth, and encourages innovation.

THE THEORY OF LIMITS TO GROWTH

BACK IN SEPTEMBER 1994, the international environmental community gathered in Cairo for the World Population Conference. The delegates from more than 100 nations signed a document urging that the world community should join together to work toward a policy of population stabilization. "What is needed," the conference report stated, "is a sustainable balance between human numbers and the resources of the planet." Among world statesmen, there was little dissent from this opinion.[7]

The Cairo report was a restatement of a prevalent theory among ideological environmentalists that human population growth on the planet must inevitably lead to environmental decline and natural resource scarcity. This neo-Malthusian theory was popularized in 1968 by biologist Paul Ehrlich of Stanford University, author of *The Population Bomb.* Ehrlich has claimed that "[w]e are literally using up in a few generations the biological and mineral wealth of the earth that took millions and millions of years to create."[8] Lester Brown, former head of the activist Worldwatch Institute, which issues an annual *State of the World* report, a volume that has recorded millions in sales worldwide, concurs with this antieconomic growth vision as the only way to save the planet. Brown writes that "current notions of economic growth . . . are at the root of so much of the earth's ecological deterioration."

In the 1960s and 1970s, a number of governmental agencies also famously warned of impending environmental catastrophe due to economic growth and rapid population increases. Thirty years ago, for instance, the Club of Rome released its highly influential *The Limits to Growth* report, which predicted that unbridled population growth would lead to mass famines and severe shortages of energy, minerals, trees, and other precious resources.[9] The book predicted that "shortages of natural resources will lead to a dismal and depleted existence by the beginning of the next century."

In 1980, this apocalyptic vision of the future received the official sanction of the U.S. government when the Carter administration released its alarmist *Global 2000 Report.*[10] The $1 million report sponsored by the Department of State and 12 other federal agencies predicted that most resources—energy, minerals, food, and forests— would be in severe shortage by the year 2000 "if present trends continued." It also predicted that "the world's people would be much poorer than today [1980]."

The terrifying predictions of Professor Ehrlich, the Club of Rome, *The Global 2000 Report,* and other ideological environmentalists can be summarized as follows. Before the year 2000 the world would experience:

- Massive worldwide famines due to inadequate world food supplies
- Worsening levels of air and water pollution due to economic growth
- Global disease and death rates would dramatically increase due to worsening environmental problems
- Severe energy shortages and even the depletion of the Earth's supply of oil
- Minerals and metals becoming more expensive and more scarce

IMPROVING AIR QUALITY

LET US NOW EXAMINE pollution trends in the United States. Pollution trends in the United States can be seen as harbingers for the future trends in other countries as their economies expand and their people grow wealthier. It is very well established that wealthier people demand and get a cleaner natural environment. For example, a World Bank analysis found that the amount of smoke and soot in the air begins to fall in city air when average annual per capita incomes reach $3,300 and that sulfur dioxide in the air begins falling when incomes reach $3,700. Even before improvements in air quality begin, people whose average incomes average $1,400 per capita demand and get clean water.[11]

> Pollution trends in the United States can be seen as harbingers for the future trends in other countries as their economies expand and their people grow wealthier.

Nevertheless, the prevailing attitude of most people, and promoted by ideological environmentalists and the media, is that the giant leaps forward in industrial production have come at the expense of degrading our air and water quality. In the 1960s, Harvard economist John Kenneth Galbraith wrote in his bestseller, *The Affluent Society,* that there was a fundamental tension between environmental and economic progress. In that book he warned that "[t]he penultimate western man, stalled in the ultimate traffic jam and slowly succumbing to carbon monoxide, will not be cheered to hear from the last survivor that the gross national product went up by a record amount."[12] Then Vice President Al Gore claimed in his book, *Earth in the Balance,* that we have been mortgaging our environmental future through our mindless pursuit of economic growth.[13] The good news is that the economic progress of the last century has not come at the expense of clean air. Rather, economic growth has generally corresponded with improvements in the natural environment.

The national picture on air quality is shown in Figure 4.1. It shows improvement for almost every type of pollution. Lead concentrations have fallen by more than 90 percent since 1976.[14] In fact, the total volume of lead emissions was lower in 1990 than in 1940 (the farthest back we have reliable data) and was lower than in every intervening year. That is a truly astonishing accomplishment given that our economy and our production levels are at least five times higher today than 60 years ago. According to a 1999 report by the Pacific Research Institute, based on EPA air quality data between 1976 and 1998:[15]

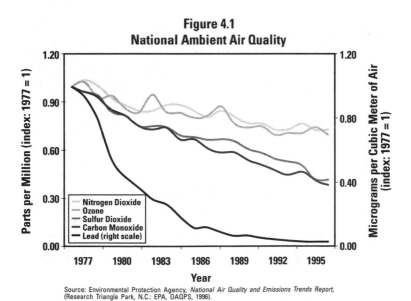

Figure 4.1
National Ambient Air Quality

Source: Environmental Protection Agency, *National Air Quality and Emissions Trends Report,*
(Research Triangle Park, N.C.: EPA, OAQPS, 1996).

- Sulfur dioxide levels decreased 66 percent.
- Nitrogen oxides decreased 38 percent.
- Ozone decreased 31 percent.
- Carbon monoxide decreased 66 percent.
- Particulates decreased 25 percent (between 1988 and 1997).

An incredible success story is the decline in pollution per unit of output. From 1940 to 1990, air pollution emissions fell by 3 percent per year relative to output, suggesting that America has become far more environmentally efficient in recent decades.[16] In fact, we now produce about six times more output per ton of emission of air pollution than we did prior to 1940. (See Figure 4.2.)

What about the smog levels in particular high-pollution cities? It was just a bit more than 30 years ago that doomsayer Paul Ehrlich wrote in an article entitled "Eco-Catastrophe!" that "smog disasters" might kill 200,000 people in New York and Los Angeles by 1973.[17] The reality is that air pollution in American cities has been falling for at least the past three decades. In fact, since the 1950s, air pollution in major cities has dramatically declined.[18] For example, air pollution, or soot, over Manhattan has fallen by two-thirds since the end of World War II.

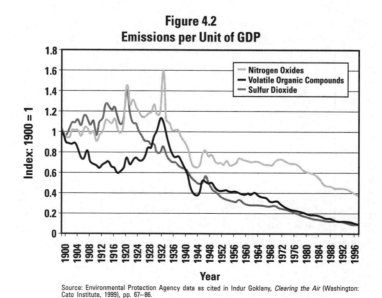

Figure 4.2
Emissions per Unit of GDP

Source: Environmental Protection Agency data as cited in Indur Goklany, *Clearing the Air* (Washington: Cato Institute, 1999), pp. 67–86.

Over the 25-year period from 1962 to 1987, smog levels fell by more than half using an index of all urban areas and improved further since 1987. Figure 4.3 indicates that air pollution over Chicago, Denver, Philadelphia, and Washington, D.C., declined by more than 50 percent between 1972 and 1996. Perhaps the most impressive success with regard to air pollution in recent years has been the rapid reduction in smog levels over Los Angeles in just the past decade. From 1985 to 1995, the number of days in the year of unhealthy air quality has fallen from about 160 to about 80.[19]

> The reality is that air pollution in American cities has been falling for at least the past three decades.

Pittsburgh's air quality improvements over the past 40 years have been even more spectacular. In the 1920s through the 1950s, as the steel mills' smoke stacks belched out black soot, there were typically more than 300 "smoky" days a year. Since the late 1960s, that number has fallen to about 60 smoky days a year.[20] There are now fewer smoky days over Pittsburgh than there were in 1900 (Figure 4.4).

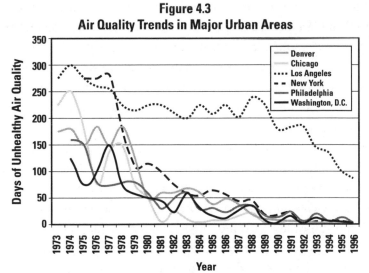

Figure 4.3
Air Quality Trends in Major Urban Areas

Legend:
— Denver
— Chicago
···· Los Angeles
– – New York
— Philadelphia
— Washington, D.C.

Y-axis: Days of Unhealthy Air Quality (0 to 350)
X-axis: Year (1973 to 1996)

Source: Council on Environmental Quality, *Annual Report*, (Washington: Government Printing Office, various years) and Environmental Protection Agency, *National Air Quality and Emissions Trends Report, 1996*, Table A-17 (Research Triangle Park, NC, EPA, OAQPS, 1997).

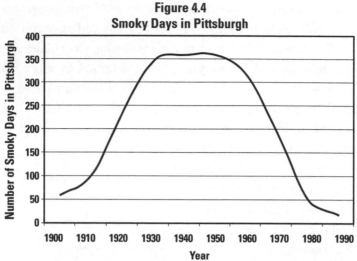

Figure 4.4
Smoky Days in Pittsburgh

Source: Cliff I. Davidson, "Air Pollution in Pittsburgh: A Historical Pespective," *Journal of the Air Pollution Control Association* vol. 29 (1979), pp. 1035-41; and Council on Environmental Quality, *Annual Report* (various years).

One reason that many Americans are surprised by the positive trends in healthier air is that automobile travel is much more common today than in earlier periods. It turns out, however, that the automobile, although it emits carbon monoxide into the air, replaced a far more polluting form of transportation, the horse, which left huge piles of smelly and messy dung in the roads. As economists William Baumol and Wallace Oates have noted, from an environmental standpoint, the automobile is "certainly an improvement from the incredibly filthy streets and waterways of medieval and Renaissance cities.[21] It is also true that emissions from automobiles are much lower nowadays than in the 1950s and 1960s, which is a major contributing factor to reduced smog levels.[22]

These air quality improvements have led to measurable health gains. Bronchitis death rates have fallen by more than 10-fold since 1900, for example.[23] According to the Pacific Research Institute's *Index of Leading Environmental Indicators*, "Due largely to the introduction of unleaded gasoline, the 97 percent reduction of lead in the air has generated a huge improvement in blood-lead levels. Between the periods 1976 to 80 and 1988 to 81, the average blood-lead levels in children dropped 76 percent. High blood-lead levels in children retard brain development, but levels are now far below the harmful range."[24]

WATER QUALITY TRENDS IN LAKES, RIVERS, AND STREAMS

ONE MEASURE OF the improvement in water quality over this century has been the dramatic reduction in outbreaks of disease from drinking water. At the start of the 20th century, many life-threatening illnesses, such as diarrhea, were a result of Americans drinking and using impure water. In fact, waterborne diseases were a leading cause of death in the 19th century. In the 1930s and 1940s, there were about 25 waterborne disease outbreaks a year; now there are maybe one or two in a bad year.[25] Thanks to improved technology in water purification, the water we drink is much cleaner and safer than in any earlier times, and the reduction in illnesses caused by bacteria in drinking water is one reliable way to measure the improvement. Anecdotal evidence suggests that in earlier eras the water was not nearly so spring fresh and natural as we like to imagine. Many waterways were filthy in and around cities across the globe. For example, in the Middle Ages, the waste from humans, horses, and manufacturing industries was bad enough to impede navigation on the River Thames.

Unfortunately, there is not much reliable long-term data on the pollution levels of American lakes and rivers. Official measurements come from the Environmental Protection Agency and start around 1960—a decade or so before the Clean Water Act was signed into law. Over the past quarter century, our lakes and streams and rivers have become much less polluted, and the trend is toward continued improvement. Since 1970 an estimated $500 billion has been spent on water cleanup. That spending has apparently paid off. The percentage of water sources that were judged by the Council on Environmental Quality to be poor or severely polluted fell from 30 percent in 1961 to 17 percent in 1974 to less than 5 percent today.[26]

We have made huge progress in purifying industrial and municipal waste before it is emitted into streams, rivers, and lakes. In 1960 only 40 million Americans—22 percent of the population—were served by wastewater treatment plants. By 1996 that had risen to 190 million Americans, or 72 percent of the population.[27] (See Figure 4.5.) According to the Pacific Research Institute's *Index of Leading Environmental Indicators*, industrial water pollution has plummeted since 1980. Organic wastes fell by 46 percent, toxic organics by 99 percent, and toxic metals by 98 percent.[28]

One consequence of these gains is that many streams, rivers, and lakes, which were at one time severely polluted, are now much more pristine. In 1969, the Cuyahoga River famously caught on fire in downtown Cleveland, but ever since that infamous incident, the water quality of the Great Lakes has improved dramatically. Lake Erie has in recent years been yielding record fish catches and is routinely used for recreational purposes nowadays. Similarly, the salmon catch on Lake Ontario is thriving again after several decades of decline. In 1994, 86 percent of U.S. rivers and streams measured were usable for fishing and swimming; 91 percent of U.S. lakes were also safe for these purposes, up from 36 percent in 1972.[29] (See Figure 4.6.)

There were also far fewer oil spills in recent years than in previous times. The world still recalls vividly the scenes from the *Exxon Valdez*

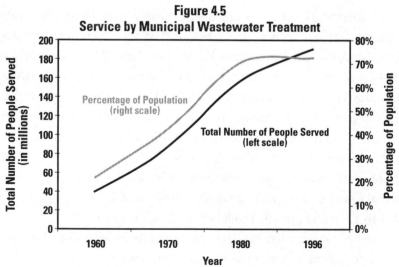

Figure 4.5
Service by Municipal Wastewater Treatment

Source: *Statistical Abstract of the United States, 1998*, no. 397; and U.S. Environmental Protection Agency, Office of Wastewater Management, *Clean Water Needs Survey Report.*

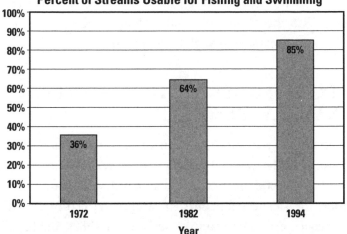

Figure 4.6
Percent of Streams Usable for Fishing and Swimming

Source: Council on Environmental Quality, *Annual Report* (various years).

oil spill in 1989. Fish and birds were washed ashore enwrapped in black tar. The good news is that the trend in oil spills by volume has been falling from 1973 to 1993, as shown in Figure 4.7.[30] Moreover, the latest news from Prince William Sound in Alaska, where the *Exxon Valdez* accident tragically occurred, is that fish and wildlife are proving much

Figure 4.7
Oil Spills Reported In and Around U.S. Waters (by volume)

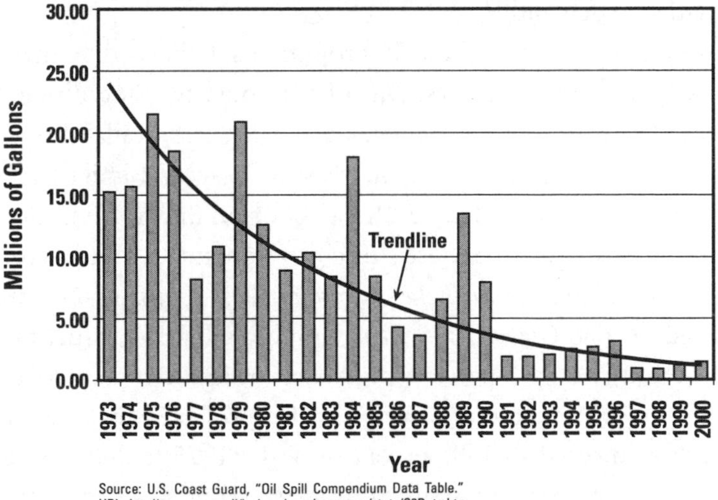

Source: U.S. Coast Guard, "Oil Spill Compendium Data Table."
URL: http//www.uscg.mil/hq/g-m/nmc/response/stats/C2Data.htm

more resilient than the experts predicted. Stan Senner, the government's chief science coordinator for monitoring the impact of the spill, declared in 1999 that "[a]lthough full ecological recovery has not been achieved . . . the ecosystem is well on its way to recovery."[31]

HOW DO WE MEASURE THE SCARCITY OF A NATURAL RESOURCE?

IT IS GENERALLY recognized that price is the most objective long-term measure of the availability of a natural resource. A rising price of a commodity, good, or service is a signal that demand is outstripping supply (or is expected to outstrip supply in the future) and that a shortage may emerge. For example, in the early 1980s, Cabbage Patch dolls doubled and tripled in price as parents' demand for the dolls rose well beyond the number available in stores.

This same law of supply and demand applies to natural resources. If there were an impending shortage of coal, silver, rice, or wheat, then buyers and sellers would consistently bid *up* their price. Conversely, if a huge new reserve of oil were discovered, or demand for oil were expected to drop because of the sudden introduction of an alternative energy source, buyers and sellers would consistently bid *down* oil prices. In sum, a rising price of a resource indicates increasing supply relative to demand; a falling price indicates declining supply relative to demand.[32]

Even *The Limits to Growth* proponents believe that increased scarcity leads to higher prices. One of the consistent and dire predictions of *The Limits to Growth* was that with less availability of resources, we can expect ever increasing prices. Similarly, Barry Commoner has written that "each barrel of oil drawn from the earth causes the next one to be more difficult to obtain. . . . The economic consequence is that it *causes the price to increase continuously*"(emphasis added).[33] The *Global 2000 Report* predicted that nonfuel mineral prices would rise by 5 percent per year through the year 2000, as a consequence of impending scarcity. It also projected that real energy would "rise more than 150 percent over the 1975 to 2000 period."[34] Lester Brown has written in his *State of the World Report* that the first "signs of scarcity in food" would be "rising world grain prices."[35] So it would seem to be a generally accepted proposition, from committed ideological environmentalists and free marketeers alike, that if humanity is entering an age of resource scarcity, we *must* observe rising prices. Falling real prices would be incompatible with the concept of resource exhaustion.

Some skeptics still maintain, however, that the price of a resource or raw material may only reflect the available supply today, *not* the relative abundance or scarcity in future years. If world population growth were to place enormous new demand pressures on resources, then even if the prices had been falling in the past, they may suddenly and sharply rise in the future. Yet this argument reveals a misunderstanding of how the modern–day price system operates.

Today's price of oil reflects not only the availability of that resource today relative to demand but also its expected availability in the future. An asset's value is determined by the discounted present value of its future return. If the market believed that oil were going to be in short supply in 10 years, then owners would bid up prices today. And any single market analyst who firmly believes that oil prices will soar in the future could buy oil at today's prices, hold on to it, and sell it in the future at the expected higher price. One would not even need to take physical possession of the resource. There are now futures markets for most resources, which allow traders to purchase the future resale rights of oil, pork bellies, or other commodities. And indeed, thousands of speculators do this; they hoard gold, copper, chickens, farmland, or whatever the resource that is expected to grow scarce might be.

> If the market believed that oil were going to be in short supply in 10 years, then owners would bid up prices today.

In sum, the price of a natural resource today not only equilibrates current supply and demand, but the market's best estimate about the future levels of supply and demand. There is no law of nature that says that the market always sets the right price. Speculators who bought oil futures in the early 1970s and then sold them in the late

1970s made a fortune. Speculators who bought oil futures in the 1980s lost fortunes. But the market price does incorporate all of the best and most relevant information we have available about a resource.

One of the first modern-day economists to note the long-term trends in falling food and resource prices was the late Julian Simon, author of *The Ultimate Resource*. One of Simon's great and lasting contributions to the debate over natural resource availability was his insight that the best measure of scarcity of a resource is its price. He also demonstrated in his work that the best measure of price over time is in relation to wages. Simon argued that the number of hours that one has to work to purchase the resource in question is the most meaningful gauge of whether we are running out. For this reason, this analysis indexes prices over time to wage rates.

MINERALS AND METALS: THE END OF SCARCITY

MINERALS AND METALS are typically classified by ideological environmentalists as "finite" or "nonrenewable" resources, because once they are used up, they are gone forever. And they are limited by the mass weight of the Earth. There is particular anxiety over future supplies of fossil fuels, copper, zinc, aluminum, and electricity.

The surprising good news is that the long-term price trends relative to wages—which is, again, the length of time we have to work to purchase these resources—show decreasing scarcity for almost all minerals and metals. Figure 4.8 shows the price trend for copper since 1800.[36] The cost of a ton of copper is now only about one-tenth of what it was 200 years ago. This trend of falling prices of copper has been going on for a very long time. In the 18th century B.C.E. in Babylonia under Hammurabi—almost 4,000 years ago—the price of copper was about 1,000 times its price in the United States now relative to wages. At the time of the Roman Empire, the price was about 100 times the present price. Copper was scarce then, not now.

Copper's downward price trend is fairly representative of the trend in almost all minerals. In fact, of the 13 most commonly used minerals, including, silver, tin, aluminum, lead, and so on, 12 of them

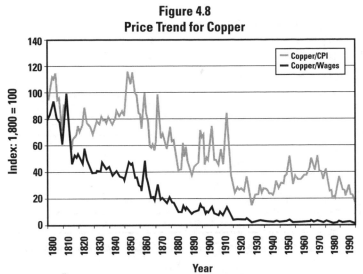

Figure 4.8
Price Trend for Copper

Source: U.S. Geological Survey, *Commodity Statistics* (various years).

fell substantially in price relative to wages over the past 100 to 200 years. (The exception was platinum.) On average, these minerals were 5 to 10 times more expensive in 1900 than they are today in terms of the numbers of hours of work an American needed to purchase them. Figure 4.9 shows the decline of a broad index of minerals over the past century.

The steady decline in mineral prices is attributable to several factors. One of these has been the constant discovery of new mines. A second has been new technological innovations in mining techniques, which lower the cost of resource recovery and allow mining from areas where excavation was previously technologically and economically infeasible. Finally, the introduction of less expensive or superior substitutes for the use of some minerals—such as the use of more efficient fiberoptic cables in place of copper telecommunication cables—has lowered demand for some of these commodities. The result of these factors is that proven reserves of most minerals are at all-time highs (Table 4.1).

In the 1960s and 1970s, ideological environmentalists predicted a reversal in these price trends of minerals. Instead, the past two decades have seen prices for natural resources plummet. There is an index of

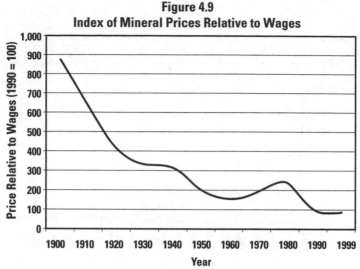

Figure 4.9
Index of Mineral Prices Relative to Wages

Source: Ronald Bailey, *The True State of the Planet* (1995) and *Earth Report 2000* (2000).

mineral and metal prices that commodity traders use called the CRB index. In the 1980s it fell by about 20 percent. At that time, economist G. F. Ray reported that the 1980s "will go down in economic history as a period when [the price] of primary products hit rock bottom, whatever method is used to illustrate their real value of purchasing power. There have been hardly any exceptions to this decline."[39] He was only wrong on one count. Prices didn't hit rock bottom in the 1980s. In the 1990s real commodity prices fell still faster, by nearly 25 percent on average. Those unfortunate investors who believed the modern Malthu-

Table 4.1.   Proven Mineral Resources, 1950–2000

Resource	1950[37]	2000[38]	Change (%)
	(Million Metric Tons)		
Bauxite	1,400	25,000	1,786%
Chromium	70	3,600	5,143%
Copper	100	340	340%
Iron Ore	19,000	140,000	737%
Lead	40	64	160%
Manganese	500	660	132%
Nickel	17	49	288%
Tin	6	9.6	160%
Zinc	70	190	271%

sians and bet their money on rising prices of natural resources in the 1980s and 1990s have suffered major financial losses because the theories of scarcity have not panned out in practice.

THE CONFOUNDING STORY OF ENERGY

IN THE SUMMER OF 2001, it appeared that another energy crisis might have been back upon us. Gasoline prices had risen in some areas to nearly $2 a gallon, California cities had been experiencing electricity brownouts, and the dependency of the United States on OPEC oil continued to mount.

But is there really a long-term energy crisis in America? Are we running out? Should we mount a massive national campaign of energy conservation to make sure that we are not unforgivably depleting future supplies of oil, natural gas, and electricity that will no longer be available to our children and grandchildren?

Here we need some historical perspective on the "energy crisis." It turns out that there have been periodic "energy shortage crises" in the United States now for at least 100 years. In the early years of the 20th century, for example, there was a great panic over scarcity of oil. In the 1920s, many geologists predicted that the United States faced certain depletion within 50 years. That never happened.

> Those unfortunate investors who bet their money on rising prices of natural resources in the 1980s and 1990s have suffered major financial losses because the theories of scarcity have not panned out in practice.

The gloomy prognostications became far more frightening in the inflationary 1970s. In 1971, the vice chairman of the Federal Power Commission, John A. Carver, described the energy crisis ahead as "endemic and incurable." He continued, "We can anticipate that before the end of this century energy supplies will become so restricted as to halt economic development around the world."[40] In late 1977— in the midst of the OPEC-created energy crisis—President Jimmy Carter announced, "We could use up all of the proven reserves of oil in the entire world by the end of the next decade."[41] The Club of

Rome had predicted a few years earlier that oil prices would skyrocket upward to $100 a barrel.

None of this happened. Energy prices plummeted in the 1980s and 1990s following a long-term trend of greater affordability of oil, gas, and other fuels. Why? Because the world is not running out of energy. In fact, proven reserves of oil continue to grow. Global oil reserves are up from 659.9 billion barrels at the end of 1980 to 1,064.4 barrels at the end of 2000.[42] Recently, prices have risen, but they still remain far below their historical price level. Today, oil sells at about $25 to $30 a barrel, a far cry from the $100 a barrel predicted in the 1970s. See Figure 4.10 for the price trends in oil, electricity, and coal.

Energy prices in the United States have fluctuated substantially since 1900. But the overall trend has been one of greater affordability. Adjusted for wage growth, oil today is about five times cheaper than in 1900 and still slightly cheaper than in 1950, notwithstanding the huge and temporary spike in the world price in the 1970s and then in 2000 to 01. Electricity prices have fallen more than eightfold since 1900. Coal was almost seven times more expensive back then.[43]

Before the 1950s, it was almost unthinkable that oil could be drilled and extracted from the bottom of the sea. In 1965, one of the

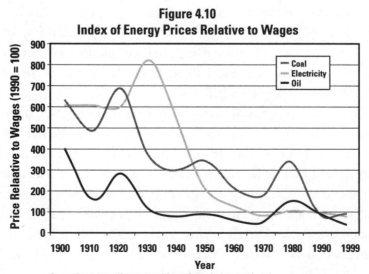

Figure 4.10
Index of Energy Prices Relative to Wages

Source: Department of Energy, *Annual Energy Review* (various years).

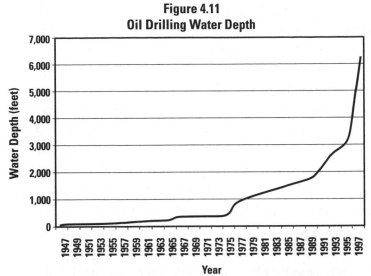

Figure 4.11
Oil Drilling Water Depth

Source: *Offshore Magazine*. URL: http://www.images.pennwellnet.com/ogj/images/off2/1098shell2.gif

first offshore oil rigs drilled oil from 600 feet deep off the coast of California. By the late 1980s the record for offshore oil drilling reached 10,000 feet. (See Figure 4.11.) It has been precisely this kind of innovation that has confounded the doomsayers, who in the 1960s and 1970s, predicted global oil shortages and even depletion.

Gasoline prices paid at the pump have been on a steady rate of decline since the 1920s, with the obvious exception of the 1970s and 2000 to 01. In 1920 the real price of gas (excluding taxes) was nearly twice as high as today. If the cost of gasoline relative to wages cost what it did 75 years ago, we would be paying almost $10 a gallon at the pump.

The experience of the 1970s in the United States, however, demonstrates that there is no inevitability of declining prices of natural resources. Unwise government intervention into the marketplace for natural resources can often have economically and ecologically debilitating consequences. For example, most economists today agree that a rash of new energy regulations introduced in the mid-1970s after the OPEC embargoes worsened the disruptions to the oil market in the ensuing years and produced severe hardships for Americans as lines at the gasoline pump lengthened, home heating bills skyrocketed, and the pace of industrial production slowed to a crawl. It was the deregulation of oil and natural gas prices under President Ronald Reagan that created a wave of innovation in the area of energy exploration and helped generate today's low prices.

Alas, in recent years, we have stumbled onto many of the same energy policy mistakes of the past and are now paying a price for those blunders. Our current "energy crisis" is a political problem, not a technological problem. U.S. energy policy has foolishly overemphasized uncompetitive alternatives to oil and natural gas, has subsidized energy use through such programs as LIHEAP, and has left the United States needlessly captive to OPEC production cutbacks and price spikes. In many states, activists have restricted oil drilling, power plant construction, and electricity generation lines. Given current technological capabilities, the world is awash in oil, but our political rules currently prevent us from tapping that unlimited potential to lower energy costs.

Yet even in this era of hostility to new production of electricity and new drilling for oil, history is very clear on one point: Any rise in prices probably won't last for long. Known oil reserves on the Earth are higher today than at any other previous time in history.

WASTE NOT, WANT NOT: TRENDS IN ENERGY EFFICIENCY

THE RECENT PRICE hikes in oil and electricity have also renewed calls in Washington, D.C., for a greater emphasis on energy efficiency in the workplace and at home. The Europeans and Asians who tax energy use much more heavily than we do in the United States (for example, other industrialized nations typically have gasoline taxes that are $1 or $2 a gallon, compared to about 50 to 60 cents a gallon here in the United States) often complain that Americans are irresponsible overconsumers of energy. Wrong. The United States is becoming ever more energy-efficient. According to calculations by the National Center for Policy Analysis, "The amount of energy needed to produce a dollar of GNP (in real terms) has been steadily declining at a rate of 1 percent per year since 1929. By 1989, the amount of energy

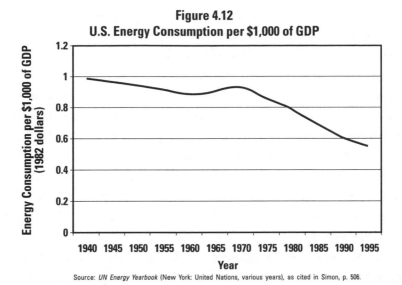

Figure 4.12
U.S. Energy Consumption per $1,000 of GDP

Source: *UN Energy Yearbook* (New York: United Nations, various years), as cited in Simon, p. 506.

needed to produce a dollar of GNP was almost half of what it was 60 years earlier."[44] (See Figure 4.12.) Energy efficiency continued to surge so much in the 1990s that today we produce almost twice as much output per unit of energy as in the first half of this century. One often overlooked benefit of the digital and the information age is the huge gains registered in energy efficiency in the world economy.

Economic development and free markets are the keys to increasing energy efficiency. In 1986, a few years before the collapse of the Berlin Wall, the United States and other developed countries used less than half the amount of energy per dollar of GDP that the socialist economies used. Communist North Korea still uses roughly three times as much energy to produce a dollar of output as South Korea does.[45]

GAINING GROUND: THE FALSE THREAT OF LOST LAND AND TREES

WE SOMETIMES HEAR it said that economic progress in the United States has come at the expense of one of our most treasured national assets: our land. Urban sprawl and increasing population are said to be imperiling our ability to feed ourselves in the future as we pave hundreds of thousands of additional acres in concrete every year. From 1960 to 1990, the number of acres classified as "urban land" more than doubled, from 25 million to 56 million.[46] Yet the percentage of land in the United States that is devoted to urban/suburban use is only about 3 percent of the total land area of the continent (Figure 4.13). The rate at which land is being converted to suburban development is about 0.0006 percent per year, which is hardly a worrisome trend.[47] In fact, protected lands from development have outpaced urban land conversion over recent decades. According to Pacific Research Institute (PRI), "The ratio of protected lands to urban and agricultural lands rose from 6.4 percent to 22.9 percent from 1959 to 1987."[48]

While there may be some cause for concern about preserving tropical rain forests in Brazil and other developing nations, and old growth forests in the United States, the fact remains that forests are not shrinking and trees are not disappearing. Here is some impressive evidence to that effect:

- Currently, the Forest Service reports that the United States is growing about 22 million net new cubic feet of wood a year and harvesting only 16.5 million, a net increase of 36 percent per year. This contrasts with the situation in the early years of

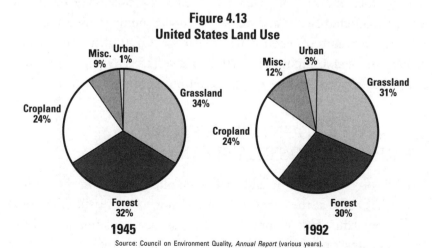

Figure 4.13
United States Land Use

1945

1992

Source: Council on Environment Quality, *Annual Report* (various years).

this century, where about twice as many trees were cut as were planted. (See Figure 4.14.)[49]

- In this century, despite a fourfold increase in population, the percentage of land space that is covered by forest has remained remarkably constant at about one-third of the land area of the United States.[50]
- The amount of world forest has held remarkably steady over the course of the past 50 years. There are now nearly 4 billion hectares of forest on the globe, up from about 3.6 billion in the late 1940s. Nor are rain forests disappearing at an alarming rate.[51]
- Russian forests have grown substantially in recent years, increasing Russia's forest cover by more than a million hectares in just the last 10 years.[52]

As always, the most reliable indicator of whether we are running out of trees and wood products is the price data for paper and other forest products. The price data for forest products over the past century should dispel overblown fears that we will soon be suffering a timber famine. Lumber prices relative to wages are about one-third the

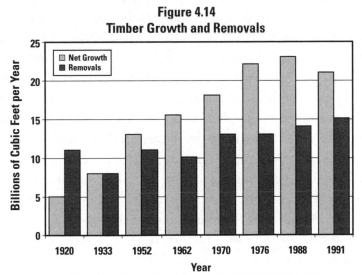

Figure 4.14
Timber Growth and Removals

Source: "The Great Forest Debate," *Reader's Digest,* vol. 143, no. 859 (November 1993), p. 125.

level of 1950 and about one-sixth the level of 1900. Economists Roger A. Sedjo and Marion Clawson of Resources for the Future have documented the long-term improvement in the inventory of U.S. forests and their overall assessment of the status of the world's forests:

> *As a result of dramatically higher wood growth in the United States, and as a result of timber harvest at a rate less than growth, inventories of standing timber have increased significantly since 1920. The popular view is that the United States is consuming its wood faster than it is growing and that we are denuding our forests. In fact, exactly the reverse is happening—we are building them up.*[53]

No, we are not running out of farmland, trees, or forests. Initiatives in Washington and state capitals to plant trees are wonderful public relations for politicians but create a false impression that we are a nation of Darth Vaders with chainsaws. That portrayal is a far cry from the reality of our resource picture.

THE NEW AGE OF RESOURCE ABUNDANCE

THE EVIDENCE PRESENTED above shows that when it comes to natural resources, Americans of each generation have tended to create a bit more than they use up. Not only must this be true to account for the increase in our wealth and population, but if this were not so—if we used up a bit more than we created and our assets deteriorated like a many-times-patched tire deteriorates until it is no longer useful—we simply would have become extinct as a species by now. The essential condition of fitness for survival of our species is that each generation creates a net surplus on average, or at least breaks even. Since we have survived and increased, this condition must have been present.

A question then immediately arises: Must not we, like other species, cease our growth when we have reached the natural limit of the available resources? One cannot answer this question with assurance, of course, because with each increase of wealth and numbers, we proceed into a situation with which we have no prior experience. All we have to go on is the record of the past. And we know that it has been the optimists like Julian Simon and Herman Kahn who have been right and the pessimists like Paul Ehrlich and Lester Brown who have been consistently wrong in their dire predictions. They have been wrong in their forecasts because ideological environmentalists with Malthusian beliefs have always underestimated man's ability to adapt and innovate. The Malthusians saw population growth trends in the first three quarters of the 20th century as catastrophic and unsustainable. What they did not envision was the computer age. The world's population may have more than doubled in 50 years, but the speed of microchips is doubling every 18 months. That's (Intel cofounder Gordon) Moore's Law.[54] This is a geometrical rate of growth that is several magnitudes larger than population growth.

The increasing availability of natural resources throughout history as measured by their declining prices—especially food, metals, and energy—suggests that there are no absolute limits on our resources in the future. There are limits at any moment, but the limits continually expand, and constrain us less, with each passing generation. In this way we are quite unlike all other species. The great 19th-century economist Henry George once wrote the following parable about the uniqueness of the human species as a net resource creator: "Both the jayhawk and the man eat chickens, but the more jayhawks, the fewer chickens, while the more men, the more chickens."[55]

All of this is to say that the gains in environmental progress and resource abundance are a result of the most precious resource of all: the human intellect. This is the primary reason that we should be optimistic that the gains that have been recorded over the past 100 to 200 years will continue in the 21st century rather than reverse themselves. Almost all of the progress laid out in the previous sections is primarily the result of wondrous advances in the storehouse of human knowledge. That knowledge can never be erased even if barbarians or Luddites were to burn every library to the ground. Encyclopedias of knowledge can now be stored on a five-inch, $1 optical disc.

We now stand on the shoulders of our ancestors, able to draw upon the accumulated knowledge and know-how of the past two centuries of immense scientific and technological progress. This knowledge is our communal wealth. Much more than the power to enjoy gadgets, our wealth represents the power to mobilize nature to our advantage rather than to just accept the random fates of nature. We now have all the evidence at hand to say definitively that Malthus was wrong, and so were his legions of modern-day doomsday followers. In the 1960s and 1970s, many people wore buttons that read "Stop the planet, I want to get off!" Their pessimism was misguided. When it comes to the environment, humanity has been a good custodian of the Earth over this past century. If present trends continue in the 21st century, food and natural resources will be more abundant than ever before and the environment should be cleaner and safer.

CHAPTER FIVE

SUSTAINABLE DEVELOPMENT VERSUS SUSTAINED DEVELOPMENT

Barun S. Mitra and Rakhi Gupta

ECO-MYTHS DEBUNKED

- *Sustainable development as currently conceived cannot lead to economic development and an improved natural environment.*
- *Sustained development that encourages rapid economic growth and technological progress will improve living standards and protect the natural world.*
- *Sustainable development is misconceived because it argues that natural resources are becoming scarcer when in fact they are becoming more abundant over time.*
- *Proponents of sustainable development by slowing technological innovation and economic growth will put both people and the natural world at greater risk.*
- *The best way to maximize the welfare of human beings and to protect the natural world is to encourage rapid economic growth and technological progress by means of open markets and democratic governance.*

THE TERM *sustainable development* entered the mainstream of policy discourse with the publication of *Our Common Future,* a report issued by the World Commission on Environment and Development (the Brundtland Commission) in 1987. The report defined sustainable development as "development that meets the needs of the present without compromising the ability of the future generations to meet their own needs." However, sustainable development as envisaged by ideological environmentalists cannot lead to economic development and an improved natural environment. Instead, what is needed is *sustained development* rather than sustainable development.

The concept of sustainability originated in the context of discussions about harvesting and managing renewable resources, such as forests and fisheries, in such a way as not to damage future supplies.[1] Most proponents of sustainability take it to mean the maintenance of the existence of ecological conditions necessary to support human life at a specific level of well-being through future generations.

Sustainable development encompasses three main notions:

- Conservation of natural resources
- Global and intergenerational equity
- Promotion of economic development through environmental protection

In 1993, eminent economist Robert Solow, in his paper "Sustainability: An Economist's Perspective," stated that "sustainability is an essentially vague concept, and it would be wrong to think of it as being precise, or even capable of being precise."

In order to avoid this charge of vagueness, some thinkers and economists have attempted to provide an operational definition of sustainable development. From this effort has emerged the concept of strong and weak sustainable development. Two of the world's eminent thinkers of sustainable development, economist David Pearce and Jeremy Warford, suggest that sustainable development means "a process in which the natural resource base is not allowed to deteriorate."[2] This is known as the "strong" definition of sustainability. The "weak" definition allows the natural resource base to be diminished as long as biological resources are maintained at a minimum critical level and the wealth generated by the exploitation of natural resources is preserved for future generations who would otherwise be "robbed" of their rightful inheritance.[3] Weak sustainability, then, can be thought of as "the amount of consumption that can be sustained indefinitely without degrading capital stocks."[4]

Both the "strong" and "weak" definitions of sustainable development pose problems. Sustainable development embodies seven basic principles:

- Natural resources are scarce.
- Natural resources should be conserved.
- Intergenerational equity should be maintained.
- Modern commercial technologies necessarily degrade the natural environment.
- Environmental protection leads to sustainable economic development.
- Government's role is central to ensuring sustainability.

• Command and control regulations are needed to protect people and the natural environment from the vagaries of the market.

SCARCE NATURAL RESOURCES?

LET US START by examining the first two principles of sustainable development. Advocates of sustainable development claim that natural resources are scarce and should be conserved.

The "strong" definition of sustainable development does not allow natural resources to be consumed faster than they can be renewed. But the fact is that supplies of natural resources are increasing. Take, for example, the agriculture sector and land. Farmers around the world are growing more food than ever before and on less land, too. Figures 5.1–5.7 show how much food production and productivity has improved in both developed and developing countries. In the last three decades, the production of food grains in the United States increased by 82 percent, whereas the planted area decreased by 11 percent in the last seven decades. (See Figures 5.1 and 5.2.)

> Farmers around the world are growing more food than ever before and on less land, too.

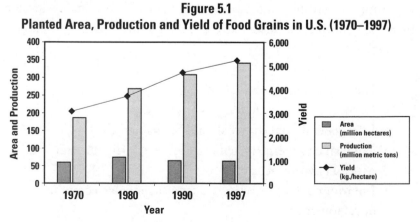

Figure 5.1
Planted Area, Production and Yield of Food Grains in U.S. (1970–1997)

Source: Central Intelligence Agency, Directorate of Intelligence, *Handbook of International Economic Statistics* (1998).

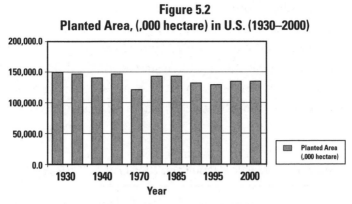

Figure 5.2
Planted Area, (,000 hectare) in U.S. (1930–2000)

Source: United States Department of Agriculture, National Agricultural Statistics
Service, *Historical Track Records*

This trend is observed for all the countries irrespective of their developed or developing status. In the case of China, the decrease in planted area in the last three decades is 34 percent while food production increased by 41 percent (Figure 5.3). In the case of developed countries, the decrease in planted area in recent times is not that high because their farmers started practicing modern intensive agriculture decades ago and long since stabilized their agricultural sector. In the last 40 years, India doubled its population and more than doubled its food production, but the cultivated land acreage increased only by 5 percent, leading to the expansion of forest area by more than

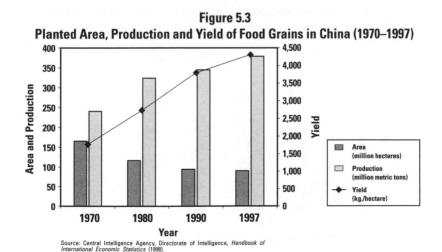

Figure 5.3
Planted Area, Production and Yield of Food Grains in China (1970–1997)

Source: Central Intelligence Agency, Directorate of Intelligence, *Handbook of International Economic Statistics* (1998).

20 percent. In other words, Indian farmers are growing a lot more food on the same amount of land. Since the 1990s, Indian farmers have been growing more food on less land. (See Figures 5.4 and 5.5.) The world currently produces a huge surplus of food. Farmers have intensified the use of resources in order to produce more food from the same amount of land. Relatively speaking, land has become more

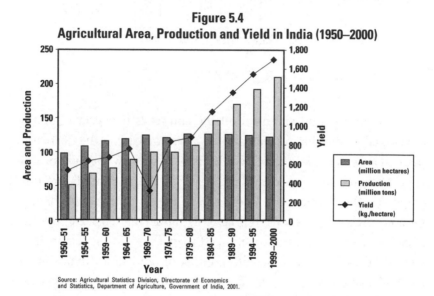

Figure 5.4
Agricultural Area, Production and Yield in India (1950–2000)

Source: Agricultural Statistics Division, Directorate of Economics and Statistics, Department of Agriculture, Government of India, 2001.

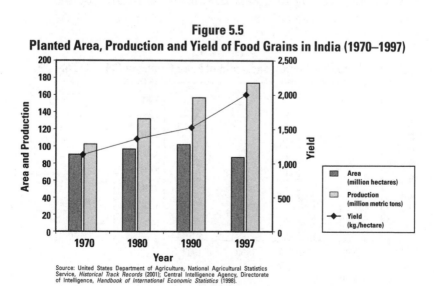

Figure 5.5
Planted Area, Production and Yield of Food Grains in India (1970–1997)

Source: United States Department of Agriculture, National Agricultural Statistics Service, *Historical Track Records* (2001); Central Intelligence Agency, Directorate of Intelligence, *Handbook of International Economic Statistics* (1998).

Figure 5.6
Planted Area, Production and Yield of Food Grains in Germany (1970–1997)

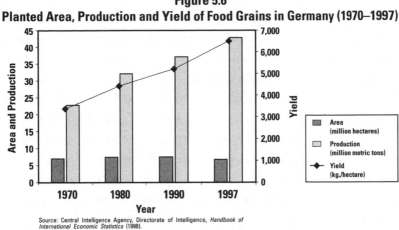

Source: Central Intelligence Agency, Directorate of Intelligence, *Handbook of International Economic Statistics* (1998).

Figure 5.7
Planted Area, Production and Yield of Food Grains in UK (1970–1997)

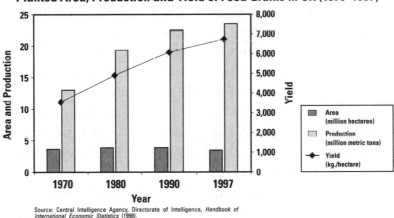

Source: Central Intelligence Agency, Directorate of Intelligence, *Handbook of International Economic Statistics* (1998).

abundant rather than scarcer, and as a result, now more and more land is available to be set aside for forests, watershed protection, nature preserves, recreational purposes, and so forth.

Strangely, some proponents of sustainable development, such as Vandana Shiva, the founder of the Indian environmental organization Research Institute for Science, Technology and Ecology, want to devote more land to agriculture. These activists claim that converting farm smallholdings into larger export-oriented farms is ecologically damaging. However, the evidence shows that larger farms are managed more sensitively than are small farms because farmers with larger farms have access to better technologies, better seeds, and better cultivation practices. Shiva also objects to the adoption of new land legislation by various states in India that makes the conversion of land from agricultural to industrial uses easier.[5] The question is whether India needs more land for agricultural purposes or not. Per capita availability of food grains in India has increased by 27 percent between 1951 and 1995.[6] India remains a net agricultural exporter and is usually self-sufficient or surplus in food grains, though inadequate incomes leave many malnourished. Higher incomes from new industries established on former farmland could go a long way toward helping the poor improve their diets.

Technological advancement has led to an increase in production of agricultural crops and yield in India without the usage of land increase. According to Norman E. Borlaug, the Nobel Peace Prize Laureate and the father of Green Revolution technologies, if India had continued with low-yielding pre-Green Revolution technology, the usage of area under cultivation would be an additional 67 million hectares to equal current wheat harvested. On a global scale, world cereal production increased from 650 million metric tons in 1950 to 1,887 million metric tons in 1998. Whereas if farmers had had to use 1950s technology to produce the cereal harvest of 1998, the cultivated area would have had to have been increased to 1,150 million hectares over the 650 million hectares that was actually used.

If we examine the data of agricultural area, production, and yield in India, it would be easy to understand how the food production has increased over the years with no increase in land area under cultivation. (See Figure 5.4.) In 1950, the production was about 50 million metric tons, area under cultivation was about 100 million hectares, and the total yield was about 500 kilograms per hectare. In 1975 to 1980, the production was less then 100 million metric tons, area under cultivation was about 125 million hectares, and the total yield was about 750 to 800 kilograms per hectare. If we compare these figures with 1995 and 1999, a decline can be noticed in the area under cultivation and a drastic increase in production and total yield. In 1995, the production was about 190 million metric tons, area under cultivation was about 123 million hectares, and the total yield about 1,500 kilograms per hectare. And in 1999 the production was about 205 million metric tons, the area cultivated was about 123 million hectares, and the total yield was about 1,700 kilograms per hectare.

Clearly, the impact of agricultural technologies in reducing pressure on agricultural land can be seen even in a low productivity country such as India. In the last 50 years, the agriculture production has increased about fourfold to 200 million metric tons per annum, while during the same period, the area brought under the plow has grown by only 25 percent to about 125 million hectares. In the last 20 years, following the spread of Green Revolution technologies in India, agricultural production has doubled, without any increase in cultivated land. In fact, since the mid-1980s, there has been a distinct decline in area under agriculture. For the first time, India, even with its 1 billion people, looks set to reduce pressure on land. By adopting today's technology practiced in the developed world, India can at the same time triple its agricultural production and dramatically reduce the demand for land. This land, not needed for agriculture, will then become available for various other uses, including conservation—exactly the kind of productivity gains that has enabled today's developing countries to lower the demand for land and labor for agriculture. Compare the area and agriculture yield trends between India (Figure 5.4) and the United States (Figure 5.1).

Sustained agricultural development fueled by advances in technologies will lead to more production from less land. The Green Revolution technologies moved the world along that path more than two decades ago, and now agricultural biotechnology is poised to improve upon that record. The genetically improved Bt cotton, which is resistant to the bollworm pest, has been shown in trial fields to require reduced spray of chemical pesticides in the range of 50 to 80 percent. In addition, the lower risk of crop failure has in effect shown an increase in yield between 14 and 38 percent. The increased productivity and lower environmental stress has led Indian cotton farmers to demand access to this new technology. Today, the average yield of cotton in India stands at about 300 kilograms per hectare, about half the world average and about a third of that in China. Clearly, modern agricultural practices and technologies have the potential to increase production, improve farm income, reduce demand for agricultural land, and lower environmental stress, resulting in all-around improvement in social, economic, and environmental quality.

The development in agriculture provides one of the best illustrations of sustained development that leads to a win-win situation. A far cry from the typical zero-sum game promoted by the sustainable development model. In other words, modern high-yield agriculture, which is often paradoxically opposed by ideological environmentalists, is a form of sustainable development.

Proponents of sustainable development often claim that the world is running out of nonrenewable resources. However, one of the best indicators to judge whether or not a natural resource is becoming scarce is its price. Considerable data showing trends in raw material prices for the last 200 years are available, and these data show that the costs of extractive materials clearly have fallen over the course of recorded price history. The price of one metric ton of aluminum came down from about $5,500 in 1890 to less than $1,000 in 1990.

The basic measure of cost of any resource is the ratio between the price of that resource and the price of another resource. One such

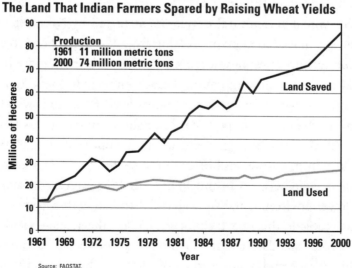

Figure 5.8
The Land That Indian Farmers Spared by Raising Wheat Yields

Production
1961   11 million metric tons
2000   74 million metric tons

Land Saved

Land Used

Millions of Hectares

Year

Source: FAOSTAT.

measure is the price of the resource related to wages. And this measure shows that the price of copper has declined very sharply. This means an hour's work now purchases much more copper now than in 1800. In the case of copper, this purchasing power has increased by 50-fold.[7] The same trend is observed for other minerals.

Another way to think about the cost of natural resources is the proportion of our total income we must pay to buy them. This measure also reveals a steady decline in cost. The extraction of natural resources has been rising and the kinds of natural resources being used have been increasing, but our expenditures on them have been falling as a proportion of total expenditures. "The gross volume of extraction output (including agriculture, oil, and coal) relative to value of national production has declined subsequently and steadily from 1870 to the present. In 1890, the extractive share was nearly 50 percent. By the turn of the century, it had fallen to 32 percent, and by 1919, to 23 percent. In 1957, the figure was 13 percent and still trending downward."[8] By 1988, the figure had fallen all the way to 3.7 percent. In 1988, minerals plus energy accounted for only 1.6 percent of the U.S. GNP.[9] This trend makes it clear that the cost of natural resources is almost irrelevant to our current standard of living. Historical evidence of falling prices of most raw materials shows a trend of increasing availability and declining scarcity. In other words, for most natural resources, their volumes are increasing, their prices are generally decreasing, and their quality is improving.

Ideological environmentalists often claim that air pollution is increasing. But the fact is that it is getting better with time. The United Nations lists more sites worldwide with improvement on three measures (sulfur dioxide, smoke, particles) than deterioration. For example, the air quality of Singapore has been rated as good or moderate on the U.S. Environmental Protection Agency's Pollution Standard Index (PSI). Concentration of TSP (total suspended particulates), sulfur dioxide, and nitrogen oxides shows a declining trend there. In recent years, total city emissions have decreased by approximately 4 percent in St. Petersburg.[10] In Hong Kong, too, sulfur dioxide emissions have been significantly reduced. Similar trends are observed in many developing countries also. A general decline in the annual average concentration of suspended particulate matter (SPM), essentially smoke and dust, has occurred in Hyderabad, a major city in India, although it is still above the World Health Organization guideline. Chennai, another major Indian city, has also seen a decline in SPM concentration levels since 1979, and its sulfur dioxide and nitrogen dioxide levels have also declined in recent years. Lead concentrations are also below the WHO levels in Hyderabad and Chennai.

The preceding examples make the point that natural resources and environmental goods like clean air are not becoming increasingly scarce. Economic growth and social modernization in the industrialized countries have brought about major changes in the use of resources. Energy and material consumption rose rapidly during the 19th and first half of the 20th centuries to meet demands from intensified agriculture, construction, and industrialization. This phase has been followed by a decrease in the growth rate of resource use as developed economies matured and became more efficient. Materials use is still changing. The emphasis now is on lighter, higher-value metals and composites rather than on heavy, bulk commodities. Materials intensity has fallen rapidly, at nearly 2 percent per year since 1971.[11] As incomes increase, people expand their universe of consumption. Though the total consumption is rising, the mix of resources consumed has changed over time. Resource consumption per unit of output is declining, leading to less resource use. The world is creating new resources at an ever-increasing rate.

Some ideological environmentalists claim that the low development in the poorer countries is due to the lack of natural resources or capital goods. Because resources are scarce, these environmentalists conclude that the resources must be preserved. It is true that the availability of natural resources has often been the key to economic success. Egyptian civilization flourished on the strength of the fertile Nile Valley, Britain thrived on iron ore and coal, and the southern U.S. states once prospered on cotton and tobacco. But many countries, such as Japan, Korea, Denmark, and Switzerland, show striking economic success today with poor endowments of natural resources. Japan's endowment of natural resources has not increased much since 1950, yet its economy is much bigger and its people much more prosperous today. On the other hand, Mexico, Nigeria, Brazil, and Russia, though rich in natural resources, provide relatively poor standards of living for their people. It is not the natural resources, but good ideas that developing countries lack.

Natural resources are not in any relevant sense finite, so preserving them in the name of sustainable development makes no sense. Actually, preservation for the sake of preservation is a threat to human well-being and economic development. Ideological environmentalists urge people to consume less in order to save natural resources. In fact, we should do the opposite. We should consume more in order to encourage the development of more abundant resources in the future. The price of any resource increases only when there is relative scarcity due to high rate of consumption. This rise in price encourages the creation and discovery of new resources. The rise in the price of wood gave an impetus to develop coal, and similarly, the rise in the price of whale oil for lighting drove the drilling of petroleum in the 19th century. Conservation for the sake of conservation is harmful for development. Stable resource prices due to conservation would lower the incentives to find new resources and substitutes for the old ones.

> Preservation for the sake of preservation is a threat to human well-being and economic development.

For example, if the prices of fossil fuels rise considerably, there would be greater incentive for researching substitutes. It should also be noted that the increase in price of any resource acts as an incentive for achieving greater efficiency in its use, thus encouraging people to conserve it.

INTERGENERATIONAL EQUITY?

ONE OF THE main principles of the sustainable development concept is intergenerational equity. But how do we know what the needs of future generations will be? Fundamentally "needs" and resources change with time, technology, and demand. Uranium, for example, was not considered a resource a century ago, but certainly it is an important resource today. Petroleum was not a significant resource 150 years ago, but today it is considered to be vital. Conserving what we consider resources today does not ensure that tomorrow is secure, and drawing down today's does not necessarily mean that tomorrow is in jeopardy.[12]

Just how nonsensical the notion of intergenerational equity is becomes clear when you consider the conundrum that if the choice to draw down resources is held exclusively by future generations, then we, being the future generations of previous generations, have been deprived of that right. Does it make sense for us to condemn our ancestors, who were much poorer and less secure than we are, for using resources to support themselves? Does sustainable development really imply that no generation has the right to use resources, no matter how urgent their needs may be? Besides, future generations, who will be wealthier and more technologically sophisticated, will have much wider choices and opportunities than we do.

TECHNOLOGY DEGRADES NATURAL ENVIRONMENT?

ADVOCATES OF SUSTAINABLE development often oppose modern commercial technologies on the grounds that they degrade the environment. But the fact is that modern technologies improve environmental quality as well as economic well-being. Actually, natural resources are more abundant because of the development of more efficient technologies. Technological change, recycling, innovation, and discovery of substitutes ease any temporary natural resources scarcities. Technological progress conserves and increases the effective supplies of natural resources. Greater technological efficiency reduces the quantity of resources necessary to produce a given unit of goods or services. For example, according to the U.S. Energy Department's Energy Information Administration, the amount of petroleum and natural gas necessary to produce a dollar's worth of GDP has declined by 29 percent since 1980.[13] Computers have helped to reduce energy consumption per unit of GDP by one-third in the last

25 years in the United States.[14] Bridges and cars are built with much less steel today using CAD-CAM design systems.

The difference between rich nations and poor nations is not that the rich just have more money than the poor, but that the rich nations produce more goods and services. The chief reason they can do that is because their technology is better. Economic growth depends on increases in the stock of human knowledge, which is practically expressed as technological progress. Since medieval times, technological change has been one of the chief factors determining economic growth and income. By 1700, Europe was already richer than any of the non-European economies, and technological progress was mainly responsible for this gap.[15] Faster economic progress also worked as a demand factor that encouraged the search for newer technologies. In the short run, technological progress has had some deleterious environmental consequences, such as air and water pollution and deforestation. But in the long run, the benefits more than compensate for the losses. Take, for example, the advent of coal mining in 16th century Europe and oil drilling in the 19th century. These inventions saved the forests that were being cut for fuelwood and whales that were being hunted for lighting oil. The Italian academic Cesare Marchetti has traced how humanity's source of primary power has gradually shifted from wood to coal to oil to gas during the last century and a half. "Each of these fuels is successively richer in hydrogen and poorer in carbon than its predecessor, so we seem to be moving towards using pure hydrogen. . . . In other words, de-carbonization of the world economy, accompanied by a shift from dirty to cleaner technologies, is occurring without any political direction"[16] and it is driven by human inventiveness.

If we want to protect the natural environment, humanity needs to take advantage of the ever-improving efficiencies that come from technological progress. Many policies advocated by ideological environmentalists actually end up harming the natural world. Take the case of modern pesticides and modern agricultural practices. Many environmentalists argue that the modern chemical-intensive production and distribution system disturbs the environment and has proved itself to be undemocratic, wasteful, and nonsustainable. Strangely, ideological environmentalists have managed to overlook the fact that agriculture itself is inherently a disruption of the environment that involves defending crops and livestock from weeds, insect pests, predators, and disease microorganisms. Most agricultural land is not suitable for farming without modification by humans. Since the advent of agriculture, people have continually invented new technologies that have led to increased productivity and the present high level of global food security. Unfortunately, this does not mean that people all across the world are well fed or have enough food, but definitely the situation has improved and now relatively few people die of starvation as compared to the earlier centuries.

Crops need protection to grow, and the nutrient renewal of the soil is also necessary to increase the productivity. To achieve these goals, new fertilizers and pesticides were introduced. In the early 1900s, before the introduction of modern pesticides, arsenical pesticides and other poisons were widely used for crops and livestock protection. Agriculture is still dependent on a variety of chemicals, though the dosage level has been greatly reduced. Many studies have shown that banning the use of chemical pesticides would greatly reduce the agricultural productivity, putting the world's growing population at risk of starvation and the world's wildlands at further risk of being plowed down by desperate, hungry people.

> Many studies have shown that banning the use of chemical pesticides would greatly reduce the agricultural productivity, putting the world's growing population at risk of starvation.

According to ideological environmentalists in the thrall of the myths of organic farming, animal manure is better for the soil than are artificial fertilizers. However, animal manure can have toxic chemicals or high salt content, and it often provides refuge to harmful bacteria, insects, worms, and other pests. Even if we agree that animal manure is superior, it would be impossible to sustain the soil nutrients needed to raise crops and feed the world's population by using manure only. In the late 1980s, about 4.4 billion tons of composted organic animal manure would have been needed to produce the equivalent of the 65 million metric tons of chemical nitrogen used at that time. And with the increasing demand for food before world population stabilizes, ever-greater volumes of manure would be needed to replace artificial fertilizers. This would mean a three- to four-fold increase in world animal production along with concomitant increases in feed grain production and expanded pasturage. Going organic would spell disaster for both people and the natural world.

Many ideological environmentalists point to the alleged harmful effects of the Green Revolution and intensive agriculture in India. But they forget that farmers now produce far more food from every hectare than they could have dreamed about producing two generations ago. (See Figure 5.4.) Hybrid seeds, inorganic fertilizers, pesticides, irrigation, and mechanization have made it possible to provide India's people with more and more food at less and less cost. In 1950, India and sub-Saharan Africa both produced the same amount of grain. Today, more than 50 years later, India produces three times more, while sub-Saharan Africa is still producing about the same amount it did in 1950.[17] India was transformed from a starving nation to an exporter of food. Nothing like the Bengal famine in the 1940s, the world's worst recorded food disaster, can happen in India again. While the Green Revolution has had some deleterious environmental side effects, if food were still produced at a low intensity by traditional methods, a majority of the Indian population would have starved to death in the past three decades. Besides, low-intensity, traditional methods of agricultural practice would have destroyed most of India's remaining forests. Also, the Green Revolution enabled productivity enhancements that caused food prices to decline dramatically. Lower food prices are of special value to the poor since they spend far more of their income on food than do wealthy people.

Because of the Green Revolution, the real prices of rice and wheat declined globally by more than 70 percent since the 1970s.[18] According to the economist Indur Goklany, had farm technology and yield been frozen at 1961 levels, producing as much food as was actually produced in 1998 would have required increasing the acreage farmed and devoted to pasturage from 12.2 billion acres to 26.3 billion acres, or from 38 percent to 82 percent of global land area. That would have meant destroying forests, draining swamps, irrigating deserts, and exterminating species on an unimaginable scale.[19]

Meanwhile, biotechnology holds tremendous promise for the developing world. The use of high-yielding, disease-resistant, and pest-resistant crops would have a direct bearing on improved food security, poverty alleviation, and environmental conservation in developing countries. Plant biotechnology may have some environmental side effects, but with time, these side effects will be reduced as has happened in the case of other technological innovations. Technological progress is the best hope for economic as well as environmental improvement. Of course, the benefits are exactly what ideological environmentalists who oppose agricultural biotechnology claim they favor.

If ideological environmentalism in the name of sustainable development succeeds in outlawing pesticides and restricting the use of new technologies, farmers will get less food from their land, which in turn means that they would need to clear more land to feed the world's growing population. And putting more land under cultivation means the destruction of more forests and wilderness. Low-tech organic farming may be environmentally orthodox, but adopting it on a widespread basis would have horrendous effects on the natural environment. The increased productivity that biotechnology makes possible will help agriculture costs and prices to plunge. New technologies like plant biotechnology have created a world where natural resource availability is growing far faster than demand. Turning back the clock and adopting the medieval patterns of farming technology in the name of environmental protection would do far more harm to the natural world than any modern farming technologies have done.

Keep in mind that technological advances have reduced the amount of resources necessary to produce a unit of goods or services resulting in improvements in environmental quality. Advances have been made in many areas. Cables carrying information long distances are now typically made of glass-fiber rather than copper. A cable made from 60 pounds of silica can carry 1,000 times as much information as a cable made from a ton of copper. Computers offer perhaps the most startling example of this "dematerialization." In the

1950s, computers were the size of a two-bedroom flat and could process only about 1,000 instructions per second. Today, computers the size and weight of a book can process 200 million instructions per second. These advances in computer technology have also led to more efficient use of resources in other areas.[20]

"When economists invented growth accounting in the late 1950s, they found that technical change accounted for almost 90 percent of U.S. economic growth in the first half of the 20th century. Accumulation of physical capital—investment in machines, construction, heavy metal—explained less than one-eighth of the fourfold increase in prosperity of then-recorded history's most dynamic economy," according to economist Danny Quah from the London School of Economics.[21] History is replete with examples of how technological innovations driven by market forces have reduced both the use of natural resources and stresses on the natural environment.

ENVIRONMENTAL PROTECTION = SUSTAINABLE ECONOMIC DEVELOPMENT?

IDEOLOGICAL ENVIRONMENTALISTS ASSERT that environmental protection leads to sustainable economic development. However, it is clear that the less developed a country is, the worse are the effects on the natural world caused by poverty and the use of low-grade technology. History shows that initially economic development and environmental protection cannot generally be achieved simultaneously. However, once the economy of a nation develops, its people can afford to clean up and protect their natural environment. This process has been observed in all the developed countries. Eighteenth-century London was full of smog, but now for a major city, London's air quality is one of the best in the world. Wealth helps to clean up the environment. In fact, developing nations today are in a better position than was the earlier developed world. Because of the availability of modern technologies, whatever the developed world could achieve in 200 years, developing nations can achieve in relatively less time and by polluting their environments relatively less. One of the best examples is Japan, which grew rapidly by adopting technologies already developed in the West.

A study of the European countries confirms that increased income brings about decreased pollution. During the 1970s and 1980s, the richer countries had significantly greater decreases in carbon monoxide and sulfur dioxide concentrations than did the poorer countries.[22] A study comparing cities from both developed and developing countries reveals that the environmental quality, especially air quality, started improving in the developed world a long while ago, whereas the air quality in developing countries has been deteriorating. For example, the annual average concentrations of sulfur dioxide increased sharply in both Calcutta and Kuala Lumpur in the 1980s.[23] This sudden increase in sulfur dioxide emissions in cities in less-developed countries is attributed to their increased economic activity and growing vehicular populations. In fact, this kind of emissions trend was historically seen in the developed countries when they were going through the process of development. The history of soot and other air pollutants in the developed countries includes a long period of increasingly dirty air accompanying the growth of industrial activity, followed by rapid improvements in air quality. So understanding the long-term trends in the United States and other developed countries will help to predict the future course of air pollution in poor countries still undergoing the process of development.

In the developing countries, economic development usually means higher energy consumption, and more energy consumption temporarily means more air pollution. But in the long run, ever-wealthier developing countries will be able to improve their energy efficiency and thus also improve their air quality. In addition, pollution levels in the developing countries will not necessarily reach levels found earlier in the rich countries during their development period. In the present era of globalization, developing countries can gain access to the modern technology quite easily. So the developing countries can achieve a high level of economic as well as environmental development in a much shorter period than did the developed countries.

The level of energy consumption in a developing country like India is extremely low, currently standing at 226 kilograms of oil equivalent per capita as compared to 7,759 kilograms of oil equivalent in the United States. Though per capita energy consumption is low in India, the pollution level is quite high in India as compared to the Western developed countries. Clearly, this contradicts the assertions made by ideological environmentalists that more energy consumption leads to more environmental degradation.

High-energy efficiency due to high technological development in the developed countries has resulted in less utilization of natural resources and higher environmental quality. At the global level, energy intensity has fallen by about 1 percent per year since 1800, and it declined even faster during the 1970s and 1980s, at about 2 percent per year.[24] If we consider only the developed countries, the decline in energy intensity would be much more.

THE ROLE OF GOVERNMENT

ADVOCATES OF SUSTAINABLE development claim that government must play the key role in ensuring sustainability and that command and control regulations are the best approach to ensuring sustainability. Specifically, government must restrict the use of natural resources and limit economic activities in order to safeguard the environment. This claim that command and control is an effective way to preserve the environment and direct sustainable economic development flies in the face of the evidence from the collapse of the Soviet Union. In fact, imposing command and control systems on the management of the natural environment will likely have the same effect on the environment as it had on the Soviet Union's economy.

> Data clearly shows that less government control is highly correlated with more freedom and more economic development.

Data clearly shows that less government control is highly correlated with more freedom and more economic development. Figure 5.9 shows the higher the economic freedom, the higher the per capita GNP. And the higher the per capita GNP, the higher the overall development, as is quite evident from Figures 5.10, 5.11, 5.12, and 5.13.

Figure 5.9
Index of Economic Freedom Rankings 2000 and per Capita GNP

Source: Gerald P. O'Driscoll, Jr., Kim R. Holmes, and Melanie Kirkpatrick, *Index of Economic Freedom* (*Wall Street Journal*, The Heritage Foundation, and Dow Jones & Company, Inc., 2000).

Figure 5.10
Life Expectancy at Birth (1995–2000) in Selected Countries

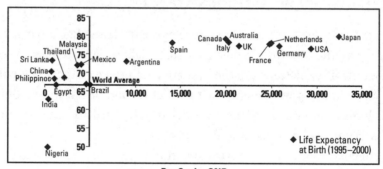

Source: Human Development Report 2000, Entering the 21st Century, World Development Report 1999/2000.

Figure 5.11
Under 5 Mortality Rate (per 1,000 live births 1998) in Selected Countries

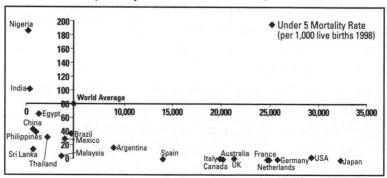

Source: Human Development Report 2000, Entering the 21st Century, World Development Report 1999/2000.

Figure 5.12
Access to Safe Water (% of population with access 1995)
in Selected Countries

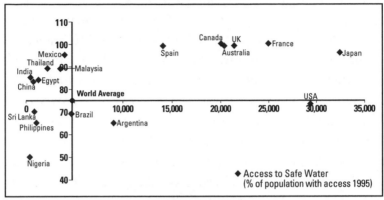

Per Capita GNP

Source: Human Development Report 2000, Entering the 21st Century, World Development Report 1999/2000.

Figure 5.13
Main Telephone Lines (per 1,000 people 1998) in Selected Countries

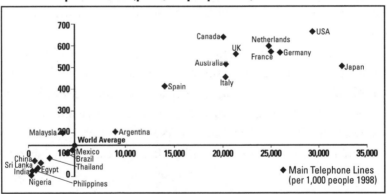

Per Capita GNP

Source: Human Development Report 2000, Entering the 21st Century, World Development Report 1999/2000.

COMMAND AND CONTROL APPROACH

HOW THE COMMAND and control approach can harm the economy as well as the environment can be briefly illustrated by looking at recent developments in the automobile industry in India. India's automobile industry made a humble beginning in the 1950s. Until the late 1970s, India's car industry was considered a low-priority sector and was protected from competition by high tariff barriers. There were only a couple of major manufacturing plants. The volume of production was limited and the technology used was obsolete. Because of foreign exchange constraints, there was no serious attempt to upgrade the technology or to attract foreign investment and technology. The result of this protectionism was the production of low-efficiency cars that emitted clouds of pollution and caused air quality to deteriorate.

In the last 15 years, the automobile sector has grown tremendously. Fuel efficiency has also dramatically increased, and this improvement can be traced directly to trade liberalization. Free trade induced competition, leading to the improvement in technology, which thus improved fuel efficiency and air quality. Due to the trade liberalization, environmentally friendly and fuel-efficient technology was introduced in India's automobile industry for the first time. Efforts are being made to meet international emission norms by installing catalytic converters, emission control devices, and fuel injection systems. Since 1991, emissions from passenger cars have dropped by 84.4 percent (combined carbon monoxide, hydrocarbons, and nitrogen oxides).

Though overall air pollution has increased in some cities because of the dramatic increase in vehicles, pollution per vehicle has decreased. Over time, the polluting capacity of the cars will decrease constantly as technology improves. The eventual result will be improved air quality like that found in Western countries. Had India's government permitted economic liberalization earlier, the air quality of India would already have been improving.

Advocates of sustainable development and ideological environmentalism are generally opposed to free markets and globalization because they believe that free markets lead to the overexploitation of natural resources. In fact, open markets help preserve resources and protect the environment. Open markets invite competition that leads to increases in people's choices among a greater variety of products. And this competition in turn induces innovation in ideas and technologies. Cleaner production, supply, recycling, wise residue management and disposal, and increased waste minimization are far more visible and viable now as a result of free markets and improved technologies. Take, for example, the packaging industry. Packaging improves the quality of products as well as reduces costs. Packaging protects items from damage during transport and thereby reduces waste.

Packaging also enhances the shelf life of food products and ensures that less food will be wasted on the journey from the producer to the consumer. Thus food can be sold at a lower price, satisfying more consumers and increasing the profits of the manufacturer and retailer. Moreover, as packaging itself uses resources, over time entrepreneurs have developed packaging systems that use less material in order to reduce their costs and to survive in the market. For example, lightweight plastic bottles and laminated cartons today have replaced the heavy glass bottles used for the packaging of milk and other soft drinks. These modern alternatives are very cheap to produce, and their lighter weight and more rectangular shape have also reduced transportation costs. Figure 5.14 shows how the weight of soft drink containers has been reduced over time in the United States. Reduction in the weight of the packaging material means reduction in the use of natural resources, and that means preservation of natural resources.

It is clear that free trade can promote high economic development and protect the natural environment. Nevertheless, the ideological environmentalists are strongly opposed to free trade, technology, and globalization. But globalization is a crucial instrument for economic and environmental improvement. Globalization can help the developing countries access the best technologies available and thus

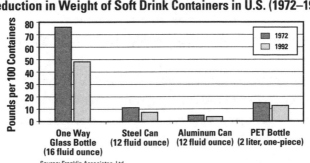

Figure 5.14
Reduction in Weight of Soft Drink Containers in U.S. (1972–1992)

Source: Franklin Associates, Ltd.

achieve great strides in both economic and environmental improvement in a short time. Developing countries like India, where conventional agricultural practices are still prevalent in many parts of the country, can use modern technology to achieve the high crop productivity levels of developed countries. Agriculture accounts for 30 percent of India's GDP. Though India is self-sufficient in food production now, increasing productivity creates a surplus for export. Export earnings can then be used to fund more investments aimed at overall economic improvement. Since 1991, farmers have already benefited from the removal of export controls on rice and wheat as part of the liberalization program in India.[25] For example, the removal of export restrictions has led to an increase in cereal exports, which rose from 12 percent to 27 percent of agricultural exports between 1991 and 1996.[26]

It is quite clear that if the principles of sustainable development as propounded by ideological environmentalists are adhered to, neither economic nor environmental development can be achieved. Sustainable development is a static and closed model. Strict adherence to the tenets of sustainable development would harm the welfare of present as well as future generations. The ultimate constraint is not resources but knowledge.

In contrast, *sustained* development can help humanity, especially the poor in developing countries, to achieve economic growth and protection of the natural world. In contrast to sustainable development, *sustained development* can be defined as an economic development that increases productivity and thus enhances the quality of consumption, including environmental quality. The concept of sustained development leads us to principles that actually are quite opposite of the principles of sustainable development.

The principles of sustained development are as follows:

- There are no permanent natural resource scarcities, so there is no need to forbid the consumption of natural resources.
- Increased consumption can increase the resource base and improve the economy and the environment.

- Intergenerational equity does not exist. However, intergenerational inequity can put future generations in an advantageous position at the expense of the current generation.
- Technological innovation improves environmental quality.
- Economic development improves environmental quality.
- Government intervention in economic and environmental activities often has deleterious side effects on both.
- Markets and technological innovations protect people from the vagaries of nature.

These principles of sustained development provide the incentives for technological advances and economic development in competitive markets that lead to the improvement of qualities at affordable prices. Environmental quality is like any value-added product that becomes available to an increasing number of people as a society develops economically. History has demonstrated that sustained development can be achieved only through the spread of globalization in the form of economic liberalization and expanding free trade.

Human civilization has experienced sustained development for approximately 3,000 years without following the principles of sustainable development and the guidance of would-be environmentalist central planners. The result is not only a world that is healthier and wealthier but also a world with more natural resources at its disposal than ever before. In fact, sustainable development as conceived by ideological environmentalists is ultimately unsustainable. The best way to maximize the welfare of human beings and to protect the natural world is sustained development that encourages rapid economic growth and technological progress by means of open markets and democratic governance.

CHAPTER SIX

CHEMICAL WARFARE: IDEOLOGICAL ENVIRONMENTALISM'S QUIXOTIC CAMPAIGN AGAINST SYNTHETIC CHEMICALS

Angela Logomasini

ECO-MYTHS DEBUNKED

- *Ever since Rachel Carson's Silent Spring (1962), ideological environmentalists have claimed that chemicals are creating a cancer epidemic, but data from the National Cancer Institute (NCI) shows that both cancer incidence and mortality are declining.*
- *Environmental pollution only accounts for 2 percent of all cancer cases. By contrast, tobacco use accounts for about 30 percent of all annual cancer deaths. Dietary choices account for 35 percent of annual cancer deaths.*
- *Cancer incidence among children is stable, and we are experiencing dramatic declines in mortality, according to the NCI.*
- *Despite claims by environmental activists that childhood brain cancer is on the rise, the NCI reports that brain cancer incidence has stabilized among children. Better detection makes it appear that there was an increase.*
- *Contrary to the claims made by environmental lobbyists, no study has ever shown that anyone in the public has developed cancer from legal application of pesticides.*
- *Eliminating modern pesticides, herbicides, and fertilizers would have devastating ecological effects, forcing farmers to plow down as much as 10 million additional square miles of land (more than the area of all of North America) to produce the same amount of food as they produce today.*
- *Banning of pesticides has had real-world health consequences for millions. After many nations stopped using the pesticide DDT because of environmentalist pressure, malaria cases have skyrocketed. According to the World Health Organization (WHO), malaria alone infects 300 to 400 million people a year and kills more than 1 million.*

E VER SINCE THE publication of Rachel Carson's 1962 bestseller, *Silent Spring*, the alleged health and environmental effects of synthetic chemicals have been a central concern of ideological environmentalism. Carson highlighted alleged harms that agricultural chemicals were having on wildlife and also claimed that the chemicals might be responsible for an epidemic of cancer in people. "The most alarming part of all man's assaults upon the environment is the contamination of air, earth, rivers, and sea with dangerous and even lethal materials. This pollution for the most part is irrecoverable; the chain of evil it initiates not only in the world that must support life but in the living tissues is for the most part irreversible," Carson declared. She claimed that synthetic chemicals, particularly pesticides such as DDT, were wreaking havoc on nature and would produce a world in which "no birds sing."[1]

Carson also warned that, besides harming wildlife, the increasing use of synthetic chemicals would cause a cancer epidemic among humans. Carson's "solution" to the problem of modern chemicals has been the solution for ideological environmentalism ever since—ban them. Carson declared, "The most determined effort should be made to eliminate those carcinogens that now contaminate our food, our water supplies, and our atmosphere, because these provide the most dangerous type of contact—minute exposures, repeated over and over throughout the years."[2]

> Carson also warned that, besides harming wildlife, the increasing use of synthetic chemicals would cause a cancer epidemic among humans. She was wrong.

Carson closed her cancer chapter, "One in Every Four," by claiming that "the most eminent men in cancer research" believe that "malignant diseases can be reduced significantly by determined efforts to identify the environmental causes and to eliminate them or reduce their impact."[3] A ban on modern chemicals must be implemented because "for those not yet touched by the disease [cancer] and certainly for the generations yet unborn, prevention is the imperative need."[4]

Following in Carson's footsteps, the infamous eco-doomster Paul Ehrlich sketched a scenario in a 1969 article entitled "Eco-Catastrophe!" in which American life expectancy would be reduced to only 42 years by the 1980s because of an epidemic of cancer caused by modern chemicals and pesticides.[5]

Forty years later, the antisynthetic chemical zeal of ideological environmentalists inspired by Carson is still going strong. In his introduction to the 1994 edition of *Silent Spring*, Vice President Al Gore noted, "For me personally, *Silent Spring* had a profound impact . . . Rachel Carson was one of the reasons why I became so conscious of the environment and so involved in environmental issues."[6]

"The production, trade, use, and release of many synthetic chemicals is now widely recognized as a global threat to human health and the environment,"[7] declares Greenpeace. Greenpeace has even called for the global elimination of chlorine. In 1993, Greenpeace's Joe Thornton stated that "[t]here are no known uses for chlorine which we regard as safe."[8]

"Our enthusiasm for new chemicals and the products and services they allow has outstripped our attention to their long-term effects," says a Worldwatch Institute report.[9] Worldwatch is more circumspect than Greenpeace in its condemnation because "questions no doubt remain" about the impact of chemicals on health. But "[g]iven the shadow this casts over these 'conveniences' of modern life, overturning the presumption of innocence about chemicals is long overdue," Ann Misch of Worldwatch concludes. Pesticide Action Network of North America seeks alternatives to pesticides because they claim "[p]esticides are hazardous to human health and the environment, create resistant pest populations, contribute to declining crop yields, undermine local and global food security and threaten agricultural biodiversity."[10]

The notion that man-made chemicals are a problem is widely echoed within media reports. In "27 Reasons to Worry About Toxic Exposure," a *Washington Post* journalist tells us that "[t]he unprecedented chemical assault on our bodies is cause for major alarm and major action."[11] *Newsweek* reports, "Over 1 million children consume more than the 'safe' adult dose of organo-phosphates (insecticides that affect the nervous system) daily."[12] In 1993, a reporter on *CBS Evening News* explained that "[a]dvocacy groups say contamination of the environment may be the biggest and most overlooked cause of today's [breast cancer] epidemic."[13] "Half a century into the chemical revolution, there is a lot we don't know about the tens of thousands of chemicals around us," declares a narrator to a PBS program on the alleged dangers of synthetic chemicals. "So, we are flying blind. Except the laboratory mice in this vast chemical experiment are the children,"[14] the narrator concludes.

CHEMICALS AND CANCER

WHILE MOST OF her book focused on alleged dire impacts on wildlife, Carson also included a chapter claiming that chemical use would eventually lead to a cancer epidemic among people in the future.[15] With the introduction of industrial chemicals, Carson claims that "[i]t is hardly surprising, therefore, that we are now aware of an alarming increase in malignant disease."[16] As evidence for the impending cancer epidemic caused by exposure to pesticide residues, Carson chiefly cited cases of leukemia and lymphoma that Dr. Malcolm Hargraves, Mayo Clinic hematologist, provided. She reported that Dr. Hargraves told her that "almost without exception these patients have had a history of exposure to various toxic chemicals, including sprays which contain DDT, chlordane, benzene, lindane, and petroleum distillates."[17] Carson then recounted the actual cases to illustrate the carcinogenic dangers of DDT and other pesticides.

"One concerned a housewife who abhorred spiders," wrote Carson. "In mid-August she had gone into her basement with an aerosol spray containing DDT and petroleum distillate. She sprayed the entire basement thoroughly, under the stairs, in the fruit cupboards and in all the protected areas around ceiling and rafters. As she finished the spraying she began to feel quite ill, with nausea and extreme anxiety and nervousness. Within the next few days she felt better, however, and apparently not suspecting the cause of her difficulty, she repeated the entire procedure in September, running through two more cycles of spraying, falling ill, recovering temporarily, spraying again. After the third use of the aerosol, new symptoms developed: fever, pains in the joints and general malaise, acute phlebitis in one leg. When examined by Dr. Hargraves she was found to be suffering from acute leukemia. She died within the following month."[18]

Carson also details the case of a man embarrassed by an infestation of roaches in his office. "He spent most of one Sunday spraying the basement and all secluded areas. The spray was a 25 percent DDT concentrate suspended in a solvent containing methylated naphthalenes," records Carson. "Within a short time he began to bruise and bleed. He entered the clinic bleeding from a number of hemorrhages. Studies of his blood revealed a severe depression of the bone marrow called aplastic anemia."[19] Carson goes on to tell readers that after 59 transfusions and nine years, the roach sprayer died of leukemia.

Today, epidemiologists and toxicologists would dismiss Carson's anecdotes as urban legends that have no scientific foundation. In fact, there is no evidence to show that either event is related, and decades of research have failed to discover definitive cause-and-effect relationships between household pesticides and serious public health ailments like cancer and leukemia. Furthermore, it should be noted that Carson, in the now canonical antisynthetic chemical strategy, often cited high-level acute exposures to insinuate that low-level chronic exposures would have similar deleterious health effects. That's like saying because an overdose of vitamins can make you sick, low levels of vitamins are going to make you sick as well.

A more fair scientific perspective would caution against linking pesticide exposures and health ailments that merely happened to occur later.

Carson's ideological grandchildren still find it useful to recite the claim that synthetic chemicals cause cancer. "If you think there's a link between heavy pesticide use and human health problems, you're not alone," writes Pesticide Action Network Program Director Monica Moore in a spring 2001 fund-raising letter. Just in case you don't make the link, the letter helpfully notes in bold type at the top: **"Childhood cancer is increasing 1% per year"** and **"Breast cancer is increasing nearly 2% per year."** On its Web page, the Environmental Working Group (EWG) declares that "[c]ancer incidence in the American population has skyrocketed—up 48% from 1950 through 1990, according to National Cancer Institute statistics. These statistics are adjusted for an aging population and exclude lung and stomach cancers where the causes are generally well-understood."[20]

ACTUAL HEALTH TRENDS SHOW NO CANCER EPIDEMIC

IF THE IDEOLOGICAL environmentalists and Carson had turned out to be correct, we would expect to see some increase in the cancer rate. Yet both incidence and mortality are declining. "A typical commentary blamed 'increasing cancer rates' on 'exposure to industrial chemicals and run-away modern technologies whose explosive growth had clearly outpaced the ability of society to control them,'" researchers from the University of Alabama Schools of Medicine and Public Health note. But their research finds that "[t]here is no denying the existence of environmental problems, but the present data show that they produced no striking increase in cancer mortality."[21]

Environmental activists have been able to claim otherwise by ignoring many other factors that can affect rates, such as longer lives (cancer most often occurs later in life) and better screening. For example, one researcher failed to account for population increases in a chart plotting cancer incidence between 1900 and 1990. By not accounting for the fact that population increased from 77 million to 250 million, the chart made it appear as if cancer rates skyrocketed.[22] Instead, cancer rates should be measured in units of population, such as the number of cancers per 100,000 people.

In addition, reporting on cancer trends should consider the age of various segments of the population. Cancer is a disease of old age—the longer one lives, the greater the chances that one will have cancer. Since cancer increases with age, if the segment of senior citizens enlarges compared to the others, you should expect more cancers per 100,000. Hence as the baby-boomer generation ages, the cancer rate will naturally go up and we should not confuse those numbers with other causes, such as chemical exposure.

Another problem includes the failure to consider the impact of smoking. Smoking has indeed increased the number of lung cancers profoundly. Counting those cancers to demonstrate that air pollution or other chemicals are causing a cancer epidemic is wrong. The University of Alabama researchers report that smoking is responsible for making lung cancer, which was once a rare occurrence, one of the most common cancers. They note, "When the mortality from all smoking-related cancers is excluded, the decline in other cancer from 1950 to 1998 was 31 percent (from 109 to seventy-five deaths per 100,000 person years)."[23] Hence the increase in cancer at that time was not the use of synthetic chemicals or pollution, but personal lifestyle choices.

The NCI[24] produces an annual report on cancer trends that attempts to take into consideration such factors. Its figures are age adjusted, and they measure cancers per 100,000 people. These reports also attempt to explain increases or decreases within the various categories.

According to its latest report, "Cancer incidence for all sites combined decreased from 1992 through 1998 among all persons in the United States, primarily because of a decline of 2.9 percent per year in white males and 3.1 percent per year in black males. Among females, cancer incidence rates increased 0.3 percent per year. Overall, cancer death rates declined 1.1 percent per year."[25]

In recent years, cancer among women is up because of an increase in breast cancer, which has increased 40 percent between 1973 and 1998.[26] The NCI notes that these trends in large part reflect better screening and increased detection "since the increase was limited to the early stage of the disease."[27] This scenario is highly likely given the percent of woman aged 40 to 49 who obtained mammograms doubled between 1987 and 1998, from 32 percent to 63 percent. The percent of woman aged 50 to 64 who received a mammogram increased from 31 to 73 percent in that same time period.[28] Looking at more recent trends, the NCI finds that "[b]reast cancer incidence rates have shown little change in the 1990s."[29]

Not emphasized by environmentalists is the fact that modern medicine and its chemicals are saving women from breast cancer. The NCI report notes that, despite incidence increases, death rates from breast cancer decreased by 1.6 percent for all races combined from 1989 through 1995. Between 1995 and 1998, the death rate declined even faster, at a rate of 3.4 percent.[30]

Figure 6.1
Age-Adjusted Cancer Death Rates,* Females by Site, U.S., 1930–1998

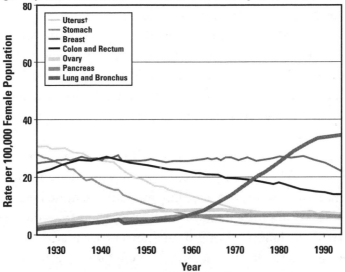

*Per 100,000, age-adjusted to the 1970 U.S. standard population. †Uterus cancer death rates are for uterine, cervix, and uterine corpus combined.

Note. Due to changes in ICD coding, numerator information has changed over time. Rates for cancers of the liver, lung and bronchus, and colon and rectum are affected by these coding changes.

Source: US Mortality Public Use Data Tapes 1960–1998, US Mortality Volumes 1930–1959, National Center for Health Statistics, Centers for Disease Control and Prevention, 2001.

Figure 6.2
Age-Adjusted Cancer Death Rates,* Males by Site, U.S., 1930 1998

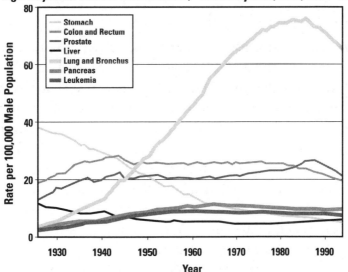

*Per 100,000, age-adjusted to the 1970 U.S. standard population.

Note: Due to changes in ICD coding, numerator information has changed over time. Rates for cancers of the liver, lung and bronchus, and colon and rectum are affected by these coding changes.

Source: US Mortality Public Use Data Tapes 1960–1998, US Mortality Volumes 1930–1959, National Center for Health Statistics, Centers for Disease Control and Prevention, 2001.

During the past several decades, cancer among women has also increased because of a rising number of smoking-related lung cancers. The NCI reports that starting in 1975, the number of men smoking declined more rapidly than the decline of the number of women smoking, but the rate of decline began to coincide between the sexes in 1985.[31] Because of such trends, the reduction in lung cancer among women is taking longer. Fortunately, lung cancer incidence among women has leveled off[32] and hopefully will begin its decline in the near future.

Likewise, the NCI reports that prostate cancer incidence increased after 1973 at a rate of 2.9 percent annually and then at a steeper rate when improved screening methods identified more cases. Some increases in prostate cancer could also result from the fact that people are living longer. Most prostate cancers occur after age 55, and most are not detected until age 70.[33] Nonetheless, prostate cancer cases began to decline by 11 percent annually between 1992 and 1995 and have since leveled off. Mortality follows a similar trend, with mortality declining between 1995 and 1998 at a rate of 4.7 percent for white males and 3 percent for African American males.

CAUSES OF CANCER

IN THEIR LANDMARK 1981 study of the issue, cancer researchers Sir Richard Doll and Richard Peto set out to determine the causes of preventable cancer in the United States. They note that 80 to 90 percent of cancers are caused by "environmental factors." Activists often point to this assertion as evidence that pollution and chemicals are indeed the culprits. But in their 1981 study, Doll and Peto noted, "Unfortunately, the phrase 'intrinsic factors' (or the phrase 'environmental factors' which is often substituted for it) has been misinterpreted by many people to mean only 'man-made chemicals,' which was certainly not the intent of the WHO. The committee included, in addition to man-made or natural carcinogens, viral infections, nutritional deficiencies or excesses, reproductive activities, and a variety of other factors determined wholly or partly by personal behavior."[34]

They found that exposure to man-made chemicals, including pollution, accounts for just 2 percent of all cancer cases. The more significant causes of cancer are things over which people have control. Tobacco use accounts for about 30 percent of all annual cancer deaths.[35] Dietary choices account for 35 percent of annual cancer deaths.[36] University of California researchers Bruce Ames and Lois Swirsky Gold have come to similar conclusions, noting that smoking causes about a third of all cancers. They underline the importance of diet by pointing out that the quarter of the population eating the fewest fruits and vegetables have double the cancer incidence. Accordingly, if public health officials and activists really seek to reduce cancer rates, they would do better to promote improved diets and less smoking rather than campaigning for more expensive and ineffective federal regulations to control trace amounts of synthetic chemicals in the environment.

> They found that exposure to man-made chemicals, including pollution, accounts for just 2 percent of all cancer cases.

One should also be wary of environmentalist claims that chemicals cause human cancers because they give cancer to rodents exposed to massive doses. Doll and Peto note that some chemicals found to be carcinogenic in humans have not produced cancerous tumors in rodent experiments. In fact, for many years, cigarette smoke failed to produce malignant tumors in laboratory animals despite the fact that tobacco is perhaps the leading cause of cancer in the United States. These discordant effects of chemicals on animals and humans underline the difficulty of relying on animal results to estimate human risks.[37]

Moreover, toxicologists have long contended that "the dose makes the poison." Small quantities of substances can be helpful or benign, but at high doses, they can sicken or kill. In fact, when researchers administer rodents with high levels of healthy foods—such as apples, bananas, carrots, and celery—the animals developed tumors.[38] Some scientists have concluded that often high doses of nearly any chemical will kill cells in test animals directly, provoking cell division to replace the dead cells. This process of cell proliferation increases the possibility of mutations that can lead to cancer.[39]

Ames and Gold found that "rodent carcinogens" pose no more of a risk of causing cancer than those posed by many natural, unregulated substances that are common and accepted parts of a healthy diet. They point out that while 212 of the 350 synthetic chemicals examined by various agencies were found to be carcinogenic at the massive doses given to rodents, 37 out of 77 of the natural substances tested also were found to be carcinogenic in rodent studies employing the same methodology.[40] Essentially, natural and synthetic chemicals are equally likely to cause cancer in rats.

CHILDREN'S HEALTH AND SYNTHETIC CHEMICALS

RACHEL CARSON WAS an effective popularizer of the idea that children were especially vulnerable to the carcinogenic effects of synthetic chemicals. "The situation with respect to children is even more deeply disturbing," wrote Carson in 1962. "A quarter century ago, cancer in children was considered a medical rarity. *Today, more American schoolchildren die of cancer than from any other disease* [emphasis original]."[41] In support of this claim, Carson reported "twelve percent of all deaths in children between the ages of one and fourteen are caused by cancer." Of course, this statistic is essentially meaningless unless it's given some context, which Carson failed to supply. Were numbers of children dying of cancer going up? Were the percentages of children dying of cancer increasing or were they rising because other causes of death were decreasing? In fact, it was the latter—the percentage of children dying of cancer was rising because other causes of death were declining.

Carson then tried to make the link between cancer in children and exposure to trace amounts of synthetic chemicals by citing the speculations of Dr. W. C. Hueper of the National Cancer Institute, whom she described as "a foremost authority on environmental cancer." Dr. Hueper, as well-meaning as he might have been, had been long fixated on the chemical induction of cancer ever since his experiments with dogs in the 1920s and 1930s. Hueper was so certain that trace amounts of synthetic chemicals were the cause of cancer that he simply dismissed the real damage caused by cigarettes. Carson wrote that Dr. Hueper "has suggested that congenital cancers and cancers in infants may be related to the action of cancer-producing agents to which the mother has been exposed during pregnancy and which penetrate the placenta to act on the rapidly developing fetal tissues."[42]

As additional backing for her claim that synthetic chemicals were harming children, Carson reported that Dr. Francis Ray of the University of Florida had warned that "we may be initiating cancer in the children of today by the addition of chemicals [to food]. . . . We will not know, perhaps for a generation or two, what the effects will be."[43]

In recent years, the antichemical activists have resuscitated Carson's claims that synthetic chemical residues are more harmful to children than to adults. In 1989, the Natural Resources Defense Council (NRDC) launched its Children's Environmental Health Initiative with a report on apples treated with the chemical Alar, a growth regulator that prevents red apples from falling from trees before harvest and improves their appearance. The NRDC alleged that Alar had dangerous health impacts based on Environmental Protection Agency (EPA) rodent tests. The environmentalist group gave the exclusive story to CBS's *60 Minutes*. The program claimed that Alar-laced apples were the "most potent cancer-causing chemical in our food supply" and quoted a congressman who suggested that cancer wards around the nation were filled with children suffering from Alar's impact.[44]

The CBS program set off a national hysteria. Newspapers carried terrifying headlines, such as "Fear: Are We Poisoning Our Children?" (*USA Today*),[45] "Hazardous Apples" (*Washington Post*),[46] and "Red, Delicious—and Dangerous" (*St. Louis Post-Dispatch*).[47]

Yet this critical event in the growing children's environmental health movement was based on fiction. The apples were never dangerous. According to scientists and regulators of Alar, the NRDC's faulty methods for calculating risks had exaggerated them by as much as 400 to 500 times the actual risk level.[48] The EPA, the Food and Drug Administration, and the Department of Agriculture all reported that

Alar was safe at the very low levels found on apples.[49] A United Nations panel of medical and agricultural experts and the American Medical Association issued statements stating that Alar did not pose a health threat.[50]

Nevertheless, Alar was withdrawn from the market. Shortly after the NRDC launched its anti-Alar campaign, schools around the nation pulled apples from their cafeterias,[51] importers canceled orders for U.S. apples,[52] supermarkets and schools stopped selling and serving apple juice,[53] and the EPA ordered the phase-out of the chemical. In the end, apple growers lost $250 million and apple product manufacturers lost $125 million, and many small growers were put out of business.[54]

The renewed emphasis on "children's environmental health" spawned by the Alar scare led to a report, *Pesticides in the Diets of Infants and Children*, issued by the National Research Council of the National Academy of Sciences in 1993. In that report, the NRC investigated the issue of whether children might be more susceptible to the impacts of synthetic chemicals.

But even before the NRC released its report, *Newsweek* reported that the "panel is expected to conclude that children are more vulnerable to carcinogenic and neurotoxic pesticides than adults are, and to slam the EPA for failing to protect children."[55] The study did more moderately note "exposures occurring earlier in life can lead to greater or lower risk of chronic toxic effects such as cancer than exposures occurring later in life."[56] So just to be safe, the NRC report recommended that the EPA employ a 10-fold safety factor when setting pesticide regulations, in addition to the 100-fold safety factor the agency already applied. But probably the most important conclusion of the NRC study was largely overlooked: The NRC did not find that most children were being exposed to unsafe levels of pesticide residues.

Following the NRC report, the EPA published a national children's health policy[57] and Congress amended the federal pesticide law directing the EPA to apply a 10-fold safety factor when setting pesticide regulations unless data demonstrated the safety factor was not necessary. In 1997, President Clinton issued Executive Order 13045[58] creating a presidential task force involving all federal departments and the EPA to coordinate executive branch efforts related to children's environmental health. The EPA then set up the Office of Children's Health Protection to help implement the order.[59] The stated mission of the Office of Children's Health Protection is "to make the protection of children's health a fundamental goal of public health and environmental protection in the United States."[60]

CHILDREN'S GENERAL HEALTH TRENDS POSITIVE

IF THE DIRE warnings by environmental ideologues about children's health were correct, we would expect some negative trends. However, between 1980 and 1998, the death rate for children aged 1 to 4 declined 50 percent.[61] The death rate for children aged 5 to 14 declined about 10 percent during that same period.[62] The death rate for adolescents and young adults (ages 15 to 24) has declined from 115 per 100,000 in 1980 to 82 per 100,000 by 1998.[63] American children have never been healthier. But what about cancer rates so often cited by alarmists?

In a report on the impact of chemicals on children, the NRDC claims that "[w]hile human exposure to synthetic chemicals in the environment is on the rise, the overall incidence of childhood cancer also increased 10.5 percent between 1973 and 1994, with childhood cancers of the brain and other sites in the central nervous system rising 35.1 percent in the same time period."[64] At a 1997 EPA conference on children's health, EPA Administrator Carol Browner exclaimed, "We've got to know more about the links between the environment and the alarming increase in new incidences of childhood cancer. . . . In the past two decades, we have seen higher rates of acute lymphoblastic leukemia in children, higher rates of types of brain cancer in children, and higher rates of Wilms' tumor of the kidney. Testicular cancer in young men is up by nearly 70 percent."[65]

But according to the NCI, the trends are anything but alarming. Cancer incidence among children is stable, and we are experiencing "dramatic declines" in mortality. In 1999 the NCI concluded:

There was no substantial change in incidence for major pediatric cancers, and rates have remained relatively stable since the mid-1980s. The modest increases that were observed for brain/CNS [central nervous system] cancers, leukemia, and infant neuroblastoma [cancer of the sympathetic nervous system] were confined to the mid-1980s. The patterns suggest that the increases likely reflected diagnostic improvements or reporting changes. Dramatic declines in childhood cancer mortality represent treatment-related improvement in survival . . . . recent media reports suggest that incidence is increasing and that the increases may be due to environmental exposures. However, these reports have not generally taken into consideration the timing of changes in childhood cancer rates, or important development in the diagnosis classifications of childhood cancers.[66]

The bottom line is that despite the alarming claims driven by fund-raising needs of groups like the Pesticide Action Network, there is no growing epidemic of childhood cancer.

Nevertheless, cancer scaremongering continues to impact public perceptions. One of the latest claims is that children's exposures to chemicals—particularly pesticides—have produced an explosion of childhood brain cancer. But again, the NCI studies indicate otherwise.

In 1999, the NCI reported "brain cancer incidence has stabilized over the past decade for all major age groups with distinctive age-specific groups."[67] The NCI did note "a rapid, although relatively small," increase of childhood brain cancer between 1984 and 1986, but that was followed by a decade of stable rates. The increase is linked to better detection as it coincided with the period of increased use of magnetic resonance imaging (MRI), which dramatically improved diagnosis. The NCI also suggests that changes in classification of cancers as well as changes in neurosurgical practices may have led to more diagnoses of cancer. The good news is that there has also been a "continuous, although modest, decline in mortality during the period from 1975 to 1995."[68] Again, the actual scientific data do not

> Cancer scaremongering continues to impact public perceptions.

support the claim that there is an epidemic of childhood cancer as alleged by the activists.

CANCER CLUSTERS

NEWS REPORTS FREQUENTLY appear describing cancer clusters in communities that apparently experience higher than average rates of cancer, ranging from stories about high breast cancer rates on Long Island, New York,[69] to reports on a cluster of leukemia cases in Fallon, Nevada.[70] Generally, news reports reflexively attribute such clusters to exposures to man-made chemicals.

For example, ABC's *World News Tonight* recently reported that more than two dozen former students of a high school located on a former industrial site eventually contracted cancer. "Many people claim that the chemicals in the ground are to blame,"[71] said ABC journalist Michele Norris.

But such claims are often based on the misuse of science, especially the misuse of epidemiological studies. When assessing whether such clusters are related to chemicals, epidemiological studies attempt to link a particular chemical exposure to a specific health problem. Many times media and environmental groups cite such studies as proof that a chemical causes cancer when all the study found was an "association." But an association is not proof of anything. For example, there might be an association between driving and listening to the radio, but listening to the radio does not cause driving. Associations can result simply by accident, by other factors (called confounding factors), by problems with the study design because of bias on the part of the researcher or those interviewed in the data collection process, and so on. Eliminating all other possible causes can strengthen a relationship or show that it doesn't exist at all.

Citing a single study is also a tactic frequently used by ideological environmentalists, but rarely, if ever, does a single epidemiological study prove conclusively a cause-and-effect relationship. As Marcia Angell of the *New England Journal of Medicine* notes, "What medical journals publish is not received wisdom but rather working papers ... rarely can a single study stand alone as definitive proof."[72] As a result, the public has heard contradictory reports, such as the dangers or benefits of butter versus margarine, because the media tends to report each epidemiological study as if it were the final word.

Hudson Institute Senior Fellow Michael Fumento identifies some tenets that the average person can use to avoid the pitfalls of what he calls "amateur epidemiology."[73] In sum, his key tenets include the following: (1) most cancers are unexplained, (2) being either a victim or a physician treating a victim of a disease does not make you an expert on its causes, (3) miscarriages and birth defects are both common and unexplained, (4) epidemiology is a complex, inexact science conducted by humans who have their own biases and who make mistakes, (5) rare diseases happen and you can't simply make assumptions about the causes because they are rare, and (6) cancer clusters almost always mean nothing at all.

The last tenet is based on the fact that thousands of clusters occur by mere chance. Raymond R. Neutra of the California Department of Health Services finds that we can expect 4,930 such random cancer clusters to exist in any given decade in the United States.[74] Not surprisingly, when the CDC reported on 22 years of studies that covered clusters in 29 states and 5 foreign countries, they could not establish a clear cause for any cluster.[75]

To see the pitfalls of amateur epidemiology in action, consider how it fueled fears in upstate New York in the famous "Love Canal" case. National attention focused on this community when the nation learned of a leaking waste disposal site called Love Canal.[76] When results of an incomplete epidemiological study on chromosome abnormalities were leaked to the press, terrifying headlines warned of imminent danger: "Upstate Waste May Endanger Lives" (*New York Times*, August 2, 1978); "Vapors from Love Canal Pose Serious Threat" (*Washington Post*, May 25, 1978); "Devil's Brew in Love Canal," (*Fortune*, August 2, 1978).

Residents became "experts." Lois Gibbs, then president of the Love Canal Homeowners Association, testified at a congressional hearing: "I believed there was a hazard immediately after reading . . . a series of articles that were being printed in the newspaper in the area."[77] Frightened residents attributed every possible illness in the area to the contamination. "I was never sick until we moved in here," said one resident. "We were here about a year when I got this big lump on my neck," he continued.[78] People attributed what they thought were unusually high occurrences of cancer, birth defects, and miscarriages to the leak. Eventually, the government relocated more than 1,000 families. Congress reacted to Love Canal by passing the federal Superfund law, which was designed to speed up the cleanup of waste sites but has proven to be an expensive failure.

Later, a panel convened by the EPA eventually concluded that the Love Canal chromosome study was poorly conducted and of no value.[79] And researchers did not find that the area suffered from higher than normal birth defects or miscarriages.[80] The New York State Department of Health also did not find elevated rates of any cancers among former Love Canal residents.[81]

Environmental groups provide numerous other examples of amateur epidemiology when they issue "studies" condemning chemicals. The Environmental Working Group is the master at this craft. In a recent public relations campaign against chemicals, the EWG released a report called *Consider the Source,*[82] attacking chlorine. According to this "study," "137,000 pregnancies a year face an increased risk of miscarriage and birth defects each year from CRPs [chlorination by-products] in tap water." These ominous by-products of water chlorination supposedly are giving thousands cancer, too. Sounds scary! But why don't we have any actual cases? The science doesn't support the claims.

The EWG employs the classic approach: Cite a bunch of largely inconclusive epidemiological studies and claim that "collectively" they prove something. But when the EPA set an onerous standard for disinfection by-products in 1998, even it noted that the science underlying the rule was very weak. The EPA notes that "a causal relationship between exposure to chlorinated surface water and cancer has not yet been demonstrated."[83] The agency had noted earlier that the studies "generally showed weak statistical significance and were not always consistent among the studies." These inconsistencies are better called outright contradictory data that makes even the claims of "weak statistical significance" highly questionable. "For example," the EPA explained, "some reviewers believe that two studies showed statistically significant effects only for male smokers, while two other studies showed higher effects for nonsmokers. One study showed a significant association with exposure to chlorinated surface water but not for chlorinated groundwater, while others showed the opposite result."[84]

Grasping for some justification for its rule, the EPA turned to potential adverse reproductive effects but admits that again the science falls short. The EPA finds only "limited evidence to substantiate the hypothesis that DBPs [disinfectant by-products] in drinking water cause adverse reproductive or developmental effects since the bulk of the findings are inconclusive."[85]

The terrifying aspect of such junk science in action is that it may imperil public health. Disinfectant by-product regulations could curtail the use of disinfectants that are vitally important to protect consumers against microbial contamination, a cause of approximately 50,000 deaths daily worldwide.[86] Underscoring that concern, the EPA's own Science Advisory Board (SAB) reported in 1993 that the EPA lacked the hard data necessary to justify passing a disinfectant by-product regulation. The SAB warned that a "key concern is the possibility that chlorination . . . may be replaced by processes with poorly understood health impacts, both chemically and microbiologically."[87]

Despite the near impossibility of attributing causes to cancer clusters and the propensity for amateur epidemiology to rule the day, states and activist groups such as the EWG are developing "cancer registries" to identify cancer clusters and attribute causes.[88] One private effort, called Health Track, is supposed "to help American families and communities identify and track the links between environmental hazards and illnesses and to provide researchers and public health officials with the necessary tools to prevent disease." But it is very unlikely that families and communities could use this information to determine links between diseases and environmental hazards since decades of scientific research have not been able to establish such links. The likely result is that such well-meant tracking systems will only confuse and unnecessarily frighten the public further.

Such cancer tracking systems will undoubtedly prove all too useful to trial lawyers looking for opportunities to pin the blame for any random cancer cluster on an industry with deep pockets. The use of cancer clusters by trial lawyers has gained the public's attention in two major motion pictures, *A Civil Action* and *Erin Brockovich*. Both are based on actual communities that were alarmed by the possibility that the illnesses some residents were suffering might have been due to chemical contamination. In these cases, trial lawyers claimed that drinking water contaminated by industry caused health-related problems in nearby areas.

A Civil Action highlighted a tragic case of a cluster of 12 leukemia cases, 8 of which were among children in Woburn, Massachusetts. The parents in this neighborhood naturally wanted answers to these horrible, unexplained illnesses. Trial lawyers target this genuine desire among the public to find answers to target the companies in the area with the deepest pockets, which is what happened in that case.[89]

The plaintiffs claimed that the chemical trichloroethylene (TCE), which the companies located near the community had disposed of improperly, entered the water supply and caused several cases of leukemia. However, federal agencies at the time noted the chemical contamination but had concluded that there was no scientific case to support the idea that exposure to chemicals was responsible for the leukemia cases in Woburn. In 1980, the U.S. Centers for Disease Control and Prevention (CDC) issued a study noting there was an unusually high incidence of leukemia but concluded that contaminated drinking water was not the cause.[90] "As far as I know, there is no evidence in the literature of TCE's effect on the immune system," declared Renate Kimbrough of the CDC. The Agency for Toxic Substances and Disease Registry does not list TCE as a cause of leukemia.[91] In addition, there is evidence that some of the leukemia cases occurred before the community could have been exposed to TCE.[92]

But even if TCE were carcinogenic, were residents exposed to levels that could even have had an impact? A researcher from the Harvard School of Public Health noted that exposures to TCE in Woburn were so low that assuming TCE were responsible for the leukemia cluster would require "a major revision of our ideas about chemical carcinogenesis."[93] This cluster, like most others, was probably the result of mere chance. "Diseases don't fall evenly on every town like snow . . . there are clusters of any kind of cancer," noted one epidemiologist on the inevitability of chance clusters.[94] Still, the trial lawyers in the Woburn case were able to win a huge settlement because the costs of litigation were too high for the firm involved, so it settled.

Erin Brockovich is the tale of how a crusading legal secretary accidentally discovers some medical records in office files that allegedly indicated that a "cluster" of cancers in Hinkley, California, might be linked to particular chromium chemicals emitted from an industrial facility. But this case of underdogs versus corporate malefactors was based on very dubious scientific grounds. First, to prove that a specific chemical caused a particular cancer cluster, one would expect that most cases would be the same type of cancer. Yet the cancers in the Hinkley cluster were all over the map. The Hinkley plaintiffs suffered from cancers of the lung, breast, nasal passages, and prostate. And the legal settlement even included such noncancer illnesses as arthritis, the flu, and clubfoot.

Second, researchers would expect that the chemical alleged to cause the cancer cluster would be linked through scientific studies to the type of cancers found in that area. The supposed chemical culprit in this case was chromium, which some scientists linked to lung and nasal cancers. Out of the more than 600 Hinkley claimants, there were only a handful of lung cancers. One plaintiff had nasal cancer. These incidences, although heartrending, do not constitute a cluster.

Finally, the Hinkley case also ignored the importance of exposure levels and pathways. Some researchers found that chromium causes cancer only when workers are exposed to relatively *high* levels of *airborne* chromium in enclosed areas. Hinkley residents were supposedly exposed to relatively *low* levels, which they *ingested* in drinking water. According to the EPA, there is no evidence that ingesting chromium through drinking water causes cancer.[95]

Trial lawyers, nonetheless, can win such cases by paying junk scientists to serve as "expert witnesses" and by displaying plaintiffs' truly awful cancer stories. Defending against such tactics is expensive. Consequently, firms often find it cheaper to settle even when they are innocent, which is what the company in this case, Pacific Gas & Electric, chose to do. The trial lawyers then pocketed $133 million of the $333 million settlement. The attorneys later took a luxury cruise with some of their close friends—which included three of the judges that managed the alternative dispute resolution for the Hinkley case.

CHILDREN AND PESTICIDES

No DEFINITIVE SCIENTIFIC study has ever shown that anyone in the public has been harmed by the legal application of pesticides.[96] Yet, as was shown above, influential activist groups like the Pesticide Action Network continue to claim that exposure to trace amounts of pesticides causes cancer. Since the epidemics of cancer that exposure to synthetic chemicals were predicted to cause have failed to materialize, ideological environmentalists have now concocted a new scare campaign against synthetic chemicals like pesticides. Now they are supposed to be neurotoxins, chemicals that affect children's brain development. The most exhaustive review of studies on neurotoxins is found in *Pesticides in the Diets of Infants and Children*. It does not cite any studies that show that pesticides now in use have neurotoxic effects.[97] The study does note that some rodent studies show that polychlorinated biphenyls (PCBs) and lead impair neurological development in young rats and mice exposed to high levels of these chemicals. PCBs have never been used as pesticides (they were used as coolants in electrical equipment). The levels of PCBs in the environment have declined in recent decades, as has lead since its elimination from gasoline.[98] These studies are of highly questionable relevance to human children exposed to parts per billion of completely different chemicals.

In a recent report on carcinogens in the human diet, the NRC concluded that "the great majority of individual naturally occurring

> Ideological environmentalists have now concocted a new scare campaign against synthetic chemicals like pesticides.

and synthetic chemicals in the diet appears to be present at levels below which any significant adverse biological effect is likely, and so low that they are unlikely to pose any appreciable cancer risk."[99] Similarly, the American Academy of Pediatrics declares that "[t]he risks of pesticides in the diet are remote, long-term, and theoretical, and there is no cause for immediate concern by parents. The risks to children over their lifetime of experiencing the major chronic diseases associated with the typical American diet far exceed the theoretical risks associated with pesticide residues."[100]

The risks posed by synthetic chemicals are low because we are exposed to very low levels of these chemicals. University of Texas Professor Frank Cross highlights a number of studies showing that EPA's conservative risk estimates on public exposure to pesticides that they use to set regulatory standards overstated exposure by as much as 99,000 to 463,000 times actual exposure levels.[101] When researchers recalculated risks by considering actual pesticide exposure levels measured by the Department of Agriculture, they found that risks were "from 4,600 to 100,000 times lower than EPA estimates."[102]

In addition, rarely is the public ever exposed to pesticide levels even approaching the very stringent regulatory limits. Various government agencies test pesticides for residues to ensure they meet safety standards. In its most recent study, the Food and Drug Administration (FDA) found nearly 70 percent of domestic vegetable samples had no detectable residues, and nearly 39 percent of fruit had no residues. The FDA found no trace of pesticides in domestic infant formula or baby food out of 38 samples. Overall, the report found no violations of federal pesticide limits on 96.9 percent of all imported fruit and vegetable samples. And one study shows that washing fruits and vegetables can reduce exposure by 97 percent for some pesticides.[103]

CHILDREN'S HEALTH AND ENDOCRINE DISRUPTERS

IN 1997 VICE President Al Gore wrote the foreword to a book that he described as the "sequel" to *Silent Spring*. The book, *Our Stolen Future*, Gore claims, "takes up where Carson left off and reviews a large and growing body of scientific evidence linking synthetic chemicals to aberrant sexual development and behavioral and reproductive problems."[104] The book helped launch a new attack against man-made chemicals by suggesting that they had become key "endocrine disrupters"—agents that can impact human and animal reproductive systems. In this new campaign against synthetic chemicals, ideological environmentalists claim that people and wildlife are experiencing increased infertility, neurological disorders, cancer, and developmental problems because of exposure to these man-made endocrine disrupters.

Much of the endocrine disrupter theory is based on findings that children of women who took diethylstilbestrol (DES; a drug that was used between 1940 and 1970 to prevent miscarriages) experienced a higher incidence of reproductive tract problems. But the relevance of comparing the effects of a medicine administered at high therapeutic doses to the alleged effects of very low-level environmental exposures to other potential endocrine modulators is highly tenuous. As Texas A&M University toxicologist Stephen Safe notes, "DES is not only a potent estrogen, but it was administered at relatively high doses. . . . In contrast, synthetic environmental endocrine-disrupting compounds tend to be weakly active."[105]

Along the same lines, the American Council on Science and Health puts environmental exposures to synthetic chemicals in perspective by comparing their potencies to that of natural human-produced estrogen, 17b-estradiol. Scientists have found the synthetic chemicals DDT and PCBs (the most studied chemicals claimed by activists to be endocrine disrupters) to be up to 1 million times less potent than 17b-estradiol.[106]

The endocrine disruption theory took a blow in 1999 when the NRC published *Hormonally Active Agents in the Environment*. While there are impacts on wildlife exposed to high levels of chemicals, the council could find no human health effects from endocrine disrupters in the environment.[107] The report noted that male reproductive disorders "cannot be linked to exposures to HAAs [hormonally active agents] at this time,"[108] data on immunologic effects are "inadequate to support any definitive conclusion,"[109] collectively and alone "studies do not support an association between DDE [a metabolite of the pesticide DDT] and PCBs and breast cancer,"[110] testicular cancer increases are "unlikely to be related to DDT,"[111] and studies show no association between PCB exposure and incidence of prostate cancer.[112] The most "damning" information the NRC could find is that data of several studies combined "suggest" a correlation between PCBs and cognitive and behavioral development in children, which reveals the council could come to no real conclusion. The NRC does note that, "for the most part," the data exposure to PCBs in breast milk (which has been the key concern) "does not appear to significantly contribute to these outcomes."[113]

Environmentalists' endocrine disruption theory is further called severely into question when considering exposures to naturally occurring endocrine modulators. Plants naturally produce endocrine modulators called phytoestrogens. Humans consume these chemicals every day without adverse effects, and some contend that these chemicals promote good health. In fact, hundreds of different plants appear to contain natural endocrine disrupters, and such compounds are found in 43 foods in the human diet, such as corn, carrots, rice, and soybeans.[114] Soy products, particularly soybean oil, are found in hundreds of products that people safely consume on a regular basis.[115] However, phytoestrogens are 1,000 to 10,000 times more potent than synthetic estrogens. Because we consume far more phytoestrogens in our diet, the estrogenic effects of the total amount we consume are as much as 40 million times greater than the quantity of the synthetic chemicals in our diets.[116] However, that is not a problem since normal consumption of dietary phytoestrogens is not a health risk either.

WHAT WE STAND TO LOSE

ALTHOUGH WE DON'T think much about it, man-made chemicals are essential to almost everything we do. They make our cars run; they clean everything from our teeth to our dishes; they reduce illnesses by disinfecting our bathrooms at home and the operating rooms in our hospitals; they are used on food products such as poultry to eliminate *E. coli* and other deadly pathogens; and they keep our computers, television sets, and other electronic equipment running. Consider what the world would be like if we succumbed to the unscientific scare campaigns of ideological environmentalists and we eliminated pesticides.

The elimination of all herbicides (weed killers) could cause U.S. corn, wheat, and soybean exports to plummet by 27 percent.[117] A ban on insecticides could decrease supplies of corn, wheat, and soybeans by a devastating 73 percent.[118] According to one study, a ban on fungicides alone could reduce production of fruits by 32 percent, vegetables by 21 percent, peanuts by 68 percent, and corn by 6 percent.[119]

The use of high-yield farming, employing chemical fertilizers, pesticides, and herbicides, means we feed more people while farming less land—leaving more land for wildlife. Controlling weeds decreases the need for tilling soil, which in turn reduces soil erosion by 50 percent to 98 percent.[120] If we had continued to farm with 1950's technology—when most of the world did not use pesticides and fertilizers—some estimate that today we would have to plant as much as 10 million square miles of additional land to generate the food we now produce.[121] That's more land than all of the United States, Canada, and Central America combined (which is about 8.5 million square miles) and almost as much as all the land in Africa (which is just under 12 million square miles).

Banning pesticides already leads to real-world health consequences for millions of people around the globe. Ever since Rachel Carson first attacked DDT for its effects on wildlife, ideological environmentalists have campaigned ceaselessly to ban that pesticide. However, DDT is the best available tool for controlling the spread of malaria-carrying mosquitoes. Not only is it effective, but it is much more affordable for poor people in developing nations. For mosquito control, DDT is used in tiny amounts in and around homes, preventing mosquitoes from entering and infecting inhabitants. Such limited use does not affect wildlife.

The results of the environmentalist campaign to ban DDT have been devastating to poor people living in developing nations. Lacking adequate control methods for mosquitoes, malaria cases have skyrocketed in recent years. According to the WHO, malaria alone infects 300 to 400 million people a year and kills more than 1 million.[122] For example, South Africa nearly eradicated malaria-carrying mosquitoes when it used DDT, but cases soared again after the nation caved to environmental activists who pressed the country to switch to another pesticide. Cases rose from 4,117 in 1995 to 27,238 by 1999 (or possibly as many as 120,000 if one considers pharmacy records).[123] In response to this crisis, South Africa has decided to resume DDT use.

Tropical medicine specialist Dr. Don Roberts and his colleagues explain that "[s]eparate analyses of data from 1993 to 1995 showed that countries that have recently discontinued their spray programs are reporting large increases in malaria incidence. Ecuador, which has increased use of DDT since 1993, is the only country reporting a large reduction (61%) in malaria rates since 1993."[124]

Despite the rising death toll, environmentalists continue to push for a ban on DDT. Greenpeace, the World Wildlife Fund, Physicians for Social Responsibility, and the Pesticide Action Network have been "some of the most vociferous campaigners for a ban of DDT," notes one report.[125] Nevertheless, in the face of this pressure by environmentalist lobbies, the public health community mobilized in support of the continuing use of DDT. Faced with this opposition, the environmental lobby has softened its attacks on DDT.[126] Still, Greenpeace continues fighting to shut down one of the few facilities left in the world that produces DDT.[127]

Even in the United States, where we do have more alternatives, pesticide regulation may jeopardize public health. In 1992 a National Academy of Sciences report warned that a "growing problem in controlling vector-borne diseases is the diminishing supply of effective pesticides." Because all pesticides must go through an onerous registration process at the federal EPA, "some manufacturers have chosen not to reregister their products because of the expenses of gathering safety data. Partly as a result, many effective pesticides over the past 40 years to control agricultural pests and vectors of human disease are no longer available."[128]

SUMMARY AND CONCLUSIONS

IDEOLOGICAL ENVIRONMENTALISTS CONTINUE to campaign against synthetic chemicals despite the fact that there is little evidence that they are causing health problems for people or causing widespread damage to nature. All their earlier predictions about cancer epidemics caused by exposure to synthetic chemicals have turned out to be false. Cancer incidence rates are down for all major types of cancer, and minor increases in some cancers are explained by improvement in medical diagnostic technology that enables us to detect and treat more cancers. Accordingly, cancer mortality is also down, and more people are living longer, healthier lives than in any time in history.

Dire predictions about the impact of synthetic chemicals on children's health are also unsubstantiated by the facts. Brain cancer, childhood leukemia, and other cancers among children are not on the rise. The National Cancer Institute reports that any slight increases in some cancers seen in recent years are best explained by better detection methods, and these detection methods are improving treatment and survival rates. Nor is there any convincing scientific information demonstrating that children are suffering brain damage caused by exposure to pesticides, as some environmental groups have suggested. In a review of the scientific literature, the NRC did not identify a single study demonstrating that pesticides in use today impact children's cognitive development. Nor are there any studies showing that anyone in the public has suffered from proper use of legal pesticides.

A real concern is that activist campaigns may undermine the public's ability to use chemicals for critical needs. In particular, ideological environmentalist efforts to ban and heavily regulate pesticides threatens the public's ability to produce a stable food supply and control deadly pests. Nowhere is this danger more apparent than in the efforts to ban the pesticide DDT, which has led to millions of deaths every year around the world.

In January 2000, Worldwatch Institute founder Lester Brown ominously noted, "Every human being harbors in his or her body about 500 synthetic chemicals that were nonexistent before 1920." Considering that average American life expectancy has increased by 20 years—from an average of 56 years in 1920, to 71 years in 1970, to 76.7 years today—it is fair to say that synthetic chemicals are helping to prolong our lives. They are part and parcel of the modern, wealthy technological world, in which they continually help reduce risks of all kinds to our health and our lives.

CHAPTER SEVEN

THE ATTACK ON PLANT BIOTECHNOLOGY

Gregory Conko and C. S. Prakash

ECO-MYTHS DEBUNKED

- *A century's worth of genetic improvements in plants and animals has made food more abundant and less expensive today than at any other time in history. Continuing improvements in productivity will be necessary to feed the world in the 21st century without having to bring millions of acres of undeveloped wilderness into agricultural use.*

- *Despite opposition from ideological environmentalists, biotechnology— the next step in the continuum of genetic improvement—has been endorsed by countless scientific and health organizations, including the American Medical Association, the U.S. National Academy of Sciences, and the United Nations Food and Agriculture Organization.*

- *Around the world, more than 70 bioengineered plant varieties are grown commercially on approximately 109 million acres, in countries including the United States, Argentina, Australia, Brazil, Canada, Chile, China, Mexico, and South Africa.*

- *Bioengineered varieties of corn, cotton, potato, soybean, and others are raising yields, reducing pesticide use, conserving topsoil, and making other contributions to environmental protection.*

- *Biotechnology is helping scientists breed plants that mature faster, tolerate drought or extremes of heat and cold, and have improved nutrition. It is also being used to develop healthier cooking oils that are low in saturated fats, vegetables with higher levels of cancer-fighting antioxidants, and foods with better taste and longer shelf life. It is even possible to use bioengineered plants to create biodegradable plastics and better medicines and to help clean up hazardous wastes.*

- *Due to activist pressures, governments around the world have created harmful regulations that make it harder for researchers to use biotechnology to improve crop plants and livestock.*

O N A BLUSTERY November day in 1999, U.S. Food and Drug Administration scientists kicked off the first of three nationwide public meetings on biotechnology and bioengineered foods at the Plaza Club in Chicago. In the wake of substantial and growing concern about the technology in some European countries, FDA officials wanted to gauge the public mood in the United States and head off any growing domestic crisis of confidence. What they found was not surprising—no scientific evidence supporting claims that biotechnology was particularly dangerous either for consumers or the environment, but a small and growing segment of the public that believe bioengineered crop plants to be truly hazardous. Outside, members of Greenpeace and several other activist environmental groups protested with signs declaring, "Genetically engineered food is poison."[1]

Many Americans have never even heard of bioengineered crops, and most who have hold a neutral or positive opinion about them.[2] But beneath this otherwise calm surface, there is a growing campaign led by ideological environmentalists against plant biotechnology. The U.S. Public Interest Research Groups argue that bioengineered foods "pose unacceptable risks to human health," risk "spawning new superweeds," or pose hazards to beneficial insects and soil organisms.[3] The activist group Friends of the Earth warns that biotech crops could "seriously threaten biodiversity in agricultural areas" and that they "may also be toxic to humans."[4] And when the United States Agency for International Development sent a shipment of corn and soy meal that happened to contain some bioengineered varieties in the mix to aid the victims of a cyclone in the Indian province of Orissa, Vandana Shiva, director of the New Delhi–based Research Foundation for Science, Technology and Ecology, argued that "[t]he U.S. has been using the Orissa victims as guinea pigs for [bioengineered] products."[5]

Other critics are even more shrill. Jeremy Rifkin, a notorious and longtime opponent of all forms of genetic research, calls the introduction of bioengineered plants "the most radical, uncontrolled experiment we've ever seen."[6] Mae-Wan Ho, a biologist at London's Open University, argues that biotech crop plants are "worse than nuclear weapons or radioactive wastes."[7] What is it about agricultural biotechnology that inspires such attacks?

Ever since the 1962 publication of Rachel Carson's *Silent Spring*,[8] ideological environmentalists have warned that mankind's use of modern farming technologies would lead to widespread ecological and human health catastrophes. Then the villain was synthetic chemicals—particularly the use of insecticides, herbicides, and fungicides on farms to protect growing crop plants. Thirty years later, scientific evidence clearly shows that those concerns were wildly exaggerated. Nevertheless, the use of agricultural chemicals can have some negative environmental effects. Ultimately, humanity must choose between using chemicals that can cause some minor harm on the one hand or sacrificing tremendous gains in food productivity on the other.

> Thirty years later, scientific evidence clearly shows that those [modern farming technology] concerns were wildly exaggerated.

For many, the choice is simple. At its heart, all of agriculture requires a never-ending struggle against the destructive forces of nature: pests, diseases, weather, and many others. Despite the steadily growing use of insecticides, herbicides, and fungicides on farms around the world, as much as 40 percent of crop productivity in Africa and Asia, and about 20 percent in the industrialized countries of North America and Europe, is lost to insect pests, weeds, and plant diseases.[9] Without any means for controlling those pests, crop losses would climb to as much as 70 percent.[10] Thus, something clearly must be done to prevent crop losses, or agricultural production would fall dramatically, possibly even subjecting humanity to the widespread famines predicted by Thomas Malthus more than 200 years ago.[11]

Today, a new crop protection revolution is under way that will help farmers combat pests and pathogens more effectively while also reducing humanity's dependence upon agricultural chemicals. Agricultural biotechnology[12] (alternatively known as bioengineering, genetic engineering, plant biotechnology, and genetic modification) uses 21st-century advances in genetics and cell biology to move useful traits from one organism to another, allowing plants to better protect themselves from insects, weeds, diseases, and even such environmental stresses as poor soils and drought. Biotechnology can also improve the nutritional quality of staple foods like corn and rice by adding healthful vitamins and minerals. The technique is so beneficial that it has been endorsed by dozens of scientific and health associations, including the U.S. National Academy of Sciences,[13] the United Kingdom's Royal Society,[14] the United Nations Development Programme,[15] and many others.

Farmers around the world planted more than 109 million acres (44.2 million hectares) with biotech crops by the year 2000, just five years after their introduction on the market.[16] It's easy to see why. In the United States alone, bioengineered varieties of corn that are resistant to some insect pests were about 5 percent more productive on average than conventional varieties during the period from 1996 to 1999.[17] Biotech cotton varieties generated more than 10 percent higher yields and simultaneously reduced chemical insecticide use by an average of about 14 percent during that time.[18] Not surprisingly, farmers have a very favorable view of the development of biotech seeds. By 2001, 26 percent of all corn, 68 percent of all soybeans, and 69 percent of all upland cotton grown in the United States were bioengineered varieties.[19]

Although improved agricultural productivity might seem like a luxury that industrialized countries can do without, it is an absolute necessity for less-developed nations. In a report published in July 2000, the United Kingdom's Royal Society, the national academies of science from Brazil, China, India, Mexico, and the United States, and the Third World Academy of Science embraced agricultural biotechnology, arguing that it can be used to advance food security while promoting sustainable agriculture. "It is critical," declared the science academies, "that the potential benefits of [genetic] technology become available to developing countries."[20]

Importantly, the increased productivity made possible by these advances will allow farmers to grow substantially more food and fiber on less land. Such productivity gains will be essential if we are to outpace the projected increase in global population over the coming decades while sparing more land for nature. During the second half of the 20th century, in which the population increased from 3 billion to 6 billion, advances in conventional plant and animal breeding and improved use of synthetic fertilizers, pesticides, and herbicides allowed food production to grow much faster than population growth. But the average annual per acre increase in cereal yields has been slowing, from 2.2 percent per year in the late 1960s and 1970s, to only 1.5 percent per year in the 1980s and early 1990s,[21] to as low as just 1 percent in the second half of the 1990s.[22] More important, there has been little or no increase in the theoretical maximum possible yields of rice and corn in a decade.[23]

Worldwide, farmers already use approximately one-third of the Earth's land surface area (excluding Antarctica) for agriculture,[24] of which about one-third, or 5.8 million square miles, is dedicated to growing crops.[25] If the average annual increase in productivity per acre for the cereal grains that make up the bulk of food and animal feed remains at its current rate of around 1 percent, the world will have to bring more than 700 million acres of new land into agricultural use by the year 2050 to meet projected demand.[26] Nobel Peace Prize–winning plant scientist Norman Borlaug argues that "[e]xtremists in the environmental movement, largely from rich nations and/or the privileged strata of society in poor nations, seem to be doing everything they can to stop scientific progress in its tracks."[27]

The rate of increase in grain yields is slightly higher on average in less-developed countries than industrialized ones, but population growth is higher there as well. And even this average obscures the fact that Africa was almost totally excluded from the productivity gains generated during the Green Revolution. Crop productivity there has much room for growth, but for a variety of reasons, Africa has not been able to take advantage of such production increasing inputs as fertilizers, irrigation, and pesticides. Yields of sorghum and millet in sub-Saharan Africa have not increased since the 1960s.[28] Thus the productivity gains expected to be generated by biotechnology-enhanced crop plants can not only help to reduce the use of agricultural chemicals, but they could also save millions of acres of sensitive wildlife habitat from being converted into farmland. Explaining his strong support for biotechnology to a Reuters interviewer, Borlaug said, "You have two choices. You need [biotechnology] to further improve yields so that you can continue to produce the food that's needed on the soil that's well-adapted to agricultural production. Or, you'll be pushed into cutting down more of our forests."[29]

One might expect environmental activists to be pleased with the development of a technology that can make man's footprint on the environment lighter. But ideological environmentalists have launched a global campaign to suppress this vital technology on the specious grounds that it is unsafe for humans and the environment. Bioengineered products are denounced as "Frankenfoods," and claims that the new technology could result in "Andromeda strain"–like plagues abound. Lord Peter Melchett, former head of Greenpeace's United Kingdom chapter, declared that his organization's opposition to biotechnology is "a permanent and definite and complete opposition based on a view that there will always be major uncertainties."[30]

Never mind that the weight of scientific evidence does not support such outlandish claims or the belief of most crop scientists that biotechnology will have substantial benefits for environmental stewardship, as well as for farmers and consumers in poorer regions of the world. Kenyan crop scientist Florence Wambugu believes that biotechnology "can help us increase the production of food and other commodities, lowering their prices to consumers while raising the incomes of poor farmers."[31]

That may not be enough to satisfy most ideological environmentalists though. At an Organisation for Economic Co-operation and Development Conference in March 2000, Greenpeace antibiotech campaigner Benedikt Haerlin "dismissed the importance of saving African and Asian lives at the risk of spreading a new science that he considered untested."[32]

One might expect environmental activists to be pleased with the development of a technology that can make man's footprint on the environment lighter.

WHAT IS PLANT BIOTECHNOLOGY?

EVER SINCE THE dawn of agriculture, which began thousands of years ago with domestication of wild plants and animals from their natural habitats, humans have continuously transformed the crops

BOX 7.1 AMERICAN PUBLIC REACTS TO PLANT BIOTECHNOLOGY

Although most Americans have not succumbed to the ideological scaremongering campaign against biotechnology, some do view agricultural bioengineering with ambivalence. Other food safety issues are far more important to average consumers, but when prompted, they express opinions ranging from mild support to strong opposition (see Table 7.1).

The one thing that is known for certain about the public's opinion of biotechnology is that most people don't really know what they think. But when they're confronted with the issue, they typically pose lots of questions about biotech crops, including the following:

Is the genetic modification of crops inherently hazardous? Could we unwittingly make foods unsafe? What are the long-term consequences of consuming such foods? Do biotech crops affect the environment or wild ecosystems? Could they lead to the development of dangerous "superweeds"? Is it ethical for scientists to modify living organisms around us? Is it morally right to tamper with our food supply?

Answering these questions requires a discussion that places biotechnology in the context of how agriculture developed through crop domestication over many millennia and how plant breeders created modern crop varieties during the past century. A review of the history of agriculture will illuminate and allay the concerns that some people may harbor over the alleged risks posed by crop biotechnology.

Table 7.1 Public Attitudes Regarding Biotechnology

Q. What, if anything, are you concerned about when it comes to food safety? [33]

	Jan. 2001	Sept. 2001
Packaging	27%	25%
Food Handling/Preparation	23%	32%
Disease/Contamination	16%	30%
Chemicals/Pesticides in Food	10%	11%
Ingredients	8%	9%
Altered/Engineered Food	2%	2%
Other	19%	14%
Nothing	9%	3%
Don't Know/Refused	3%	20%

Percentages do not add up to 100% because multiple responses were allowed.

Q. All things being equal, how likely would you be to buy a variety of produce, like tomatoes or potatoes, if it had been modified by biotechnology to *taste better or fresher*? Would you be very likely, somewhat likely, not too likely, or not at all likely to buy these items?[34]

	1997	Feb. 1999	Oct. 1999	May 2000	Jan. 2001	Sept. 2001
Total Likely	55%	62%	51%	54%	58%	52%
Very Likely	19%	20%	18%	19%	19%	16%
Somewhat Likely	36%	42%	33%	36%	39%	36%
Total Not Likely	43%	37%	43%	43%	38%	42%
Not Too Likely	21%	18%	18%	21%	19%	21%
Not at All Likely	22%	19%	25%	22%	19%	21%
Don't Know/Refused	2%	1%	6%	2%	4%	6%

Q. All things being equal, how likely would you be to buy a variety of produce, like tomatoes or potatoes, if it had been modified by biotechnology to be *protected from insect damage and required fewer pesticide applications*? Would you be very likely, somewhat likely, not too likely, or not at all likely to buy these items?[35]

	1997	Feb. 1999	Oct. 1999	May 2000	Jan. 2001	Sept. 2001
Total Likely	77%	77%	67%	69%	70%	65%
Very Likely	39%	34%	28%	30%	32%	25%
Somewhat Likely	38%	43%	39%	39%	38%	40%
Total Not Likely	23%	21%	27%	28%	27%	30%
Not Too Likely	11%	11%	11%	14%	14%	15%
Not at All Likely	12%	10%	16%	14%	13%	15%
Don't Know/Refused	1%	2%	6%	3%	3%	5%

Q. How much have you seen, read, or heard recently regarding genetically modified foods/biotechnology in the production of food that is sold in grocery stores?[36]

	March 2001
A Great Deal	9%
Some	35%
Not Much	29%
Nothing	25%
Don't Know	1%

Q. Do you think genetically modified foods are basically safe, are basically unsafe, or don't you have an opinion on this?[37]

	March 2001
Safe	29%
Unsafe	25%
Don't Know	46%

(continues)

Table 7.1   Public Attitudes Regarding Biotechnology, continued

Q. **Now, as you may know, more than half of products at the grocery store are produced using some form of biotechnology or genetic modification. Knowing this, do you think genetically modified foods are basically safe, are basically unsafe, or don't you have an opinion on this? After hearing that more than half of the foods in grocery stores are genetically modified, one in five of those who initially said genetically modified foods are unsafe changed their minds.[38]**

	Then Said Safe	Then Said Unsafe	Then Said Don't Know
Initially Said Safe	89%	6%	5%
Initially Said Unsafe	19%	65%	17%
Initially Said Don't Know	37%	8%	55%

and animals that we have come to depend upon for food and animal feed.[39] Over many millennia, the crop varieties that were chosen for domestication have been gradually modified by selecting individual plants that grew the best and produced the best grains, vegetables, and fruits. Over time, this process of artificial selection resulted in profound changes in the stature, productivity, and taste of crop varieties. Modern corn is derived from a wild Central American grass plant called teosinte. Through successive generations of selection, breeders developed an entirely new species of plant—corn—that shares very few of its characteristics with the wild teosinte.[40]

Entirely new plant varieties were also developed by crossbreeding plants from different but related species with one another. The progeny of such hybridizations expressed new traits resulting from the random mixing of literally tens of thousands of genes from the two parent plants. With these "natural" breeding techniques, entirely new proteins and other plant chemicals were routinely introduced into food crops, often from wild species never before part of the food supply.[41] Bread wheat, for example, resulted several hundreds of years ago from the crossing of at least three different species of wild grasses from two different genera. And in the 20th century, wheat and rye, plants from two different genera, were crossed to produce a new variety called triticale, which is used as food and animal feed.[42] Hundreds of useful crop plants were developed with selection and hybridization techniques. But the flexibility of these techniques is limited by the need for the parent plants to be from species that can breed sexually.

The discovery of genes, chromosomes, and other mechanisms of plant genetics during the 20th century opened up new avenues for modifying plants. Scientists developed many novel tools that expanded the range of modifications that could be used to improve crop varieties. For example, in the late 1940s, agronomists began using X rays, gamma rays, and caustic chemicals on seeds and young plants to induce random genetic mutations.[43] Such mutations generally kill the plants (or seeds) or cause detrimental changes in the DNA. But on rare occasions, the result is a desirable mutation—for example, one producing a useful trait, such as altered height, more seeds, or larger fruit. In these cases, breeders have no real knowledge of the exact nature of the genetic mutation(s) that produced the useful trait or of what other mutations might have occurred in the plant. But more than 2,250 mutation-bred varieties of corn, wheat, rice, and dozens of other varieties have been commercialized over the last half century, and they are grown in more than 50 countries around the world.[44]

More sophisticated breeding techniques also permit agronomists to overcome natural barriers to ordinary sexual reproduction. They include methods such as protoplast fusion and embryo rescue, which join cells from sexually incompatible plants in a laboratory and overcome their natural inability to produce offspring. These techniques for genetic modification permit the artificial hybridization of plants of the same species, different species, and even different genera.[45] "Wide crosses" of plants from different species or genera allow scientists to add into an existing crop species traits for disease and pest resistance, increased yield, or different nutritional qualities. They can even be used to create entirely new plant species.[46] Examples of such artificial wide crosses include a wheat-barley hybrid, a tomato-potato hybrid, and a radish-rapeseed hybrid.[47] Yet none of these techniques are considered to be bioengineering, so they escape the wrath of ideological environmentalists.

These techniques underpinned the last century's spectacular increases in food productivity in all major crops around the world, including the Green Revolution in developing countries.[48] This dramatic increase in food production has been critical in ensuring an affordable supply of food. For example, U.S. corn growers averaged 134 bushels per acre in 1998 compared to only 26 bushels of corn per acre in 1928.[49] It will be possible to achieve additional productivity improvements through conventional breeding. But these techniques are crude and slow, and the traits that descendant plants eventually carry are not easily predictable. Typically, one or more unwanted traits are transferred to the offspring plants with any of these more conventional breeding techniques, so the breeder's job is not yet done. After the initial modification, agronomists must crossbreed the offspring again and again with the original plant for several generations to eliminate any undesirable traits.[50] And many agronomists believe that we are already nearing the maximum possible gains in yield that can be achieved with conventional breeding.[51] Fortunately, with the advent of modern biotechnology, an alternative for boosting crop productivity is now available.

In the 1980s, scientists in the United States and Europe independently developed new and more precise methods for moving single genes directly into plants. This overcame the limits imposed by sexual incompatibility among species and opened up immense possibilities for developing novel crop varieties with improved traits. A naturally occurring soil bacterium, *Agrobacterium tumefaciens*, which transfers its own DNA into plants, was modified to deliver desirable genes into plant cells instead of its own infective genes. Subsequently, a few other methods of gene transfer to plants were developed, including a "Gene Gun" that literally shoots gene fragments into the plant chromosomes. Since then, scientists have identified thousands of genes of potential value for agriculture from a wide variety of organisms and have developed methods to reliably insert genes into every major crop plant. Genes are recipes for producing proteins, and those proteins can improve a crop's nutritional value or protect it against pests. These are the various techniques that are now known as genetic engineering, bioengineering, genetic modification, or biotechnology.[52]

In modern biotechnology, the genes coding for specific traits are inserted into plant cells, which are then cultured for development into full plants. The bioengineered plants will then express the new trait—such as resistance to an insect pest. Added genes are taken up into the plant's DNA in random positions, opening biotechnology to questions about unintended and unexpected effects. But such pleiotropic effects, brought about by the rearrangement of DNA, occur even in the conventional breeding of plants from the same species.[53] Compared with the mass genetic alterations that result from using wide-cross hybridization or mutagenic irradiation, the direct introduction of one or a few genes into crop plants results in much more subtle and far less disruptive changes that are relatively specific and predictable.

The process differs from more conventional breeding methods of hybridization, induced mutation, and others in that only one or two specifically identified additional genes are typically introduced into an existing background of tens of thousands of genes. But because DNA is identical from organism to organism, bioengineering techniques can transfer genes, not just between plants, but from any living organism to any other—such as between plants and animals, or bacteria and plants.[54] This new flexibility aside, scientists see biotech gene transfer techniques as a logical extension of the continuum of methods used to improve crop plants. A report published by the U.S. National Academy of Sciences in 1989 concluded the following:

> *[Bioengineering] methodology makes it possible to introduce pieces of DNA, consisting of either single or multiple genes, that can be defined in function and even in nucleotide sequence. With classical techniques of gene transfer, a variable number of genes can be transferred, the number depending on the mechanism of transfer; but predicting the precise number or the traits that have been transferred is difficult, and we cannot always predict the [characteristics] that will result. With organisms modified by molecular methods, we are in a better, if not perfect, position to predict the [characteristics].*[55]

Thus, with biotechnology, plant breeders are actually less likely to produce unanticipated effects in crops. As biotechnology researcher

Nina Federoff of Pennsylvania State University notes, "This is like the difference between having to depend on a lightning strike for the fire to cook your evening meal and learning how to make matches to be able to make a fire when and where you want it."[56]

To date, more than 70 biotech plant varieties have been commercialized in the United States expressing a range of improved traits, such as heightened resistance to certain insects and diseases, tolerance to herbicides, and longer shelf life.[57] Globally, bioengineered varieties are grown commercially on approximately 109 million acres, in countries ranging from the United States, Argentina, Australia, Brazil,[58] Canada, Chile, China, Mexico, and South Africa.[59] Some critics have suggested that biotech crops are primarily an industrialized country interest. But the proportion of bioengineered crops grown in less-developed nations has grown consistently since their introduction, from 14 percent in 1997 to 24 percent in 2000. (See Table 7.2.)[60]

Some of the most successful crop varieties have been modified by adding a bacterial gene that produces a protein toxic to predatory insects but not to people or other mammals. By reducing the need for spraying chemical pesticides on crops, such crops are environmentally friendly. Another popular trait is tolerance to a particular herbicide. Herbicide tolerance can be developed in some crop varieties through selection and breeding methods, but biotechnology can achieve the same goal much more quickly and effectively. Today, varieties of canola, corn, cotton, rice, soybean, and sugar beet have all been bioengineered to tolerate one or another broad spectrum herbi-

Table 7.2. Commercial Planting of Bioengineered Crops Area by Country (in Millions of Hectares)

Country	1996	1997	1998	1999	2000	% of Global Total in 2000
United States	1.45	7.16	20.83	28.64	30.3	68.6%
Argentina	0.05	1.47	3.53	5.81	10.0	22.6%
Canada	0.11	1.68	2.75	4.01	3.0	6.8%
China	1.00	1.00	1.10	1.30	0.5	1.1%
Brazil	0.00	0.00	0.00	1.18	Not Available	Not Available
Australia	0.00	0.20	0.30	0.30	0.2	<1.00%
South Africa	0.00	0.00	0.06	0.18	0.2	<1.00%

Sources: EC Directorate General for Agriculture, "Economic Impacts of Genetically Modified Crops on the Agri-Food Sector: A First Review," Working Document, Revision 2 (Brussels: Commission Of The European Communities, 2000); and Clive James, *Global Status of Commercialized Transgenic Crops: 2000*, ISAAA Issue Brief, No. 21-2000 (Ithaca, NY: International Service for the Acquisition of Agri-Biotech Applications, 2000).

Table 7.3. Traits Included in Currently Cultivated Bioengineered Crops

The purpose of the current generation of bioengineered crops is primarily to improve pest resistance and weed control. In turn, this should reduce the use of crop protection products and/or increase yields.

Herbicide Tolerance
The insertion of a herbicide-tolerant gene into a plant enables farmers to spray wide spectrum herbicides on their fields, killing all plants but the crop.

Insect Resistance
By inserting genetic material from the *Bacillus thuringiensis* (Bt) into seeds, scientists have modified crops, allowing them to produce their own insecticides. For example, Bt cotton combats bollworms and budworms, and Bt corn protects against the European corn borer.

Virus Resistance
To date, a virus-resistance gene has been introduced into squash, tobacco, potatoes, and papaya. The insertion of a potato leaf roll virus-resistance gene protects the potatoes from the corresponding virus, which is usually transmitted through aphids. For that reason, it is expected that there will be a significant decrease in the amount of insecticide used. The introduction of virus-resistance genes into other plants may offer similar benefits. Virus-resistant papaya varieties have single-handedly revived the Hawaiian papaya industry, nearly totally destroyed by the rampant papaya ring-spot virus.

Quality Traits
Today, quality trait-improved crops are only sown marginally and represent less than 125,000 acres in Canada and the United States. They are high-oleic soybeans, high-oleic canola, and high-laurate rapeseed (see Table 7.4).

Source: Adapted from: EC Directorate General for Agriculture, "Economic Impacts of Genetically Modified Crops on the Agri-Food Sector: A First Review," Working Document, Revision 2 (Brussels: Commission Of The European Communities, 2000).

cide.[61] Herbicide-tolerant varieties allow farmers to control weeds by spraying fields without damaging growing crops. This in turn eliminates the need to plow under weeds, which loosens topsoil and contributes to erosion.[62] And because the spraying of herbicides is more efficient, herbicide-tolerant crops have even led to a modest reduction in herbicide use.[63] (See Table 7.3.)

THE REGULATION OF BIOTECH CROPS

SOON AFTER THE creation of the first bioengineered organisms, scientists and policy makers began to ask themselves what type of regulatory oversight would be appropriate. During the last 30 years, dozens of scientific bodies—including the U.S. National Academy of Sciences (NAS),[64] the American Medical Association,[65] the Institute of Food Technologists,[66] and the United Nations Food and Agriculture Organization and World Health Organization[67]—have studied the scientific literature and made recommendations about the oversight that is appropriate for bioengineered organisms, arriving at remarkably similar conclusions. The level of risk an individual plant might pose to human health or the ecology has nothing to do with how it was developed; it has solely to do with the characteristics of the plant that is being modified, the specific gene or genes that are added, and the local environment into which it is being introduced.[68]

When introduced into new ecosystems, all types of plants, whether they are wild types or are developed with biotechnology or more conventional breeding methods, pose a danger of becoming invasive weeds and harming local biodiversity. Similarly, both conventional and modern plant breeding involve introducing new genes into established crop plants. Thus they both pose a risk of introducing potentially harmful proteins and other substances into the food supply, some of which could be allergens or toxins. However, the mere fact that new genes are being added to plants, even from wholly unrelated organisms, does not make them less safe either to the environment or to people.[69]

> The mere fact that new genes are being added to plants does not make them less safe either to the environment or to people.

An analysis published by the Institute of Food Technologists, a professional society of food scientists, concluded that the evaluation of biotech food "does not require a fundamental change in established principles of food safety; nor does it require a different standard of safety" than those that apply to conventional foods.[70] Under U.S. federal law, developers and marketers of all new foods have a responsibility to ensure that the products they sell are safe and in compliance with all legal requirements.[71] Yet that's where the similarity in regulation of conventional and bioengineered foods ends. Biotech plants are regulated much more stringently, even though scientists agree that the same practices used to regulate new crop varieties produced by means of conventional techniques are sufficient to ensure the safety of plants developed with biotechnology.

For plants developed with more conventional techniques, regulators rely on plant breeders to conduct appropriate safety testing and to eliminate plants that exhibit unexpected adverse traits before they are commercialized.[72] No specific testing is required, nor is premarket approval necessary, even though new varieties produced with these more conventional methods often contain hundreds of unique proteins and other chemicals that may never have been in the food supply before. Most of those newly introduced substances will be totally unidentified (and unidentifiable) by the plant breeders.[73] But this rarely poses any real danger. Decades of accumulated scientific evidence confirm that even the use of relatively crude and unpredictable genetic techniques for the improvement of crop plants poses minimal risk to human health and the environment.

But bioengineered plants, in which breeders actually know which new genes and proteins are being introduced into the plant, are subjected to heightened scrutiny in every country in the world where they are grown. In the United States, they are regulated by the U.S. Department of Agriculture (USDA), the Environmental Protection Agency (EPA), and the Food and Drug Administration (FDA).[74]

The USDA is charged with making sure that biotechnology-enhanced plants do not become environmental nuisances or problematic weeds, directly addressing the activists' concerns about "superweeds."[75] The EPA has jurisdiction over bioengineered plants that have a built-in resistance to insects, plant diseases, or other substances—including those that are resistant to herbicides.[76] They are regulated as strictly as synthetic chemical pesticides, and the agency is responsible for ensuring that "pest-protected" biotech plants are safe both for the environment and for human health. And the FDA is responsible for ensuring that foods made from biotech plants are safe for people and livestock to eat.[77]

> The regulation of biotechnology is actually far more stringent than necessary to ensure that bioengineered crops are safe.

The differences in the way conventionally bred and bioengineered plants are regulated are clearly substantial. For example, some varieties of canola and soybean have been selectively bred with conventional methods to be herbicide tolerant, but only bioengineered herbicide-tolerant plants are subject to special field-testing requirements by the USDA.[78] Other plants, such as kidney beans, peaches, and potatoes, are known to contain naturally occurring pest-resistant chemicals that are toxic in very high doses and pose a small risk to human health,[79] but only bioengineered pest-resistant plants require premarket approval as pesticides by the EPA before they can be commercialized. Both soybeans and potatoes are known to occasionally contain proteins that are allergenic,[80] but only biotech plants face strict testing requirements for toxicity and allergenicity.

In short, dozens of new plant varieties produced through less precise techniques like selection, hybridization, induced mutation, embryo rescue, and other nonbiotech methods enter the market every year without any special premarket testing requirements. But every single bioengineered plant on the market has been tested and retested, going through several hundred—and in some cases, several thousand—different tests to ensure environmental and human health protection. Contrary to the assertions of ideological environmentalists, the regulation of biotechnology is actually far more stringent than necessary to ensure that bioengineered crop varieties are at least as safe as conventional ones.

ARE BIOTECH CROPS SAFE?

OPPONENTS OF BIOTECHNOLOGY have long claimed that bioengineered plants are unnatural and dangerous. Complaints range from general charges of random, unintended effects that could make the plants unsafe to more specific criticisms alleging the possible introduction of new toxins or allergens into the food supply. Ideological environmentalists also claim that bioengineered plants are more likely to have negative environmental impacts, including the destruction of wild biodiversity. But as mentioned above, all bioengineered crop varieties are subjected to much greater regulatory scrutiny than conventional crops, and the regulatory mechanism has been designed specifically to prevent such potentially harmful side effects.

Because different plant varieties will have different characteristics, and thus different risks, the regulatory approach for biotech plants focuses on identifying the source of potential hazards to the environment and human health that specific plants might pose. Regulators draw upon the existing risk assessment process for chemicals and novel foods and factor in additional analyses specific to biotechnology. For example, all methods of crop breeding run the risk of unintended and unexpected disruptions in the normal functioning of specific genes—called *pleiotropic effects*.[81] So crop breeders always conduct a number of evaluations to eliminate potentially harmful side effects before commercialization.

But for biotech plants, regulators require tests to compare the biological, chemical, and agronomic equivalence of the modified varieties with their closest related conventional varieties. This is done to ensure that no pleiotropic effects have changed the new bioengineered plant in a way that would make it unsafe—such as changing the normally existing levels of plant nutrients or other phytochemicals.[82] Modest changes in the level of phytochemicals can occur with any type of breeding, but no bioengineered plants that have shown a significant change in important nutrients or toxins have ever been put on the market. However, several new plant varieties with intentionally altered phytochemicals are now being developed, such as tomatoes, peppers, and rice with added or higher levels of beta-carotene and soybeans with higher levels of vitamin E.[83]

Regulatory evaluations also pay special attention to the genes that are added to bioengineered plants, the source of those genes, the traits that the genes produce, and whether or not they have a history of safe use in the food supply. Scientists generally know a great deal about the safety of genes that come from other plants or microorganisms that are already part of the food supply. For those that are not, additional tests to ensure the safety of the genes and their traits are required. The action of most genes is to help create proteins, which could be toxins or allergens. So several additional studies are then required to ensure that the proteins are not toxic and to measure the similarity of the proteins with known allergens to ensure that no new allergenic substances are introduced into the food supply. And numerous feed evaluations have shown no adverse effects on livestock, or their meat or milk.[84]

The potential for added genes to make bioengineered plants allergenic is among the most widely cited concerns about biotechnology.

Although all forms of plant breeding pose some risk of introducing new allergens into the food supply, biotechnology has been singled out by activists for special attention. Professional scaremonger Jeremy Rifkin argues that "[i]n the coming years, agrichemical and biotech companies plan on introducing hundreds, even thousands, of genes into conventional food crops . . . raising the very real possibility of triggering new kinds of allergenic responses about which little is known and for which there exist no known treatments."[85] But Professor Steve Taylor, a noted allergen researcher at the University of Nebraska, thinks the risk is very small because "there are good ways of predicting the potential allergenicity of a genetically modified food."[86] In fact, one of the most important potential advantages of biotechnology is actually to eliminate existing allergens from foods like peanuts, wheat, and milk by "silencing," or "turning off," the genes that generate allergenic proteins. Taylor says, "[I]n the long term, we will have foods that are less hazardous because biotechnology will have eliminated or diminished their allergenicity."[87]

One of the most important potential advantages of biotechnology is actually to eliminate existing allergens from foods like peanuts, wheat, and milk.

Just as with human safety, the ecological impact of any new crop depends on the type of introduced trait and the nature of the altered crop. Specific traits are focused on for assessing potential toxicity to beneficial insects, wild birds, and other animals. And the impacts of the whole plants are studied by assessing their similarity to traditional counterparts. New biotech plants are also assessed for their potential to cross-pollinate with wild or weedy plants, which could move the bioengineered traits into wild species with potentially negative consequences. Ecological aspects, such as potential to become problematic weeds and a range of other potential environmental effects, are studied prior to commercialization in small field trials. These effects are also monitored carefully after commercialization. Although some complaints have been lodged by farmers regarding the agronomic performance of certain bioengineered crop plants, no genuine environmental problems have yet been identified.[88]

There is a risk that genes from biotech varieties could be transferred to wild plants through cross-pollination, but only in regions where there are closely enough related wild species for ordinary sexual reproduction. Moreover, this outcrossing is really only problematic when the genes in question could enhance the reproductive fitness of the recipient weeds—that is, enable weeds to produce and scatter seeds that survive better in the wild. Gene flow between crops and wild plants has been going on for a long time and is by no means unique to biotechnology. It has not been a problem though because most genes that are introduced into crop plants, conventional or biotech, have little value in the wild. In fact, while some traits added with either bioengineering or conventional breeding methods could provide an ecological advantage, most crop traits tend to make plants less likely to survive the rigors of the wild.

For example, herbicide-tolerant rapeseed plants have been produced with conventional breeding for 20 years, and no unmanageable weed problems have been reported as a result of their use.[89] So while the transfer of a gene for herbicide tolerance into a wild relative could create a nuisance for farmers, it is unlikely to have any impact on wild biodiversity because the herbicide-tolerance trait wouldn't give the wild plant any selective advantage relative to other weeds. Even in the extremely unlikely event that herbicide-tolerance genes were transferred to a weed species, it wouldn't run amok in farmers' fields. Farmers could still control it by using other herbicides to which it was not tolerant.

Still, ideological environmentalists insist that any outcrossing of genes from bioengineered plants into conventional or wild plants will be negative. In one recent case, ecologists from the University of California at Berkeley reported in *Nature* that genes from bioengineered corn varieties had been transferred into local varieties of corn in Oaxaca state in southern Mexico where no bioengineered varieties have yet been approved for commercial cultivation.[90] Concerns arose among some ideological environmentalists that the presence of biotech genes could only be explained by cross-pollination from bioengineered varieties and that their presence posed a threat to the genetic diversity of the many landrace or heirloom varieties in what is considered to be the birthplace of corn. One Greenpeace activist from Mexico argued that "[i]t's a worse attack on our culture than if [biotech companies] had torn down the Cathedral of Oaxaca and built a McDonald's over it."[91] Several other university-based scientists later found the Berkeley research to be invalid—the ecologists misinterpreted their results, which did not actually indicate the presence of biotech genes. In the face of this evidence, *Nature*'s editors later publicly admitted that they should never have published the badly flawed study. Nevertheless, the possibility that biotech genes could eventually outcross into nonbiotech varieties is real. However, this is highly unlikely to pose a genuine threat to the diversity of landrace varieties.

Traditional farmers reproduce their varieties by carefully selecting the seed they save from year to year. Thus, if an undesirable gene is transferred into certain plants, seed from those plants will not be planted the following year and will be eliminated from the gene pool. This practice has worked very well for millennia and explains why Mexican farmers can plant many different varieties next to one another, without worrying about cross-pollination. Luis Herrera-Estrella, a noted plant scientist and director of the Center for Research and Advanced Studies in Irapuato, Mexico, has noted that "gene flow between commercial and native varieties is a natural process that has been occurring for many decades," so "there is no scientific basis for believing that outcrossing from biotech crops could endanger [corn] biodiversity."[92] Indeed, the presence of certain genes from biotech varieties could actually enhance genetic diversity by improving the ability of landrace varieties to resist insect pests, making them more productive.

Given concerns about the spread of bioengineered genes, you might think biotech opponents would welcome innovations designed to keep them confined. But when scientists at the USDA and the Delta Pine Land Company did just that, environmentalists were infuriated. The process, called the Technology Protection System (TPS), was designed to make plant seeds sterile by interfering with the development of plant embryos.[93] Hope Shand, research director for the Rural Advancement Foundation International, dubbed it "Terminator Technology."[94] Jeremy Rifkin calls it "pathological"[95] and has spread fears that escape of the TPS genes into weed populations through cross-pollination could destroy great swaths of plant life. But in the remote possibility of cross-pollination with weedy relatives, genes for traits such as herbicide tolerance or pest resistance wouldn't create "superweeds," because the TPS trait would prevent the wild plants from reproducing. Biotechnology companies like TPS because preventing farmers from replanting saved seeds from the prior year's harvest would protect the breeders' considerable invest-ment in the development of new varieties. But critics see TPS as one more facet of global corporate hegemony. Mark Ritchie, president of the Institute for Agriculture and Trade Policy, argues that "[i]t is a threat globally to food security, which is a basic human right."[96]

The presence of certain genes from biotech varie-ties could actually enhance genetic diversity by improv-ing the ability of landrace varieties to resist insect pests, making them more productive.

Like many other concerns about biotechnology, this issue, too, has a non-biotech analogue. High-yielding hybrid varieties of plants like corn don't breed true, so most crop growers in the United States and western Europe have been buying seed annu-ally for decades. Thus technology protected seeds wouldn't represent a big change in the way many American and European farmers farm. Many farmers in less-developed countries have resisted hybrid tech-nology because they prefer to have the option to plant saved seed.[97] Similarly, if farmers didn't want the advantages offered in the en-hanced crops protected by TPS, they would be free to buy seeds with-out the technology protection, just as farmers are free to buy nonhybrid seeds. Nevertheless, some of the biggest biotechnology companies have succumbed to pressures from environmental activists and aid organizations and have promised not to commercialize the TPS technology.[98] In any case, gene flow from bioengineered crops creating "superweeds" is not very likely.

Also consider that the biotech plants themselves are not likely to "escape" from farm fields and become weeds themselves, because crop plants of all varieties are generally not suited for existence in the wild—they need to be pampered. One noteworthy result of the extensive transformation of wild plants into crop varieties was the loss of many traits required for wild existence and the creation of a true dependency of modern crop plants upon human care for their survival.[99] A 10-year study by British scientists found that neither biotech nor conventional crop plants survive well in the wild, and biotech varieties are no more likely than their conventional counterparts to invade wild ecosystems.[100] Researchers have identified at least 12 genetic traits that are necessary for plants to be successful weeds. And crop plants typically have only six of them.[101] For example, one of the most important traits shared by all weeds is their ability to disperse seeds beyond the immediate area. But crop varieties are bred specifically for their ability to hold seeds and thus have lost their dispersal ability. The fact is that modern cultivated plants, such as corn or soybeans, are incapable of invading and taking over forests and meadows.

Naturally, farmers and scientists are nevertheless vigilant against the unlikely chance that plants could outcross with weeds or that the crop plants themselves could become weedy as a result of adding new traits. But this is the case whether or not a particular plant was modified with conventional or biotech methods. The risk of gene transfer to weeds is similar with both conventional and biotech varieties and has no relation to the methods used in altering the plants.[102] And because farmers are the first people affected by new weeds, they have a direct and strong incentive to prevent their development. The testing and monitoring of biotech crops, combined with hundreds of years of experience with conventional varieties, provides more than sufficient safeguard that such risks will be minimal and manageable.

The effect of biotechnology on crop biodiversity is another often-cited concern. The popularity of high-yielding varieties has narrowed the genetic variation found in major crops because more and more farmers are planting the same or similar varieties. But biotechnology, if employed strategically, can reverse this trend by permitting the recovery of older varieties that were discarded for lack of certain features (such as resistance to new disease strains). With modern bio-engineering techniques, older heirloom and landrace varieties can be modified to add such traits without destroying genetic diversity.[103] Biotechnology researchers are also developing better methods for the preservation of germ plasm in laboratories, such as cryopreservation, where plant cells with valuable genes are being stored and thus saved from extinction.[104]

Despite the record of safety in biotech and the existence of a strict regulatory system, ideological environmentalists remain obdurate in their opposition to the technology. They seize on even the most tenuous evidence to justify their continued attacks. In 1998, for example, a Scottish scientist named Arpad Pusztai claimed that his research showed a variety of bioengineered potatoes had negative health effects in lab rats.[105] Pusztai fed rats with conventional potatoes and an experimental biotech potato variety that was never put on the market. He claimed to have found that the bioengineered variety damaged the immune systems and stimulated abnormal cell division in the digestive tracts of the lab rats. But many scientists have shown that Pusztai's research methodology was critically flawed and that no conclusions about the safety of biotech foods can be drawn from his data.[106]

Pusztai fed the rats only potatoes, making no attempt to provide nutritionally balanced diets. So all the rats in the study experienced adverse health effects.

> With modern bioengineering techniques, older heirloom and landrace varieties can be modified to add such traits without destroying genetic diversity.

In addition, because Pusztai used an experimental variety and not one that was likely to be commercialized, the bioengineered potatoes were nutritionally impaired, lacking several key vitamins. Any effects that Pusztai might have observed were almost certainly due to these two factors.[107] After an extensive review, the British Royal Society issued a statement explaining why the experiment was fatally flawed, and noted that "[o]n the basis of this paper, it is wrong to conclude that there are human health concerns with the process of genetic modification itself, or even with the particular genes inserted into these [biotech] potatoes."[108]

To date, no scientist has replicated Pusztai's study with bioengineered potatoes to confirm his results. But a team of Chinese scientists conducted their own studies of bioengineered sweet peppers and tomatoes and found no such biological changes.[109] A Japanese study likewise found no negative effects on the immune systems of rats fed with biotech soybeans.[110] And nearly two dozen publications evaluating the effect of various biotech feeds on livestock have found no evidence of harm.[111] Nevertheless, Arpad Pusztai's flawed research has become a touchstone for antibiotechnology activists, who persist in claiming that it highlights the "dangers" of bioengineered food.[112]

Although the Pusztai story made headlines in Europe, it was largely ignored by the mainstream press in the United States. But U.S. activists were provided with their own antibiotech scare story in 1999, when the results of a laboratory test were published finding that pollen from a type of bioengineered corn dusted on milkweed could kill monarch butterfly caterpillars.[113] This was hardly news to plant scientists, though, because the corn had been engineered to kill other types of caterpillars, which are the major insect pests of corn. Nevertheless, the paper's publication triggered an immediate frenzy of antibiotech stories in the media coverage.

A *USA Today* headline declared "Engineered Corn Kills Butterflies."[114] The Associated Press led with "Lab-Designed Corn May Harm Insects,"[115] a report the *Boston Globe* published with the headline "Butterfly Deaths Linked to Altered Corn."[116] A review of the news coverage by one journalism researcher found that, between 1997 and 2000, the *New York Times* and the *London Times* used fewer and fewer university-based scientists as sources, and they were more than twice as likely to quote representatives from such activist groups as Greenpeace, the Environmental Defense Fund, and the Union of Concerned Scientists.[117] Such adverse coverage primed readers to be skeptical of biotechnology. So when a second monarch study, which attempted to simulate field conditions of corn pollen dispersal, found that pollen distribution onto milkweed plants—on which monarch caterpillars must feed—in and around cornfields could be high enough to kill the monarch caterpillars, plant biotechnology's future looked gloomy.[118]

Many scientists, however, pointed out that neither study accurately simulated real-world conditions. Corn pollination happens at a different time of year than the time of monarch larval development, and the amount of pollen that is spread falls dramatically beyond about 20 to 30 feet from the edge of cornfields.[119] Moreover, all types of insects—monarchs included—would be killed if farmers sprayed synthetic chemical insecticides instead of using the biotech crop varieties. So most scientists concluded that a tiny effect on monarchs should not condemn biotech corn. Ultimately, the gloomy scenario predicted by the initial research seemed to be contradicted by several factors, including the fact that monarch butterfly populations had actually increased since the introduction of biotech corn in the United States.[120]

Nevertheless, even the speculation that pollen could contribute to the spread of potentially risky genes moved some scientists to accelerate research into ways of avoiding such a problem in the future. One idea, already under investigation, is to insert transferred genes into a specific part of the plant DNA that controls cellular organelles called chloroplasts, which contain the machinery for photosynthesis. There is no chloroplast DNA in the pollen of most crop plants, so isolating bioengineered genes there would normally be expected to contain the genes and the proteins made by them inside the plant.[121] This chloroplast engineering technique is also being investigated as a potential way to prevent, or reduce, the possibility of bioengineered genes being transferred to weedy relatives through cross-pollination.[122]

Fortunately, at least in the case of Bt corn and monarch butterflies, chloroplast engineering doesn't appear to be necessary, because doubts about the dire implications of the monarch butterfly research have been confirmed. Six peer-reviewed papers published in the highly respected *Proceedings of the National Academy of Sciences* in October 2001 should eliminate concerns about the effects of biotech corn pollen on monarch caterpillars.[123] The papers describe two full years' worth of intensive field research by 29 scientists—including three of five authors of the two critical reports—who found little or no effect of Bt pollen on monarchs. Other research shows little or no impact on other beneficial insects and soil organisms.[124] Nevertheless, these robust scientific results have not stopped activists from using monarch costumes in their street theaters and protests against biotechnology. The Union of Concerned Scientists (a leading ideological environmentalist organization) continues to use images of monarch butterflies on its Web site and fund-raising envelopes as a way of perpetuating the politically useful myth that crop biotechnology is causing environmental damage.[125]

What is all too often overlooked by antibiotech activists, however, is the fact that bioengineered crop varieties have substantial positive impacts on the environment. In addition to the significant reduction in chemical insecticide applications mentioned above, the introduction of biotech crops has made agriculture more efficient, promoting the conservation of important resources. Scientists from Louisiana State University and Auburn University found that when farmers plant bioengineered pest-resistant crop varieties, fewer natural resources are consumed to manufacture and transport pesticides. Their study, which examined only pest-resistant cotton, estimated that in 2000, 3.4 million pounds of raw materials and 1.4 million pounds of fuel oil were saved in the manufacture and distribution of synthetic insecticides. Additionally, 2.16 million pounds of industrial waste were eliminated. On the user end, farmers used 2.4 million gallons less fuel and 93 million gallons less water and were spared some 41,000 10-hour days needed for applying pesticide sprays.[126]

Perhaps most important is the fact that the increased productivity generated by bioengineered crop varieties will make it easier to conserve valuable wildlife habitats around the world. The loss and fragmentation of native habitats caused by agricultural development in the poorer regions of the world experiencing the greatest rates of population growth is widely recognized as among the most serious threats to the conservation of biodiversity.[127] Thus, increasing agricultural productivity is an essential environmental goal, and one that would be much easier in a world where agricultural biotechnology is in widespread use.

> The increased productivity generated by bioengineered crop varieties will make it easier to conserve valuable wildlife habitats around the world.

Consider just one example. Rice is the major staple food for about 2.5 billion people, almost all of whom live in the less-developed regions of the world where the bulk of 21st-century population growth is expected to take place. The International Rice Research Institute estimates that reducing yield losses of rice by just 5 percent worldwide could feed an additional 140 million people.[128] Highly promising field tests in 1999 and 2000 showed a bioengineered rice variety to produce 28.9 percent higher yields than conventional hybrid rice varieties.[129] The environmental benefit of just this one biotech variety could be tremendous, if only wrongheaded international regulations inspired by ideological environmentalism do not doom its future.

INTERNATIONAL RULES

WHILE U.S. REGULATION of biotechnology is overly strict, it pales in comparison with that in many other countries—particularly those countries that are part of the European Union (EU). Environmental activists in the EU, and in the United Kingdom in particular, have been aided and abetted by a sympathetic media willing to report uncritically activists' scaremongering as a way to sell more newspapers and magazines.[130] Great Britain's *Express* ran such headlines as "Mutant Crops Could Kill You" and "Is Baby Food Safe?"[131] The *Daily Mail* chimed in with "Mutant Crops' Threat to Wildlife," and the *Guardian* added "Gene Crops Could Spell Extinction for Birds."[132] Thus the general public in most EU nations has become far more skeptical of biotechnology than the public in the United States.[133] Theories abound regarding why this suspicion arose.[134] But one thing is certain: The greater public sensitivity to the issue of biotechnology has had a direct and deleterious impact on the development of European regulatory policy.[135]

Beginning in 1990, the European Commission implemented a set of biotechnology regulations for all EU member countries. The rules are far more onerous than those in the United States, and the regulatory process is complex and difficult to navigate. For example, 18 varieties of biotech crop plants—including varieties of corn, canola, cotton, potato, tomato, and soybean—have been approved for commercial cultivation.[136] But only two varieties—one corn and one soybean—have been approved for use in food.[137] None of this matters much, however, because EU rules also require bioengineered foods to be labeled.[138] And due to the strong negative opinion of biotech foods held by a sizable portion of the public, few grocery stores will stock products labeled as being bioengineered.[139]

Further problems stem from the fact that new bioengineered plant varieties must be approved by all 15 member nations in the EU before they can be grown by farmers or sold as food.[140] The objection of any one government can prevent the new variety from being granted EU approval. Since 1998, Austria, Denmark, France, Greece, Italy, and Luxembourg have blocked the EU's approval of all new bioengineered varieties.[141] In 1998, the highest French court suspended commercialization of three biotech corn varieties, even though the French government had supported their approval at the EU level just two years earlier.[142] And in November 1999, the U.K. government announced a moratorium on commercial planting of bioengineered crops, pending a three-year program of farm-scale evaluations to assess environmental impacts.[143] But test crops are routinely destroyed by antibiotech activists, delaying completion of the research.[144] And under persistent threat of attack, many farmers are dropping out of the program.[145]

To make matters worse, an even stronger set of biotech regulations were being finalized by the European Commission in 2001. The rules, which EU politicians boast to be "the toughest [biotechnology] legislation in the world," are touted as just the trick to restore public confidence in the technology.[146] But because they are so much more strict, more complex, and more costly, they are likely to make it more difficult to grow and sell biotech crops, not less so. Any positive impact on public opinion is likely to be swamped by the negative impact of trussing biotech researchers and farmers in ribbons of red tape.

Although dangerously wrongheaded, the European hysteria over biotech foods initially was seen as a regional problem. Increasingly, however, poor countries in East Asia are taking a far more cautious approach to biotechnology regulation. Japan, which has been a long-time leader in biotechnology research, has recently tightened restrictions on biotech food imports.[147] And the EU is pushing its overly strict rules into international treaties affecting countries around the world. The EU was the primary advocate of the Cartagena Protocol on Biosafety, for example, which regulates the planting of bioengineered crops and the international trade in harvested biotech grains, vegetables, and fruits.[148]

Finalized in January 2000, the Biosafety Protocol is intended to ensure that the introduction of bioengineered organisms into the environment is "undertaken in a manner that prevents or reduces the risks to biological diversity."[149] But it also encourages countries to create unnecessarily severe biotechnology regulations based upon the precautionary principle that overemphasize biotechnology's very modest risks and ignore its vast potential benefits.[150] (See chapter 10 on the precautionary principle in this volume.) Thus, laws enacted under the auspices of the Biosafety Protocol are likely to slow the research and development of new biotech products needlessly. Moreover, by making it easier for countries to create scientifically unjustifiable restrictions, the protocol will undoubtedly be abused by politicians seeking trade protection for their domestic agriculture and food processing industries.[151]

Importantly, countries whose exporters are adversely affected by biotechnology rules based on the precautionary principle might be able to challenge them through the dispute settlement processes of the World Trade Organization (WTO). The WTO trade rules generally prohibit countries from restricting trade with environmental or public health laws that are not based upon a scientifically demonstrated risk.[152] For a variety of reasons, however, it is not altogether clear that WTO rules would take precedence over the Biosafety Protocol, nor even that the WTO would be inclined to rule against biotechnology restrictions enacted to meet the protocol's requirements.[153]

Another important feature of the Biosafety Protocol is its requirement that bulk shipments of harvested agricultural products be labeled if they contain any biotech grains, fruits, or vegetables.[154] To comply, farmers, shippers, and other food handlers would have to create hugely expensive segregation and record-keeping mechanisms and test the foods at each step of the production process to isolate conventional varieties from bioengineered ones. The EU's Directorate General for Agriculture estimates that the "identity preservation" costs alone for such a labeling requirement would range from 6 percent to 17 percent for commodity grains.[155] The newly proposed

European biotechnology law is set to go even further, by requiring not just mandatory labeling but also "traceability" of biotech foods—an array of technical, labeling, and record-keeping mechanisms that require food processors to keep track of grains, fruits, vegetables, and other ingredients from the plant breeder, to the farm, to the grain handler, and beyond—from dirt to dinner plate.[156]

Labeling requirements like those enforced in the EU represent serious obstacles that could all but destroy the affordability of biotechnology products and impede their adoption in the poorer regions of the world that need them most, without adding any safety benefits.

Ultimately, labeling requirements like those enforced in the EU represent serious obstacles that could all but destroy the affordability of biotechnology products and impede their adoption in the poorer regions of the world that need them most. The *2001 Human Development Report* issued by the United Nations Development Programme laments that "[t]he opposition to yield-enhancing [bioengineered] crops in industrial countries with food surpluses could block the development and transfer of those crops to food-deficit countries."[157]

WHAT ABOUT LABELING?

REGULATORY AGENCIES AROUND the world could learn a thing or two from the FDA's treatment of calls for biotech food labeling. Just as in Europe, some activists in the United States have called upon the government to mandate the labeling of all bioengineered foods. They assert that consumers have a "right to know" how their foods have been altered and that a mandatory label would best allow consumers to choose between bioengineered and conventional foods.[158] Biotechnology proponents and free speech advocates, on the other hand, have argued against mandatory labeling because such a requirement would unnecessarily raise food costs, mislead consumers into believing that the labeled products pose a heightened safety risk,[159] and violate constitutional free speech rights.[160]

Despite harsh attacks and considerable political pressure from environmentalist and consumerist organizations, the FDA has held firm in its respect for the judgment of the scientific opinion about the value of such labeling. In its 1992 statement of policy, the FDA concluded that there was no reason to believe "that bioengineered foods differ from other foods in any meaningful or uniform way."[161] But sensing some activist support for labeling, the FDA decided to reevaluate that decision in 1999. It held three public meetings and received more than 50,000 written comments on it policy, most of which favored mandatory labeling. Nevertheless, when all was said and done, the agency reaffirmed its decision to not require special labeling of all bioengineered foods.[162]

The American Medical Association,[163] the Institute of Food Technologists,[164] and others have consistently argued that there is no scientific justification for special labeling of biotechnology-derived foods per se. Thus, the FDA only requires labeling of biotech foods if the genetic modifications change the food in a way that has a real impact on consumer health. Examples would include alterations in the plants that could increase the level of naturally occurring but potentially harmful chemicals; introduce new substances, such as potential allergens, into foods that did not previously have them; or change the nutritional composition or a food's storage or preparationrequirements.[165] To date, no bioengineered food products put on the market in the United States have required such labeling, though the very first bioengineered fruit, the Calgene corporation's Flavr-Savr slow-ripening tomato, carried a voluntary notice that it had been engineered, and it was initially well received by consumers who were willing to pay a premium for the improved flavor promised on the labels.[166]

Similarly, the FDA believes that requiring food labels to indicate the presence of bioengineered ingredients could mislead consumers into believing that the foods differ in safety or nutrition when they do not.[167] Labels are a valuable source of information for consumers, so U.S. federal law prohibits label statements that are likely to be misunderstood by consumers, even if not technically false.[168] For example, labeling the vegetable broccoli as being "cholesterol-free" could run afoul of the FDA's rules because no broccoli contains cholesterol, and such a statement could suggest to consumers that while the particular broccoli is cholesterol-free, other broccoli is not.[169] Thus, rather than serving an educational or "right-to-know" purpose, mandatory labels on biotech foods could be misunderstood by consumers as a warning about some important difference.

A government-mandated label on all bioengineered foods would also raise important First Amendment free speech issues. In 1996, a U.S. Court of Appeals, in the case of *International Dairy Foods Association, et al. v. Amestoy*, ruled unconstitutional a Vermont statute requiring the labeling of dairy products derived from cows treated with a bioengineered growth hormone, noting that food labeling cannot be mandated simply because some people would like to have the information. "Absent . . . some indication that this information bears on a reasonable concern for human health or safety or some other sufficiently substantial governmental concern, the manufacturers cannot be compelled to disclose it."[170] In other words, to be constitutional, labeling mandates must be based in science and confined to requiring disclosure of information that is relevant to health or nutrition.

Ultimately, though, consumers do not need to rely on mandatory labeling of biotechnology-enhanced foods to truly have a choice. Real-world examples show that market forces are fully capable of supplying information about the methods in which foods and other products are produced if consumers truly demand it.[171] Kosher and organic production certification are prime examples. Neither kosher nor organic labels convey relevant information about the safety or nutritional value of those products, but both meet a demand by consumers for information about the way the foods were produced.

The same can be said about biotechnology. Some producers of nonbioengineered products are already making label statements to convey that information to consumers.[172] And the FDA recently published proposed guidelines to assist producers in voluntarily labeling both biotech and nonbiotech foods in a way that is not misleading.[173] In addition, under USDA requirements, food products labeled as "organic" cannot contain bioengineered ingredients.[174] Consequently, consumers wishing to purchase nonbiotech foods need only look for certified organic products.

THE ROAD AHEAD

SINCE THE INTRODUCTION of the very first bioengineered crop plant on the market in 1994, farmers, consumers, and food processors have experienced considerable benefits—from lower production costs to reduced pesticide use. But these benefits are dwarfed by the vast potential of agricultural biotechnology to aid in combating the even more serious problem of global food security.

During the next 50 years, global population may rise by 50 percent to 9 billion people, with nearly all of that growth coming in the poorest regions of the world.[175] Fortunately, mankind will face the extraordinary challenge of hunger and poverty with the very powerful tool of crop biotechnology. As many have noted, the problem of hunger and malnutrition is not now primarily caused by a global shortage of food. At current levels, world food production could provide more than 2,600 calories every day for all 6 billion people on Earth.[176] The primary causes of hunger during the past century have been political unrest and corrupt governments, poor transportation and infrastructure, and, of course, poverty.[177] All of these problems and more will need to be addressed if we are to truly conquer worldwide hunger. But ensuring true food security in a world of 8 or 9 billion will require greater productivity.

As population increases, farmers must be able to grow more and more nutritious food on less land. Biotechnology can provide one very powerful way to do just that. Without such gains in productivity and nutrition, the growing need for food will require plowing under millions of hectares of

> Without such gains in productivity and nutrition, the growing need for food will require plowing under millions of hectares of wilderness—an environmental tragedy surely worse than any imagined by biotechnology's opponents.

wilderness—an environmental tragedy surely worse than any imagined by biotechnology's opponents. Furthermore, 650 million of the world's poorest people live in rural areas where agriculture is the primary economic activity.[178] They are highly dependent upon the income that comes from growing and selling crops, so boosting the productivity of their crops would make a tremendous contribution to the battle against hunger and poverty.

Fortunately, the next generation of bioengineered products, now in research labs around the world, is poised to bring improved nutrition, longer shelf life, and greater productivity in the poor soils and harsh climates that tend to be characteristic of impoverished regions.[179] And many of these products are being developed primarily or exclusively for poor subsistence farmers and consumers in less-developed countries. Some improved plants include the same or similar traits for resistance to insects and plant diseases that are now used in industrialized countries, but in crops that are grown more typically in less-developed nations, including rice, corn, cassava, sweet potato, and tropical fruits, such as bananas and papayas.[180] Other bioengineered traits include faster maturation,[181] drought tolerance,[182] the ability to be irrigated with salty water or to grow in soil contaminated with excess salt,[183] tolerance to extremes of heat and cold,[184] and tolerance to soils with high acidity that are common in the tropics.[185] These traits for greater tolerance to environmental conditions would be tremendously advantageous to poor farmers in less-developed countries, and no one more so than in Africa.

Farmers in sub-Saharan Africa never saw the same productivity gains that countries in Asia and South America enjoyed from the Green Revolution.[186] The primary focus of Green Revolution plant breeders was on improving such crops as rice, wheat, and corn, which are not widely grown in Africa. Plus much of the African dry lands have little rainfall and no potential for irrigation, which play an essential role in productivity success stories of crops such as Asian rice. And the remoteness of many African villages and poor transportation infrastructure in landlocked African countries make it difficult for African farmers to obtain agricultural chemical inputs such as fertilizers, insecticides, and herbicides, even if they had the money to purchase them.[187] Thus by packaging technological inputs within seeds, biotechnology can provide the same, or better, productivity advantage as chemical or mechanical inputs, but in a much more user-friendly manner. Farmers could be able to control insect pests, viral or bacterial pathogens, extremes of heat or drought, and poor soil quality, just by planting their crops.

Still, antibiotech activists like Vandana Shiva and Miguel Altieri argue that poor farmers in less-developed nations will never benefit from biotechnology because it is controlled by multinational corporations. Altieri says that "[m]ost innovations in agricultural biotechnology have been profit-driven rather than need-driven. The real thrust of the genetic engineering industry is not to make third world agriculture more productive, but rather to generate profits."[188] But that sentiment is not shared by the thousands of academic and public sector researchers actually working on biotech applications in those countries. Cyrus Ndiritu, former director of the Kenyan Agricultural Research Institute, argues that, "[i]t is not the multinationals that have a stranglehold on Africa. It is hunger, poverty, and deprivation. And if Africa is going to get out of that, it has got to embrace [biotechnology]."[189]

Researchers are also improving the nutritional quality of plants, by boosting their ability to produce important vitamins, minerals, and proteins.[190] The diet of more than 3 billion people worldwide includes inadequate levels of many important micronutrients such as iron and vitamin A. Deficiency in just these two micronutrients can result in severe anemia, impaired intellectual development, blindness, and even death.[191] Fortunately, a substantial amount of research into improving the nutritional value of staple crops is well under way. Perhaps the most promising recent advance in this area is the development of a rice variety that has been genetically enhanced to add beta-carotene, which is converted in the human body to vitamin A.[192] By boosting the availability of vitamin A in developing-world diets, this "Golden Rice" could help prevent as many as a million deaths per year and eliminate numerous other health problems.[193]

But for critics of biotechnology, like India's Vandana Shiva and New York food journalist Michael Pollan, Golden Rice is just a "Great Yellow Hype"—another ploy by multinational biotechnology corporations to

Table 7.4. Biotechnology Research Useful in Developing Countries

Traits Now in Greenhouse or Field Tests	Traits Now in Laboratory Tests
Input Traits	**Input Traits**
Resistance to insects, nematodes, viruses, bacteria, and fungi in crops such as rice, maize, potato, papaya, and sweet potato	Drought and salinity tolerance in cereals
	Seedling vigor in rice
Delayed senescence, dwarfing, reduced shade avoidance, and early flowering in rice	Enhanced phosphorus and nitrogen uptake in rice and maize
Tolerance of aluminum, submergence, chilling, and freezing in cereals	Resistance to the parasitic weed Striga in maize, rice, and sorghum, to viruses in cassava and banana, and to bacterial blight in cassava
Male sterility/restorer for hybrid seed production in rice, maize, oilseed rape, and wheat	Nematode resistance and resistance to the disease black sigatoka in banana
New plant types for weed control and for increased yield potential in rice	Rice with the alternative C4 photosynthetic pathway and the ability to carry out nitrogen fixation
Output Traits	
Increased beta-carotene in rice and oilseed rape	**Output Traits**
Lower phytates in maize and rice to increase bioavailable iron	Increased beta-carotene, delayed postharvest deterioration, and reduced content of toxic cyanides in cassava
Modified starch in rice, potato, and maize and modified fatty-acid content in oilseed rape	Increased vitamin E in rice
Increased bioavailable protein, essential amino acids, and seed weight and delayed ripening in banana sugar content in maize	Apomixis (asexual seed production) in maize, rice, millet, and cassava
Lowered lignin content of forage crops	Use of genetically engineered plants such as potato and banana as vehicles for production and delivery of recombinant vaccines to humans
	Improved amino-acid content of forage crops

Source: Gordon Conway and Gary Toennissen, "Feeding the World in the Twenty-First Century," *Nature* Vol. 402, No. 6761 (December 2, 1999) pp. C55–C58.

get the world hooked on bioengineering.[194] Never mind that the research, which added genes taken from daffodils and a bacterium to rice, was funded primarily by the New York–based Rockefeller Foundation, which has promised to make the rice available to developing-world farmers at little or no cost.[195] Ismail Serageldin, director of the UN-sponsored Consultative Group on International Agricultural Research, asks opponents, "Do you want 2 to 3 million children a year to go blind and 1 million to die of vitamin A deficiency, just because you object to the way golden rice was created?"[196] Apparently, the critics find it important to oppose biotechnology in any form.

But the benefits of agricultural biotechnology will by no means go exclusively to less-developed countries. In industrialized nations such as the United States, consumers and farmers will continue to share in the benefits of improved productivity and reduced agricultural chemicals use. Agricultural biotechnology can also be used to develop healthier cooking oils that are low in saturated fats, vegetables with higher levels of cancer-fighting antioxidants, and foods with better taste and longer shelf life.[197] It is also possible to use bioengineered plants to create biodegradable plastics and better medicines[198] and to help clean up hazardous wastes.[199]

Although the complexity of biological systems means that some of these promised benefits of biotechnology are many years away, the biggest threats that consumers awaiting the bioengineering revolution currently face are restrictive policies stemming from unwarranted fears that the technology poses unique and dangerous threats to human health or the environment. No one thinks that biotech innovators should not be cautious, as all new technologies have both risks and benefits. But appropriate regulatory approaches involve weighing the risks and benefits of moving into the future against the risks and benefits of forgoing the new technology—not pointing to hypothetical risks and saying no. The bottom line is that scaremongering and overregulation are slowing progress in agricultural biotechnology and inflating the costs of research and development. Ultimately, this hurts both poor farmers struggling to feed their families and the natural environment upon which we all depend.

CHAPTER EIGHT

AVOIDING WATER WARS

David Riggs

ECO-MYTHS DEBUNKED

- *Although ominous scenarios about future water quantity and quality are widespread, the fact is that water conflicts are avoidable. The dire predictions can be averted by relying on markets to balance the supply and demand for water and take into account environmental values.*
- *Across the world, only about 8 percent of renewable freshwater resources are withdrawn for domestic, industrial, and agricultural purposes. The problem is not that there is insufficient water but that current institutional arrangements offer no incentive to use water efficiently.*
- *In most parts of the world, water is still treated as a collectivized public good, its provision and distribution handled almost exclusively by state authorities and heavily influenced by special interest politics.*
- *In publicly administered systems of water allocation, water is often used wastefully and has resulted in politically influential groups getting easier access to water while many of the poor are not served and must resort to buying their water at relatively high prices. Experience clearly shows that the best way to allocate water is through a flexible marketplace rather than an inflexible bureaucracy.*
- *Maintaining water resources in an open-access commons leads to depletion and degradation. In a commons arrangement, no one owns water and therefore no one is responsible for it or has an interest in protecting and preserving it.*
- *Freely operating markets are the most effective means for distributing goods, whether they be bread, apartments, shoes, or water. Water markets discourage users from wasting valuable water, they channel supply to those who value it most, and they help to reduce poverty by providing income and employment to the poor.*

WATER IS ONE of the world's most plentiful natural resources. Abundant as it may be, water is also a scarce resource in many places. Increasingly, ideological environmentalists are promoting the view that globally freshwater is an overused, precious resource that we are running out of. Consequently, many people have come to believe that countries across the world will

soon face serious and debilitating freshwater shortages. These shortages, it is feared, could lead to major conflicts, even war among nations.[1]

Water scarcity, like that of other natural resources, is often por-
trayed in terms of infinite demand versus finite supply. For example,
after a 2001 United Nations–sponsored conference on global water
supplies held recently in Stockholm, Sweden, many newspapers
widely interpreted those discussions as indicating that soon the demand for freshwater may outstrip supplies.[2] Professor Frank Rijsber-
man, director general of the International Water Management
Institute, told the press, "If current trends continue, the shortage of
water will extend beyond the semi-arid and arid regions. Expanding
demand for water will drain some of the world's major rivers, leaving
them dry throughout most of the year."[3]

Worries about impending disaster are not limited to just water
shortages but also extend to concerns about diminishing water quality. The 1996 edition of the Worldwatch Institute's *State of the World*
warns, "At every level of organization, from genes to species to as-
semblages to ecosystems, there are indications that the ecological in-
tegrity of freshwater systems has been simplified, degraded, and
jeopardized."[4] Klaus Toepfer, executive director of the United Nations Environment Programme, said, "The diminishing availability of
usable water in the face of exponentially increasing demand indicates
the potential for disputes and even con-
flict, both within and among states over
water resources."[5]

While the world is by no means physically running out of water, people have,
in many locales, already tapped the most
accessible—and therefore the cheapest—
sources of freshwater. This is why some
analysts have voiced concerns over possible severe future water shortages.

In many instances, these concerns
about water stem not from an absence of
supplies but from the absence of a proper market that would ensure a
balance between supply and demand. Sadly, defective institutional

frameworks that encourage profligate water use are the primary cause for the current anxiety over water supplies. And the failure to assign and enforce property rights and avenues of recourse is the primary reason for water quality problems. Water can and should be managed like any other scarce resource through the use of markets. Freely operating markets are the most effective means for distributing goods, whether they be bread, apartments, shoes, or water. Generally, it's not the lack of physical quantities of water that causes shortages, but rather a lack of proper institutional arrangements.

Although ominous scenarios about future water quantity and quality are widespread, the fact is that water wars are avoidable.

To forestall water supply conflicts, ideological environmentalists believe that only governments can ensure sufficient water for all those who want or need it. Only by means of regulation and centralized control, claim the activists, can governments create and manage adequate water supplies and ensure equitable distribution. However, the record of governments in controlling and providing water supplies is not good. Governments across the world have engaged in massive public-works water projects—from the Aswan High Dam in Egypt to the Klamath basin in California—but they have neither solved the potential shortage problems nor ensured distribution of water to those persons who need and value it most.[6]

Given the well-documented failures of government control over water resources, an alternative path beckons. If government regulations and subsidies distorting water use were eliminated, water markets would allow those with excess supplies of water to sell or lease them to those who desire more. In this way, a market would replace inflexible bureaucratic controls, enabling water to be more properly valued, assuring a balance between the supply and demand for water—just as markets do for other goods and services in the economy.

So what is the state of the blue planet?[7] Is humanity running out of water? What causes the shortages that do occur? How can looming water shortages in the Middle East, China, India, and the western United States be resolved so as to avoid conflict? Finally, how can water markets help humanity to more wisely manage this important resource for the benefit of future generations and the natural world upon which we all depend?

WATER QUANTITY AND QUALITY

THE EARTH'S WATER supply is governed by the hydrologic cycle, where water runs through a cycle of precipitation, evaporation, runoff, percolation, and storage. Each year only a fraction of the enormous quantities of water that flow through this cycle is withdrawn by humans. Experts estimate that more than 41,000 cubic kilometers of renewable water resources are available annually.[8] That volume is more than three times the size of Lake Superior, the largest freshwater lake in the world in terms of surface area and the third largest in terms of volume.[9] Of that total, only about 8 percent is withdrawn for domestic, industrial, and agricultural purposes.[10] Thus on a global scale, renewable water supplies exceed demand by a factor of about 12. Yet as comforting as that statistic may be, it does not take into account water allocation difficulties and growing demand in some geographic areas.

Available supplies are derived from surface water (freshwater in rivers, lakes, and reservoirs) and groundwater (water that collects in porous layers of underground rock known as aquifers). Figure 8.1 compares how each continent divides its freshwater withdrawals among three different uses: industrial and energy, irrigation, and commercial and residential. Although there are "uncertainties in the data,"[11] general comparisons across uses and continents shows that Asia holds about 61 percent of the world's population and accounts for about 56 percent of the world's total freshwater withdrawal.[12] Europe and North America collectively account for about 20 percent of world population and 37 percent of its water withdrawal.

Americans use large amounts of water—due to our highly industrialized economy, dispersed population, and agriculturally intensive landmass—but we use water efficiently. Today we consume less water per person than we did 25 years ago (see Figure 8.2) and our consumption continues to fall. In the 1950s the dominant water use was irrigation,

Figure 8.1
World Freshwater Resources: Water Withdrawals by Continent

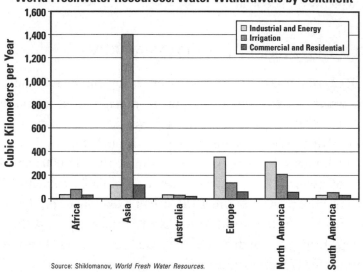

Source: Shiklomanov, *World Fresh Water Resources.*

Figure 8.2
U.S. Water Withdrawals and Consumptive Use per Day

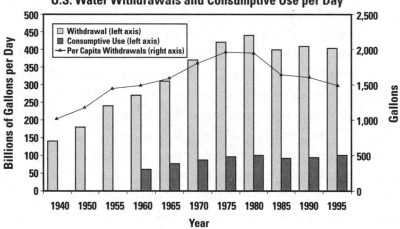

Data on Consumptive Use not available for 1940, 1950, and 1955.
Source: *Statistical Abstract of the United States: 2000.*

but since the mid-1960s thermoelectric water use has been the largest water consumer (see Figure 8.3). Although irrigation use has remained stable, U.S. farm productivity has increased at least fivefold over that time period.[13] Improved irrigation techniques, such as sim-

Figure 8.3
Trends of Estimated Water Use in the United States, 1950–1995

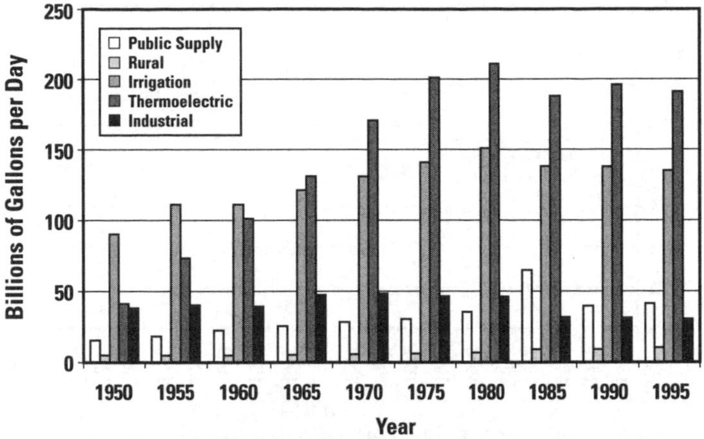

Source: U.S. Geological Survey, *Trends in Water Use, 1950–1995*.
http://www.water.usgs.gov/watuse/pdf1995/pdf/trends.pdf

ply moving from flood irrigation to drip or spray irrigation, have been contributing factors in per capita water consumption decreases.

While efforts are presently under way to improve and upgrade the quality of water data, both in the United States and abroad, one source of consistent data from which we can draw a limited but reliable trend of ambient water quality in the United States does exist: the U.S. Geological Survey's National Stream Quality Accounting Network (NASQAN).[14] NASQAN consists of 420 monitoring stations located on major rivers nationwide. While this network is not designed to provide a statistical sample of water quality, it is useful in tracking the reduction in pollution from factories and municipal sewage treatment plants. Municipal sewage, the main source of fecal coliform bacteria, combines with industrial waste to reduce the dissolved oxygen content of river water, leading to "dissolved oxygen deficit." Phosphorus pollution comes from both point (e.g., the end of pipe) and nonpoint (e.g., agricultural runoff) source pollution.

Figure 8.4 shows that the percent of NASQAN readings exceeding clean water standards for fecal coliform has declined since its peak in 1975. Phosphorus levels have shown little decline, yet even in 1975, only 5 percent of the readings exceeded the standard. And finally the number of readings exceeding dissolved oxygen standards has improved slightly.

Figure 8.4
Ambient Water Quality in U.S. Rivers and Streams: Violation Rates, 1975–1995

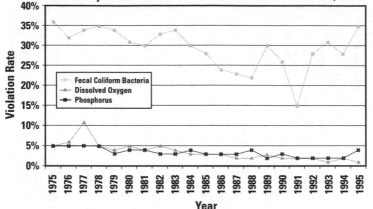

Source: *Statistical Abstract of the United States* (various years).

As a further proxy to compare water quality improvements, Figure 8.5 shows how pesticide contaminant levels found in bird eggs at Lake Superior have dropped over time.[15] The annual values for each of the pollutants are converted to a base year, which makes it possible to compare water quality in later years to the base year level. The contamination fell considerably between 1974 and 1995. All five of the contaminants show about an 80 percent or better improvement over the 20-year period. These favorable trends can be observed in other Great Lakes as well.

POTENTIAL WATER CRISES?

STORIES ABOUT VARIOUS impending environmental apocalypses have appeared in the popular press and captured the public's attention for decades. It is not surprising that polls find that most Americans think that environmental problems will get worse.[16] About 80 percent of Americans are, however, optimistic that environmental problems will be under control in the next 20 years, according to a Gallup poll.[17] Americans also consistently rank water quality as one of the nation's leading environmental problems, and 87 percent are concerned about the pollution of rivers, lakes, and reservoirs.[18]

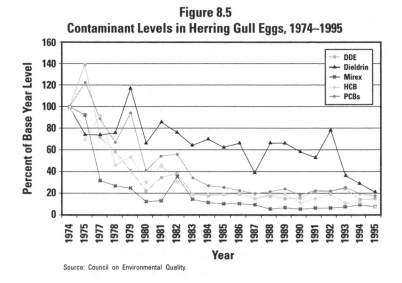

Figure 8.5
Contaminant Levels in Herring Gull Eggs, 1974–1995

Source: Council on Environmental Quality.

While Americans have their concerns about the environment and water quality, many ideological environmentalists warn that mankind is not only in danger of degrading and depleting the Earth's water resources but also in danger of generating fierce conflict. As noted earlier, Klaus Toepfer, head of the UNEP, has warned that the growing demand for water could soon spark conflicts between and within countries. Toepfer further asserted, "Severe water shortages already exist in many parts of the world and the global water cycle is unlikely to be able to cope with demands that will be made on it in the coming decades."[19]

Sandra Postel, director of the Global Water Policy Project, issued a similar warning: "Water scarcity is now the single biggest threat to global food production. Just two decades ago, serious water problems were confined to manageable pockets of the world. Today, however, they exist on every continent and are spreading rapidly."[20]

These cataclysmic predictions about running out of natural resources is in the infamous tradition of the *The Limits to Growth* report in 1972 to the Club of Rome. According to this report, the world would run out of gold, lead, natural gas, petroleum, and a host of other natural resources.[21] The sequel to this report, *Beyond the Limits*, which was published in 1992, is only slightly less frantic, stating:

> *Globally water is in great excess, but because of operation limits and pollution, it can in fact support at most one more doubling of demand, which will occur in 20 to 30 years. Even if it were possible to stop all pollution, trap every drop of flood, move either the water to the people or the people to the water, even if it were possible and desirable to capture the planet's full 40,000 cubic kilometers of annual runoff for human use, there would be enough water for only 3 to 4 more doublings—a mere 100 years away if current growth rates continue.[22]*

Citing such judgments, many analysts concur that water crises will be inevitable in various parts of the world. Three regions, the Middle East, India, and China, are seen as being especially susceptible to these crises, and the United States also has its problems to sort through.

MIDDLE EAST

Perhaps potential conflicts over water are nowhere more volatile than in the Middle East, where the watersheds of three rivers form the backbone of water supply: the Jordan, the Tigris-Euphrates, and the Nile. Former Senator Paul Simon recently declared that "in 10 years or less the area is likely to explode over water."[23] Water supplies in the region are indeed stretched very thin and population growth keeps the demand for water rising. Moreover, because the region has an arid climate, food production is heavily dependent on irrigation.

Israel, Jordan, Syria, and Palestine (the West Bank and Gaza) obtain much of their water from the Jordan River basin as well as groundwater supplies. The water withdrawals of all of these countries from the Jordan River and their underground aquifers exceed their internal renewable water resources. Israel, for example, consumes 109 percent of its available water resources, while Jordan and Syria consume 145 and 206 percent, respectively.[24] This means, of course, that each country relies on water sources that originate in other countries.

With population growth rates on the rise for each of these countries, absent improvements in efficiency, the rising demand for water is likely to continue. Depending on population growth rates and water use per capita, Israel, Jordan, and Palestine are projected to run a water deficit of 1 to 2 billion cubic meters a year by 2020, which amounts to about 20 to 40 percent of current consumption.[25]

Conflicts over water could also occur in the Tigris-Euphrates watershed. Both rivers originate in the mountains of eastern Turkey, with the Tigris flowing through Iraq and the Euphrates running through Syria and Iraq before they join together to flow to the Persian Gulf. Despite a current surplus in the watershed, Iraq and Syria stand to lose from a large water project in Turkey that could reduce flow in both rivers below the minimum they claim to need.[26]

Finally, the watershed of one of the most famous rivers on all the earth, the Nile, is also likely to experience substantial water conflicts in coming years. About 80 percent of the Nile's flow originates with the Blue Nile, which flows through Ethiopia and Sudan. Most of the remaining flow comes from the White Nile, which originates at Lake Victoria in Tanzania and flows through several countries, including Sudan. Egypt, where the Nile reaches the Mediterranean Sea, built the Aswan Dam, creating Lake Nassar. Despite agreements on how much water each country in the Nile watershed is entitled to annually and projects slated to increase supplies, the region could still be headed toward conflict.

> The watershed of one of the most famous rivers on all the earth, the Nile, is also likely to experience substantial water conflicts in coming years.

Egypt's population is projected to grow by more than 11 million people in the next 10 years.[27] With virtually no new sources of water immediately available, conventional wisdom holds that Egypt had better squeeze more out of its existing supplies by upgrading and better managing its systems. Through government edict, Egypt could require its agricultural sector to move away from water-intensive crops like cotton and sugarcane in order to free up water to grow more food. Or worse, Egypt may decide to unilaterally move forward with large-scale river basin schemes to increase water supplies.

With 97 percent of total water flow originating outside Egypt's borders,[28] "unilateral actions to construct a dam or river diversion in the absence of a treaty or institutional mechanism that safeguards the interests of other countries in the basin is highly destabilizing, often spurring decades of hostility before cooperation is pursued."[29] Such was the case between Egypt and Sudan in the 1950s when Egypt unilaterally planned construction of the Aswan High Dam. The signing of a treaty in 1959, however, defused tensions between the two countries.[30] Today, Egypt's increasing demand for water and lack of formal agreements with neighboring countries in the basin dealing with future demand leaves open the possibility for conflict.

INDIA

With more than 1 billion people, India faces serious challenges from its limited and sporadic water resources.[31] India's climate varies from region to region, but most rainfall comes to most of the regions during the monsoon season, which typically runs from June to September.[32] During that season, the challenge is to control flooding and capture enough runoff from floods to prepare for the dry season. Like many other countries, India's government has invested enormous sums of money to build dams (the country has 4,291 dams, according to one estimate[33]) to increase supply. But many of these efforts have either come up short or failed to allocate water to desired areas. In the spring of 2000, for example, India's western state of Gujarat was hit by the worst drought in a century with nearly 10,000 villages reeling from severe water shortages.[34] The drought and the gross mismanagement of water resources left 50 million people desperate, and many fled the parched lands.

Much of India's current problems with water shortages may date back to large-scale public-works irrigation projects begun under British rule in the 19th and early 20th centuries. "By 1900, India had 13.4 million hectares under irrigation, an area larger by two-thirds than the entire world's irrigated area 100 years earlier," according to one analyst.[35] Today, India irrigates 50.1 million hectares compared to 21.4 million hectares in the United States.[36]

CHINA

With more than 20 percent of the world's population and roughly 7 percent of the world's internal renewable water resources, China, one could argue, faces very severe water problems.[37] Indeed, Lester Brown of the Worldwatch Institute has asserted that "[t]he water scarcity that now plagues much of China reflects the extent to which demand is outrunning the sustainable yield of rivers and aquifers."[38] Chinese government officials estimate that nearly two-thirds of China's 668 cities face water shortages, many of these cities being in northern China.[39] "Experts say the shortages are a result of overgrazing, overlogging, and overpopulation during the past century,"[40] runs the conventional environmentalist litany.

While the above factors may have contributed to China's water woes, the Chinese government's policy of encouraging national food self-sufficiency is also a big part of the problem. China uses approximately 87 percent of its freshwater withdrawals for agriculture.[41] Most of China's farms still use flood irrigation, which consumes considerably more water than much more efficient "sprinkling" or "trickling" irrigation.[42] The adoption of more efficient irrigation technologies combined with abandoning the quixotic pursuit of food self-sufficiency would go a long way toward easing China's freshwater supply problems.

UNITED STATES

U.S. water supplies are generally abundant in the east, but as settlers moved westward into more arid regions, the lack of water became the chief factor in determining where people settled. (See Figure 8.6)

For example, after a drought in California beginning in the late 1980s, increased pressure was put on municipal water supplies as reservoirs were lowered. Yet at that time, agriculture consumed about 80 percent of all water used in California, and farmers paid about one-tenth the price of that paid by urban customers. Since taxpayers heavily subsidized water use by farmers, farmers wasted water while urban homeowners grew desperate for new supplies.

Figure 8.6
Freshwater Withdrawals in Western States

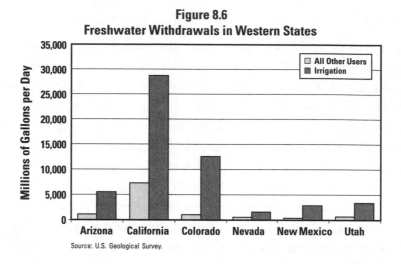

Source: U.S. Geological Survey.

In the past, rather than create markets for water, the public's response to impending shortages was to press for new major government-
financed water projects to recycle existing supplies or to secure new
sources. Yet constraints on government budgets make funding for
major new water projects difficult to obtain. And across the world,
there is growing public concern over the damage caused to aquifers
and rivers from creating new water supplies. In Florida, for example,
increased pumping from the aquifers is exceeding the natural rate of
recharge from river and rainwater seepage. When an aquifer's water
level drops in coastal areas, salty ocean water can be drawn underground, harming the aquifer.

There's not much use in blaming Florida's water crisis on the
weather. As one of the wettest regions in North America—with average annual rainfall ranges from 40 inches in the Keys to nearly 66
inches in the state's panhandle—the state has an average of 150 billion gallons of rainwater per day. Almost three-fourths of that total
evaporates or is consumed by plant life, but even after subtracting this
amount, rainfall provides the equivalent of 3,076 gallons per person
per day in Florida.

Difficulties like those discussed above have persuaded many analysts that a global water crisis is unavoidable. The World Commission
on Water for the 21st Century, for example, declared that water

should be managed in a framework that recognizes it as the scarce resource that it is.[43] Viewed narrowly as a strict supply-and-demand problem within current institutional arrangements, water shortages and the potential conflicts they could bring do appear inevitable. Water supplies are being depleted and degraded, while water demand is rising. But there is an alternative.

FROM COMMON POOLS TO PROPERTY RIGHTS

BECAUSE WATER IS a necessity for life, it is often viewed as too important to leave to markets. This view is badly mistaken.

As we have seen, the conventional wisdom is that water resources are being used up too rapidly and that political controls should be instituted to conserve water for future generations. This simplistic notion of conservation as refraining from use, however, provides no guidance as to the proper rate of resource use over time. The relevant conservation question for water is, what is the optimal rate of use over time?

The simplistic premises of the old-style conservation movement and modern ideological environmentalists has led to public management and public ownership of most freshwater resources. The result is the impending water shortages described earlier.

Postel finds that "measures to reduce demand for water through conservation, recycling, and higher efficiency are typically more economical than efforts to gain new supplies of freshwater. Costing between 5 and 50 cents per cubic meter of water, nearly the entire spectrum of conservation options—including leak repair, the adoption of more efficient technologies, and water recycling—cost less than the development of new water sources and much less than desalination."[44] But current dependence on publicly owned and managed water projects strongly discourages efforts to take advantage of the innovations and efficiencies identified by Postel and others.

So public managers and politicians ignore Postel's analysis and focus on building more publicly financed water systems as the solution to impending water crises. The World Bank, for example, estimates that over the 1995 to 2005 period more than $600 billion will need to be spent in developing countries on water projects to avoid water shortages.[45] There is, however, growing recognition that large-scale water projects are no longer the answer to increasing water demands.[46] Because of cost overruns, long delays, and budgetary difficulties, public investment in hydraulic infrastructure has proven to have costs that exceed what their eventual benefits were worth. In fact, a recent research report shows that many publicly financed water systems in numerous countries have low or negative rates of return.[47] Moreover, many governments are becoming less willing to spend public resources on water infrastructure or even on maintaining and operating existing infrastructure due to increasing fiscal pressures.

All of these so-called solutions, ranging from government-mandated conservation programs to expanded public-works projects, overlook the fundamental fact that water shortages are an inevitable result of the exploitation of an open-access commons resource. Such open-access resources always end up depleted and degraded. Why? Because no one owns the resource and no one is responsible for it or has an interest in protecting and preserving it. However, when property rights to water are clearly defined, fully enforced, and cheaply transferable, the owner of the water has an incentive to protect the body of water so that it can provide future benefits, mitigating the potential for shortages or pollution.

> When property rights to water are clearly defined, fully enforced, and cheaply transferable, the owner of the water has an incentive to protect the body of water so that it can provide future benefits.

Garrett Hardin's "The Tragedy of the Commons" helps explain why water that is left open for any and all to access leads to overuse and overexploitation.[48] Hardin describes a village commons, or common-access pasture, used by villagers for cattle grazing. In Hardin's story, villagers cannot exclude one another from the common pasture and do not have to pay for the right to graze their cattle on the pasture. Overgrazing results because self-interested villagers wish to reap the benefits of the pasture for their cattle before the next villager grazes his cattle. In short, the villagers lack the incentive to protect the commons from degradation.

Similarly, this problem arises when the common-access resource is water. Water users cannot exclude other users from tapping into the resource, leading to overuse. In many cases, such as the Middle East, the competing users are countries squabbling over how much water one country will leave a downstream country. In the absence of property rights to water, users face an incentive to withdraw as much water as possible before someone else does and they have no incentive to maintain downstream water quality.

WATER MARKETS

THERE ARE BASICALLY two methods of organizing the use of water resources: the market and bureaucratic central direction. Analysis of past water crises provides important lessons in how best to manage water problems in the future.

Ownership is no less important for water than for other natural resources and assets. The problem associated with the use of open-access common property resources is that people have greater regard for what they own than for what they possess in common with others. Private ownership, in sharp contrast to ownership in common, encourages water users to conserve for the future because current market values reflect the value of future income. That is, the market values a privately owned water resource based on the income it will generate in the future. Actions that lessen future income lessen the asset's current market value, everything else being the same. So long as the water resource can be bought and sold, a current water owner will have strong incentive to take the preferences of future generations into account even though the current owner may not expect to personally reap the benefits of future water sales.

A market for water works like any other market. Owners of water supplies offer their water for sale and users offer to buy it, with the two parties negotiating an agreeable price. As other buyers and sellers repeat these transactions, an efficient and competitive water market develops, which balances supply and demand—without the need for bureaucratic control over water distribution.

Water markets would discourage users from wasting valuable water, they would channel supplies to those who value them most, and they would moderate demands among would-be users, thus preventing overuse and damage to the natural environment.

One of the best working examples of water markets is found in the country of Chile, which under its 1981 water code granted existing water users property rights to both surface and groundwater. The owners of these water rights may sell them to anyone for any purpose at negotiated prices. Mateen Thobani, senior economist at the World Bank, describes Chile's success with water markets:

> *In Chile, farmers sold or leased their surplus water rights to more efficient neighboring farmers, industrial users, or water companies. The sales and leases have allowed some water companies and industrial users to obtain reliable access to water without expensive infrastructure investment. The results . . . have been large gains to society. For example, the city of La Serena was able to purchase 28 percent of its water rights from neighboring farmers, allowing the government to postpone the construction of a proposed dam. Similarly, the city of Arica, in the arid north, has been able to meet the needs of urban residents by leasing groundwater from farmers. Such measures have contributed to Chile's success in providing water to virtually all urban residents.*[49]

Success with water markets has not been isolated to a few areas within Chile. Mexico has also experienced success by allowing holders of water rights to sell or lease their rights as long as the water rights of other users are not negatively affected. Tradable rights have given owners an incentive to sell to those with a higher valued use and given buyers an incentive to conserve to keep their costs to a minimum. As a result, Mexico has diverted water to more productive uses, benefiting many small farmers whose operations were previously unprofitable due to the accumulation of unsustainable debt.[50]

The benefits of water markets are not just limited to communities and industry groups. Environmental groups, especially in the United

States, have participated in water markets, often for the benefit of increased in-stream flow. The Oregon Water Trust, for example, "obtains water rights through gifts, leases, and outright purchases, and then transfers them to in-stream flows. Improving these flows into some of Oregon's rivers and streams not only protects fisheries and aquatic habitats, but also enhances their recreational value and ecological health."[51] Other environmental groups, like the Environmental Defense Fund, have negotiated willing seller-willing buyer contracts to enhance in-stream flows in parched western states.[52]

Despite the success of water markets, they have not been without problems. A casual look at the riots that occurred in Bolivia in the spring of 2000, for example, might indict water markets as the cause of Bolivia's president declaring martial law in the city of Cochabamba and the deaths of six people.[53] In Cochabamba, a consortium of private companies was to supply residents of the city and nearby farmers with water. Riots broke out, however, when people discovered that their water rates were to rise by 35 percent. Following months of unrest, the companies decided to scrap the project and left Bolivia.

A closer look at the Bolivia privatization experiment reveals that the government was hoping to finance another expensive scheme by forcing the private companies to subsidize its costs. So the increase in water rates was merely an attempt by the consortium to increase revenues to pay for a $350 million irrigation and hydroelectric program that the government had imposed on them.[54] The consortium made the mistake of passing those costs along to consumers before having noticeably improved service quality. Nevertheless, the rioting was less the result of privatizing water supplies than an imposition of additional costs by the public sector.

The Bolivia case highlights the importance of discovering effective ways to supply water in developing countries—that is, of supplying water in the poorer areas of the world. However, ideological environmentalists find danger around every corner in privatizing water systems, declaring, "For developing nations like Bolivia, this is a calamity in the making."[55] But these contentions are not supported by the facts.

Water markets help to reduce poverty by spurring new supply in high-demand areas and by providing income and employment to the poor. By allowing water to move to its highest valued use, water markets improve efficiency and increase production, both of which serve to enhance income and employment. Moreover, because water markets are based on secure water rights, they encourage investment in new enterprise. Thobani, for example, finds that "[i]n Mexico, investors built a water-bottling plant after negotiating for the water rights from a farmer. Not only was the farmer better off, but the increased investment also generated additional employment."[56]

Water markets help to reduce poverty by spurring new supply in high-demand areas and by providing income and employment to the poor.

Besides balancing supply and demand, markets for water offer additional benefits. By requiring users to pay the full market price of supplies, prices rise when supplies are short, thus automatically encouraging conservation. In addition, a market price for water encourages existing users of subsidized cheap water, such as farmers cultivating arid land, to consider selling water to those who value it more highly for things like maintaining in-stream flows or supplying to urban dwellers, but who cannot obtain supplies because of rigid bureaucratic allocations.

The principles of water markets—clearly defined and enforced rights, which are freely transferable—also aid in resolving international water conflicts, where a water body forms an international boundary or water flows across an international boundary. In either situation (boundary or cross flow), without established water rights between countries, water could be treated as a common-access resource, subject to overuse and pollution. Similar to the previous examples of establishing water markets within a country, the challenge in international water agreements is to shift the resource from a system of political dispensation to private allocation; that is, shifting water use decisions from countries to actual water users.

The conventional approach to international water conflicts is bilateral agreements on the apportionment of transboundary water. Although these agreements may result in better outcomes than if countries act unilaterally (where war is a potential consequence), they rarely incorporate the vested rights of water users within affected countries. "These apportionments have often been vaguely defined and have been subject to frequent renegotiation. The resulting uncertainty of supply has made private rights less definite, which in turn has discouraged water rights transfers. More importantly, the national apportionment approach to transboundary water allocation inevitably has had little if any regard for the relative productivity of water on opposite sides of national borders," according to resource economist James Huffman.[57]

An alternative approach to national apportionment agreements lies in an emerging field of study that examines the possibility of designing transnational institutions of limited authority. A transnational institution for water markets would require transboundary countries to give up some sovereignty—a highly contentious issue. However, sovereignty is often a contentious aspect in the transnational apportionment approach as well. Given sovereignty aspects with both approaches, the transnational institutional approach may offer a workable solution due to the tremendous efficiencies to be gained from transnational water markets. Moreover, the transnational institutional approach for water markets is a division of sovereignty rather than a unification of governments.

The power of the transnational water market authority must be narrowly defined to only govern water markets and carefully limited so that the natural consequence of human freedom from competing sovereignties is not jeopardized. Importantly, "a transboundary water market requires a unified system of property rights which are enforceable and transferable without regard to national borders."[58] Transboundary water institutions could create a more efficient allocation of water and "change the focus from the acquisition and exercise of political influence to the greatest productivity of water."[59]

Markets for water resources thus offer efficient means for allocating water supplies both within and between countries. They also offer a powerful mechanism for balancing demands for new water supplies with concerns about the natural environment. The political pressure for expensive new publicly funded water projects would disappear if proponents had to pay their full market costs. The natural environment would be better protected if markets were more widely accepted as a way to resolve competing interests.

IMPEDING THE FLOW OF WATER MARKETS

SWITCHING TO WATER markets will not be easy. One of the major obstacles will be bureaucratic resistance from public officials who currently manage publicly built water infrastructure. In Los Angeles, California, for example, private companies have offered to pay to use publicly built aqueducts and canals to deliver water to potential buyers. In order to get their product to buyers (e.g., cities and water districts), private companies are willing to pay to use these public delivery systems.

However, exactly what constitutes "fair compensation" for use of these systems has proven to be difficult to determine. Private companies contend that public managers attempt to preserve control over water by setting exorbitant rates for using the system. Northern California–based Western Water Company, for example, is having difficulties with officials at the Metropolitan Water District of Southern California, owner of southern California's 242-mile-long Colorado aqueduct. As one news report described, "Michael George, president of Western Water, accuses the water district of attempting to preserve its control over water by setting an exorbitant price for using its system."[60]

Critics of water markets typically deploy two arguments in opposition to them. First, they contend that markets would prompt owners of water rights and supplies to hoard their supplies to drive up prices for water consumers. However, the evidence is that this occurs far more readily under publicly financed and managed water systems than under a market approach. Consider, for example, the behavior of the managers of an irrigation district receiving its water at a below-market rate that is a fraction of the price nearby cities are willing pay. With a regulatory system that prohibits water sales, the irrigation district managers have no incentive to economize on their water usage and make supplies available to thirsty cities. Meanwhile, the stymied municipalities have a strong incentive to press for the construction of new water projects and for taxpayer subsidies. If irrigation districts could legally sell any water in excess of their minimum requirements, they would have strong incentives not to hoard or waste water. Thus, existing supplies would be used far more efficiently and the natural environment would be spared from another disrupting water project.

The second common objection to water markets is the claim that they may not allocate water to the most important uses. "The creation of water markets amounts to destruction of the commons and denial of water rights to weaker sections of society,"[61] claims one prominent activist. Ideological environmentalists often invoke images of parched schoolchildren and hospitals in crisis under a market-oriented water allocation system as a rhetorical ploy. In fact, under the current system, supplies often go to powerful politically connected interests while water remains scarce for industries and communities with less influence. Markets allow one group to purchase water from the other, which then generates an alternative source of revenue for the seller. This potential income stream is a strong incentive for powerful interests in control of water supplies to take into account the needs of other users. Thus, decisions over water supplies are removed from the win/lose arena of politics to the win/win dynamic of markets.

Before a farmer or other user of water can sell or trade his supplies to a municipal water system, of course, he must have a firmly established ownership right in the water. Private property rights are a prerequisite for a functioning market. Markets cannot develop or operate when ownership rights are unclear or when there is a constant threat of confiscation by the government. This is a major impediment to water markets today. Governments do not provide the legal framework within which water markets can function.

However, the idea of water markets is beginning to catch on: Water is beginning to be viewed as an asset instead of a limitless, common-access resource.[62]

SUMMARY AND CONCLUSIONS

Although water is essential to life, conflicts, even wars, are not inevitable. Water is a commodity, similar to other essentials like food, shelter, and clothing. The most efficient, humane, equitable, and just method for the production and distribution of commodities is a system of ownership rights and market exchanges.

The potential for domestic and international conflict over water arises because it is still treated as a collectivized public good: Its provision and distribution are handled almost exclusively by state authorities and heavily influenced by the political arena.

The problem is not that there is insufficient water but that current institutional arrangements offer no incentives to use supplies efficiently or opportunities to avoid conflict. When resources are handled through the marketplace, impending shortages lead to higher prices, which encourage conservation, new production, and the development and marketing of alternatives, which eventually leads to increased supply and lower prices. The process is not perfect, but experience shows that water markets are more effective at supplying the needs of people and protecting the natural world than are the current systems political management.

The blue planet faces a serious challenge of trying to satisfy the growing thirst of its people and the agriculture that sustains them. With nearly one-fifth of the world's population not having access to safe drinking water and a potential for greater conflict between nations with rising water scarcity, water markets are a moral imperative. Feeding a hungry planet requires that we repair leaky water distribution systems and use better irrigation techniques. Only water markets can create the incentives to reduce waste and send water to its most productive and necessary uses. By treating water as a tradable commodity, by including water in market processes, people across the world and the natural environment will be better served.

> Only water markets can reduce waste and send water to its most productive and necessary uses.

CHAPTER NINE

FUELING THE FUTURE

John Jennrich

ECO-MYTHS DEBUNKED

- *Earlier predictions that the world would soon run out of oil and natural gas by now and that energy prices would skyrocket have proven to be dramatically off the mark.*
- *In the 1990s, fossil fuels supplied 85 percent of the world's production of primary energy.*
- *In 1999, market shares for primary energy production worldwide were as follows: petroleum, 39 percent; natural gas, 23 percent; coal, 22 percent; hydropower, 7 percent; nuclear, 6.6 percent; and all renewables, 0.7 percent.*
- *The U.S. Energy Information Administration (EIA) notes that non-hydro renewables supplied only 3.7 percent of total U.S. energy consumption and projects that figure will rise to only 4.6 percent by 2020.*
- *Solar and wind power systems contributed only 0.1 percent of U.S. energy consumption in 2000 and the EIA projects that will rise to 0.25 percent by 2020.*
- *A single 555-megawatt natural gas-fired electric power plant in California produces more electricity than all 13,000 windmills in that state.*
- *Current renewable energy technologies cannot meet humanity's energy needs, so fossil fuels will likely supply the bulk of humanity's energy for the immediate decades ahead.*

THE WORLD'S OIL reserves were supposed to be depleted by 1992 at exponential growth rates or, more optimistically, if consumption rates didn't increase, world oil reserves might last as long as 2003, according to the famous *The Limits to Growth* report in 1972.[1]

Similarly, at exponential growth rates, global reserves of natural gas were supposed to be gone by 1994, and again, if somehow consumption didn't increase, they would last until 2010.

More recently, Princeton University professor Kenneth S. Deffeyes forecasts in his book *Hubbert's Peak: The Impending World Oil Shortage* that global oil production will peak in the first decade of the 21st century.[2]

On the other hand, some environmentalists worry that there is *too much* fossil fuel on the planet. David Nemtzow, president of the Alliance to Save Energy, claims, "It's not the finite nature of fossil fuels that's harming the global climate; it's their abundance. It's not the scarcity of oil that endangers pristine and public lands; it's the profusion."

Therefore, Nemtzow argues, "We need a more sustainable energy economy with highly efficient cars, houses, offices and factories powered primarily by solar, wind, geothermal and other clean, renewable sources of energy."[3]

So, what's a concerned citizen to think? Are we running out of oil, natural gas, coal, or whatever . . . or aren't we?

Often ideological environmentalists paint with a broad brush and use innuendo and expected inference to make questionable points. The Sierra Club, for example, is adept at this tactic. The Sierra Club claims, "Few Americans realize that even today much of our electricity comes from dirty, heavily polluting, coal-fired power plants. In fact, fossil fuels—coal, oil and natural gas—account for over 85 percent of fuel use in the United States. These power plants spew hundreds of millions of tons of global warming pollution into our atmosphere each year."[4] The Sierra Club further claims that "[t]here are viable alternatives to fossil fuel. Clean, renewable energy from the sun and wind offer nonpolluting, economical and durable alternatives for generating electricity."

> So, what's a concerned citizen to think? Are we running out of oil, natural gas, coal, or whatever . . . or aren't we?

In the Sierra Club's commentary, there are three sentences. The first and third deal with power generation in highly negative terms. The middle sentence cites the fossil fuel contribution to *total* energy use (not just power generation). In this, it includes oil, which is used overwhelmingly as a transportation fuel and for lubricants, not for power generation. In fact, oil products in 2000 were used for only 2.7 percent of power generation in the United States; notably, the use of renewable fuels for making electricity is more than three times as great

(9.3 percent).[5] With regard to power generation, the only fossil fuels that matter significantly are coal and natural gas, which together in 2000 constituted less than 46 percent of energy consumption in the United States.[6] Alas, that's not as big a wallop as "over 85 percent" in the Sierra Club's misleading commentary.

But what about the comparison between coal and natural gas, two fossil fuels whose emissions—from production or mining through transportation to consumption—are far different? There are those who think that natural gas (which constitutes 24 percent of energy consumption and 27 percent of primary energy production) is the answer to the problems caused by coal.

For example, the environmentalist group Scientists for a Sustainable Energy Future professes to be concerned about global warming caused by burning fossil fuels. In a recent open letter, SSEF offered a solution: "more energy from natural gas, renewable hydrogen and geothermal sources, and less coal and oil."[7]

So then is natural gas the problem as the Sierra Club claims, or is it the solution as Scientists for a Sustainable Energy Future argue?

Again, what's a concerned citizen to think?

John P. Holdren, who is a professor of environmental policy at Harvard University, recently claimed that energy depletion is a nonissue. "The belief that the world is running out of energy," according to Holdren, is a belief "that few if any environmentalists actually hold."[8]

Holdren adds: "That 'the energy problem' is not primarily a matter of depletion of resources in any global sense but rather of environmental impacts and sociopolitical risks . . . has in fact been the mainstream environmentalist position for decades." Specifically, he says, "It was, for example, the position I elucidated" in 1971 in a Sierra Club publication and in 1977 in the book *Ecoscience* that he coauthored with Paul and Anne Ehrlich. It is true that Holden focused his analysis in his 1971 Sierra Club book, *Energy: A Crisis in Power,* on the sociopolitical and environmental impacts of energy use, but interestingly, Holdren also declared, "[I]t is fair to conclude that under almost any assumptions, the supplies of crude petroleum and natural gas are severely limited. The bulk of energy likely to flow from these sources may have been tapped within the lifetime of many of the present population."[9]

Despite Holdren's revisionist interpretation of his earlier views, he and the infamous environmental doomsters Paul Ehrlich and Anne Ehrlich, both of Stanford University, also very much took a depletionist approach in 1977 in their book *Ecoscience:*

> *[B]y any method of analysis, U.S. supplies of petroleum and natural gas are severely limited. World supplies of those fuels, moreover, are almost as small in relation to projected demands as the U.S. supplies. Both for the United States and the world, any significant increase in consumption of oil and gas will lead to the substantial depletion of the recoverable resources of those materials by early in the next century. And if the pessimists are correct, U.S. domestic production of petroleum was already near or even past its peak in 1974, with domestic natural gas not far behind.*[10]

And in 1976 environmentalist energy guru Amory Lovins, who heads the Rocky Mountain Institute, claimed in his influential 1976 *Foreign Affairs* article "Energy Strategy: The Road Not Taken?" that despite intensive electrification, "we are still short of gaseous and liquid fuels, acutely so from the 1980s on, because of slow and incomplete substitution of electricity for the two-thirds of fuel use that is now direct. Despite enhanced recovery of resources in the ground, shortages steadily deepen in natural gas—on which plastics and nitrogen fertilizers depend."[11]

Most readers would reasonably interpret those statements as warnings about depletion.

The quixotic activist Hazel Henderson, in her 1981 book, *The Politics of the Solar Age,* touted solar power and argued in favor of a more *labor*-intensive society.[12]

In promoting the use of solar and other renewable alternatives in the United States, Henderson claimed, "The fact that with the steady declines in consumption of electricity over the past few years, largely due to its skyrocketing price, there may be no need to build anymore electricity-generating capacity in most parts of the country."[13] Her prediction proved to be spectacularly wrong.

According to U.S. Energy Information Administration (EIA) statistics going back to 1949, there had been a steady increase in electricity consumption to the time that Henderson wrote her book—including growth of more than 200 percent in the prior 20 years, with only a 0.4 percent hiccup in 1974—so her claims about "steady declines"[14] in electricity consumption are pure nonsense. And in the two decades since her book was published, electricity consumption in the United States has increased by more than 70 percent, even as end-use efficiencies have increased.[15]

NATURAL GAS FUELS THE FUTURE

HENDERSON ALSO CITES a Texas petroleum geologist who, speaking in 1978, noted that the price of natural gas had risen tenfold over the previous six years but concluded that not a lot more would be produced because the "laws of physics and geological occurrence transcend the laws of men."[16] While it is true that production of natural gas in Texas since 1978 has declined 1 percent, production elsewhere has grown so that total production—matching consumption—has increased by 16 percent, according to the EIA.

> With natural gas production and consumption now greater than they were in the mid-1970s, natural gas is expected to be an abundant fuel source for many decades to come.

For the record, with natural gas production and consumption now greater than they were in the mid-1970s, natural gas is expected to be an abundant fuel source for many decades to come. Gas production in the United States was about the same in 2000 (19.22 trillion cubic feet [Tcf]) as it was in 1975. However, a great deal more natural gas is being produced in Canada, which is linked by pipeline to the United States, making the two nations essentially one production zone. Imports, mostly from Canada, have increasingly helped supply the consumption in the United States, a gas demand that rose 16 percent between 1975 and 2000 to a volume of 22.7 Tcf.[17]

However, as the earlier quotation from Lovins shows, a belief in the abundance of natural gas was not always widely held. Both an unfortunate Supreme Court decision in 1954 and misguided legislation in 1978 were based on the premise that natural gas was a rapidly depleting resource. The High Court's decision extended the 1938 Natural Gas Act's provisions to production of natural gas sold in interstate markets, filling what was perceived to be a gap in the regulation of the transmission and distribution of natural gas. The result was the imposition of federal price controls on natural gas, which discouraged production and led to the natural gas "shortages" of the 1970s. Once price controls were lifted, production surged and estimated resources of gas continue to grow.

Thirty years after the "energy crisis" of the 1970s, it is now apparent that the United States—and the world, too—is awash in energy resources. This specifically includes an abundance of natural gas.

Data from the U.S. Geological Survey (USGS), for example, show that yet-to-be produced resources of natural gas in the United States amounted to 923 Tcf in 1975, a volume that grew to 1,412 Tcf, an increase of 53 percent, as of January 1, 1994 (January 1, 1995, for the federal offshore assessment).[18] The USGS has begun an update of that mid-1990s assessment with work begun in FY2000 and expected to continue to FY2004.[19]

According to a report of recent resource assessments by the Potential Gas Committee (PGC), an industry group supported by the Potential Gas Agency (PGA) at the Colorado School of Mines, North American natural gas resources are "growing with time." Not physically, of course, but "through improvements in technology and our knowledge," according to John B. Curtis, director of the PGA.

"The total estimated natural gas resource for the United States, as of December 31, 2000, was 1,258 trillion cubic feet," according to the report of the PGC assessment. "That's up 4.5 percent over the previous estimate of 1,204 Tcf, made two years ago, even though 38 Tcf of gas was produced and consumed during that time."[20]

And new natural gas reserves are being discovered each year. In decades past, natural gas was considered a by-product, often unwanted, of oil production. That has changed and, with it, there has been a change in philosophy about exploring for natural gas. Geologists now look for natural gas where they think the gas should be, not (as they did in the past) where they thought the oil would be.

"We usually find gas in new places with old ideas. Sometimes, also, we find gas in an old place with a new idea, but we seldom find much gas in an old place with an old idea," says PGA director Curtis, paraphrasing geologist Parke A. Dickey. "Several times in the past we have thought that we were running out of gas, whereas actually we were only running out of ideas."[21]

So, What About Renewable Energy?

Regardless of what ideological environmentalists, government agencies, or even some members of the energy industry said decades ago about energy resources, the indisputable fact today is that the United States and the world have enough to supply human needs for many more generations.

> Regardless of what ideological environmentalists, government agencies, or even some members of the energy industry said decades ago about energy resources, the indisputable fact today is that the United States and the world have enough to supply human needs for many more generations.

That said, there remain obstacles to providing energy reliably at a reasonable cost, to supplying it more evenly throughout the world, and to minimizing adverse environmental effects.

It also is an indisputable fact that fossil fuels—coal, oil, and cleaner-burning natural gas—currently supply the overwhelming volume of energy and will continue to do so for decades to come. What about recent predictions that oil production is about to peak? Professor Deffeyes bases his analysis on the work of geologist M. King Hubbert, who correctly predicted the peak of U.S. oil production in 1970. Of course, even if it turns out that a global oil production peak is reached in the next few years, that hardly means that production ends. In the United States, oil production in 2000 was 81 percent of what it was in the peak year of 1970.

Worldwide, between 1990 and 1999, fossil energy continued to supply more than 85 percent of the world production of primary energy. While petroleum production grew 10 percent over that time and gas production (the second largest source of primary energy, after oil) grew 15 percent, coal production declined 12 percent. During that time, hydroelectric power grew 20 percent and power generation from renewables like geothermal, solar, wind, and wood and waste grew by 76 percent.

But growth rates can be deceiving. In 1999, market shares for primary energy production worldwide were as follows: petroleum, 39 percent; natural gas, 23 percent; coal, 22 percent; hydro, 7 percent; nuclear, 6.6 percent; and the renewables, 0.7 percent.[22] (See Figure 9.1.) Some activists argue that the United States uses an inordinate amount of fossil fuels, but, notably, the United States led the world in the use of non hydro renewables for power generation in 1999, producing 83 billion kilowatt-hours. Japan, ranked second, produced only 30 percent of that total.[23]

In the United States, the EIA, in its *Annual Energy Outlook 2002* (AEO2002) reference case, shows that renewable energy of all types,

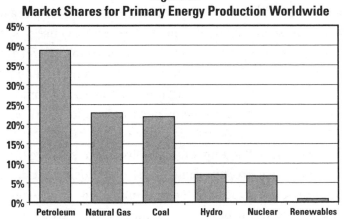

Figure 9.1
Market Shares for Primary Energy Production Worldwide

Source: Energy Information Administration, *International Energy Annual 1999: World Energy Overview.*
http://www.eia.doe.gov/emeu/iea/overview.html

including hydropower, accounted for 6.5 percent of total energy consumption in 2000.[24] That category is expected to grow only to 6.8 percent of the total by 2020. This is true despite the expectation that renewables will grow an average of 1.6 percent a year over the two-decade span, second only to the expected 2 percent growth in the use of natural gas.

But even ideological environmentalists, those who favor solar and wind power, admit that the bulk of the renewable energy contribution comes from hydropower, an energy source that most of them dislike almost as much as coal and nuclear power. EIA statistics show that in 2000, hydropower supplied 85 percent of the renewables contribution to electricity generation; even with growth in solar and wind power by 2020, hydropower is expected to provide 74 percent of the renewables contribution.[25]

Worldwide, according to the International Energy Agency (IEA), renewables are expected to play a slightly larger role.

In an article titled "Benign Energy?" the IEA noted, "Until the 1970s, renewable energy was widely considered to be a minor and declining energy source. Since then, the importance of renewables for electricity generation (including biomass, geothermal, hydro, photovoltaics, solar thermal electric and wind) has increased so that they now provide nearly 20 percent of the world's total primary energy requirement in this sector."[26] The great bulk is hydropower.

"Despite . . . significant environmental benefits," the IEA added, "renewables are not without some environmental disadvantages. In recent years, the increased deployment of renewable energy schemes has resulted in growing awareness of all their impacts and this has proved to be an obstacle to their deployment." The IEA concluded that if renewables are to fulfill their "potential as part of an integrated energy system, then these problems need to be addressed."[27] These impacts range from odors associated with the burning of animal wastes to significant flooding of lands for large-scale hydropower projects. Geothermal projects can emit carbon dioxide and hydrogen sulfide and can cause groundwater contamination. And wind power can involve noise, visual intrusion, significant land use, bird strikes (especially for migratory species), and interference with electromagnetic communications.

One recent analysis concluded that a global solar-energy system would consume at least 20 percent of the world's known iron reserves and would cover at least 500,000 square miles of land, an area more than three times the size of California. In addition, the analysis pointed out that a wind farm equivalent in output and capacity to a 1,000-megawatt fossil fuel or nuclear power plant would occupy 2,000 square miles of land and would produce electricity at double or triple the cost of fossil fuels.[28] One thousand megawatts is enough energy to supply the needs of only about 100,000 homes. Incidentally, 100,000 homes built on half-acre lots would occupy just over 78 square miles of land.

> One recent analysis concluded that a global solar-energy system would consume at least 20 percent of the world's known iron reserves and would cover at least 500,000 square miles of land, an area more than three times the size of California.

In early 2001, the Bush administration released its national energy plan. Noted energy analyst Glenn R. Schleede, who heads up Energy Market & Policy Analysis Inc., recently issued a critique of the plan, entitled "It's Time for a National Energy Policy Reality Check." Schleede is a former official with the White House's Office of Management and Budget and a senior energy industry executive, working with the New England Electric System.

Before the Bush administration's national energy plan was released, Schleede noted that President Bush and Vice President Cheney were "criticized for not relying more on renewable energy. The administration responded by proposing various subsidies, including tax credits, to encourage investments in various renewable energy sources. Most were identical to those advanced by the Clinton-Gore administration and already introduced in various bills by members of Congress."[29]

Two key points in Schleede's analysis:[30] First, energy conservation and energy efficiency cannot be expected to replace the need for new energy supplies, although they can slow the rate of growth in energy requirements, depending on which technologies are chosen and how they are promoted. Mandated appliance energy efficiency standards and much of the taxpayer-funded research and development designed to pick winners better chosen by the competitive economy deserve little credit for the substantial progress made in reducing energy intensity in the U.S. economy. Why? Because most gains in U.S. energy efficiency have been due to three key factors:

1. Relatively high prices, especially during the 1970s and early 1980s, led many individuals and businesses to focus on their energy costs and find ways to reduce those costs in ways that made sense for them, such as reducing energy losses, changing equipment and processes to reduce energy requirements, and reducing energy-intensive activities.

2. Improved energy efficiency has occurred as an unplanned by-product of the adoption of new technologies such as computerization and telecommunications and the use of lighter-weight materials. New technologies have permitted increased productivity and required less energy than the equipment and activities they replaced.

3. The makeup of the U.S. economy has changed significantly, resulting in a higher proportion of less energy-intensive manufacturing and services.

> For the foreseeable future, hydropower remains the only significant source of economical renewable energy.

Clearly, these are not the kinds of improvements that stem from energy regulation or from most federal R&D aimed at developing products for use in the private economy.

A second key point from Schleede is that renewable energy sources will remain niche technologies that will do little to relieve the necessity for the nation to continue relying on traditional energy sources—coal, oil, natural gas, and nuclear energy—for virtually all its energy requirement.

For the foreseeable future, hydropower remains the only significant source of economical renewable energy. But renewable-energy advocates do not like hydropower, favoring only non-hydro renewables. However, non-hydro renewables will provide little usable energy. These sources—wind, solar, geothermal, biomass (including wood and wood wastes), and municipal solid wastes—are essentially niche resources and niche technologies "that are not likely to *ever* make a significant contribution towards supplying U.S. energy requirements."[31]

The reasons why non-hydro renewables will fail to make large-volume contributions to the nation's energy supply are as follows:

- They are more costly than traditional sources except in niche applications, such as solar-powered calculators and highway signs, and where building electric distribution lines in remote areas is prohibitively expensive.
- There is little evidence that technological improvements will bring costs down to competitive levels.
- Most facilities that use non-hydro renewables do so not for economic reasons but because of subsidies or government mandates or in an attempt to achieve good public relations. These uneconomic promptings include investment tax credits, accelerated depreciation, production tax credits (1.7 cents per kilowatt-hour from the federal government), state tax breaks, mandates such as "renewable portfolio standards" in several states, and decisions by corporate executives to "look green" or to appease advocacy groups in an attempt to ease rate cases and environmental permit proceedings.

All of these actions, concludes Schleede, have the effect of shifting costs from renewables developers to taxpayers.

Schleede notes that in the past 20 years, the U.S. Department of Energy (DOE) has spent "hundreds of millions in tax dollars on renewable energy R&D" and "millions more have been allowed in tax credits." Despite this federal largesse, non-hydro renewables are making only a small contribution to overall energy requirements and to electric generation. According to EIA statistics, non-hydro renewables in 2000 supplied only 3.7 percent of total U.S. energy consumption, a figure that is expected to rise to 4.6 percent by 2020. Of these volumes, the contributions of solar and wind systems contributed only 0.1 percentage point in 2000, with an expected contribution of 0.25 percent in 2020.

The contribution of non-hydro renewables to electricity generation is even less. According to a recent policy analysis by the Cato Institute, the current contribution of solar, wind, geothermal, and biomass is about 2 percent, a figure that rises to only 2.8 percent by 2020.[32]

Cato analysts Jerry Taylor and Peter VanDoren, citing government and industry statistics, note that "no renewable energy source was competitive with combined-cycle natural gas turbine technology, the primary source of new electric power capacity, which produces electricity at about 3 cents per kilowatt-hour."[33] Like Schleede, Taylor and VanDoren point to the poor economics of renewables, and they include capital costs as well as production costs. Of several electricity-generating technologies, the Cato authors cite capital costs per installed kilowatt-hour as follows:

- Gas/oil combined cycle, $445
- Advanced gas/oil combined cycle, $576
- Wind, $983
- Coal, $1,092
- Coal gasification cycle, $1,306
- Waste and landfill gas combustion, $1,395
- Geothermal, $1,708
- Biomass, $1,732
- Fuel cells, $2,041
- Advanced nuclear, $2,188
- Solar thermal, $2,946
- Solar photovoltaic, $4,252

"Without policy privileges, the renewable energy industry (at least the portion that generates electricity for the power grid) would cease to exist,"[34] conclude Taylor and VanDoren.

It appears that natural gas will be an increasingly important energy source in the future. In fact, one recent analysis declared, "EIA has forecast that natural gas consumption will reach 30 Tcf by 2012, with the largest increases accounted for by electric generation."[35]

A study released in January 2002 by the INGAA Foundation, a research arm of the Interstate Natural Gas Association of America, projects growth in natural gas consumption of more than 34 percent from 2000 to 2015, starting at 23.3 Tcf in 2000 and rising to 29.6 Tcf in 2010 and to 32.3 Tcf in 2015. The largest growth sector is for gas use in power generation, which rises 106 percent over the 15-year period. That's five times greater than the growth in the next-largest specified sector (consumption for industrial use).[36]

Natural gas offers substantial environmental benefits when compared to burning coal, the largest energy source for power generation at present. For example, gas use results in virtually no sulfur dioxide emissions, and in new generating units, emissions of nitrogen oxides are roughly one-third of those from a coal-fired unit. Emissions of carbon dioxide from natural gas are 55 percent to 60 percent lower than from coal.[37]

Among ideological environmentalists, wind power is often cited as a benign and increasingly inexpensive source of renewable power. However, as Schleede points out, wind power is both costly and unreliable.

" . . . windmills are huge structures, high cost, produce very little electricity, destroy scenery and damage neighbors' property values."

Responding to an August 16, 2001, *USA Today* article, "Green Power Gets Second Wind," Schleede warned that the article had unfortunately contributed "to the false impression in the public, media and Congress that windmills actually might be a realistic way to supply electricity when, in fact, *windmills are huge structures, high cost, produce very little electricity, destroy scenery and damage neighbors' property values*" (emphasis in original).[38]

Schleede added, "False claims about wind energy are leading members of Congress to extend unwise wind energy subsidies." He further noted that "[o]ne gas-fired electric generating plant in northern Oregon (Hermiston) produced six times more electricity in 2000 than can be expected from the entire 396-turbine 261-megawatt Stateline (Oregon-Washington) Wind Farm described in [the *USA Today*] story."[39] He also pointed out that "[m]any windmills built in California in the 1980s are already being abandoned, are falling down, and are becoming a part of California's 'windmill junkyards.'"[40]

In fact, the new electric generating plant inaugurated in July 2001 by Governor Gray Davis of California produces more electricity each year than *all* of California's 13,000-plus windmills produced during 1999. This fact illustrates dramatically the small amount of electricity produced by large windmills and the small role that wind energy can play in supplying U.S. electricity requirements. Rated at 555 megawatts, the new gas-fired plant, operating at 72 percent of capacity, would produce 3.5 billion kilowatt-hours (kWh) of electricity, slightly more than the 3.4 billion kWh produced in 1999 by all of the California windmills.[41]

Nevertheless, ideological environmentalists continue to promote large expenditures for renewable energy projects that will have a small payoff in energy production. California is a state that did everything it could to foster alternative fuels and stop the building of major power plants. It paid the price and is now blaming deregulation and a whole host of power companies for its largely self-inflicted problems.

Despite the failure of renewables in the past, might they contribute more in the future?

"The failure of renewables to emerge more prominently in the nation's energy portfolio," noted Joel Darmstadter, an analyst with Resources for the Future, in a September 2000 report, "is intimately linked to the concurrent decline in the cost of conventional generation. Consider that in 1984, the [EIA] projected nationwide electric generation costs to rise from 6.1 cents/kWh to 6.4 cents/kWh in 1995; in fact, they declined to 3.6 cents/kWh. That 41 percent decline, though less percentagewise than what was achieved by wind power, nonetheless preserved a sufficiently large margin of advantage—3.6 cents/kWh vs. 5.2 cents/kWh—for conventional over wind power as to foreclose more than a minute niche for the latter."[42]

Darmstadter attributed the decreased costs for conventional generation technologies to more competitive energy supply markets; the successful deregulation of natural gas, oil pipelines, and railroads (the last a major factor in reducing coal-shipping costs); technological progress in generation, such as the introduction of combined-cycle gas turbine systems; and the continuing restructuring of the electricity industry.

Despite significant sums spent on renewable technologies, Darmstadter concluded that "progress on the part of more traditional energy systems is sure to parallel further development of renewables, and there is no reason to expect that dynamic state of affairs to flag in the future."[43] In other words, conventional energy production is likely to remain cheaper and more efficient than renewable energy production for the foreseeable future.

BENIGN ENVIRONMENTALISTS?

WITH REGARD TO the hype about renewables purveyed by environmentalist ideologues, Michael Economides and Ronald Oligney offer this arresting vignette in their 2000 book *The Color of Oil:*

The World Wildlife Fund produces television commercials, the themes of which "go something like this: A beautiful landscape is shown . . . then the camera zooms in on a subject, in one case, a female rhinoceros and her baby." The story continues:

In the foreground, a hunter appears, kneeling and taking aim with his rifle. The picture freezes. Then it takes the shape of a jigsaw puzzle, and the hand of a little girl appears, removes the piece with the hunter, and replaces it with another piece—minus the hunter and his rifle.

The voice-over implores us to give the little girl a better Earth to live on. Fair enough.

Yet, the sequence of a similar TV spot is very troublesome: Again, a big landscape is shown. This time, the camera zooms in on a power plant, unidentified, but either nuclear or fossil fuel. The picture again freezes and breaks into jigsaw puzzle pieces. The little girl removes the piece with the power plant and replaces it with one showing three windmills.

Again, the voice-over implores for a better world.

Lost completely is the fact that a typical 2,000-megawatt power plant would need to be replaced by 20,000 windmills of the typical 100-kilowatt capacity, not three. For this imagery to have any semblance of accuracy, the entire landscape (before the camera zooms in on the power plant) would need to be covered with windmills.[44]

Economides and Oligney draw a sharp distinction between ideological environmentalism and proper stewardship of land, water, and air.

"Environmentalism, couched in difficult-to-combat superficial imagery, has taken a sinister turn," according to Economides and Oligney. "Now highly politicized, it has a gross disregard for the impact that the energy industry has on the world economy. Using moralistic, yet blatantly dishonest slogans and pseudo-science, the environmental movement has digressed dangerously and has replaced some of the most radical movements for social experimentation of the century. One of the most fundamental truths rarely surfaces from the movement: There is no credible alternative to hydrocarbons in either the near or distant foreseeable future.

"Modern-day environmentalism—the New Green that stands so tall among the elitist community, multibillionaires and movie stars in the industrialized world—must be distinguished from environmentalism of the stewardship variety, to which we subscribe."[45] They conclude, "Latent political or ideological motives, cloaked in pseudo-science, are perhaps the ultimate form of dishonesty."[46]

FUEL CELL SOLUTIONS?

PREDICTING WHAT HUMANITY'S energy needs will be in a hundred years would be like expecting even very smart people to have predicted in 1900 what we would be using in 2000. The best scientific panel available in 1900 would simply not have been able to plan for hundreds of millions of automobiles and trucks, ubiquitous electric lighting in tens of millions of houses and office buildings, fuel for thousands of jet planes, and tens of millions of refrigerators, air-conditioners, computers, telephones, radios, televisions, and the like. Virtually none of the devices on this nearly endless list had even been invented by 1900. Given the increasing rate of technological innovation, we undoubtedly have even less chance of foreseeing the future than people in 1900.

However, there are promising technologies that can help reduce the environmental impact of fuels that are abundant, have existing infrastructures, and are comparatively inexpensive. One of these is the greater use of fuel cells.

Fuel cells have been around for a while; they have been used in spaceships for years. Now newer types are based on new technologies and offer new applications for both stationary and mobile applications.

Predicting what humanity's energy needs will be in a hundred years would be like expecting even very smart people to have predicted in 1900 what we would be using in 2000.

A fuel cell involves no combustion. Therefore, there are no emissions related to burning. It uses a chemical process involving super-clean hydrogen to produce electrical energy. Various technologies and sizes of fuel cells are used to provide backup or supplemental power for hospitals in urban centers or for vehicles.

One thing is clear, however, although the fact frequently gets lost in the hype: A fuel cell is not now a renewable energy source. The hydrogen has to come from some source, and that source often is natural gas, propane, or even gasoline.

Energy analysts Robert L. Bradley Jr. and Richard W. Fulmer note, "Fuel cells are very efficient and very clean—their only 'effluent' is pure water. They have few moving parts and are therefore quiet, reliable and maintenance-free. Their chief drawback is their high cost—about $4,500 per kilowatt of capacity as compared to $800 to $1,500 per kilowatt for a diesel generator."[47]

In the current state of fuel cell technology, it makes more sense to compare fuel cells with diesel turbines because fuel cells are competing against diesel generators in today's market. For example, companies

looking for backup power for their computer equipment find both to
be practical alternatives. On the other hand, fuel cells are not yet a
practical alternative power source for automobiles.

While hydrogen use is clean, a cradle-to-grave analysis of the fuel
must also consider how hydrogen is obtained. Bradley and Fulmer
note, "From an environmental standpoint, hydrogen is nearly an ideal
fuel since its only products of combustion are water and a little ni-
trous oxide. Unfortunately, hydrogen is very reactive and does not
exist in a pure state on earth. Hydrogen is usually produced by water
electrolysis (a process that consumes a lot of electricity), although it
can also be extracted from hydrocarbons, including coal." According
to the American Petroleum Institute, "Unless the electricity that produces the hydrogen is generated by the sun, a hydroelectric facility or
a nuclear energy plant, its creation would produce at least some emissions, including greater carbon dioxide emissions than reformulated
gasoline."[48]

Of course, environmentalists favor the nonfossil-fuel approach to
producing hydrogen, but even the environmentally orthodox Worldwatch Institute, at least, understands the huge step needed to get
there. Worldwatch researcher Seth Dunn argues, "As the shift towards hydrogen accelerates, one of the most important outstanding
issues is how to pick the quickest, least-expensive path from today's
fossil fuel-based economy. Today, about 99 percent of the world's hydrogen is extracted from fossil fuels, most of this by treating natural
gas with steam. In the long run, hydrogen will be derived from renewable energy through electrolysis—using electricity from the sun,
wind and other sources to split water into hydrogen and oxygen—
thereby eliminating the use of fossil fuels altogether."[49]

According to the Worldwatch report, "Dunn's research suggests
that, in many instances, the best route to a renewable energy-based
hydrogen economy would be to pipe natural gas to fuel stations, and
turn the gas into hydrogen at the station for use in fuel cell vehicles.
This infrastructure could then be converted to handle hydrogen produced from renewable energy. But despite the apparent advantages of
this natural gas-to-renewable hydrogen route, industry and governments are currently devoting substantially more resources to extract-

ing the hydrogen from gasoline or methanol on board the vehicles—a path that will cause the transition to hydrogen to be more incremental, more polluting and ultimately more expensive."[50]

On the other hand, of course, the infrastructure already exists to deliver liquid fuels to stations everywhere, and drivers are accustomed to the quickness of transferring liquid fuel to their vehicles. In years past, there was a movement to get people to drive compressed natural gas vehicles, which require a gas-based infrastructure and longer fueling times for vehicles. Except for a few central-station-fueled commercial vehicles (e.g., Postal Service and other delivery services), the movement failed.

Although fuel cells use a chemical reaction that can be twice as efficient as burning a fuel,[51] Bradley and Fulmer also note, "[H]ydrogen contains only about one-sixth the energy of an equal volume of gasoline. Hydrogen-powered cars, therefore, require very large tanks and frequent refills. Also, as with other alternative fuels, there is, as yet, no distribution network for hydrogen, so refilling the tank would be a problem."[52]

In January 2002, the U.S. Department of Energy terminated a partnership with automakers, begun in 1993, to triple automobile fuel efficiency, and replaced it with a fuel-cell program. The new program, Freedom CAR (CAR stands for Cooperative Automotive Research), is aimed "at developing a fuel-cell operating system for tomorrow's cars and trucks," according to Energy Secretary Spencer Abraham. Abraham added that Freedom CAR "has a long, but realistic time horizon. Our vision spans several decades as together the [DOE] and the automobile industry look to develop cost-effective hydrogen fuel cells."[53]

Of course, this new program has the political advantage of having a goal several decades in the future, thus allowing President Bush and Secretary Abraham to be long gone before the accounting time is due.

CONCLUSION

IDEOLOGICAL ENVIRONMENTALISTS claimed nearly three decades ago that renewable energy sources would supply the nation with a significant part of its energy needs.

They were wrong.

Today they're saying the same thing—and they're still wrong.

Is renewable energy, especially solar and wind power, useful?

Yes, of course it is. There are numerous applications (such as using solar panels to supply electricity to remote locations) where renewables are better suited than conventional energy sources. To say otherwise is like saying a candle is useless because a lighthouse is brighter.

But renewable energy sources, especially non-hydropower sources, remain niche technologies. Important, yes, but not on the scale of energy sources such as natural gas, coal, and oil. This is true in America. It is true worldwide.

In the near term—the next several decades—humanity will remain heavily dependent on fossil fuels as its chief source of energy. Renewables, especially non-hydro renewables, simply are too costly, inefficient, and unreliable to depend on as the mainstays of developed, growing economies, much less for use by underdeveloped countries.

Ultimately, what the future of energy will be is unknowable. However, this much is certain: It is a process, not a fixed goal.

It is limited only by the ingenuity of humans.

CHAPTER TEN

THE PRECAUTIONARY PRINCIPLE'S CHALLENGE TO PROGRESS

Jonathan H. Adler

ECO-MYTHS DEBUNKED

- *Environmental policy increasingly incorporates the "precautionary principle," which calls upon governments to impose regulatory measures based upon the barest potential of environmental harm.*
- *The precautionary principle holds that "[w]hen an activity raises threats of harm to human health or environment, precautionary measures should be taken even if some cause and effect relationships are not fully established scientifically."*
- *A corollary to the precautionary principle is that the proponent of an activity or new technology should bear the burden of proof to demonstrate that it is without risk.*
- *Applied in even a mild formulation, the precautionary principle will create "bottlenecks" in the development and distribution of new technologies.*
- *Some proponents of the precautionary principle call for moratoria on the development and use of biotechnology and the phaseout of chlorinated chemical compounds.*
- *The precautionary principle was adopted in the Maastricht Treaty of the European Union, referenced in numerous international environmental treaties, and incorporated into the operative provisions of the Cartagena Protocol on Biosafety.*
- *Adopting the precautionary principle can increase risks to human health and environmental protection by focusing on the risks posed by the introduction of new technologies while ignoring the risks that new technologies can alleviate or prevent.*
- *Advocates of the precautionary principle tend to assume that economic growth and development are themselves a threat to public health and environmental protection, yet the rise of industrial society has coincided with a massive explosion of wealth and health that is unprecedented in the history of human civilization.*
- *To enhance public health and environmental protection, the precautionary principle should not be adopted. Rather, the risks of new chemicals or products must be weighed against the risks that they ameliorate or prevent.*

I DEOLOGICAL ENVIRONMENTALISM INCREASINGLY seeks to incorporate the precautionary principle into national and international environmental regulatory schemes. The principle calls upon governments to impose regulatory measures based upon the barest potential of environmental harm. If a chemical substance *might* be causing harm, it should be controlled or eliminated. If a new technological innovation *could* have unknown environmental effects, it should not be permitted. The precautionary principle may appeal to common-sense notions of safety, but its application will not produce a safer, cleaner world. Quite the opposite. The incorporation of the precautionary principle in environmental, health, and safety regulation is itself a threat to environmental protection and optimal safeguards for public health. Ideological environmentalists are campaigning worldwide to get the precautionary principle widely adopted.

- At the 1999 meeting of the World Trade Organization (WTO) in Seattle, Washington, environmental activists protest alongside union organizers, anticapitalist agitators, anarchists, and other opponents of globalization. Among other things, the protesters demand global trade rules to permit the imposition of environmental trade barriers even in the absence of scientific support. Inside the official WTO sessions, representatives from several countries and various nongovernmental organizations (NGOs) echo the call to allow for precautionary environmental measures to restrict trade.
- In Great Britain, members of Greenpeace trespass on a field to destroy a crop of genetically engineered maize undergoing field trials. The activists claim their action was necessary to prevent potential "contamination" of the countryside by pollen from the maize crop. Despite a lack of evidence that such contamination is possible, Greenpeace argues direct precautionary measures are justified until the British government adopts a complete moratorium on the testing and introduction of genetically engineered crops. In response to such environmental concerns, some European nations prohibit the importation of

genetically engineered crops despite the lack of a scientific basis
for doing so.[1]

• Children's health activists in the United States and Europe
launch a campaign against phthalates, a class of plastic soften-
ers commonly used in toys and medical supplies, for their potential to cause cancer or other health problems. Numerous
studies fail to find such effects from products containing phthalates, and scientific bodies in the United States and Europe
reject the activists' claims. Nonetheless, the European Union
acts to ban phthalates in products used by children, and the
U.S. Consumer Product Safety Commission recommends that
American manufacturers withdraw such products until further
studies are conducted.[2]

THE PRINCIPLE DEFINED

THE PRECAUTIONARY PRINCIPLE appeals to the common-sense idea
that it is better to be safe than sorry. At its core, the precautionary
principle embodies "the belief that society should seek to avoid environmental damage by careful forward planning, blocking the flow of
potentially harmful activities."[3] Simple safety measures, such as
wearing a seat belt or motorcycle helmet, can greatly reduce the risk
of substantial harm at relatively modest cost. In many instances, preventing harm can be easier and less costly than repairing damage after
the fact. While the precautionary principle appeals to conventional
notions of "safety" and "taking care," it calls for more drastic measures than the adoption of cost-effective safety measures. Rather, it
calls for a presumption that government action is required to address
every potential risk. The principle is premised on the idea that all
technologies and chemical substances are dangerous until proven safe.
Drastic changes in regulatory policy are therefore required. In the
words of its proponents, "new principles for conducting human affairs are necessary" as it is time to "adopt a precautionary approach to
all human endeavors."[4]

A conventional formulation of the precautionary principle is outlined in the Wingspread Consensus Statement, a document drafted

by several dozen ideological environmentalists in January 1998.[5] (See Box 10.1.) Under the Wingspread formulation, "When an activity raises threats of harm to human health or environment, precautionary measures should be taken even if some cause and effect relationships are not fully established scientifically."[6] As applied in the environmental context, this means that it is better to err on the side of regulating or controlling new technologies than to risk new or unforeseen problems; "decision makers should act in advance of scientific certainty to protect the environment (and with it, the well-being of future generations) from incurring harm."[7] In this sense, the precautionary principle establishes a default rule for regulating new innovations, irrespective of the relative risk that they actually pose to human health or the environment. At its extreme, the principle calls for the elimination of substances that are not proven safe: "[T]he precautionary principle calls for the prohibition of the release of substances which might cause harm to the environment *even if insufficient or inadequate proof exists regarding the causal link.*"[8]

> The principle is premised on the idea that all technologies and chemical substances are dangerous until proven safe.

On the one hand, this aspect of the precautionary principle does not call for much. Scientific certainty is rare, and few environmental regulations would exist if absolute scientific certainty were required before their imposition. Rather, policy makers traditionally consider the weight of the evidence for or against a given causal relationship, and the costs involved with implementing a particular policy. In some cases, such as the link between cigarettes and lung cancer, the causal connection is easy to identify. In other cases, such as a postulated connection between water chlorination and the incidence of bladder cancer, the connection is more suspect, and the costs of reducing the risk are substantial. Most environmental laws nonetheless authorize regulation of potentially dangerous substances or activities with less-than-absolute proof or quantification of environmental risk.

On the other hand, by emphasizing the need to act in the face of scientific uncertainty, before there is clear scientific evidence of harm,

BOX 10.1 WINGSPREAD STATEMENT ON THE PRECAUTIONARY PRINCIPLE

The release and use of toxic substances, the exploitation of resources, and physical alterations of the environment have had substantial unintended consequences affecting human health and the environment. Some of these concerns are high rates of learning deficiencies, asthma, cancer, birth defects and species extinctions; along with global climate change, stratospheric ozone depletion and worldwide contamination with toxic substances and nuclear materials.

We believe existing environmental regulations and other decisions, particularly those based on risk assessment, have failed to protect adequately human health and the environment—the larger system of which humans are but a part.

We believe there is compelling evidence that damage to humans and the worldwide environment is of such magnitude and seriousness that new principles for conducting human activities are necessary.

While we realize that human activities may involve hazards, people must proceed more carefully than has been the case in recent history. Corporations, government entities, organizations, communities, scientists, and other individuals must adopt a precautionary approach to all human endeavors.

Therefore, it is necessary to implement the Precautionary Principle: When an activity raises threats of harm to human health or the environment, precautionary measures should be taken even if some cause and effect relationships are not fully established scientifically.

In this context the proponent of an activity, rather than the public, should bear the burden of proof.

The process of applying the Precautionary Principle must be open, informed, and democratic and must include potentially affected parties. It must also involve an examination of the full range of alternatives, including no action.[9]

the precautionary principle lowers the threshold for what is considered reliable evidence of a potential effect. "Better safe than sorry" can be used to call for regulatory measures when there is little, if any, evidence of an actual health or environmental impact. After all, it is impossible to disprove the existence of risk. As noted in chapter 7, there is no evidence that even a single individual has suffered a negative reaction from the consumption of genetically engineered food. Yet proponents of the precautionary principle call for moratoria on the development and marketing of such products because such risks are possible and have yet to be *un*proven.

A related corollary to the principle is a shift in the burden of proof for new technologies and inventions. Government agencies would not be required to demonstrate that a technology poses a likely risk. Rather, "the proponent of an activity, rather than the public, should bear the burden of proof" of demonstrating that it is risk-free.[10] Greenpeace's Jeremy Leggett explains: "[T]he modus operandi we would like to see is: 'Do not admit a substance unless you have proof that it will do no harm to the environment.'"[11] The World Charter for Nature incorporates this position, holding that "where potential adverse effects are not fully understood, the activities should not proceed."

Applied in even a mild formulation, the reverse onus idea will dramatically retard the development of new technologies. As precautionary principle advocate Joel Tickner acknowledges, the principle "establishes a type of 'speed bump,' which creates bottlenecks in the development process" to slow down the introduction of new technologies.[12] Applied in a more rigorous fashion, however, and the

> Proving that a new technology or product will cause no harm requires proving a negative, something that science cannot do.

reverse onus could stop the flow of new innovations altogether. "The truth of the matter is that whoever has the burden of proof loses," explains Boston University bioethicist George Annas.[13]

Application of the principle to existing technologies, such as various industrial chemicals, would require eliminating thousands of substances from economic use. Proving that a new technology or product will cause no harm requires proving a negative, something that science cannot do. "It is not possible to prove something is harmless, any more than it is possible to prove that there are no fairies at the bottom of one's garden," notes environmental analyst Julian Morris.[14] The scientific process can test the robustness of a given hypothesis—substance X will cause cancer in mice or substance Y disrupts amphibian reproduction—but it cannot prove that a given substance is risk-free. Substance X might not cause rodent tumors, but it could always cause something else. For this reason, scientists fear that the precautionary principle could "block the development of any technology if there is the slightest theoretical possibility of harm."[15] Indeed, "taken literally, the directive would be: 'Don't do anything.'"[16]

Another corollary to the precautionary principle that is equally problematic is that the consideration of a given technology or environmental decision must "involve an examination of the full range of alternatives, including no action."[17] Taken literally, this corollary calls for paralysis by analysis. It is simply impossible to consider the full range of alternatives. Some advocates of the precautionary principle suggest that this corollary would merely require a consideration of likely or possible alternatives as a part of the decision-making process, much like federal agencies in the United States must consider alternatives to proposed actions when undergoing Environmental Impact Statements under the National Environmental Policy Act. Thus, before a company could introduce a new pesticide, a regulatory agency would need to consider alternative means of controlling the target pest and whether the pest needs to be controlled at all. Even in this more mild form, the additional burden placed upon new technologies could be substantial, while doing little to improve public health or environmental protection. If existing alternatives were adequate, it is unlikely that a new product would be purchased in the marketplace.

THE ANTICHLORINE CRUSADE

MOST PROPONENTS OF the precautionary principle seek to regulate or eliminate specific technologies or chemical by-products. Groups such as Friends of the Earth and Environmental Defense appeal to the precautionary principle in calling for greater limits, if not complete moratoria, on the development and marketing of genetically engineered crops. The "Safe Trade" campaign organized by Greenpeace seeks to incorporate precautionary regulation into global trade rules under the WTO. The advocacy group Health Care Without Harm seeks to ban the use of phthalate plasticizers in medical supplies for fear they might have, as-yet-unproven, negative health impacts. The precautionary principle is also a driving force behind arguments for adoption of the Kyoto Protocol on climate change.

Perhaps the most ambitious manifestation of the precautionary principle in environmental policy is the effort to eliminate the use of chlorine compounds, from the manufacture of pesticides and solvents, to pharmaceuticals and water purification. The application of the precautionary principle to chlorine was initiated by Greenpeace but is supported by more mainstream environmental organizations as well, such as the National Wildlife Federation.[18] Ellen Silbergeld, a toxicologist with Environmental Defense, has argued that chlorine compounds should be presumed dangerous until proven safe.[19] The U.S.-Canada International Joint Commission (IJC), which oversees environmental protection of the Great Lakes, recommended that the United States and Canada "consult with industry and other interests to develop timetables to sunset the use of chlorine and chlorine-containing compounds as industrial feedstocks, and [examine] the means of reducing and eliminating other uses,"[20] and the Clinton administration proposed a national study to outline a chlorine phaseout in 1994.[21]

Several chlorine compounds, including polychlorinated biphenyls (PCBs), dioxins, and chlorofluorocarbons (CFCs), have been linked to public health or environmental problems. CFCs, for example, are largely responsible for depletion of stratospheric ozone. On this basis, Greenpeace and others call for applying the precautionary principle to *all* chlorine-based compounds, sunsetting existing uses and prohibiting new uses unless they can be proven to be perfectly safe. "The only rational, protective policy would be to phase out all chlorinated chemicals as a class. All of them," explains Peter Montague of the Environmental Research Foundation.[22] "What the world needs is a reduction in the total burden of chlorinated chemicals, not just a reduction in one or two or 10 specific compounds."[23] All chlorine compounds should be banned because chlorine is contained in some compounds—dioxin, PCBs, CFCs—believed to have negative health or environmental effects at sufficient doses. "We decided you can't distinguish among different compounds of chlorine as to which is harmful and which is not," said one member of the IJC, explaining the basis for a chlorine sunset.[24] "Phasing out chlorine is the only way to virtually eliminate dioxin, especially in industrial processes and products," counsel analysts with the Science and Environmental Health Network, sponsor of the Wingspread conference.[25]

No distinction is made between more or less harmful uses of chlorine, or what offsetting benefits some uses of chlorine provide. "There are no uses of chlorine that we regard as safe," declares Joe Thornton, a former analyst at Greenpeace and author of *Pandora's Poison: Chlorine, Health, and a New Environmental Strategy.*[26] According to Thornton:

> *We need to treat organochlorines as a class. There are 11,000 in commerce plus thousands more that are produced as by-products. It would be truly impractical to regulate them one-by-one. . . . It makes sense to treat organochlorines as guilty until proven innocent.*[27]

By this logic, it would make sense to ban oxygen and carbon because they are contained in compounds that contribute to smog. To many scientists, this idea is absurd. "It isn't taken seriously from a scientific point of view," Dr. Mario Molina told *Science* magazine.[28] Nobelist Molina was coauthor of the studies of stratospheric ozone that led to the phaseout of chlorofluorocarbons. Dr. Stephen Safe, a toxicologist at Texas A&M University, agrees: "The idea of banning chlorine is patently ridiculous and scientifically indefensible."[29]

The effort to phase out chlorine illustrates the potentially extreme consequences of adopting the precautionary principle in public policy. It is estimated that chlorine is used in the production of more than 80 percent of all pharmaceuticals.[30] It is also used to purify nearly all of the American drinking water supply. "None of the alternative disinfection processes that have been proposed to date are equally effective or economical," report experts at the Harvard Center for Risk Analysis.[31] Not purifying water can be disastrous. In 1991, failure to chlorinate drinking water supplies in Peru contributed to a massive outbreak of cholera that infected more than 300,000 people, killing several thousand.[32]

Chlorination may well present some risks. Some scientists believe that excess water chlorination could contribute to bladder and rectal cancer. The risk of untreated water, however, is clearly far greater.[33] Worldwide, more than 5 million deaths per year are attributable to unsafe drinking water or inadequate sanitation, according to the World Health Organization.[34] Diarrhea alone kills 2.2 million children per year—or one child every 15 seconds—a toll that could be reduced dramatically by greater use of water chlorination.[35] "Chlorination and disinfection of the water supplies are the public health success story of the century," argues Carol Henry of the International Life Sciences Institute. "To start altering this in some way has very grave and immediate consequences."[36] It is anything but a "safe" precaution against environmental risks.

> By this logic, it would make sense to ban oxygen and carbon because they are contained in compounds that contribute to smog.

Activists who apply the precautionary principle to chlorinated compounds nonetheless advocate a sunset on all chlorine use. This is not a policy that will maximize the protection of public health and environmental protections. Nor is it scientifically justified. A handful of chlorinated chemicals have been linked to environmental problems, while thousands of others are used for myriad productive purposes. Yet these concerns do not phase proponents, as it is an essential element of the precautionary principle that scientific evidence is not required for precautionary government action. According to Thornton, "Waiting to take preventative action until cause-effect linkages are proven between individual chemicals and large-scale health effects is no longer acceptable."[37]

PRINCIPLE SPREAD

MOST PROPONENTS OF the precautionary principle trace its origins to the German principle of "foresight" or "forecaution"—*Vorsorgeprinzip*.[38] In the 1970s, this principle became the basis for social democratic environmental policies in West Germany and eventually provided the impetus for aggressive environmental measures to address acid precipitation and other environmental concerns.[39] Germany was not unique in this regard, however, as other nations adopted precautionary measures in the post–World War II period as well. In the United States, for example, the so-called Delaney Clause prohibited food additives, at any level, that were linked to cancer in laboratory animals. Over time, this led to increasingly stringent regulation as scientists were able to detect ever smaller traces of pesticides or other chemicals in processed foods, until the clause was repealed in 1996.[40]

Despite its analog in the United States, the precautionary principle has had the most influence on European environmental policy. In the early 1980s, West Germany led efforts to incorporate precautionary measures into the Convention on Protection of the North Sea. At the Second North Sea Conference, ministers endorsed a "precautionary approach . . . which may require action to control inputs of such substances even before a causal link has been established by absolutely clear scientific evidence."[41]

The Second North Sea Ministerial Declaration was but the first of several European agreements that would explicitly endorse precautionary policies to one degree or another. In 1990, the Bergen Ministerial Declaration on Sustainable Development completely endorsed the precautionary principle, stating:

> *In order to achieve sustainable development, policies must be based on the precautionary principle. Environmental measures must anticipate, prevent, and attack the causes of environmental degradation. Where there are threats of serious or irreversible damage, lack of full scientific certainty should not be used as a reason for postponing measures to prevent environmental degradation.*[42]

Soon thereafter, the precautionary principle became official European policy. Article 130R(2) of the Maastricht Treaty, creating the

European Community, declares environmental policy of EC member nations is to be based upon "the precautionary principle and on principles that preventative actions should be taken."[43]

Since the signing of the Maastricht Treaty, the precautionary principle has been incorporated into various aspects of European policy. Some nations have cited the principle as justification for prohibiting the importation of genetically modified crops. The European Council of Ministers adopted a formal resolution in April 1999, calling upon the European Commission "to be in the future even more determined to be guided by the precautionary principle" in its legislative proposals. This led to the European Commission's *Communication from the Commission on the Precautionary Principle*, which declared that the EU would apply the precautionary principle "where preliminary objective scientific evaluation indicates that there are reasonable grounds for concern that the potentially dangerous effects on the environment, human, animal, or plant health may be inconsistent with the high level of protection chosen for the community."[44]

The precautionary principle as devised in Europe has now spread to international environmental agreements. The Rio Declaration, agreed to at the 1992 United Nations Earth Summit, declares that "[w]here there are threats of serious or irreversible damage, lack of full scientific certainty shall not be used as a reason for postponing cost-effective measures to prevent environmental degradation," and that "[i]n order to protect the environment, the precautionary approach shall be widely applied by States according to their capabilities."[45] The preamble to the Convention on Biological Diversity similarly declares that "where there is a threat of significant reduction or loss of biological diversity, lack of full scientific certainty should not be used as a reason for postponing measures to avoid or minimize such a threat."[46] Similar language is included in other environmental treaties and agreements as well, including the Vienna Convention for the Protection of the Ozone Layer and the United Nations Framework Convention on Climate Change (see Box 10.2).

While some U.S. policies could be characterized as precautionary in nature, the precautionary principle has not become an official part of U.S. environmental policy. Nonetheless, it has been endorsed by

BOX 10.2 PRECAUTIONARY PRINCIPLE LANGUAGE IN INTERNATIONAL AGREEMENTS

Ministerial Declaration Calling for Reduction of Pollution ("Second North Sea Declaration") (1987)

Accepting that in order to protect the North Sea from possibly damaging effects of the most dangerous substances, . . . a precautionary approach is addressed which may require action to control inputs of such substances even before a causal link has been established by absolutely clear scientific evidence. . . .

Final Declaration of the Third International Conference on Protection of the North Sea (1990)

The participants . . . will continue to apply the precautionary principle, that is to take action to avoid potentially damaging impacts of substances that are persistent, toxic and liable to bioaccumulate even where there is no scientific evidence to prove a causal link between emissions and effects. . . .

Bergen Ministerial Declaration on Sustainable Development in the ECE Region (1990)

In order to achieve sustainable development, policies must be based on the precautionary principle. Environmental measures must anticipate, prevent and attack the causes of environmental degradation. Where there are threats of serious or irreversible damage, lack of full scientific certainty should not be used as a reason for postponing measures to prevent environmental degradation.

Ministerial Declaration of the Second World Climate Conference (1990)

In order to achieve sustainable development in all countries and to meet the needs of present and future generations, precautionary measures to meet the climate challenge must anticipate, prevent, attack, or minimize the causes of, and mitigate the adverse consequences of, environmental degradation that might result from climate change. Where there are threats of serious or irreversible damage, lack of full scientific certainty should not be used as a reason for postponing cost-effective measures to prevent such environmental degradation. The measures adopted should take into account different socio-economic contexts.

The Rio Declaration on Environment and Development (1992)

In order to protect the environment, the precautionary approach shall be widely applied by States according to their capabilities. Where there are threats of serious or irreversible damage, lack of full scientific certainty shall not be used as a reason for postponing cost-effective measures to prevent environmental degradation.

Framework Convention on Climate Change (1992)

The Parties should take precautionary measures to anticipate, prevent or minimize the causes of climate change and mitigate its adverse effects. Where there are threats of serious or irreversible damage, lack of full scientific certainty should not be used as a reason for postponing such measures, taking into account that policies and measures to deal with climate change should be cost-effective so as to ensure global benefits at the lowest possible cost. To achieve this, such policies and measures should take into account different socio-economic contexts, be comprehensive, cover all relevant sources, sinks and reservoirs of greenhouse gases and adaptation, and comprise all economic sectors. Efforts to address climate change may be carried out cooperatively by interested Parties.

Convention on Biological Diversity (1992)

Where there is a threat of significant reduction or loss of biological diversity, lack of full scientific certainty should not be used as a reason for postponing measures to avoid or minimize such a threat.

Maastricht Treaty on the European Union ("Maastricht Treaty") (1994)

Community policy on the environment . . . shall be based on the precautionary principle and on the principles that preventive actions

(continues)

should be taken, that environmental damage should as a priority be rectified at source and that the polluter should pay.

Cartagena Protocol on Biosafety to the Convention on Biological Diversity (2000)

Reaffirming the precautionary approach contained in Principle 15 of the Rio Declaration on Environment and Development, . . .

Lack of scientific certainty due to insufficient relevant scientific information and knowledge regarding the extent of the potential adverse effects of a living modified organism on the conservation and sustainable use of biological diversity in the Party of import, taking also into account risks to human health, shall not prevent that Party from taking a decision, as appropriate, with regard to the import of that living modified organism intended for direct use as food or feed, or for processing, in order to avoid or minimize such potential adverse effects.

various levels of government. In 1996, the President's Council on Sustainable Development (PCSD) declared that "even in the face of scientific uncertainty, society should take reasonable actions to avert risks where potential harm to human health or the environment is thought to be serious or irreparable."[47] Similarly, as noted above, in 1992 the International Joint Commission (IJC) endorsed the precautionary principle as the basis for future environmental policy and called for the sunset of industrial chlorine use.[48]

At present, it is unclear the extent to which the administration of President George W. Bush will embrace the precautionary principle. Before her appointment as administrator of the Environmental Protection Agency, Christine Todd Whitman declared that "policymakers need to take a precautionary approach to environmental protection." Echoing the language of the Wingspread Statement, she explained that "uncertainty is inherent in managing natural resources, recognize it is usually easier to prevent environmental damage than to repair it later, and shift the burden of proof away from those advocating protection toward those proposing an action that may be harmful."[49] The administration also endorsed an international treaty calling for the reduction and eventual elimination of selected persistent organic pollutants (POPs), such as PCBs and furans, based upon precautionary concerns. On the other hand, the Bush administration thus far has rejected the Kyoto Protocol on climate change, despite arguments that it represents a precautionary approach to concerns about climate change.[50]

Speaking in January 2002, the Bush Administration's top regulatory policy official, John Graham, explained that "the US government supports precautionary approaches to risk management but we do not recognize any universal precautionary principle." The speech suggested that Graham may temper Administrator Whitman's precautionary impulses. While it is always possible to identify instances in which precautionary regulation could have averted serious harms, Graham noted that there are many instances in which postulated risks never materialized. In these cases, precautionary measures would have wasted scarce resources and done nothing to enhance public health. "Precaution is a necessary and useful concept but it is also subjective and susceptible to abuse," and therefore cannot be the focal point of regulatory policy. Graham concluded that "it may be wise to apply a precautionary approach to any attempt to recommend a universal precautionary principle."

THE CARTAGENA PROTOCOL

IN JANUARY 2000, negotiators from more than 150 nations agreed to a protocol to the United Nations Convention on Biological Diversity to regulate international transport and trade genetically engineered products. Like most contemporary environmental agreements, the so-called Cartagena Protocol on Biosafety (named for Cartagena, Colombia, where much of the negotiations took place) includes language endorsing the precautionary principle. The Biosafety Protocol, however, is the first global environmental agreement to incorporate the principle into its operative provisions.

The Biosafety Protocol creates an international framework for the regulation of bioengineered products "that may have adverse effects on the conservation and sustainable use of biodiversity, taking also into account risks to human health."[51] Specifically, the protocol creates mechanisms whereby national governments will be able to restrict, or even prohibit, the importation of genetically engineered crops. Like many environmental treaties, the preamble to the protocol "reaffirm[s] the precautionary approach" contained in the 1992 Rio Declaration.[52] The protocol goes further, however, by explicitly stating that "[l]ack of scientific certainty" about potential risks of biotech products "shall not prevent" a member nation from limiting, or even prohibiting, the importation of a given biotech product.[53] A country may even take into account "socio-economic considerations arising from the impact of living modified organisms" in deciding to block importation of a crop or foodstuff. Thus under the protocol, speculative risks to human health, the environment, or even national culture—such as traditional, and inefficient, farming practices—could provide a basis for obstructing trade.

By incorporating the precautionary principle into its operative provisions, the Biosafety Protocol marks a significant departure from traditional international trade rules. Under Article XX of the General Agreement on Tariffs and Trade, countries are authorized to enact measures "relating to the conservation of exhaustible natural resources" or "necessary to protect human, animal or plant life or health."[54] For a measure to pass muster under Article XX, it may not be a "disguised restriction on international trade" nor may it be "applied in a manner which would constitute a means of arbitrary or unjustifiable discrimination."[55] National environmental measures must be scientifically based and no more trade restrictive than necessary to meet their goals.[56] In practice, this meant that nations could regulate the importation of goods based on their actual characteristics, but not the manner in which they were produced. A nation could impose neutral food safety rules that apply to all relevant foods, domestic and imported alike, but could not prohibit importation of a food merely because it was produced using particular methods or technologies.

Nations have sought to erect trade barriers through the imposition of putative health or environmental measures. In 1989, for example, the European Union banned the importation of beef from cattle that were treated with bovine growth hormones. Injecting cattle with naturally occurring growth hormones increases cattle growth and milk production. Growth hormones are used for these purposes by many cattle producers in the United States. The EU defended the hormone ban as a precautionary step to protect European consumers from potential effects of eating beef from hormone-treated cattle. EU officials, however, were unable to point to scientific research supporting these concerns. There is no credible scientific evidence that the use of bovine growth hormones poses any threat to human health. For this reason, most observers saw the import restriction as a protectionist effort to exclude U.S. producers from the lucrative European beef and offal markets.[57] In 1997, a WTO dispute resolution panel sided with the United States, ruling that the import ban was a protectionist measure and not a neutral environmental regulation. The EU appealed, but to no avail, as the WTO panel again sided with the United States. Had the EU been able to rely on the precautionary principle, it might have prevailed.

The bovine growth hormone dispute is not an isolated instance. EU nations have also imposed limitations on the importation of genetically engineered crops, despite the lack of scientific evidence that such crops pose any risk to consumers or the environment. Under traditional GATT-WTO rules, it seems clear that such restrictions would be struck down as protectionist measures. Import restrictions lacking any scientific basis could not be defended as neutral protective measures. Under the Biosafety Protocol, however, such measures could potentially be upheld due to the protocol's explicit incorporation of the precautionary principle. Under the protocol, the lack of scientific evidence should not be an obstacle to the imposition of unscientific import restrictions.

MORE SORRY, LESS SAFE

IN THEORY, THE precautionary principle enhances protection of public health and environmental concerns by reducing the threats posed by new technologies and development. In practice, this is not

the case. By focusing on one set of risks—those posed by the introduction of new technologies with somewhat uncertain effects—the
precautionary principle turns a blind eye to the harms that occur, or
are made worse, due to the lack of technological development. Reflex-
ive efforts to regulate one risk can create other, often more dangerous
risks. "The truly fatal flaw of the precautionary principle, ignored by
almost all the commentators, is the unsupported presumption that an
action aimed at public health protection
cannot possibly have negative effects on
public health," observes professor Frank
Cross of the University of Texas.[58]

> By focusing on one set of
> risks, the precautionary
> principle turns a blind eye to
> the harms that occur, or are
> made worse, due to the
> lack of technological devel-
> opment.

The case of biotechnology provides
an obvious example of how precautionary
regulation could have negative consequences for public health and environmental protection. As detailed in chapter
7, genetic modification of crops can increase yields in many ways, ranging from
enhancing plant resistance to frost, pests,
soil toxicity or salinity, and droughts, to regulating flowering and reducing spoilage. A scientific panel convened by the World Bank and
Consultative Group on International Agricultural Research concluded that genetic engineering could increase agricultural yields by
as much as 25 percent.[59] Biotechnology not only holds the potential to
increase per-acre yields, but it could also increase the nutritional value
of the crops that are grown. Genetically modified crops may well
make food both more abundant *and* more nutritious.

Precautionary regulation that limits the development, testing, sale,
or trade in genetically engineered products will limit the benefits that
such technologies can provide. This could mean less food and lower
nutrition intake for many of the world's poor. Because agricultural
biotechnology also holds the promise of increasing per-acre crop
yields, limiting the use of genetically engineered crops will result in
greater pressure to clear tropical forests and other undeveloped land
for agricultural use. Without the contribution of new generations of
genetically enhanced crop varieties, it will be immensely difficult to

meet the rising food demands of the world's peoples and still preserve large areas of undeveloped habitat. Even if the use of genetically engineered crops allows for the further intensification of agricultural production, which has environmental impacts of its own, these impacts pose a lesser threat to biodiversity than the unabated loss of natural habitat throughout the world; "the environmental costs of expanding the area tilled are enormously greater than those of increasing yield."[60] An overemphasis on the potential risks of using agricultural biotechnology ignores the equal, if not far greater, risks of doing without such advances. "For the world's developing countries, one of the greatest risks of genetic engineering is not being able to use this technology at all," declared Calestous Juma from the Harvard University Center for International Development.[61]

> An overemphasis on the potential risks of using agricultural biotechnology ignores the equal, if not far greater, risks of doing without such advances.

Unfortunately, this is anything but an isolated example. There are numerous instances in which the adoption of precautionary measures to control a given substance or technology will have negative impacts on public health or environmental protection.

Drug Lag

Perhaps the most prominent example of the harm caused by excessive precaution in regulatory policy is drug lag, the delay in approval of potentially lifesaving medicines and treatments. The Food and Drug Administration (FDA) must approve new pharmaceuticals and medical devices before they may be used or prescribed. The purpose of FDA approval is to ensure that only those drugs are approved that are "safe and effective." In a precautionary fashion, the FDA seeks to prevent the release of an unsafe drug. Delaying the availability of potentially lifesaving treatment, however, poses risks of its own. In the simplest terms, if a new drug or medical treatment will start saving lives once it is approved, then the longer it takes for the government to approve the drug, the more likely it is that people will die awaiting treatment.[62]

This is not merely a theoretical concern. Consider the example of Misoprostol, a drug that prevents gastric ulcers.[63] Misoprostol was developed in the early 1980s and was first approved in some nations in 1985. The FDA, however, did not approve use of Misoprostol until 1988. Even though the drug was already available in several dozen foreign countries, the FDA subjected Misoprostol to a nine-and-one-half month review. At the time, between 10,000 and 20,000 people died from gastric ulcers per year. Therefore, had Misoprostol been approved more rapidly, it could have saved as many as 8,000 to 15,000 lives. In other words, the FDA's delay cost lives, just as surely as does the approval and use of unsafe treatments. Thus precautionary regulation by the FDA does not always enhance protection of public health.

PESTICIDES

Pesticides are a common target of precautionary principle advocates, but as with drug lag and biotechnology, it is not clear that more government regulation of chemical pesticides always makes people safer. In some cases, restrictions on the use of a pesticide can expose people to other risks, such as disease, or result in the use of more harmful substitutes. Ethylene dibromide (EDB), for example, was a powerful fungicide used to prevent the growth of molds on grain and other foods. Molds produce some of the most potent carcinogens known, such as aflatoxin.[64] Yet EDB was also deemed a potential carcinogen and was banned by the U.S. Environmental Protection Agency (EPA). The ban was a precautionary measure, yet the EPA did not consider whether the risk of EDB was greater or lesser than that posed by aflatoxin. Moreover, EDB was replaced with fungicides that had to be applied in greater quantities, increasing the risk for exposed workers.[65] Thus the EDB ban may have, on net, *increased* risks to human health.

Among the chemicals targeted for elimination by advocates of the precautionary principle is DDT. Once widely used for mosquito control, DDT was banned in most developed nations due to concerns that its widespread use interfered with the reproduction of several bird species, including the bald eagle. In the years after World War II, DDT became the ultimate weapon in the battle against malaria. In

Ceylon (now Sri Lanka), DDT spraying reduced the number of malaria cases from approximately 3 million in 1946 to approximately 7,300 in only a decade. By 1964 there were only 29 recorded malaria cases on the island nation.[66] In India malaria cases dropped from an estimated 75 million in 1951 to approximately 50,000 by 1961.[67] In industrialized nations DDT helped eliminate malaria completely.

Evidence that DDT contributed to egg-shell thinning in some bird species, and fears that it could harm people as well, led to a ban on DDT in the United States in 1972. Other developed countries followed soon thereafter, and many developing countries restricted its use.[68] At the time, there was concern—though little evidence—that DDT might pose a risk to public health. Rachel Carson's *Silent Spring* and media alarmism contributed to fears that DDT use was poisoning America's children. Foreshadowing later precautionary appeals for chemical phaseouts, then–EPA administrator William Ruckleshaus argued that DDT was "a warning that man may be exposing himself to a substance that may ultimately have a serious effect on his health."[69] Solid evidence of DDT's health risks never materialized, however. A few animal studies suggest some risk, but epidemiological and other research has been inconclusive, producing no more than "weak evidence of harm to human health."[70] Indeed, Harvard University's Amir Attaran notes that "[t]he scientific literature does not contain even one peer-reviewed, independently replicated study linking DDT exposures to any adverse health outcome" in humans.[71]

Continuing concerns about potential human health effects of DDT led to the pesticide's inclusion on a proposed list of POPs to be completely phased out under an international agreement sponsored by the United Nations Environment Programme. During the negotiations, however, the complete elimination of DDT was reconsidered. Although DDT is virtually synonymous with industrial pollution in Western nations, it is known as a lifesaving compound in much of the developing world. DDT is still used in nearly two dozen countries for malaria control, and for good reason.

DDT remains one of the few affordable, effective tools against the mosquitoes that transmit malaria, a plague that sickens at least 300

million and kills over one million, mainly children, in economically
underdeveloped areas of the tropics each year. Such a toll is scarcely
comprehensible. To visualize it, imagine filling seven Boeing 747s
with children, and then crashing them, every day.[72]

> The phaseout of DDT before the development of a suitable, cost-effective alternative would condemn millions of people in the developing world to malaria infection and potential death.

The phaseout of DDT before the development of a suitable, cost-effective alternative would condemn millions of people in the developing world to malaria infection and potential death. Application of the precautionary principle to DDT, and eliminating it on the basis of speculative concerns that it *might* harm human health, would leave much of the world far less safe than it is today. The use of DDT may yet be shown to cause health problems in humans; in many developing countries, doing without DDT will definitely cause health problems for millions. As two malaria researchers observe, "DDT has saved countless millions of lives, while Greenpeace struggles to find some evidence that it harms mankind."[73]

WEALTHIER IS HEALTHIER, RICHER IS CLEANER

ADVOCATES OF THE precautionary principle tend to assume that economic growth and development are themselves a threat to public health and environmental protection. The Wingspread Statement, for example, speaks of the "substantial unintended consequences" brought about by the industrial society.[74] An underlying premise of the precautionary principle is that modern industrial society is unsustainable and threatens the survival of humanity, if not much of the planet as well. This assumption is highly questionable, as the other chapters in this volume illustrate. Economic growth and technological progress have been a tremendous boon to both human health and environmental protection. Efforts to limit such progress are likely to be counterproductive. Regulatory measures that stifle innovation and suppress economic growth will deprive individuals of the resources necessary to improve their quality of life and deny societies the ability to make investments that protect people and their environs.

The rise of industrial society has coincided with a massive explosion of wealth and health that is unprecedented in the history of human civilization. For centuries, average life expectancy hovered in the 20s and 30s. U.S. life expectancy in 1900 was only 47. Today, in developed nations life expectancy is nearly 80.[75] Infant and maternal mortality plummeted over this same period, as have the incidence and mortality of typhoid, diphtheria, tuberculosis, and other lethal diseases.[76] These positive trends are largely the result of increased wealth and the benefits such wealth brings. Higher economic growth and aggregate wealth strongly correlate with reduced mortality and morbidity.[77] This should be no surprise as the accumulation of wealth is necessary to fund medical research, support markets for advanced lifesaving technologies, build infrastructure necessary for better food distribution, and so on. In a phrase, poorer is sicker, and wealthier is healthier.[78]

Cancer rates are often blamed on environmental exposures to chemicals and other synthetic substances. Were this so, one would expect cancer rates to increase with the proliferation of synthetic chemicals in our food supply and environs. This has not been the case. According to the most recent report of the National Cancer Institute, overall incidence and death rates for cancer are also declining.[79] Even lung cancer incidence, largely the result of smoking, has begun to decline.[80] Simply put, "[t]he common belief that there is an epidemic of death from cancer in developed countries is a myth, except for the effects of tobacco. . . . For most nonsmokers, the health benefits of modern society outweigh the new hazards."[81] In short, "the Western world is a remarkably healthy place to live."[82]

Economic progress is no less essential for environmental protection than for protection of public health. Environmental protection is a good and, like all goods, it must be purchased. Wealth is required to finance environmental improvements, from the purification of drinking water to invention and installation of low-emission technologies.

Not only are wealthier communities healthier than poorer communities, but on average, they tend to be more concerned about protecting environmental values as well. Wealthier societies have both the means and the desire to address a wider array of environmental concerns.[83]

Pollution, while still a serious environmental problem in much of the world, is not the mortal threat to human survival it once was. At the dawn of the 20th century, soot and smoke permeated cities, sometimes to lethal effect. In 1948, a four-day weather inversion in Donora, Pennsylvania, blanketed the town with pollution from local factories, killing 18 people.[84] Over the past several decades, pollution levels in wealthy, industrialized societies have declined, particularly in the case of those emissions for which the health impacts are most severe.[85] "Countries undergo an environmental transition as they become wealthier and reach a point at which they start getting cleaner."[86] This occurs first with particularly acute environmental concerns, such as access to safe drinking water and sanitation services. As affluence increases, so does the attention paid to conventional pollution concerns, such as fecal coliform bacteria and urban air quality.[87]

There is no doubt that chemicals pose risks. Indeed, some of the chemicals and other technologies targeted by advocates of the precautionary principle can cause problems—if misused. Yet it is notable that the proliferation of these technologies has coincided with the greatest explosion of prosperity and longevity in human history. If modern society were as risky as the ideological environmentalists who advocate the precautionary principle suggest, this should not be the case.

TOWARD A SAFER WORLD

THE STATED AIM of the precautionary principle is to enhance protection of public health and environmental concerns. In practice, however, the precautionary principle is only applied to the risks of technological change and industrial society, with little appreciation for the risks that wealth and technology prevent. New technologies can be risky things. Some industrial chemicals may cause health problems even if used carefully. But this does not justify the adoption of a blanket precautionary rule suppressing chemical use and technological development.

If the true aim is a safer world, and not merely the retardation of technological progress, the risks of new chemicals or products must be weighed against the risks that they ameliorate or prevent. The risks of change must be weighed against the risk of stagnation. In every case, "[t]he empirical question is whether the health [and environmental] gains from the regulation of the substances involved are greater or lesser than the health [and environmental] costs of the regulation."[88] Genetically modified corn may pose hypothetical risks to butterflies in the wild, but the absence of genetically modified corn will perpetuate substantial risks to the habitats of many more species in the wild. The use of chlorine may create some compounds with carcinogenic potential, but the phaseout of chlorine would eliminate a tremendously valuable feedstock and greatly reduce the safety of the food supply.

"The precautionary principle rests upon an illusion that actions have no consequences beyond their intended ends."[89] In reality, even the most well-intentioned precautionary measures can have terrible results. The precautionary principle's threat to technological progress is itself a threat to public health and environmental protection. The world would be safer without it.

CHAPTER ELEVEN

ENCLOSING THE ENVIRONMENTAL COMMONS

Fred Smith

ECO-MYTHS DEBUNKED

- *Nearly all environmental problems—air and water pollution, declining fisheries, extinctions, rain forest destruction, coral reef degradation— occur in open-access commons.*
- *In a commons, no one is in charge, no one protects the resource, so people have an incentive to exploit a resource before someone else beats them to it, leading to environmental damage.*
- *Political management of a commons has proven to be costly and ineffective and merely slows the damage caused to the natural world by the misdirected incentives in a commons. Politicizing the environment does not resolve the tragedy of the commons. Rather, it institutionalizes it.*
- *Enclosure—that is, assigning owners to environmental goods—will integrate those goods into the private sector and reveal their true values and help protect and preserve them.*

OWNERSHIP OF THE COMMONS CAN PREVENT THE TRAGEDY OF THE COMMONS—A PARADIGM FOR ENVIRONMENTAL PROBLEMS

FEW THINGS PROVE as depressing as reading the conventional environmentalist lore. Fertile topsoil is being blown off our farms. Not only are our waters unsafe to drink, but there is less available every year. Elephants in Africa, tigers in Asia, parrots in Brazil, the spotted owl in the Pacific Northwest—indeed, ever more species on our planet are threatened with extinction. The Amazon forests are disappearing like rain in the desert—and the deserts are encroaching on arable land. Around the world, coral reefs are dying, while increasingly fishermen return home with empty holds. Growing quantities of hazardous substances contaminate airsheds in our urban centers. And, of course, we face a global warming catastrophe. While it is now becoming more widely understood that ideological environmentalists have exaggerated the extent of such problems, most of us believe we can and should do better.[1]

But to do better, one must know why environmental problems arise in the first place, and here ideological environmentalists have seriously misdiagnosed the causes of environmental degradation. Lacking knowledge of the historical response to industrial pollution and disdainful of private property and markets, environmentalists have accepted unthinkingly the market failure explanation for pollution. Pollution and its impacts, they believe, are external to the market and, therefore, ignored. Thus government intervention is necessary.

Their indictment goes further. Since mankind enjoys the fruits of industry, environmental controls must extend to the population itself, our demand for goods and services, and our reliance on new and inadequately tested technologies. Environmentalists see the world in "terrible toos" terms: There are *too* many of us, we consume *too* much, and we rely *too* heavily on technology that we understand *too* little about. These factors, they argue, stress our planet and explain environmental woes. Since private action has created the problem, only political action—population control, consumption restrictions, and prior approval of technology—offer any hope of reducing the stress our insatiable demands are placing on the carrying capacity of our all too finite Earth.

An alternative explanation of pollution is found in the work of Garrett Hardin in his oft-cited *Science* article "The Tragedy of the Commons." Hardin describes an open-access resource, a pasture, that inevitably experiences environmental degradation.[2] His example deals with a village surrounding a pasturage open to all. Initially, there are few villagers and the pasture is adequate for their cattle. However, as the village grows, so also do the number of cows. Self-interest motivates the first villager to place one more cow on the commons, the second to follow suit, and so on, reducing the availability of forage and degrading the pasture with accumulating animal waste. However, while each villager gains the full value of the additional cow, he bears only a fraction of the costs. The calculus is clear: The gains of an additional cow accrue to the individual; the costs of the lower quality pasturage are borne by all. Eventually, the carrying capacity of the pasture is exceeded, resulting in the tragedy of the commons, a degraded pasture providing little value to anyone. Hardin summarized the result: "Ruin is the destination toward which all men rush, each pursuing his own best interest in a society which believes in the freedom of the commons. Freedom in a commons brings ruin to all."[3]

The problem, it should be noted, is not that demand per se is excessive, but rather that there is no gatekeeper to moderate such demands by reducing the number of cattle or by adopting ways to use the pasture more intensively. Environmental problems reflect the lack of stewardship arrangements. Factories belch smoke into the air because the people in the affected regions cannot legally stop them. The degradation of rivers and estuaries by municipal sewage reflects the fact that downstream groups—lacking any property rights in the harmed resource—have no right to block such pollution. The depletion of rain forests and fisheries results from their open access, their common property status—not from any excessive demands. To realize how these problems reflect the lack of property rights, note that steel mills do not dump slag in people's backyards (where ownership protections are explicit) but do dump soot and acid residuals into the airsheds and waterways (where private ownership is absent).

The *market failure* explanation for environmental problems ignores the basic fact that markets without property rights are a grand illusion. Without the institutional framework of property rights, no goods can be protected or valued. Environmental goods and values are at risk because they have not been integrated into the market system of property rights. No market exists and thus cannot have failed. Tragedies of the commons are not observed where property rights exist and are protected. To see this, consider a few examples. Groundwater is increasingly scarce, while oil is becoming ever more abundant (in the relevant metric of the hours of human work needed to purchase this substance). Greater demands for quality air in the indoor spaces (cars, offices, malls, workplaces) where we spend an increasing fraction of our lives are met readily; yet despite the expenditure of many billions of dollars, the air in many urban areas remains smoggy. Note also that while many species of wildlife are threatened, domesticated species—pets as well as livestock—are prospering. None of this is surprising. The late Julian Simon liked to quote the 19th-century American economist Henry George: "Both the jayhawk and the man eat chickens, but the more jayhawks, the fewer chickens, while the more men, the more chickens." The point is that people own chickens and have an incentive to produce more as demand increases.

Simon's key observation is that environmental resources are endangered—not because of the market, but rather because environmental resources have been left out in the cold. Lacking any property right protections, they are vulnerable. The resources noted above—wildlife, groundwater, urban air—all are common property resources. Everyone can use these resources—no one owns them and has a direct interest in protecting them. The result is the tragedy of the commons. But tragedy is not inevitable. It can be resolved by the creation of property rights in the resource at risk. Private ownership arrangements are pervasive in our society, allowing individuals to nurture and protect many things they care about. People can protect their backyards and their pets, so why not water or wildlife? From this perspective, the problem is not that too much of the planet is privately controlled, but rather that too little is. Our goal should be to allow more of the planet to become the moral equivalent of someone's backyard or pet and, thereby, to empower people to play a direct and immediate role in environmental protection.

> Our goal should be to allow more of the planet to become the moral equivalent of someone's backyard or pet and, thereby, to empower people to play a direct and immediate role in environmental protection.

The problem is not that people lack ecological consciousness; that problem can be addressed by value education. Indeed, Hardin argues, it would be wrong to "browbeat a free man in the commons into acting against his own interests." Moral suasion in the commons situation is worse than useless. Any sacrifice that the ecologically conscious individual might make would be pointless because the less-sensitive villager would simply take advantage of his sacrifice to place his additional cow on the commons. The pasture would still degrade, and the altruist would lose vis-à-vis his neighbors. For such reasons, the ecologically sensitive individual is disadvantaged in open-access situations.[4]

Resolving the tragedy, Hardin argues, required institutional change: Either the resource must be privatized or the resource must come under political control. Let us consider the implications of each choice. First, if we go down the political path, we would create a regulatory control agency, call it the Pasture Protection Agency (PPA), and appoint a PPA Administrator. If we take the privatization path, we would divide the pasture into plots and grant each villager a deed to a portion. In either situation, similar problems must be addressed: How many cattle can the pasture accommodate? Who will be allowed to graze their cattle and how many cows will they be allowed? How can we ensure that the allocations granted are observed? How should we respond to changes—a drought, a bountiful year, requests to graze sheep or to build a lawn tennis court? How do we improve the pasture over time? Let's see how well these tasks will be performed under each alternative.[5]

In the private property option, each villager would decide the number of cows to graze on his field. He would be free to place as many or as few as he wished. He would, of course, also have to decide whether to fence his plot or not. If not, he would have to decide how to protect his pasture from wandering cows from other farms. The initial decisions are likely to be wrong, but the farmers will have every incentive to gain knowledge quickly to improve management through trial and error. Too few cows will yield too low a return; too many may damage the pasturage. Some villagers will garner this knowledge more quickly than others, and their practices will soon be emulated by everyone. One environmentally beneficial aspect of the privatization option is the variety of experimentation it encourages.

The PPA Administrator will also seek to determine the number of cattle that can safely graze on the pasture. He may well hire an analyst to calculate that number. But again mistakes will happen. However, the Administrator operates in a political environment, and mistakes are likely to be viewed as malfeasance. If the estimate turns out to be too low, the Administrator will be criticized for depriving the village of the additional value. If the estimate is too high, the Administrator will be criticized for allowing the pasture to deteriorate. The analyst hired by the PPA has every professional reason to determine the correct number, but neither the analyst nor the PPA administration are directly affected by success or failure. Indeed, a bad decision by the PPA may even mean that the agency will be awarded a larger budget.

Note that pasture management entails gathering information on the quality and quantity of the grass, the stress placed by the cattle or other animals allowed to graze, the value of the various species grazing, and how these values would change with alternative grazing policies. The individual villagers will experiment with various strategies. Mistakes will be noted by other villagers, as will successes. The variety of approaches exercised under private management is likely to result in much faster acquisition of knowledge than under the centralized PPA approach. And again, the fact that the PPA employees do not directly lose or profit argues for slower learning. The creative bureaucrat may well garner commendation and perhaps a merit award, but those incentives are far weaker than if he were an owner who would capture the full ecological and economic value of a successful innovation.

In either case, the hope is that, over time, we will learn how to do more with less. Innovations are critical for sustainable pasture management. Along the private path, the desire for improvements creates a market. Note that incentives exist for people who have no direct linkage to the pasture to provide such innovations. Markets link the broader society to the challenge of improving pasture management. The individual villager will be eager to compensate those able to increase his profits. The PPA Administrator will seek funds to conduct similar research, but his budget may not permit extensive research. Note that any gains that such research might yield would not accrue to his budget. Bureaucracies, as a result, are slow to innovate.

Adapting to changing conditions and tastes poses further management problems. Should, for example, only cows be allowed or should we also allow sheep and goats and geese? Should the pasture be preserved for grazing only or would it be permissible to allow some to create a lawn tennis court? Should the pasture be used continuously or would it be better to put it in fallow every few years? Each villager may also face the problem of adjusting his policies in the event of a drought or a year of plenty. The private manager has every incentive to find ways to accommodate such diverse demands—the greater the demand for his land, the greater the potential profits. Problems arising from inappropriate mixes will strongly signal the villager to rethink any mismanagement.

Political resource managers are subject to political pressures. Powerful political interests are likely to be favored over political pariahs. Election concerns may well lead the PPA Administrator to ease up on restrictions, even if that would create long-term problems for the pasture. Moreover, changes in administration may cause changes in policy. The sheep contingent may prevail at the polls over the cattlemen with destabilizing impact on pasture management. Changes in stocking patterns will also occur in the private example, but the dispersal of control would normally lead to a wider variety of responses and a lowering of overall harm to the pasturage.

The foregoing discussion suggests the reasons why private ownership of grazing lands (or its equivalent in long-term leases for politically controlled areas) has become so dominant. Ownership rights create incentives for wise management today and for creative innovations over time. Political controls are likely to prove superior to open-access common property arrangements. However, a political management system lacks the reward structure essential to good management and innovation. Ultimately, the political approach does not really resolve the tragedy of the commons, but rather it institutionalizes it. Nonetheless, modern environmental policy has relied almost totally on political controls to address environmental concerns.

PROGRESSIVES INSTITUTIONALIZE THE TRAGEDY OF THE COMMONS

IF THE ENVIRONMENTAL tragedy of the commons can be better resolved by privatization, why then has the Pasture Protection Administration path so often been selected? The answer is that the market's ability to address environmental concerns had been so weakened prior to the dawn of the modern environmental age (dated roughly as April 22, 1970, the first Earth Day) that almost everyone perceived environmental problems as the inevitable result of industrial activity. Markets were seen as causing environmental problems, not solving them.

Let us briefly examine the historical record. First note these resources (minerals, food, oil) integrated (via property rights) into the market have become more abundant, not less, over the last century. Moreover, historical record suggests that market forces in both England and the United States were beginning to address environmental concerns in the early days

> Ownership rights create incentives for wise management today and for creative innovations over time.

of the Industrial Revolution (the latter half of the 19th century) far before the environmental concerns became prominent. The Industrial Revolution did pose serious and novel environmental problems. Industrial wastes were often more noxious and greater in quantity than the effluents of the preindustrial age. Early mills produced vast quantities of liquid effluents; trains belched forth vast quantities of smoke and soot. Yet the initial inclination of the courts was not to stand idle but rather to regard these nuisances as actionable. Property owners expected that their property rights would be protected—that industrial corporations could not mar private owners' rights to enjoy their properties peacefully.

Nobel Prize–winning economist Ronald Coase documents a number of those examples in his article "The Problem of Social Cost."[6] Coase describes offices disturbed by vibration from adjoining industrial operations, odors arising from distilling operations, smoke coming from railroad locomotives, and dams flooding upstream properties. The courts sought to integrate these concerns into the established property rights system. The question was whether one had created an actionable nuisance or whether one's actions constituted trespass. If so, then the individual could stop the enterprise or, at least, obtain restitution for damages. For example, early mills built dams that sometimes flooded upstream properties. That flooding, an early form of pollution, was treated as a trespass, and the dam builder was forced to reach accommodation with upstream parties or else lower the dam.[7] Similarly, early steam locomotives spewed forth not only smoke but also sparks. Those sparks sometimes ignited grain fields near the rail tracks. Again, that action was treated as trespass and the railroad was held responsible for damages.

Thus the Industrial Revolution did not inevitably mean the destruction of the natural environment, but rather prompted a response by the courts that promised to "housebreak" these newer enterprises, subjecting them to the same restraints imposed on traditional enterprises. Unfortunately, that process was short-circuited. The belief that private property was critical, that society was responsible for protecting private property, lost favor to the belief that property was a social construct to be used for the public good.

In America, this negative attitude toward private property was chiefly championed by the growing Progressive movement of the late 19th and early 20th centuries. Progressives, of course, held disparate views; however, the government's intervention in the economy, collective action, via politics was, they believed, more likely to advance the public interest, to ensure that resources were used for their greatest value. The Progressive shift brought about changes in the way courts came to view externalities and property rights. Property rights were weakened as the courts moved from common law trespass and nuisance concepts to utilitarian concepts of balancing "social" gains and losses. The language of a 1911 Georgia Supreme Court is telling: "The pollution of the air, so far as reasonably necessary to the *enjoyment* of life and indispensable to the progress of society, is not actionable" (emphasis added).[8]

Coase details this transformation, noting that in both Britain and the United States, legislatures authorized activities that were known to create environmental problems. The courts heeded these legislative acts by offering less protection against such environmental harms. Coase notes a number of cases—consider the language of one court decision: "Legislative sanction makes that lawful which otherwise might be a nuisance. Examples of this are damages to adjacent land arising from smoke, vibration and noise in the operation of a railroad

. . . unpleasant odors connected with sewers, oil refining and storage of naphtha."[9]

This Progressive bias for economic growth over ecological values is neatly captured in the phrase: Excuse our dust, but grow we must! In that political climate, it is not surprising that people came to associate economic activities with pollution.

Progressives viewed the world in utilitarian terms—resources were placed on this Earth to be used! People who held their land idle, who failed to develop resources, were squandering a precious heritage. Indeed, to gain ownership of land one often needed to demonstrate that one had put it to use—plowing the land, building a house, catching the fish, digging the mine, grazing the cattle, cutting the timber. Forests were to be logged to produce housing, fuel, paper, and wealth. Rivers were to be channeled to improve America's transportation infrastructure and to provide power to light our homes. Even "environmental agencies" such as the Department of the Interior's National Park Service viewed their mission in developmental (maximizing the number of visitor days) rather than in preservation terms. Most Americans, of course, agreed with these policies at the time.

Given this orientation, the surprise is that there wasn't even more pollution, more environmental damage. The primary reason is that markets encourage efficient use of energy and raw materials, and efficiency is not only good business, but it also reduces pollution. Pollution, after all, is that fraction of material and energy input that does not find its way into the final product. The phrase "industrial ecology" hadn't yet been coined, but industrialists, nonetheless, continually found ways of doing more with less. An excellent example was the invention of the Kraft process for papermaking. That process not only allowed the use of pines and other lower-cost woods, but also burning the noncellulose component of the wood pile provided most of the energy required to make paper. The result was less

> Markets encourage efficient use of energy and raw materials, and efficiency is not only good business, but it also reduces pollution.

waste per unit of paper produced.[10] Moreover, firms desired to have good relations with their neighbors and thus to some degree sought to reduce the nuisances attendant to their activities.

Still, the utilitarian bias of the Progressive Era that undermined property protections reduced the incentives for industry to proceed along a more ecologically sensitive path. After all, if a manufacturer could not be held responsible for his pollution, why expend monies to reduce it? Why purchase buffer zones around a facility? Why purchase pollution control equipment or install settling ponds?

Perhaps the most serious consequence of this weakening of common law property protections was that it reduced the amount of social experimentation that would have occurred. Even a century ago, there were some people who valued the environment highly. In a world where property rights were respected, companies would have found themselves forced to adjust their operations to accommodate these concerns. Firms would have learned to negotiate with adjoining property owners prior to locating a plant. Consider railroads. Had property rights been honored, firms might well have purchased buffer zones or noise easements adjacent to their tracks. Spark and smoke suppression technologies would probably have been introduced earlier. Tracks and loading yards would, more likely, have been located in nonresidential areas. The need to respect the property rights of the environmentally sensitive minority would have encouraged firms to reduce their environmental footprint during the era when few have placed high value on the environment. The result would have been that environmental management strategies would have been introduced in a few locations at an early date. As America grew wealthier and environmental concerns increased accordingly, there would have been a smoother transition to the environmentally conscious world of today, with less damage to the natural world.

Another legacy of the Progressive Era, antitrust regulation, has made it difficult to develop cooperative conservation agreements. As but one example, Gulf Coast shrimpers organized to reduce their catch and thus conserve shrimp stocks. That arrangement was disallowed by the federal antitrust authorities.[11]

The work of Ronald Coase regarding the way laws were changed during the industrialization era suggests we rethink the path along which environmental policy has proceeded for the last few decades. As discussed above, Coase examined the legal and legislative records and found that, rather than markets failing, it would be more accurate to say that markets had been blocked from operating in ways that would have better protected the natural world. Legislative bodies deliberately weakened the defenses available to property owners (specifically nuisance and trespass claims), leaving industry free to develop along a more polluting path. Environmental policy makers today remain largely unaware of this fact. Commenting on that point, Coase notes,

> *Most economists seem to be unaware of [the role played by laws weakening property defenses].... When they are prevented from sleeping at night by the roar of jet planes overhead (publicly authorized and perhaps publicly operated), are unable to think(or rest) in the day because of the noise and vibration from passing trains (publicly authorized and perhaps publicly operated), find it difficult to breathe because of the odour from the local sewage farm (publicly authorized and perhaps publicly operated), and are unable to escape because their driveways are blocked by a road obstruction (without any doubt, publicly devised), their nerves frayed and mental balance disturbed, they proceed to declaim about the disadvantages of private enterprise and the need for government regulation.[12]*

Coase's point is that property rights once had linked economic concerns to environmental concerns. Had property rights remained secure, environmental policy might well have taken a very different course. First, development would have proceeded in ways that created less environmental harm. Also, many more innovative options for addressing environmental concerns would have been explored over the last century. Pollution-minimizing technologies would have been developed and adopted much earlier. Activities that are inherently disturbing would have been sited in more remote locations; firms would have organized their work year to minimize operations in times when they would have had the greatest negative effect on the environment. Firms would have purchased larger buffer zones around their plants and negotiated in advance with neighboring property owners. Communities might well have gained the right to police their airsheds, allowing use for consideration (possibly payments by firms and adjoining jurisdictions affecting the community that would permit lower taxes, for example). Pollution-reducing technology would have a ready market. Unfortunately, when environmental activists emerged as major players in the policy arena after the first Earth Day in 1970, they had no knowledge of the role that private property had once played, nor its potential for addressing their concerns.

THE MODERN ENVIRONMENTAL AGE AND ITS PROBLEMS

TRAGICALLY, EARTH DAY activists knew little history, so from their limited perspective, markets were inherently antagonistic to environmental values. They sought immediate action to address what they viewed as pervasive and dangerous ecological problems. They gave little consideration to extending property rights to environmental resources (indeed, that idea would have seemed blasphemous to those environmental activists espousing a "This land is your land, this land is my land" ideology). The result was the rapid enactment of an array of laws governing air, water, and land pollution. The aim was to control the flow of energy and materials through the economy to prevent environmental harm. The complexity of such a cradle-to-grave monitoring and control system is incredible. Moreover, federal environmental laws in the United States generally preempt state and local government rules. As a result, environmental policy became largely federalized and thoroughly politicized. The environmental slogan "Think globally, act locally!" has never been realized.[13]

The environmental slogan "Think globally, act locally!" has never been realized.

For example, the regulatory powers of the Environmental Protection Agency (EPA) are vast, with the power to control any activity that might pollute. Since, however, every process that converts energy or material into more human-friendly forms leaves some residue, this rule literally allows the EPA to regulate every economic activity. In effect, the EPA has become America's national economic planning agency, exercising more power than almost any other agency of government. Central planning, however, does not work. That point is now well understood in the economic world; it has yet to be realized in the environmental area. That is somewhat surprising, because ecological central planning is, if anything, an even more complex task. After all, the economic planner does have a metric to determine whether focusing on one sector or another is more likely to yield higher returns. Money provides a metric for evaluating alternative policies. There is no such metric in the environmental field. Not surprisingly, therefore, the EPA has encountered serious problems.[14]

The EPA's problems are akin to those discussed earlier in the pasture example. The EPA has no ready means of establishing priorities. The EPA's priorities are based on ephemeral political concerns, and it makes little use of science and analysis.

Consider the problem of setting priorities. The EPA faces many claimants, none of whom can be ignored. Moreover, since there is no market for the various environmental resources being protected, there is no way for the claimants to bid among themselves to determine which goals should receive greatest emphasis. What is more important, African elephants or the ozone layer, recycling or population control, reducing trace elements in our water supply or increasing fuel efficiency? Priorities vary widely among individuals in the ecological area just as they do in the economic area. One of the chief virtues of the private economy is that it permits people to set priorities without any central planning agency. The challenge is to create a mechanism that would permit people to express their choices in the ecological sphere as well as they now do in the economic sphere. Absent property rights, this becomes incredibly complex.

Moreover, like all political entities, the EPA is subject to special interest lobbying. Most people lack the direct interest (the economic gains) needed to invest much time in environmental policy. Those active in such matters tend to be groups having an unusual economic or ideological stake in the outcome. The pressure groups that influence the EPA represent only a fraction of the diverse interests characterizing our complex society. The EPA will encounter primarily ideological environmentalists, along with business groups who find regulations a useful tool to tilt the playing field against their competitors. The likelihood that their combined voices are representative of the public interest is minimal. Nonetheless, the EPA listens to them and often heeds their advice. The current system clearly advances special interests not those of the public. Again, in effect, politicizing the environment does not resolve the tragedy of the commons. Rather, it institutionalizes it.

THE PATH NOT TAKEN— ASSESSING THE PRIVATIZATION OPTION

SOME WITHIN THE environmentalist community would agree with all of the above and, yet, still doubt whether private property approaches would prove superior in protecting environmental values. How, they ask, would extending private property advance environmental goals?

Wildlife ownership illustrates the rich potential of the privatization approach. Several African nations have realized that conservation laws were failing to protect their wildlife. Elephants, for example, were protected by national laws. But the enforcement of these laws— given the value of ivory—was difficult. Moreover, many in the rural regions viewed poaching as a fully legitimate activity (recall that Robin Hood was a "poacher" after all). For rural Africans, elephants provided no positive gains; yet they often cost local villagers dearly, destroying crops and even killing people. Responding to this reality, several African nations elected to grant management responsibilities (a partial "ownership right") for the elephants to the local villagers. In effect, the local jurisdictions would decide (within limits) whether elephants should be killed or protected. Communities received money from the sale of ivory and meat, from the sale of limited licenses to hunt elephants, and from the tourism trade. They now had a direct financial incentive to manage elephant herds effectively, and that change brought about dramatic gains in elephant populations. Rather than complaints about "your" elephants creating damage, the tribes began to speak of "our" elephants needing protection. The countries that adopted this private management saw their elephant populations expand dramatically, while those that continued with the old central planning model of wildlife protection suffered further severe declines in their elephant herds.

To generalize from this example, we should make it possible for individuals and groups to come forward with their ideas on providing stewardship responsibilities for some valued environmental resource. That is, we should devise an "ecological adoption" statute to encourage the transfer of environmental resources to private hands. Adoption, after all, is the procedure by which individuals volunteer to become protectors—"parents"—of an abandoned child. The adoption process involves a review procedure to ensure that the prospective parents are qualified; if the petitioners are deemed worthy, then the parents become the stewards of the child. In effect, the child is transferred from state to private control.

Something akin to this could work to protect many environmental goods and values. Government agencies are stressed; they find it difficult to do all that is expected of them. A process allowing private citizens and groups to take some of the burden would be a valued step and would also allow some changes. The local community has greater knowledge and is better positioned to determine how best to manage the resource to ensure sustainable development. Steps to allow hunting and fishing clubs or shellfish or commercial fishing cooperatives to seek title over stretches of forests, rivers, and bays should be encouraged. In these cases, we should also ensure that the groups are granted the power to protect their property in the courts.

The second principle is that environmental issues should be resolved locally whenever possible. Uniform national rules result in spending far too much on controlling some emissions that create little problem—for example, controlling water pollution in periods when river flows are high and thus assimilative capacity great, and spending too little on controls during low flow periods, when emissions are likely to have a much greater impact. Local groups have greater knowledge about such trade-offs and are better positioned to monitor compliance. Each region should be free to make its own decisions on the appropriate trade-off between environmental and developmental matters.

The third principle emphasizes efforts to simplify the task of determining which polluters are damaging which regions of the country. A property rights–oriented approach would focus on ways to unravel the complex sequence of events that relate economic activities in one place to environmental damage in another.

The fourth feature focuses on the way in which privatization creates improved fencing and trespass enforcement technology. One example—barbed wire fences separating cattle—is indicative of the innovations needed. "Beepers" or computer chip implants that would signal the location of larger wildlife (manatees, whales, Siberian tigers) might well have value.[15] Technologies also exist making it possible to determine the quantity and types of air pollution entering a region. Lasimetrics, for example, is a technology that can map atmospheric chemical concentrations from orbit. In time, that science might provide a sophisticated means of tracking transnational pollution flows. Most nations label high explosives manufactured in their countries as part of a worldwide antiterrorist program.

An excellent example of how private property better reconciles environmental and economic values is the Rainey Wildlife Refuge. This preserve, owned by a major environmental group, is located in the midst of vast natural gas and oil fields. Since the refuge was privately owned, development was at the discretion of its owner, the National Audubon Society. A "purist," no-development attitude would have lost the royalty payment of producing wells. Instead, the society elected to permit drilling under careful guidelines to reduce environmental damage. Economic and environmental gains to both parties resulted. The drillers obtained a valuable natural resource. The Audubon Society obtained revenue that could be used to better manage Rainey and other refuges. In contrast, the Audubon Society, along with most other U.S. environmental organizations, vigorously opposes energy development in the politically controlled Arctic National Wildlife Refuge. Absent a property stake in rational development, there is little reason to be rational.

The example of the English fishing club, the Pride of Derby (a river) illustrates how property rights can prevent stream pollution. In England, clubs own the right to fish along some rivers and are quick to respond to pollution threats. In the Derby case, a fishing club brought an action to stop an upstream municipality from polluting the stream. The courts viewed the issue from the property rights perspective; the municipality was harming the property of the fishing club and was required to modify its behavior. The court did not "balance the interests" of the fishing club against those of the city; rather, it enforced property rights.

In the United States, the ability of private parties such as fishing clubs to restrain municipal polluters is more limited. Under the Clean Water Act, the political authorities are told to "balance the interests" to decide what standards each polluter must meet. Not surprisingly, municipalities have been treated far more leniently than corporations. City cleanup targets are less stringent than those assigned industrial polluters; moreover, the cities are granted more lenient compliance schedules. In the political world, the status of the polluter determines the severity of the regulation. Politically preferred polluters are treated more leniently than are pariah polluters. Yet to the river and the fish, pollution is pollution.

Ownership of a pollution-sensitive species or area is a key strategy for environmental protection. By protecting privately owned fishing spots from pollution, the owners protect not only their portion of the river but also downstream areas. Similar ownership rights in oyster or shellfish beds, like those at Willapa Bay in Washington state, protect larger lakes and bays. As these examples suggest, partial ownership rights might suffice; even if only upstream or shoreline areas are privatized, the whole region can be protected.

Private ownership acts like a trip wire protecting the larger environmental commons because owners, by protecting their property, also incidentally act to protect downstream and offshore areas. For example, an owner who protects a species also protects its habitat.

Environmentalists sometimes talk about the "canary in the coal mine" safety rule. However, the canary is a far better warning signal when it has an owner that cares about it. Privatizing the commons creates multiple protections. This adoption strategy would do much to augment environmental protection efforts.

Note that the protection and conservation of groundwater is increasingly important. An advantage of the property rights approach is its flexibility. If the initial division of the property makes proper management difficult, the owner can restructure the property boundary. More than half of all drinking water now comes from aquifers. The problem is that aquifers are a classic commons. Each well drilled into the common pool benefits that owner but depletes the shared resource. Each surface property owner has a right to drill on her property. Exercising that right leads to excessive depletion and contamination.

However, new principles do not have to be devised from scratch since a similar problem has been solved routinely by the oil industry. Like an aquifer, an oil pool is an underground liquid resource subject to depletion and quality deterioration. To address this problem, the oil industry has developed a property rights restructuring program called *unitization,* which entails the assignment of all individual ownership rights in the common pool to a new entity (the unit). The unit manager then operates the field in an integrated fashion for the duration of production. Each owner receives a share of the income of the pool. Unitization illustrates the restructuring of already-existing property rights to allow more efficient management. Such reassignments of rights can be important for protecting and enhancing a resource.[16]

Unitization is not always easy. Still, it has been used successfully by the oil industry for many years. As groundwater becomes more valuable, the unitization approach might well be extended to management of groundwater.

Although many agree that command-and-control regulatory approaches to handling the problems found in environmental commons are costly and rarely achieve optimal goals, most still reject a property rights approach. For example, Harvard economist Robert Stavins states:

Does anyone really believe that acid rain can be efficiently controlled by assigning private property rights for U.S. airshed and then effecting negotiations among all affected parties? Economic-incentive mechanisms, on the other hand, avoid the impracticalities of the pure, private property approach, while retaining the merits of decentralized, market-driven policies.[17]

Stavins is right that urban air pollution control poses one of the most difficult problems to advocates of enclosing environmental commons. But he minimizes the problems associated with "green" tax and quota programs and neglects the role that private property rights could play to control air pollutants. Conceptually, one can envision a town or political jurisdiction "owning" its airshed (much as many communities do own their watershed). Practically, there has been little examination of how such properties might be "fenced" or how "trespass" might be detected and prevented. Such problems have led most environmentalists to favor political airshed management. Note, however, that these technical difficulties are not made any easier by resorting to political management. Nor has the performance of the EPA in this area been brilliant. Still, a property rights scheme suggests some directions for reforming the management of pollutants in airsheds.

One approach would involve the use of automobile emissions charges. The municipalities in which pollution is a problem could test each car to determine its emission profile. This profile could be based on emissions per kilometer, and a windshield or bumper sticker (a red, yellow, or green circle, for example) indicating the emission class of that car could be required. The owner would pay an annual fee based on the miles driven in his pollution classification. Since, however, the data suggest that many of the cars fall out of tune, there should also be monitoring sites throughout the city (some mobile to catch evaders) to detect any car emitting outside its pollution classification. Violators would pay a fine and move to a higher annual fee category.

This program would encourage owners to maintain their cars more carefully. Moreover, emission performance would become one of the features sought when buyers are choosing among vehicles to purchase. If one drives mostly outside of cities, this emissions performance would not be important; if one were driving largely in cities, one might purchase a tightly controlled vehicle in order to avoid the pollution fees.[18]

The most difficult environmental issues are global, such as the alleged greenhouse warming and ozone depletion. How serious these problems are is unclear. For many years into the future, the evidence will be ambiguous, but this is unlikely to make much difference to the policy debate. Despite the evidence to the contrary, many people are convinced that the Earth is warming, that such changes will have disastrous consequences, and that urgent global political action is needed to save Mother Earth (see chapter 1 on global warming). The major risk today is less global warming than it is that politicians might adopt antigrowth, antienergy policies.

> The major risk today is less global warming than it is that politicians might adopt antigrowth, antienergy policies.

A new layer of global regulation would be foolish. There is no reason to adopt solutions that will not work—and there is no prospect that international environmental bureaucracies will prove even as effective and reliable as their national counterparts.

How might the property rights approach be extended to the atmosphere? How might it be protected under the relatively weak rules of international property and liability law? Feasible answers are illusive. One approach is to consider the gradual evolution of private law into the international realm. In many areas, today one can make damage claims against foreign tort-feasors. Commercial liability treaties dealing with airlines, oil spills, and satellite disasters are examples of such arrangements.

Prevention, however, is not the only response to any postulated greenhouse warming. Given the uncertainties inherent in this area, the possibility that this effect might even prove beneficial on balance, and the difficulty in preventing a warming (were it valid), it would be wise to adopt a policy of resilience rather than avoidance. After all, the Earth is known to have thrived during warmer periods such as the

Medieval Climatic Optimum, which occurred some 1,000 years ago. Besides, even substantial efforts to cut energy use are only likely to delay rather than prevent these changes. Rather than spend trillions of dollars that might, at best, delay inevitable changes, a better move would be to deregulate and privatize the economies of the world, reduce the barriers to wealth creation, and thereby make the world more prosperous, more technologically adept, and better able to weather whatever harms that might emerge. Greater wealth and more advanced technologies would make possible many measures that would make whatever climate change that occurs less onerous in any event.

> The best way to enlist them is by giving them a stake in the fate of the Earth, by enclosing the environmental commons and deeding them a portion of those resources.

CONCLUSION

IN A WORLD of private property, unpopular values can be protected. In the political world, an airshed, a fishery, or a rain forest can be protected only if it garners sufficient political support. The extent of environmental values and goods at risk in the modern world is vast. Yet there are fewer than 200 governments, many of which now find it hard even to protect their own citizens. There are, however, more than 6 billion people on this globe. Only if the collective instincts of these peoples—their interests, skills, and wealth—are enlisted in the environmental cause is any appreciable fraction of the natural environment likely to receive adequate protection. The best way to enlist them is by giving them a stake in the fate of the Earth, by enclosing the environmental commons and deeding them a portion of those resources.

The challenge then is not to restrict markets, or to segregate the natural world from the global economy, but rather to integrate the ecology and the economy. By extending the institutions of markets and private property throughout the world, humanity will gain the proper incentives to save nature and better ability to do so. Ocean reefs in the South Pacific, Andean mountaintops, elephants in Africa, the shoreline of Lake Baikal—all deserve stewards, property owners, who can protect them from misuse.

Enclosing the environmental commons will not be easy. To many, open-access rules appear more just, more equitable, even when such rules pose serious threats to a sustainable ecology and society. In part, this reflects humanity's tribal prehistory—we instinctually find it hard to reject communal management approaches that served us well for many hundreds of thousands of years. Moreover, corporations have vested interests in the status quo. Current environmental rules create a complex array of penalties and subsidies. Economic actors, while unsure about the fairness or justness of the current balance, will still fear that change might make things worse. Enclosing airsheds and rivers would mean that corporations would have to pay for services (disposing of residuals) that they now get for free.

Such antiprivatization values make it hard even to move purely economic resources into the private sector. It is especially difficult to convert an informal (communal, custom-based, extra-legal) system to a modern, formal legal system. Nothing is feasible if the change is not viewed as legitimate. Yet today, many would view such a shift toward property rights as immoral, whether it was effective in protecting the resource in question or not. For example, politics has stalled efforts to privatize resources like the electromagnetic spectrum and many declining fisheries. Peruvian economist Hernando De Soto has noted the strong cultural opposition to any efforts to legitimize informal property rights in land and structures in less-developed countries.

Since we have had far less experience with ecological privatization, opposition is even more fierce. The history of the past century, where environmental values were first overridden and then supposedly advanced by massive central political intervention in the economy, has created a difficult situation. Since most people do not understand the creative role of private action, their naive view is Malthusian: If there were only fewer of us, if we only consumed less, if only we innovated less rapidly, then our footprints would be lighter, our threat to the planet less severe. Such views in a world of more than 6 billion people, where many still lack basic necessities, are immoral and impractical.

Some ideological environmentalists might object that attempts to integrate people and nature further are inherently suspect and denigrating to nature itself. Nature should be wild and free—not fenced and owned. This is a vision left over from humanity's open-access, tribal prehistory. Environmental enclosure is the path not yet taken, but both practice and theory show that it offers the best way to protect and preserve nature while building sustainable societies.

THE GLOBAL TRENDS THAT ARE SHAPING OUR WORLD

Compiled by Thomas Pearson

1

WORLD DOMESTIC PRODUCT

T HE WORLD GROSS domestic product (GDP) reflects the overall level of global prosperity. Global economic output has increased dramatically in recent decades. In constant 2000 U.S. dollars, world GDP has more than doubled from 1970 to 1997, rising from just nearly $13 trillion to just over $31 trillion. During that time, per capita GDP has also increased significantly. Spurred by advances in technology and a wave of market liberalism around the globe, individual productivity rose considerably in the latter half of the 1980s. Growth in per capita GDP slowed between 1979 and 1982 due to a worldwide global recession and the debt crisis that affected many developing countries, but it has since rebounded.

While North America and western Europe have enjoyed steady and significant economic growth for the past two centuries, many of the world's less-developed regions are beginning to catch up at an accelerated rate, taking advantage of modern methods of production and wider acceptance of free markets. As individuals and nations become more affluent, they gain the ability to devote an increasing share of their wealth to environmental protection. This "wealth effect" of a growing economy—the combination of increased economic efficiency through industrial modernization and the growing consumer preference for a clean environment—produces less air and water pollution and solid waste.

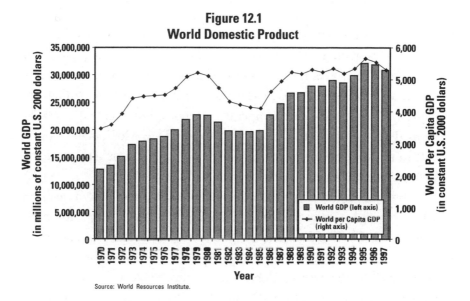

Figure 12.1
World Domestic Product

Source: World Resources Institute.

2

SATELLITE-BASED MONTHLY
GLOBAL TEMPERATURE

G
ROUND-BASED TEMPERATURE measurements indicate a warming of the planet of about 0.1 to 0.15°C per decade in the last century. This rate of increase has given rise to fears that man-made greenhouse gases may be dangerously warming the planet. The ground-based temperature record, however, suffers from many defects, such as the urban heat island effect, which make it difficult to tell whether the observed warming is real or an artifact of instrument or measurement error.

Highly accurate temperature measurements, however, have been taken from space using microwave sounding units (MSUs) aboard satellites since 1979. The data series graphed on the opposite page shows the difference between recorded temperature and the 1979 mean values. In October 2001, the average global temperature departure was 0.145°C, with a Northern Hemisphere temperature departure of 0.146°C and a Southern Hemisphere departure of 0.143°C, yielding an average increase of only 0.06°C per decade.. The satellite data are highly correlated with balloon temperature data taken from radiosonde instruments, strengthening the confidence in the accuracy of the satellite data.

MSUs measure the temperature of the lower troposphere, the atmospheric layer from the surface to 20,000 feet. This layer of the atmosphere is important for climatic research because, according to global circulation models, global warming would be much more pronounced in the lower troposphere than on the surface. The failure of the satellite data to verify rapid global warming predictions provides a strong argument against fears that man-made global warming will result in a climate catastrophe.

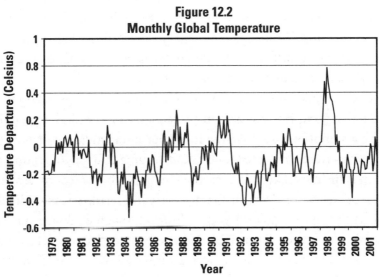

Figure 12.2
Monthly Global Temperature

Source: The University of Alabama at Huntsville.

3

WORLD POPULATION PROJECTIONS

ORLD POPULATION HAS more than doubled since 1950, chiefly because of the large reduction in worldwide death rates, not a major increase in global birth rates. The decline in death rates should continue as economic growth and scientific advances improve human health.

The United Nations issued a series of population projections for the 21st century, but population projections vary widely depending on the assumptions used. Without further understanding of how the projections were calculated, one might assume that the medium projection is the most likely. In fact, the medium UN projection assumes that acceleration or deceleration of death and fertility rates will continue as they have in recent years. However, much evidence suggests that this assumption is wrong. Historically, in a given society, after a lag period, a rapid reduction in fertility rates follows a drop in mortality rates due to economic progress. When economic development modernizes a society by improving women's education, per capita incomes, and the infant mortality rate, fertility rates tend to quickly decline to the point at which the population's growth rate is at or below zero. This process has already been completed in many Western nations. And even in Asia and Latin America, and some parts of Africa, fertility rates are dropping rapidly. Several Asian countries, including Bangladesh, India, Pakistan, and others, have experienced much faster decreases in fertility rates than previously expected. Future reductions in the world fertility rate are likely to produce populations more in line with the UN's low projection, at which point world population would reach 8 billion around 2050 and then begin to decline. In any event, population will slow at some point; even the highest projected UN trend has the world's population stop growing in 2075.

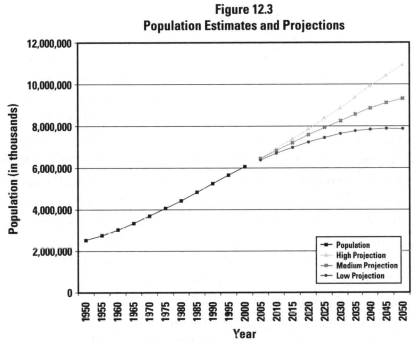

Figure 12.3
Population Estimates and Projections

Source: United Nations Population Division, 2000 Revision.

4

WORLD ESTIMATED AND PROJECTED TOTAL FERTILITY RATES

F ERTILITY RATES WORLDWIDE have been declining over the past several decades. One of the clearest indicators of fertility, the total fertility rate (TFR), corresponds to the average number of births per woman over the course of childbearing years. The world's TFR has dropped dramatically by almost half since 1950/55, from roughly 5 children per woman to around 2.7 children per woman today, and appears to be heading toward further decline. The TFR for the world's more-developed regions dropped by nearly half, from 2.8 children per woman in 1950/55 to 1.5 children per woman in 2000/05. This figure is below the replacement level of 2.1 children per woman. In the same time period, the less-developed regions of the world have witnessed a steep 53 percent reduction in their TFRs, while the least-developed regions have experienced an almost 21 percent reduction in their TFRs.

These fertility rate decreases are due, in part, to significant advancements in contraceptive technology since World War II. However, increased levels of economic development in all countries appear to be the driving force behind the reduction in fertility rates. That is, the wealth effect that allows nations and individuals to adopt environmental values also brings about a change in childbearing decisions. As people become wealthier and experience an increase in quality of life, they tend to bear fewer children.

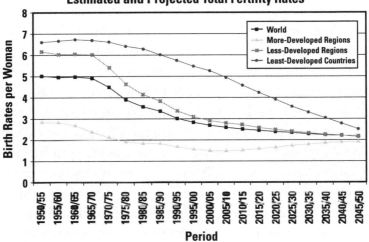

Figure 12.4
Estimated and Projected Total Fertility Rates

Source: United Nations Population Division, 2000 Revision.

5

WORLD ESTIMATED AND PROJECTED LIFE EXPECTANCY AT BIRTH

T HE 20TH CENTURY has witnessed an explosion in global health, as evidenced by the dramatic increase in human longevity. World life expectancy since 1950 has increased by more than 41 percent, from 46.5 years to 66 years. Life expectancies for populations in less-developed regions have increased by more than 50 percent, from 41 years in 1950/55 to 64.1 years currently. Life expectancies in the least-developed regions are close behind, increasing almost 45 percent since 1950/55. Populations from the world's more-developed regions have extended their average life span by just over nine years in the same period, from 66.2 years to 75.6 years.

Technological progress has been a driving force behind the extension of the human life span. Medical breakthroughs, infrastructure improvement, and innovations in communications and transport have improved the quality and capacity of medical relief to be administered to the world's populations. Improved medical care has also factored into the decline of infant mortality rates, which in turn strongly affects life expectancy at birth. Agriculture innovations also have yielded an increase in the supply and availability of the world's food. Increased food availability has averted millions of deaths from starvation that would have otherwise occurred.

Figure 12.5
World Estimated and Projected Life Expectancy at Birth

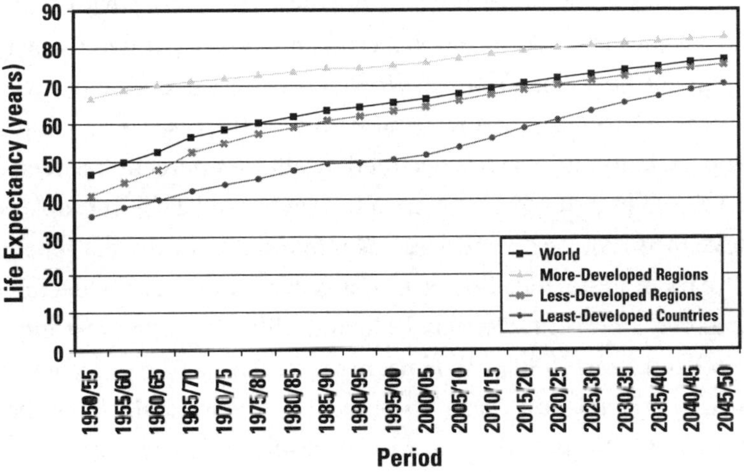

Source: U.N. Population Division, *World Population Prospects: The 2000 Revision* (2000).

6

WORLD ARABLE AND
PERMANENT CROPLAND

THE AMOUNT OF arable and permanent cropland worldwide has been increasing at a slow but relatively steady rate over the last 15 years. Global cropland area expanded by just over 2.4 percent between 1980 and 1997. While the overall trend was toward more cropland, many regions saw a decrease. The amount of European land under crops declined by about 4 percent between 1980 and 1995. Though North America has registered a slight cropland increase since 1980, cropland area has remained basically flat for the last five years. The former Soviet Union's area under crops declined by just under 1 percent between 1980 and 1993. The greatest increases in cropland from 1980 to 1993 occurred in Africa (7.2 percent), Oceania (5.7 percent), and Asia (2.9 percent). The large declines that occurred in 1991 and 1993 were the result of steep drops in food commodity prices.

Before the 20th century, the world increased its food supply chiefly by expanding the amount of land cleared and planted in crops. By dramatically increasing the amount of food grown on land already under cultivation, humanity has already managed to save up to 10 million square miles—the total area of North America—of rain forests, wetlands, and mountain terrain from being plowed down. Higher agricultural yields were achieved by substituting more productive crop varieties, pesticides, and fertilizers for extra acreage.

Figure 12.6
World Arable and Permanent Cropland

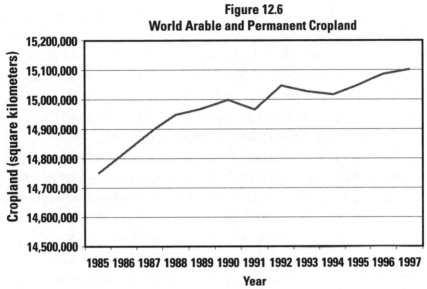

Source: Organization for Economic Cooperation and Development, *OECD Environmental Data, Compendium 1999* (Paris: OECD, 1999).

7

WORLD PRODUCTION OF CEREALS

WORLD CEREAL OUTPUT increased from close to 877 million metric tons in 1961 to more than 2.05 billion metric tons in 1998. Japan and China are the globe's greatest net importers of cereal, while the United States, Canada, and France remain the world's leading net exporters of cereals. The world's developed countries accounted for most of this period's cereal production. However, the percentage of produced cereal from developing regions climbed from 45 percent in 1961 to 58 percent in 1998.

Cereal production expanded rapidly from 1974 to 1989 as Green Revolution technologies were adopted by farmers throughout developing regions, particularly in Asia. Since 1989, a slowdown in the growth rate of aggregate cereal production is discernible. This slowdown is primarily the result of grain surpluses that have driven down commodity prices and diminished the incentive to invest in cereal production, irrigation development projects, and agriculture infrastructure.

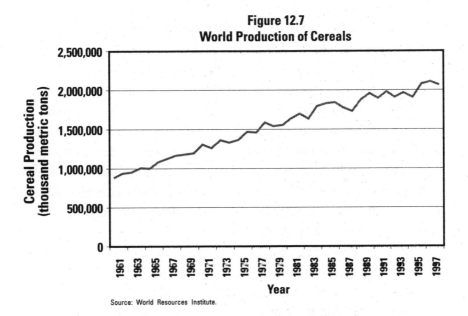

Figure 12.7
World Production of Cereals

Source: World Resources Institute.

8

WORLD AREA OF CEREALS HARVESTED

THE ACREAGE DEVOTED to cereal production increased from 1961 to 1981 and has since slightly decreased. The dispersion of Green Revolution farming technologies into Asia and other developing regions boosted cereal production through massive irrigation expansion, new high-yielding crop varieties, enhanced fertilizers and pesticides, and newer, more efficient farming methods. India was able to double its wheat yields in only a few years, and China now supports 21 percent of the world's population on just 7 percent of its arable land. Since the 1970s, global rice yields have risen 49 percent, wheat yields have risen 50 percent, and corn and sorghum have risen 28 percent.

The coming years promise even more productive cereal varieties. For example, the Veery wheats, particularly suited to Africa's subtropical climate, could boost the region's yields by up to 15 percent. Similarly, new Chinese hybrid rice and acid- and salt-tolerant plant varieties that can thrive in hot, arid, and previously uncultivable areas are under development.

Figure 12.8
Area of Cereals Harvested, World

Source: World Resources Institute.

9

WORLD INDEX OF PER CAPITA AGRICULTURAL PRODUCTION

A GRICULTURAL PRODUCTION HAS consistently outpaced population growth over the past 30 years. The pattern of per capita agricultural production has also been fairly consistent: a period of impressive growth, followed by a brief period of stagnation or decline, followed by more growth. Although there has been a recent measurable slowdown of per capita agricultural output due to economic factors, it appears to be on the upswing again. Causes of the brief slowdown included tremendous surpluses in world food supplies that prompted North America and Europe to restrain their production. Moreover, the chaos that followed the demise of communism in Eastern Europe and the former Soviet Union dramatically reduced the region's contribution to global agricultural production. Meanwhile, the developing world has managed to increase agricultural productivity (recently) at an annual rate of 5 percent.

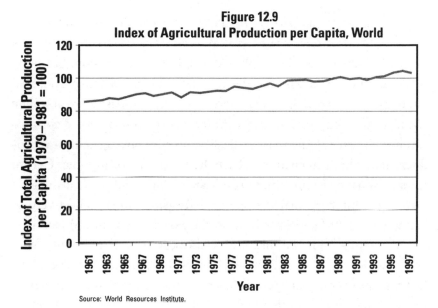

Figure 12.9
Index of Agricultural Production per Capita, World

Source: World Resources Institute.

10

WORLD TOTAL INDEX OF AGRICULTURAL PRODUCTION

LMOST WITHOUT EXCEPTION, agricultural productivity worldwide has risen year after year since 1961. Some of this increase can be attributed to cropland expansion, but most is the result of technological advances in farming, which have boosted yields per hectare of land exponentially over the past 25 years. The world's agriculture research system has proven international collaboration to be one of the most critical boons to global agricultural productivity. The International Rice Research Institute, the Centro Internacional de Mejoramiento de Maiz y Trigo, and the Consultative Group on International Agricultural Research work collectively to bring new scientific ideas to bear on the world's agricultural sectors.

The outlook for the future of yield performance is bright, especially considering the breakthroughs in the field of biotechnology. The fact that the overall yield performance of most crops shows little sign of slowing down indicates that higher yields are still attainable. Developing countries showed considerable progress with certain crops in the 1980s and into the 1990s. For example, worldwide yields of maize grew at about 47 kilograms per hectare for each year in the 1980s and 55 kilograms per hectare for each year in the 1990s. Many developing countries have enjoyed yield gains that were even higher than the world average. Chile experienced an astronomical gain, more than doubling its grain output from 2,124 kilograms per hectare in 1980 to 4,540 kilograms per hectare in 2000, according to the World Bank.

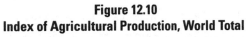

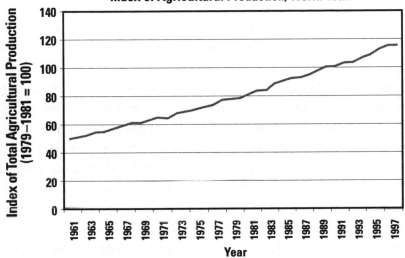

Figure 12.10
Index of Agricultural Production, World Total

Source: World Resources Institute.

11

WORLD INDEX OF PER CAPITA FOOD PRODUCTION

HE WORLD'S CONTINUING growth in population has sparked some concern that food production might not increase fast enough to feed everyone. But if trends continue as they have over the past 30 years, people will be better nourished in the future despite population gains. There is a fairly consistent upward trend in world per capita food production from 1961 to 1998, despite the fact that the world's population has more than doubled since 1950. Over this period, the amount of food produced per person increased about 23 percent, mostly due to advances in farming technology.

The same kind of research that has brought about life-extending discoveries in vaccines, sanitation, and nutrition has also fostered advances in genetic engineering, irrigation, and pesticides that have kept food productivity well ahead of global increases in population. It is important to note that population growth is closely related to food abundance. More abundant food has helped reduce starvation and malnutrition and thus cut global death rates. The result has been higher population growth rates. On the other hand, rising food production often correlates with lower fertility rates. In other words, greater food security leads to fewer children per woman. Economic growth and technological progress have kept the food supply several steps ahead of the growing population.

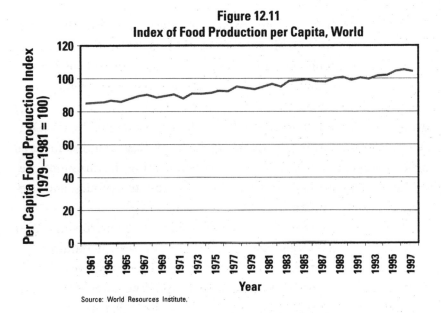

Figure 12.11
Index of Food Production per Capita, World

Source: World Resources Institute.

12

WORLD TOTAL INDEX OF
FOOD PRODUCTION

T HERE WAS A steady, nearly uninterrupted growth in total
world food production from 1961 to 1998. The growth in
production continued despite ever lower world food prices
over the same period. The majority of this increase in production is
due to the implementation of better agricultural technology resulting
from new research. This research, much of it conducted by the Consultative Group on International Agricultural Research, has fostered
major advances in pesticides, genetic engineering, fertilization, prevention of soil erosion, crop rotation, irrigation techniques, and livestock production techniques.

In general, the rate of improvement seems to be increasing. After
yields exceed 2,000 kilograms per hectare per year, it requires less
time to achieve each next 1,000 kilograms per hectare per year in productivity. The reason for this is that the shift from subsistence agriculture to technological agriculture is an initially expensive procedure.
After the shift is made, it is much easier to incorporate new scientific
findings into farming practice. Most countries in the developing
world have recently gone through this shift toward technology or will
in the near future. The potential for increased implementation of the
latest agricultural knowledge suggests that the growth in world food
production will not slow in the near term.

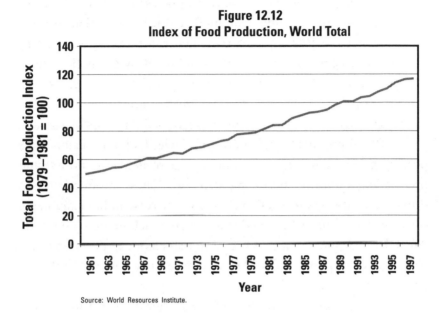

Figure 12.12
Index of Food Production, World Total

Source: World Resources Institute.

13

WORLD TOTAL FOOD COMMODITY INDEX

G LOBAL FOOD PRICES have dropped steeply since the 1960s. This index of food commodity prices shows that throughout the 1960s, prices remained somewhat steady. A large peak in price came in the mid-1970s, followed by dramatic gains in food production that greatly outpaced population increases. The price surges in 1973/74 and 1977 were related directly and indirectly to the oil crisis of those years, which increased the costs of some aspects of food production and gave the Soviet Union (a major oil exporter) the wealth to purchase grain on the world market for livestock production, radically increasing demand. These productivity improvements have led to a relatively steady increase in food abundance since the late 1970s, when food prices were much higher. This abundance has brought about a near end to mass famine. Those that have occurred in the past few decades have been caused by political strife, not lack of resources.

Several factors contribute to the reduction in world food prices. One of the most significant has been the myriad recent advances in agricultural technology. Another important factor in the drop in food prices was increased liberalization of global trade, which reduced the tariffs and price subsidies that previously had inflated food prices. Competition and increased crop specialization brought about a more efficient market in agricultural commodities.

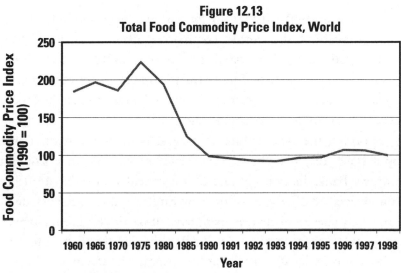

Figure 12.13
Total Food Commodity Price Index, World

Source: World Resources Institute.

14

WORLD FISH CATCH

THE GROWING DEMAND for fish products has fueled the increase of the world's commercial fishing industry. Worldwide, the fishery harvest is more than 125 million metric tons per year, an increase of more than 250 percent above the harvest of just four decades ago. Advanced technologies have enabled ocean harvesting on an unprecedented scale.

However, the current rate of harvest is depleting many marine populations. In 1994, the U.S. government shut down portions of George's Bank, historically one of the world's most fertile fishing grounds located off the coast of New England, due to fishery depletion. Many species of marine mammals, in particular, are facing serious population declines as well. Worldwide, the fish catch had declined somewhat after 1989 but has resumed its steady climb.

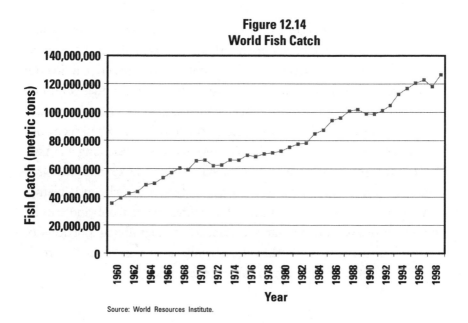

Figure 12.14
World Fish Catch

Source: World Resources Institute.

15

WORLD AQUACULTURE PRODUCTION

AS DEMAND FOR fish products has continued to climb, some people have developed methods to raise fish on the equivalent of farms. Known as aquaculture, this practice holds the potential to reduce pressures on marine fisheries; more fish would be raised for human consumption rather than caught on the open seas.

Aquaculture production increased by more than 250 percent between 1984 and 1997, with the greatest increase occurring in Asia. Successful aquaculture techniques have been developed to farm salmon, tilapia, catfish, trout, abalone, oysters, crawfish, and shrimp, among others. Already in the United States, most trout and catfish served in restaurants are farm raised, as are significant portions of crawfish and oysters. Worldwide, shrimp farms produce approximately one-fifth of the shrimp sold on the market.

Figure 12.15
World Aquaculture Production

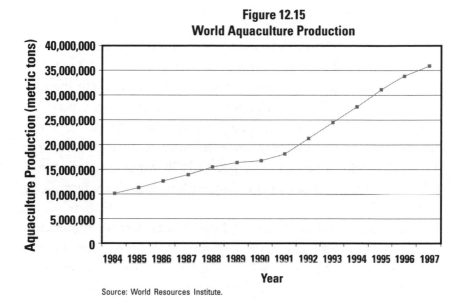

Source: World Resources Institute.

16

WORLD PER CAPITA EMISSIONS OF CARBON DIOXIDE

G LOBAL EMISSIONS OF carbon dioxide (CO_2) have increased since the 1950s, primarily driven by the rise in fossil fuel consumption throughout the world. The dramatic increase in the 1960s and 1970s has since slowed, however, with per capita CO_2 emissions actually declining from 1979 to 1983. Per capita global emission of CO_2 has leveled off over the past two decades, peaking at 1.23 metric tons of carbon per capita in 1979. Since then, per capita CO_2 emissions have fluctuated mildly, with no significant increase or decrease.

The chart also shows that over the past three decades, the amount of CO_2 released per million dollars of world GDP has fallen. That is, less CO_2 is emitted today to achieve the same increment in economic growth of the past. The decline in emissions per unit of growth is striking, falling about one-third from 1970 to 1997. Arguably, the more prosperous we become, the more the relative significance of CO_2 emissions in our global economy will diminish.

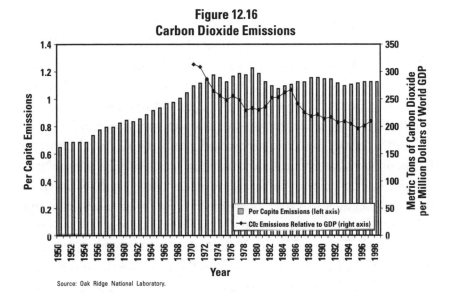

Figure 12.16
Carbon Dioxide Emissions

Source: Oak Ridge National Laboratory.

17

WORLD ESTIMATED ATMOSPHERIC RELEASES OF CHLOROFLUOROCARBONS

C HLOROFLUOROCARBONS (CFCs) WERE first used in the 1930s as refrigerants. After World War II, CFC-11 and CFC-12, the two most prominent CFCs, were also used as blowing agents for closed-cell foams (used for insulation) and as propellants for aerosol sprays. CFCs were popular because they are nonflammable and nontoxic, unlike the substances they replaced.

In the 1970s, concerns were raised about the potential impact of CFCs on the stratospheric ozone layer. Releases of CFCs into the atmosphere, it is believed, initiate a chain reaction that thins the ozone layer and potentially exposes the Earth's surface to an increase in damaging ultraviolet solar radiation. These concerns led to the ban of CFCs for use in aerosols in the United States and an overall decline in the release of CFC-11 and CFC-12 into the atmosphere. However, this downward trend was quickly overtaken by a rapid increase in the use of CFCs in the developing world. This trend was reversed with the ratification of the Montreal Protocol in 1987 (subsequently amended in 1990 and 1992), which calls for phasing out all CFC production. Due to the widespread use of CFCs, particularly in refrigeration units and air-conditioners, the phaseout will come at considerable costs: an estimated $100 billion in the United States alone.

Figure 12.17
World Estimated Atmospheric Releases
of Chlorofluorocarbons

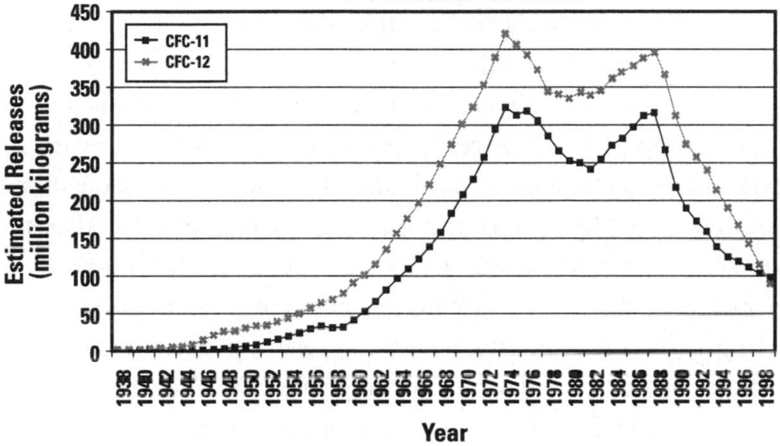

Source: Alternative Fluorocarbons Environmental Acceptability Study, 2001.

18

WORLD METALS AND MINERALS COMMODITY INDEX

T HERE WAS A sustained, though erratic, decline in the world prices of metals and minerals from 1965 to 1998. Although metals and minerals exist in fixed quantities, prices have tended to decrease rather than increase over time. The chief reason for lower prices is that the supply of metals and minerals is increasing. New supplies of these resources have been discovered with improvements in technology and scientific knowledge that allow miners to locate sources for metals and minerals more precisely. Also, new technologies have made mining of less concentrated minerals, or minerals located in previously inaccessible areas, economically feasible. Improvements in mining technology were spurred by the volatility of the market, as depicted in the graph. Despite the long-term downward trend in prices, occasional increases in price caused by sudden scarcity made advanced technologies profitable. This encourages further research, and once demand is met, market forces foster increases in efficiency, which in turn lower the price of new technology. This spiral of ever-more productive technology tends to have the effect of increasing supply faster than demand.

On the demand side, the occasional price spikes encourage conservation efforts. More abundant substitutes for the commodity were found, technologies that economize on the use of scarce resources were developed, and more efficient methods of waste recovery were discovered. Markets ceaselessly encourage the development of more efficient resource uses, essentially substituting knowledge for more physical quantities, thus making the limited supply of any physical commodity increasingly less important.

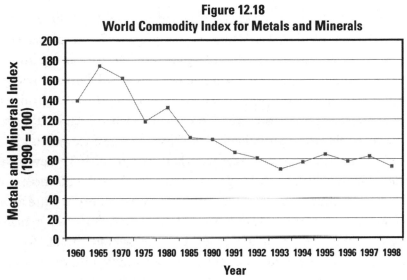

Figure 12.18
World Commodity Index for Metals and Minerals

Source: World Resources Institute.

19

CRUDE OIL DOMESTIC FIRST PURCHASE PRICES

T HE PRICE OF crude oil declined steadily from 1959 to the early 1970s. Prices increased sharply in 1974 due to the Arab oil embargo and jumped again in 1979 in response to the Iranian revolution. After regional political crises and domestic energy regulations relaxed, the price of oil dropped steeply. In 1994, crude oil prices adjusted for inflation were lower than they had been in 20 years. The years 1995 through 2000 saw volatility in prices once again.

When crude oil prices exceeded $40 per barrel in 1981, new techniques for locating and drilling for oil were developed. This increased the supply, thus loosening the OPEC nations' ability to affect oil prices. New geological research boosted the exploration of oil in many countries that had previously produced little or none. Brazil, for example, eventually produced as much as a half million barrels per day. Similar new production capabilities in countries around the globe greatly increased non-OPEC sources of oil.

Higher oil prices also encouraged switching to other sources of energy, chiefly coal and natural gas. New research in these competing energy sources yielded similar gains in production capacity, greatly increasing overall energy supplies. This diversification of energy sources and technologies has both cut oil prices to pre-crisis levels and made the oil market more resilient to other potential global crises.

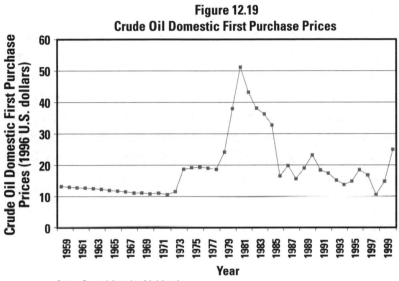

Figure 12.19
Crude Oil Domestic First Purchase Prices

Source: Energy Information Administration.

20

WORLD TOTAL CONSUMPTION OF ENERGY

A S THE WORLD'S economy has grown, so has its demand for energy. Demand has increased consistently, with only occasional lulls, such as the recession of the early 1980s that temporarily suppressed energy demand. Total final consumption of energy worldwide increased by nearly 50 percent from 1970 to 1990. This figure reflects the use of energy in all economic sectors—industrial, agricultural, residential, and commercial—as well as the nonenergy uses of fossil fuels. Over the same time period, the amount of electricity generated more than doubled, with the greatest increase occurring from the upswing in use of nuclear power to generate electricity.

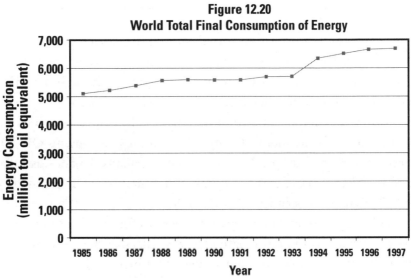

Figure 12.20
World Total Final Consumption of Energy

Source: OECD Environmental Data Compendium, 1999.

21

CONSUMPTION OF ENERGY PER UNIT OF GROSS DOMESTIC PRODUCT

E NERGY USE HAS increased substantially over the past two decades. However, as nations become more economically advanced, pursuing economic development through a market economy, energy efficiency increases significantly. Consider the trend in energy consumption per unit of GDP in developed countries. In Organisation for Economic Co-operation and Development (OECD) nations (western Europe, the United States, Canada, Japan, Australia, and New Zealand), energy consumption per unit of GDP declined by nearly 22 percent between 1980 and 1997.

The same trend toward greater energy efficiency did not occur in the former communist nations. Centralized economies lack the market pressures that constantly encourage increased efficiency and innovation. As a result, the technological breakthroughs that allow industries to produce more using a constant resource or energy base fail to materialize, and potential efficiency gains are sacrificed.

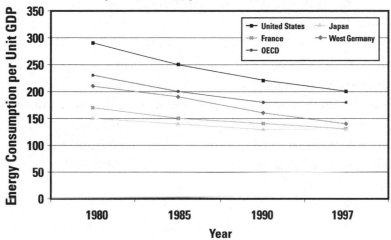

Figure 12.21
Consumption of Energy per Unit of Gross Domestic Product

Source: OECD Environmental Data Compendium, 1999.

22

U.S. WATER QUALITY VIOLATIONS

T HE PERCENTAGE OF U.S. rivers and streams violating Environmental Protection Agency (EPA) standards for fecal coliform bacteria, dissolved oxygen, and phosphorus is declining. High concentrations of fecal coliform bacteria can cause a variety of infectious diseases, including cholera and typhoid. Common sources of these bacteria are insufficiently treated sewage and runoff from pastures, feedlots, and cities. The graph shows a fairly consistent decline in the rate of fecal coliform bacteria violations until 1988. Since then violations have fluctuated rather significantly. Analysts at the U.S. Department of Interior suspect that the fluctuations are the result of unaccounted-for measurement changes rather than an actual trend.

A violation of the dissolved oxygen standard means the tested water lacks oxygen concentrations high enough to fully support aquatic life. Low levels of dissolved oxygen can reduce the solubility of trace elements and affect the taste and odor of the water. The violation rate for this standard has dropped slightly even though larger population densities have increased oxygen-demanding loads. Large technology investments in point source controls have helped keep this figure low.

Phosphorus in streams could add to oxygen depletion and increase the growth of aquatic vegetation, which can then clog water intake pipes. This figure dropped rapidly following limits put on the phosphate content in detergents in the late 1960s and early 1970s. Improvements in the 1980s can be attributed to a reduction in phosphorus fertilizer use and point source controls at sewage treatment, food processing, and other industrial plants.

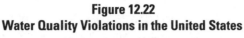

Figure 12.22
Water Quality Violations in the United States

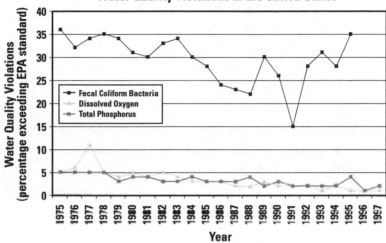

Source: Council on Environmental Quality.

23

U.S. CANCER DEATH RATES

C ANCER WAS ESTIMATED to cause about 520,600 deaths in the United States in 1996. From 1975 to 1990, cancer death rates increased from about 162 people per 100,000 in population to about 173 per 100,000. Since 1990, however, the annual cancer death rate has decreased, getting back to below its 1975 level. This decline was mostly confined to persons under the age of 65 at the time of death.

Lung, female breast, prostate, or colon/rectum cancers cause more than 50 percent of all cancer deaths. Much of the decrease can be attributed to a steep decline in lung cancer death rates due to a decline in smoking rates. In 1965, 42 percent of adults smoked compared to fewer than 25 percent in 1995.

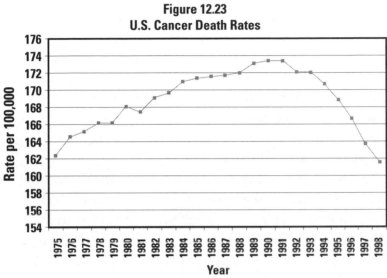

Figure 12.23
U.S. Cancer Death Rates

Source: National Cancer Institute.

24

U.S. CANCER INCIDENCE RATES

CANCER INCIDENCE RATES for all cancers combined and for most of the top 10 cancer sites declined from 1992 to 1998, reversing a 20-year trend of increasing cancer cases in the United States. Cancer incidence rates for all sites combined increased by 1.2 percent per year from 1973 to 1990, but from 1990 to 1995, the annual death rate for cancer decreased by 0.7 percent per year. The largest decreases occurred in persons between the ages 35 and 44 years and in persons who were above 75 years.

The four leading cancer sites for 1990 to 95 were lung and bronchus, prostate, female breast, and colon/rectum, which account for approximately 54 percent of all newly diagnosed cancers. The largest declines in incidence rates occurred in colon/rectum cancer (–2.3), lung cancer (–1.1), and prostate cancer (–1.0). There was no change in female breast cancer incidence rates.

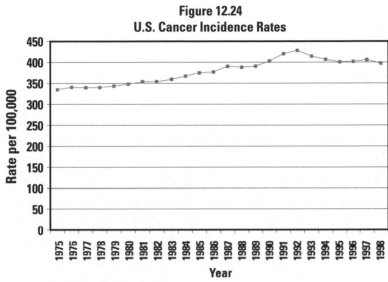

Figure 12.24
U.S. Cancer Incidence Rates

Source: National Cancer Institute.

25

U.S. AIR POLLUTANT EMISSIONS TRENDS

A GGREGATE EMISSION LEVELS for most of the six criteria pollutants have been declining fairly steadily over the last few decades, after reaching a high point in the middle of the 20th century. For example, annual carbon monoxide emissions are as low as they were in the late 1940s, even though the number of carbon-producing sources, such as industrial plants, have increased significantly since then. Lead emissions have drastically fallen, by 98 percent, since 1970.

The chart shows the annual values for each of the six pollutants after they are converted to a base year, which makes it possible to compare emission estimates in later years to the base year. Note that between 1984 and 1985, the U.S. EPA significantly overhauled its emission estimation methodology, which is prominently depicted for particulate matter. Categories of emissions were added to the total for particulate matter, such as natural wind erosion and fugitive dust, skewing the data significantly. In fact, however, the only difference is that more sources were considered as pollutants, raising the emissions estimates for this pollutant. Taking those changes into account, annual emissions for other pollutants, like particulate matter and volatile organic compounds, have dropped steadily since the 1970s as well.

Generally speaking, the downward trends in emission estimates reflect the wealth effect discussed earlier regarding other environmental trends. As a society becomes wealthier, it is able to employ a greater portion of disposable income to such things as environmental improvement. Thus we can see that as the total wealth in a society or nation increases, this translates into a cleaner environment as individuals and industries learn from past mistakes and innovate to produce more efficient and cleaner technologies. This effect explains why wealthy nations generally have improving environmental records, while less-developed nations are unable to devote resources to environmental concerns and, sometimes, experience deteriorating environments.

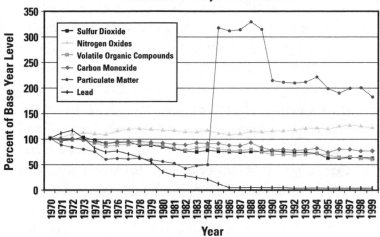

Figure 12.25
Emissions of Major Air Pollutants

Source: EPA, *National Air Quality Emissions and Trends Report.*

26

U.S. AMBIENT CONCENTRATIONS
OF POLLUTANTS

A mbient concentrations for five criteria pollutants have been declining steadily since 1980 and particulate matter has also been declining since 1990. Lead concentrations dropped by more than 93 percent from 1980 to 1999. Carbon monoxide concentrations experienced the next most significant decrease, falling 57 percent in the same period. The other pollutants fell dramatically as well.

Ambient concentration refers to the actual concentration of a pollutant in the air. The fact that these concentrations are declining suggests that air quality is improving and that our atmosphere is not trapping emitted pollutants. The declining rates of ambient concentrations are another indication that environmental problems are lessening and that the level of economic growth is positively related to the health of the environment.

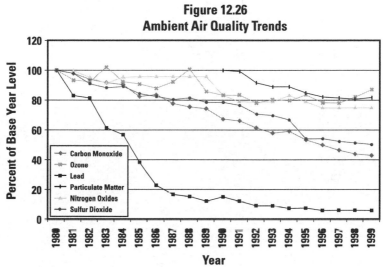

Figure 12.26
Ambient Air Quality Trends

Source: EPA, *National Air Quality Emissions and Trends Report.*

NOTES

Introduction

1. Robert C. Paehlke, *Environmentalism and the Future of Progressive Politics* (New Haven, Conn., and London: Yale University Press, 1989), p. 273.
2. Al Gore, *Earth in the Balance* (Boston and New York: Houghton Mifflin, 2000), p. 269.
3. Worldwatch Institute, *Vital Signs 2001* (New York and London: Norton, 2000), p. 122.
4. Anna Bramwell, *Ecology in the 20th Century: A History* (New Haven, Conn., and London: Yale University Press, 1989), p. 39.
5. Paul Romer, "Economic Growth," in David R. Henderson, ed., *Fortune Encyclopedia of Economics* (Warner Books, accessed at URL: http://www.stanford.edu/~promer/Econgro.htm).

Chapter 1

1. *Times* (London), July 9, 2001.
2. *New York Times*, August 19, 2000.
3. *New York Times*, August 27, 2000.
4. *Washington Post*, July 9, 2001.
5. *Time*, April 9, 2001, "Life In The Greenhouse," by Michael D. Lemonick, David Bjerklie, Robert H. Boyle, Andrea Dorfman and Dick Thompson, p. 24, et. seq.
6. P. T. Doran, J. C. Priscu, W. B. Lyons, J. E. Walsh, A. G. Fountain, D. M. Mc-Knight, D. L. Moorhead, R. A. Virginia, D. H. Wall, G. D. Clow, C. H. Fritsen, C. P. McKay, and A. N. Parsons, "Antarctic Climate Cooling and Terrestrial Ecosystem Response," *Nature* (January 13, 2002), advance online publication; and I. Joughin and S. Tulaczyk, *Science*, 295 (January 18, 2002), p. 476.
7. This information was provided through interviews with a *Time* reporter.
8. As one of 122 lead authors of IPCC 2001 Working Group I, I find the scientific text an excellent assessment of the state of the climate and climate science. Media reports generally do not convey the complex and uncertain nature expressed in the main text, however.
9. The total temperature response to human-induced greenhouse forcing is believed not to be immediate but lags behind the actual increase in the gases. Given the amount of greenhouse gases in the air today, the general thinking is that a further temperature rise is already built in (perhaps another 0.5°F). In other words, the

theory suggests that if greenhouse gases were stabilized today at their present levels, the Earth's temperature would continue to creep upward a little more, though uncertainties are quite large.

10. Intergovernmental Panel on Climate Change, 2001, *Climate Change 2001: The Scientific Basis* (Cambridge, U.K.: Cambridge University Press, 2001), pp. 190–208.

11. The model assumptions that produce the extreme 10°F warming are difficult to accept. This requires a threefold increase in CO_2 production in the next 40 years (IPCC Scenario A1F1) or a compounded rate increase of 3 percent per year. The actual rate of increase in CO_2 production by humans is less than 1 percent per year (of which half is removed by natural means).

12. R. S. Lindzen, M. D. Chou, and A. Y. Hou, "Does the Earth Have an Adaptive Infrared Iris?" *Bulletin of the American Meteorological Society,* vol. 82 (2001), pp. 417–32.

13. J. Chen, B. E. Carlson, and A. D. Del Genio, "Evidence for Strengthening of the Tropical General Circulation in the 1990s," *Science,* vol. 295 (2002), pp. 838–841; D. L. Hartmann, "Tropical Surprises," *Science,* vol. 295 (2002), pp. 811–812; and B. A. Wielicki, T. Wong, R. P Allan, A. Slingo, J. T. Kiehl, B. J. Soden, C. T. Gordon, A. J. Miller, A. K. Yang, D. A. Randall, F. Robertson, J. Susskind, and H. Jacobowitz, "Evidence for Large Decadal Variability in the Tropical Mean Radiative Energy Budget," *Science,* vol. 295 (2002), pp. 841–844.

14. B. A. Wielicki, T. Wong, R. P Allan, A. Slingo, J. T. Kiehl, B. J. Soden, C. T. Gordon, A. J. Miller, A. K. Yang, D. A. Randall, F. Robertson, J. Susskind, and H. Jacobowitz, "Evidence for Large Decadal Variability in the Tropical Mean Radiative Energy Budget" *Science,* vol. 295 (2002), pp. 841–844.

15. B. Lin, B. A. Wiclicki, L. H. Chambers, Y. Hu, and K. M. Xu, "The Iris Hypothesis: A Negative or Positive Cloud Feedback?" *Journal of Climate,* vol. 15 (2002), pp. 3–7. The authors use a new method to suggest a surface warming may induce a slight positive feedback rather than a negative feedback proposed by Lindzen.

16. *Climate Change 2001,* p. 715.

17. National Academy of Sciences, *Climate Change Science: An Analysis of Key Questions* (Washington, D.C.: National Academy Press, 2001), p. 17.

18. Ibid.

19. *Climate Change 2001,* p. 34.

20. *Climate Change 2001,* p. 641.

21. Kim Griggs, BBC News online, March 12, 2002.

22. Energy Information Administration, *Impacts of the Kyoto Protocol on U.S. Energy and Economic Activity* (Washington, D.C.: U.S. Department of Energy), http://www.eia.doe.gov/neic/press/press109.html. Costs estimated for a reduction of CO_2 by 3 percent (not Kyoto's required 7 percent) below 1990 emissions are between $125 and $280 billion per year on an economy of $9,425 billion, or about 1 to 3 percent per year.

Chapter 2

1. Paul Ehrlich, *The Population Bomb* (New York: Sierra Club-Ballantine, 1968), i.

2. Lester Brown, "The World Outlook for Conventional Agriculture," *Science* 158:604-611 (November 3, 1967) 604.

3. Vaclav Smil, *Long-Range Perspectives on Inorganic Fertilizers in Global Agriculture,* Travis P. Hignett Memorial Lecture (Muscle Shoals, Ala.: IFDC, 1999).

4. United Nations Population Division, *World Population Prospects Population Database*, at URL http://www.esa.un.org/unpp/index.asp?Panel=1)

5. Per Pinstrup-Andersen and R. Pandya-Lorch, eds., *Unfinished Agenda: Perspectives on Overcoming Hunger, Poverty, and Environmental Degradation* (Washington, D.C.: IFPRI, 2001).

6. *The World's Water, Is There Enough?* (World Meteorological Organization, 1997) at URL: http://www.unesco.org/science/waterday 2000/WMO-No.857_E.pdf.

7. United Nations Division for Sustainable Development, *Comprehensive Assessment of the Freshwater Resources of the World*, 1999 at URL http://www.un.org/esa/sustdev/freshwat.htm)

8. S. Rajaram and N. E. Borlaug, "Approaches to Breeding for Wide Adaptation, Yield Potential, Rust Resistance and Drought Tolerance" (paper presented at Primer Simposio Internacional de Trigo, Cd. Obregon, Mexico, April 7–9, 1997).

9. G. S. Khush, "Modern Varieties—Their Real Contribution to Food Supply and Equity," *Geojournal*, vol. 35, no. 3 (1995) pp. 275–84.

10. Rajaram and Borlaug.

11. A. Mujeeb-Kazi and G. P. Hettel, eds., *Utilizing Wild Grass Biodiversity in Wheat Improvement—15 Years of Research in Mexico for Global Wheat Improvement*, Wheat Special Report, no. 29 (Mexico, D.F.: CIMMYT, 1995).

12. Clive James, *Global Review of Commercialized Transgenic Crops: 2001*, International Service for the Acquisition of Agri-Biotech Applications Brief, no. 24 (Los Baños, Philippines: ISAAA Southeast Asia Center, 2002).

13. *Biotechnology and Food*, 2nd ed. (New York: American Council on Science and Health, 2000).

14. Monsanto personal communication, 2002.

Chapter 3

1. UNFPA mission statement (accessed March 29, 2002), http://www.unfpa.org/about/mission/english.htm.

2. Sierra Club, "Ecoregions: Strategy" (accessed March 29, 2002), http://www.sierraclub.org/ecoregions/strategy.asp.

3. The U.S. Census Bureau's most recent (May 2000) projections, for example, envision a decline in the population of continental Europe from 729 million in 2000 to 642 million in 2050. For Japan, the corresponding figures are 126 million in 2000 and a projected 101 million in 2050. Data available electronically from the U.S. Census Bureau Web site (accessed September 1, 2001), http://www.census.gov/ipc/www /idbagg html.

4. For 1999, Russia reported 2.144 million deaths and 1.214 million births. Data taken from the Web site of France's Institut National d'Études Démographiques (accessed September 19, 2001), http://www.ined.fr/population-en-chiffres/pays-developpes/popnaide.htm.

5. Jaya Dalal, "Population: U.N. Agency Projects Record Income for 1996," Inter Press Service (November 7, 1995).

6. Al Gore, *Earth in the Balance: Ecology and the Human Spirit* (New York: Houghton Mifflin, 2000), p. 309.

7. Vice President Al Gore on *Nightline* (ABC News), Transcript # 3467 (September 6, 1994).

8. Planned Parenthood Federation of America, Fact Sheet (accessed October 1, 2001), http://www.plannedparenthood.org/library/FAMILYPLANNINGISSUES/fpworldof difference_fact.html.

9. Gore, *Earth in the Balance*, p. 317.

10. Vice President Al Gore, "Beyond the Numbers," *CNN* Special, Transcript #350-1 (July 3, 1994).

11. Vice President Al Gore in "Beyond the Numbers," *CNN* Special, Transcript #350-1 (July 3, 1994).

12. Gore in "Beyond the Numbers."

13. Gore, *Earth in the Balance*, p. 310.

14. Gore, *Earth in the Balance*, p. xxi.

15. All data in this paragraph taken from United Nations, *Demographic Yearbook 1998* (New York: United Nations, 2000), Tables 1 and 5. Estimates of population density are for midyear 1998, and the estimate of global population density excludes uninhabited territory (e.g., Antarctica).

16. United Nations, *World Population Prospects: The 2000 Revision*, vol. I (New York: United Nations, 2001), p. 50.

17. Michael R. Haines, "The Population of the United States, 1790–1920," in Stanley Engerman and Robert E. Gallman, *The Cambridge Economic History of the United States*, vol. 2 (New York: Cambridge University Press, 2000), Table 1.

18. Gore, *Earth in the Balance*, p. 309.

19. Projections available electronically from U.S. Census Bureau International Data Base (accessed September 26, 2001), http://www.census.gov/ipc/www/idbagg.html.

20. Haines, "The Population of the United States, 1790–1920," Table 3.

21. Dennis A. Ahlburg, "Population Growth and Poverty," in Robert Cassen and contributors, *Population and Development: Old Debates, New Conclusions* (New Brunswick, N.J.: Transaction Publishers, 1994), p. 143.

22. Robert Cassen with Lisa M. Bates, *Population Policy: A New Consensus* (Washington, D.C.: Overseas Development Council, 1994), p. 15.

23. U.S. Census Bureau, "Historical Estimates of World Population," http://www.census.gov/ipc/www/worldhis.html; and U.S. Census Bureau International Data Base, http://www.census.gov/ipc/www/idbagg.html (accessed September 27, 2001).

24. Samuel H. Preston, *Mortality Patterns in National Populations* (New York: Academic Press, 1976), p. ix.

25. In 1998, for example, the United Nations Population Division projected a planetary life expectation at birth of 65.0 years for the period 1995 to 2000. (*World Population Prospects: The 2000 Revision*, vol. I, p. 38.) The U.S. Census Bureau's May 2000 projections put global life expectancy at birth for the year 2000 at 63.7 years. (U.S. Census Bureau International Data Base [accessed February 1, 2001], http://www.census.gov/ipc/www/idbagg.html.)

26. Angus Maddison, *Monitoring the World Economy: 1820–1992* (Paris: OECD, 1995), and *The World Economy: A Millennial Perspective* (Paris: OECD, 2001). Though specialists may quibble over particular figures in Maddison's detailed long-term series, the overall economic picture that his calculations paint and the general trends they outline are not matters of dispute among serious students of economic history today.

27. *Monitoring the World Economy*, Tables E-1, E-3; and *The World Economy: A Millennial Perspective*, Tables A-a, B-21, A4-c.

28. Nominal prices for corn, wheat, and rice for 1900–84 compiled from World Bank sources by Enzo R. Grilli and Maw Cheng Yang, World Bank; 1985–98 series compiled from World Bank data by Stephan Pfaffenzeller, University of Nottingham. Nominal prices adjusted by U.S. CPI (consumer price index). The author thanks Mr. Stephan Pfaffenzeller for generously sharing his research.

29. Aluminum, copper, nickel, zinc, tin, lead, cotton, timber, hides, rubber, wool 64s, wool 48s, palm oil, and coconut oil. The makeup and weighting of the index is outlined in Bjorn Lomborg's, *The Skeptical Environmentalist: Measuring the Real State of the World* (New York: Cambridge University Press, 2001), p. 382, fn. 1006.

30. "Indicators—Millennium Issue: Commodity Price Index," *Economist* (December 31, 1999), p. 139.

31. Enzo R. Grilli and Maw Cheng Yang, "Primary Commodity Prices, Manufactured Goods Prices, and the Terms of Trade of Developing Countries: What the Long Run Shows," *World Bank Economic Review*, vol. 2, no. 1 (January 1988), pp. 1–48.

32. Data utilized in this paragraph are drawn from *World Population Prospects: The 2000 Revision*, vol. I, and from U.S. Census Bureau International Data Base (accessed September 27, 2001), http://www.census.gov/ipc/www/idbagg.html.

33. Serbia's most recently reported total fertility rate (1997), for example, was 1.77; Bosnia-Herzegovina's (1998), 1.56; Macedonia's (1999), 1.76; Croatia's (1999), 1.38; Slovenia's (1999), 1.21. (Data available from Institut National d'Études Démographiques Web site [accessed September 28, 2001], http://www.ined.fr/population-en-chiffres/pays-developpes/indefcon.htm.) A total fertility rate of roughly 2.1 is necessary for long-term population stability.

34. Charles Tilly, introduction to Charles Tilly, ed., *Historical Studies of Changing Fertility* (Princeton, N.J.: Princeton University Press, 1978), p. 3.

35. Gore, *Earth in the Balance*, p. 311.

36. World Bank, *World Development Report, 2000/2001: Attacking Poverty* (New York: Oxford University Press, 2000), Tables 2 and 7.

37. Data for the preceding analysis drawn from *World Population Prospects: The 2000 Revision.*

38. Michael W. Flinn, *The European Demographic System, 1500–1820* (Baltimore, Md.: Johns Hopkins University Press, 1981), p. 94.

39. For France's 1800 total fertility rate, see Ansley J. Coale, "The Decline of Fertility in Europe Since the Eighteenth Century as a Chapter in Human Demographic History," in Ansley J. Coale and Susan Cotts Watkins, eds., *The Decline of Fertility in Europe* (Princeton, N.J.: Princeton University Press, 1986), p. 27.

40. Data derived from Thomas M. McDevitt, *World Population Profile: 1998* (Washington, D.C.: U.S. Census Bureau, International Programs Center, 1999), Table A 11; and U.S. Census Bureau International Data Base (accessed September 10, 2001), http://www.census.gov/ipc/www/idbagg.html. Data on utilization rates for modern contraceptive methods are drawn from national demographic and health surveys. "Modern contraception" is defined as all means except traditional methods.

41. For more information, see David P. Lindstrom, "The Role of Contraceptive Supply and Demand in Mexican Fertility Decline: Evidence from a Microdemographic Study," *Population Studies*, vol. 52, no. 3 (November 1998), pp. 252–74; George Martine, "Brazil's Fertility Decline, 1965–95: A Fresh Look at Key Factors," *Population and Development Review*, vol. 22, no. 1 (March 196), pp. 47–75;

and U.S. Census Bureau International Data Base, http://www.census.gov /ipc/www/idbagg.html.

42. For data and analysis, see Lant Pritchett, "Desired Fertility and the Impact of Population Policies," *Population and Development Review,* vol. 20, no. 1 (March 1994), pp. 1–55.

43. Jude Sheerin, "Population Crisis Looms Because of Failed Promises—UN," *Press Association Limited* (November 7, 2001).

44. Gore, *Earth in the Balance,* p. 308.

45. *World Population Prospects: The 2000 Revision.*

46. Wolfgang Lutz, Warren Sanderson, and Sergei Scherbov, "The End of World Population Growth," *Nature,* vol. 42 (August 2, 2001), pp. 543–45.

47. United Nations Population Division, "The Future of Fertility in Intermediate-Fertility Countries," *Expert Group Meeting on Completing the Fertility Transition* (UNPD, New York, March 11-13 2002), available electronically at http://www .un.org/esa/publications/completingfertility/PEPSPOPDIVpaper.PDF (accessed April 1, 2002).

48. Fred Pearce, "We Need More Babies," *Sunday Times* (March 17, 2002).

Chapter 4

1. See, generally, Julian L. Simon, *The Ultimate Resource II* (Princeton, N.J.: Princeton University Press, 1996) and Julian Simon, *The State of Humanity.* (Cambridge, MA: Blackwell), 1995.

2. Council on Environmental Quality, *Annual Report* (various years).

3. Steve Hayward and Laura Jones, *Index of Environmental Indicators 2002* (Pacific Research Institute, 2002), p. 16, accessed at URL: http://www.pacificresearch .org/pub/sab/enviro/ei2002-states/pri_enviro_index_2002.pdf

4. Environmental Protection Agency, Office of Air Quality, Planning, and Standards, *National Air Quality and Emissions Trends Report* (various years) accessed at URL: http://www.epa.gov/cgi-bin/epaprintonly.cgi.

5. Roger A. Sedjo and Marion Clawson, "Global Forests Revisited," *State of Humanity,* pp. 328–45.

6. Office of Technology Assessment, *Technology and the American Economic Transition* (Washington, D.C., 1988).

7. Donella H. Meadows et al., *The Limits to Growth* (New York: Universe Books, 1972).

8. Paul Ehrlich interviewed on the *Today Show,* May 3, 1989.

9. Donella H. Meadows et al., *The Limits to Growth.*

10. *Global 2000 Report to the President,* vols. I, II, and III (Washington, D.C.: U.S. Government Printing Office, 1980).

11. World Bank, *World Development Report 1992* (New York: Oxford University Press, 1992).

12. John Kenneth Galbraith, *The Affluent Society* (Boston: Houghton Mifflin, 1998).

13. Al Gore, *Earth in the Balance* (New York: Plume, 1993).

14. Environmental Protection Agency, Office of Air Quality, Planning, and Standards, *National Air Quality and Emissions Trends Report* (various years).

15. "Ideas in Action: Index of Leading Environmental Indicators," *Pacific Research Institute Fact Sheet,* April 1999.

16. Indur Goklany, *Clearing the Air* (Washington: Cato Institute, 1999), pp. 67–86.

17. Paul Ehrlich, "Eco-Catastrophe!" *Ramparts* (1969), p. 193.

18. Steve Hayward and Laura Jones, *Index of Leading Environmental Indicators 1998* (Pacific Research Institute, 1998), p. 23.

19. Council on Environmental Quality, *Annual Report* (Washington, D.C.: Government Printing Office, various years); and Environmental Protection Agency, Office of Air Quality, Planning, and Standards, *National Air Quality and Emissions Trends Report, 1996,* Table A-17 (Research Triangle Park, N.C.: EPA, OAQPS, 1997).

20. Cliff I. Davidson, "Air Pollution in Pittsburgh: A Historical Perspective," *Journal of the Air Pollution Control Association,* vol. 29 (1979), pp. 1035–41; and Council on Environmental Quality, *Annual Report* (various years).

21. William J. Baumol and Wallace E. Oates, *The Theory of Environmental Policy,* 2nd ed. (New York: Cambridge University Press, 1988).

22. "Freedom's Journey: A Survey of the 20th Century," *The Economist,* September 11, 1999, p. 7.

23. Centers for Disease Control, *Morbidity and Mortality Weekly Report,* vol. 8, no. 29; and National Center for Health Statistics, *National Vital Statistics Report,* vol. 47, no. 25.

24. *Ideas in Action: Pacific Research Institute Fact Sheet,* for the *Index of Leading Environmental Indicators 1999,* (April 1999) accessed at URL: http://www.pacificresearch .org/pub/sab/enviro/99_enviroindex/99indexfact.html.

25. "Watered Down Data," *Vital STATS* Statistical Assessment Service (November 1998), p. 2, accessed at URL: http://www.stats.org/newsletters/9811/crypto.htm.

26. Council on Environmental Quality, *Annual Report* (various years).

27. Environmental Protection Agency, Office of Wastewater Management. Clean Water Needs Survey Report to Congress, 1996 accessed at URL: http://www .epa.gov/owm/toc.htm

28. Steve Hayward and Laura Jones, *Index of Leading Environmental Indicators 1998* (Pacific Research Institute, April 1998).

29. Council on Environmental Quality, *Annual Report.*

30. *Statistical Abstract of the United States: 1998,* no. 396.

31. Traci Watson, "Wildlife Recovering from Exxon Spill," *USA Today* (February 11, 1999), p. 3A.

32. Julian L. Simon, *The Ultimate Resource* (Princeton University Press, 1981).

33. Quoted in Simon (1981), p. 100.

34. Gerald O. Barney, editor, *The Global 2000 Report to the President: Entering the 21st Century* (London: Penguin Books, 1982), p. 39.

35. Lester Brown, *The State of the World 1997,* (New York: Norton), 1997, p. 1.

36. U.S. Geological Survey, *Commodity Statistics* (various years).

37. Herman Kahn, William Brown, and Leon Martel, *The Next 200 Years* (New York: William Morrow, 1976), p. 92.

38. U.S. Geological Survey, *Mineral Commodities Summary 2001,* http://www.minerals .usgs.gov/minerals/pubs/mcs/2001/mcs2001.pdf.

39. G. F. Ray, "The Decline of Primary Producer Power," *National Institute Economic Review* (August, 1987), p. 40.

40. John A. Carver, Jr., quoted in Lawrence Rocks and Richard P. Runyon, *The Energy Crisis* (New York: Crown Publishers, 1972), p. 6.

41. Christopher Byron, "Yes, There Is an Energy Crisis," *Time* (October 10, 1977), p. 62.

42. British Petroleum, *Statistical Review of World Energy 2001,* http://www.bp .com/centres/energy/world_stat_rev/downloads/index.asp.

43. Department of Energy, *Annual Energy Review* (various years).
44. "Progressive Environmentalism: A Pro-Human, Pro-Science, Pro-Free Enterprise Agenda for Change," Task Force Report, National Center for Policy Analysis, Dallas.
45. Ibid.
46. Council on Environmental Quality, *Annual Report* (various years).
47. *Policy Review* (September/October 1998), p. 29
48. Steven Hayward, Elizabeth Fowler, and Erin Schiller, *Index of Leading Environmental Indicators* (Pacific Research Institute, April 1999).
49. "The Great Forest Debate," *Reader's Digest,* vol. 143, no. 859 (November 1993), p. 125.
50. For information documenting the improvement in the inventory of U.S. forests, see Roger A. Sedjo and Marion Clawson, "Global Forests Revisited," *The State of Humanity,* pp. 328–45.
51. Ibid.
52. Food and Agriculture Organization, *Global Forest Resources Assessment 2000,* accessed at URL: http://www.fao.org/DOCREP/004/Y1997E/Y1997E00.HTM.
53. Sedjo and Clawson, *State of Humanity.*
54. Howard Rheingold, "The Underside of Moore's Law," *IntellectualCapital.com* (May 20, 1999); and Bob Kolasky, "The Era of the Cheap PC," same publication and date.
55. John Tierney, "Betting the Planet," *New York Times Magazine* (December 2, 1990), p. 58.

Chapter 5

1. Sharachchandra M Lele, "Sustainable Development: A Critical Review." *World Development,* 1991, 19 (6): 607-621.
2. David Pearce and Jeremy Warford, *World Without End: Economics, Environment, and Sustainable Development* (New York: Oxford University Press, 1993), p. 8.
3. Jerry Taylor, "Sustainable Development: Common Sense or Nonsense on Stilts," *The Foundation for Economic Education,* vol. 48, no. 9 (September 1998).
4. Robert Costanza, "Ecological Economics: A Research Agenda," in *Structural Change Economics,* vol. 2, pp. 335-42; cited in M.J. Harte, "Ecology, Sustainability, and Environment as Capital," *Ecological Economics,* vol. 15, 1995, p. 158.
5. Vandana Shiva, "Globalisation," accessed at http://www.vshiva.net/global.htm.
6. *Agricultural Statistics at a Glance*, Directorate of Economics and Statistics, Department of Agriculture and Cooperation, Ministry of Agriculture, Government of India, (March 1996).
7. Julian Simon, *The Ultimate Resource 2* (Princeton University Press, 1999).
8. Harold Barnett and Chandler Morse, "Scarcity and Growth: The Economics of Natural Resource Availability," Resources for the Future, (Baltimore: Johns Hopkins University Press, 1963), p. 220.
9. *Economic Report of the President* (Washington, D.C.: Government Printing Office, 1991), p. 298.
10. United Nations Environment Programme and World Health Organization, *Air Quality Management and Assessment Capabilities in 20 Major Cities: Environment Assessment Report* (London: MARC, 1996).
11. "Global Change and Sustainable Development: Critical Trends," Report of the Secretary General, United Nations, Economic and Social Council, Commission on Sus-

tainable Development, January, 1997, accessed at http://www.un.org/documents/ecosoc/cn17/1997/ecn171997-3.htm, The Robinson Rojas Databank, 1997.

12. Taylor, "Sustainable Development."

13. Julian Simon, ed., *The State of Humanity* (Cambridge, Mass.: Blackwell Publishers, 1995), pp. 279–442.

14. Lester C. Thurow, "Green Growth Is No Contradiction," *Newsweek Japan* (November 1999), accessed at http://www.lthurow.com/articles.php3?qart=Environment

15. Joel Mokyr, *The Lever of Riches: Technological Creativity and Economic Progress* (Oxford University Press, 1990).

16. Matt Ridley, *Technology and the Environment: The Case for Optimism*, Prince Philip Lecture (London, May 8, 2001).

17. Indra de Soysa, "Agriculture's Role in Resolving Conflict," a talk between Indra de Soysa and Alexandra de Blas of Radio National on *Earthbeat* (February 20, 1999).

18. William D. Dar and Mark D. Winslow, *The Grey-to-Green Revolution for the Dry Tropics,* International Crops Research Institute for the Semi-Arid Tropics (ICRISAT) Andra Pradesh, India (2000) accessed at http://www.icrisat.org/text/research/Presentations/2001/gtgr/gtgr_for_dry_tropics1.htm

19. Ridley, *Technology and the Environment.*

20. Julian Morris and Charles Secrett, *Business and the Environment,* (forthcoming), London.

21. Danny Tyson Quah, ". . . and such small portions too," *CentrePiece*, Center for Economic Performance, London School of Economics, (June 1998), accessed at http://www.cep.lse.ac.uk/pubs/centrepiece/default.asp.

22. Simon, *The Ultimate Resource 2.*

23. United Nations Environment Programme and World Health Organization, *City Air Quality Trends*, vol. 3 (GEMS, 1995).

24. *The North, the South, and the Environment: Ecological Constraints and the Global Economy*, edited by V. Bhaskar and Andrew Glyn, (New York : St. Martin's Press, 1995).

25. Siddhartha Prakash, *Trade and Development Case Studies, India, Part 2 Agriculture*, 1998 World Trade Organization, Geneva, Switzerland, accessed at http://www.itd.org/issues/india2.htm#WTO

26. Siddhartha Prakash, *Trade and Development Case Studies, India, Part 2 Agriculture*, 1998 World Trade Organization, Geneva, Switzerland accessed at http://www.itd.org/issues/india2.htm#WTO

Chapter 6

1. Rachel Carson, *Silent Spring,* with an introduction by Vice President Al Gore (New York: Houghton Mifflin Company, 1994). "And No Birds Sing" is the title of one of the chapters describing how pesticides allegedly have killed off a large part of the bird population.

2. Carson, *Silent Spring,* p. 242.

3. Ibid., pp. 242–43.

4. Ibid., p. 243.

5. Paul Ehrlich, "Eco-Catastrophe!" *Ramparts* (September 1969), pp. 24–27.

6. Vice President Al Gore, introduction to *Silent Spring* (New York: Houghton Mifflin Company, 1994), p. xviii.

7. Greenpeace, Toxics Campaign, Greenpeace Web page (accessed September 23, 2001), http://www.greenpeace.org/~toxics.

8. Quoted by Ivan Amato, "The Crusade Against Chlorine," *Science*, vol. 261, no. 5118 (July 9, 1993), pp. 152–54. For more information on chlorine issues, see Michelle Malkin and Michael Fumento, *Rachel's Folly: The End of Chlorine* (Washington, D.C.: Competitive Enterprise Institute, March 1996).

9. Ann Misch, "Assessing Environmental Health Risks," in Linda Starke, ed., *State of the World 1994* (New York: W. W. Norton & Company, 1994), p. 117.

10. Pesticide Action Network of North America, PANNA Web page (accessed September 23, 2001), http://www.panna.org/panna/about/about.html.

11. Judy Mann, "27 Reasons to Worry About Toxic Exposure," *Washington Post* (April 6, 2001).

12. Sharon Begley with Mary Hager, "Pesticides and Kids' Risks," *Newsweek* (June 1, 1998).

13. Recorded in "DDT, Eco-Racism Threats: What's Not in the News," *Media Watch* (June 1994), p. 3.

14. Public Broadcasting System, *Trade Secrets: A Moyers Report* (March 26, 2001), transcript available at http://www.pbs.org/tradesecrets/transcript.html.

15. Carson, *Silent Spring*, p. 6.

16. Ibid., p. 221.

17. Ibid., p. 227.

18. Ibid., p. 227–28.

19. Ibid., p. 228.

20. Environmental Working Group, "Myth #3: Cancer Rates Are Decreasing, or: 'We're Winning the War on Cancer,'" *Pesticide Industry Propaganda: The Real Story* (Washington, D.C.: EWG, Web page accessed July 28, 2001), http://www.ewg.org/pub/home/Reports/Myths/Myth3.html.

21. Brad Rodu and Philip Cole, "The Fifty Year Decline of Cancer in America," *Journal of Clinical Oncology*, vol. 19, no. 1 (January 1, 1001), pp. 240–41.

22. Charles B. Simone, *Cancer & Nutrition* (New York: McGraw-Hill, 1983), as noted in William M. London and John W. Morgan, "Living Long Enough to Die of Cancer," *Priorities*, vol. 7, no. 4 (December 31, 1995).

23. Rodu and Cole, "The Fifty Year Decline of Cancer in America," pp. 239–41.

24. According to the National Cancer Institute, it produces its annual report in collaboration with the American Cancer Society, the North American Association of Central Cancer Registries, and the Centers for Disease Control and Prevention, including the National Center for Health Statistics and the Center for Chronic Disease Prevention and Health Promotion. See Holly L. Howe et al., "Annual Report to the Nation on the Status of Cancer (1973 Through 1998), Featuring Cancers with Recent Increasing Trends," *Journal of the National Cancer Institute*, vol. 93 (June 6, 2001), pp. 824–42.

25. Ibid.

26. Ibid.

27. Ibid.

28. U.S. Centers for Disease Control and Prevention, *CDC Fact Book 2000/2001* (Washington, D.C.: CDC, 2001), p. 46, http://www.cdc.gov/maso/factbook/Fact%20Book.pdf.

29. National Institutes of Health, National Cancer Institute, press release (May 14, 2000), http://www1.od.nih.gov/ormh/press_rel/annual_report.html.

30. Howe et al., "Annual Report to the Nation on the Status of Cancer."

31. Phyllis A. Wingo et al., "Annual Report to the Nation on the Status of Cancer, 1973–1996, with a Special Section on Lung Cancer," *Journal of the National Cancer Institute*, vol. 91 (April 21, 1999), pp. 675–90.

32. Howe et al., "Annual Report to the Nation on the Status of Cancer."

33. "Stat Bite: Incidence Rates by Age at Diagnosis for Breast and Prostate Cancers," *Journal of the National Cancer Institute*, vol. 93 (March 21, 2001), p. 425.

34. Richard Doll and Richard Peto, "The Causes of Cancer: Quantitative Estimates of Avoidable Risks of Cancer in the United States Today," *Journal of the National Cancer Institute*, vol. 66, no. 6 (June 1981), p. 1197.

35. Ibid.

36. Ibid.

37. Ibid., pp. 1192–1308.

38. National Research Council, Committee on Comparative Toxicology of Naturally Occurring Carcinogens, *Carcinogens and Anticarcinogens in the Human Diet: A Comparison of Naturally Occurring and Synthetic Substances* (Washington, D.C.: National Academy Press, 1996), Appendix A.

39. Bruce N. Ames and Lois Swirsky Gold, "Too Many Rodent Carcinogens: Mitogenesis Increases Mutagenesis," *Science*, vol. 249, no. 4972 (August 31, 1990), pp. 970–71.

40. Ibid.

41. Carson, *Silent Spring*, p. 221.

42. Ibid., p. 222.

43. Ibid.

44. As quoted by Kenneth Smith and Jack Raso, *An Unhappy Anniversary: The Alar Scare Ten Years Later* (New York: American Council on Science and Health, February 1999), p. 2.

45. Tim Friend and Nanci Hellmich, "Fear: Are We Poisoning Our Children?" *USA Today* (February 28, 1989), p. 1A.

46. "Hazardous Apples," *Washington Post* (February 7, 1989), p. A23.

47. "Red, Delicious—and Dangerous" (editorial), *St. Louis Post-Dispatch* (February 8, 1989), p. 2E.

48. As cited by Michael Fumento, *Science Under Siege* (New York: William Morrow and Company Inc., 1993), p. 35.

49. Philip Shabecoff, "3 U.S. Agencies, to Allay Public's Fears, Declare Apples Safe," *New York Times* (March 17, 1989), p. 16.

50. Quoted in Smith and Raso, *An Unhappy Anniversary* (New York: American Council on Science and Health, February 1999), p. 3.

51. Bruce Keppel and Elaine Woo, "More Schools Ban Apples in Concern over Chemical," *Los Angeles Times* (March 14, 1989), p. 1; and "More Schools Ban Apples," *Washington Post* (March 15, 1989), p. A19.

52. John Davis, "Pesticide Fears Cancel U.S. Apple Export Order," *Journal of Commerce* (March 14, 1989), p. 1A.

53. Barbara W. Selvin, "Stores Pull House Brand Apple Juice" *Newsday* (March 31, 1989), p. 45.

54. Smith and Raso, "An Unhappy Anniversary," p. 3.

55. Sharon Begley with Mary Hager, "How Much Risk Do Pesticides Pose to Children?" *Newsweek* (July 5, 1993), p. 53.

56. National Research Council, *Pesticides in the Diets of Infants and Children* (Washington, D.C.: National Academy Press, 1993), p. 359.

57. U.S. Environmental Protection Agency, *National Agenda to Protect Children's Health from Environmental Threats* (Washington, D.C.: EPA, September 1996), EPA 175-F-96-001, http://www.epa.gov/epadocs/child.htm#agenda.

58. *Federal Register*, vol. 62, no. 78 (April 13, 1997), pp. 19883–88.

59. For more information on the EPA Office of Children's Health Protection and the task force, see the EPA's Web page: http://www.epa.gov/children.

60. Environmental Protection Agency, Office of Children's Health Protection, "EPA Leadership in Children's Environmental Health," (Washington, D.C.: EPA, Web publication accessed September 23, 2001), http://www.epa.gov/children/whowe/leadership.htm.

61. U.S. Centers for Disease Control and Prevention, *CDC Fact Book*, p. 9.

62. Ibid., p. 10.

63. Ibid., p. 21.

64. Natural Resources Defense Council, *Our Children at Risk: The Five Worst Environmental Threats to Their Health* (New York: NRDC, November 1997), http://www.nrdc.org/health/kids/ocar/ocarinx.asp.

65. "Experts Study Rise in U.S. Childhood Cancers," *Cancer Weekly Plus* (September 29, 1997), p. 22.

66. Martha S. Linet et al., "Cancer Surveillances Services: Recent Trends in Childhood Cancer Incidence and Mortality in the United States," *Journal of the National Cancer Institute*, vol. 91 (June 16, 1999), pp. 1051–58.

67. Julie M. Leger et al., "Brain Cancer and Other Central Nervous System Cancers: Recent Trends in Incidence and Mortality," *Journal of the National Cancer Institute*, vol. 91 (August 18, 1999), pp. 1382–90.

68. Ibid.

69. Frank Eltman, "Congressional Hearing on Cancer Rates Held on Long Island," *BC Cycle* (June 11, 2001).

70. "Parents Seek Answers After First Fallon Cancer Cluster Death," Associated Press State & Local Wire (June 11, 2001).

71. Michele Norris, "Schools Across the Country Built near Sites Contaminated with Toxic Waste," transcripts from ABC *World News Tonight* (March 19, 2001).

72. Marcia Angell, "Clinical Research—What Should the Public Believe?" *New England Journal of Medicine*, vol. 331, no. 3 (July 21, 1994), pp. 189–90.

73. Michael Fumento, "A Fairly Brief, Nonboring Lesson on the Pitfalls of Amateur Epidemiology," in *Science Under Siege*, pp. 78–96.

74. Lori Miller Kase, "Why Community Cancer Clusters Are Often Ignored," *Scientific American*, Special Issue (September 1996), pp. 85–86.

75. G. G. Caldwell, "Twenty-Two Years of Cancer Cluster Investigations at the Centers for Disease Control," *American Journal of Epidemiology*, suppl. no. 1 (July 1990), pp. S43–47.

76. For an excellent exposé on the Love Canal myth, see Eric Zuesse, "Love Canal: The Truth Seeps Out," *Reason* (February 1981), http://www.reason.com/8102/fe.ez.the.shtml.

77. Headlines and Gibbs quote documented by Kenneth Smith in "What Price Love Canal? An Unhappy Anniversary," *Priorities*, vol. 10, no. 4, URL: http://www.acsh.org/publications/priorities/1004/lovecanal.html.

78. Ben De Forest, "Family Wonders if Their Illnesses Were Caused by Chemical Dump," Associated Press (May 22, 1980).

79. See Gina Bari Kolata, "Love Canal: False Alarm Caused by Botched Study," *Science*, vol. 208, no. 4449 (June 13, 1980), pp. 1239–42.

80. Controversy surrounded studies that showed some higher rates of miscarriages in one area of Love Canal in the 1960s, but rates returned to normal in the 1970s and 1980s. The study was criticized as not valid for many reasons, including the fact that sample size for the isolated area was criticized as too small to make the study useful. The study of the larger area indicated that the entire area had no more problems than that of the entire state. The New York state researcher involved with the study explained that he considered the area safe and urged people not to move out; see Marc Herbert, "Scientist Sees No Medical Reason for Love Canal Evacuations," Associated Press (June 24, 1980). For a detailed description of the study and the controversy surrounding it, see Aaron Wildavsky, "Love Canal," in *But Is It True? A Citizen's Guide to Environmental Health and Safety Issues* (Cambridge, Mass.: Harvard University Press, 1995).

81. Dwight T. Janerich et al., "Cancer Incidence in the Love Canal Area," *Science*, vol. 212, no. 4501 (June 19, 1981). For overviews of the scientific studies, see Aaron Wildavsky, "Love Canal," and Elizabeth Whelan, "The 'Disaster' of Love Canal," in *Toxic Terror* (Ottawa, I.L.: Jameson Books, 1985).

82. *Consider the Source*, Environmental Working Group, January 8, 2002, http://www.ewg.org/reports/ConsidertheSource/index.html.

83. *Federal Register*, vol. 63, no. 241 (December 16, 1998), p. 69407.

84. *Federal Register*, vol. 63, no. 61 (March 31, 1998), pp. 15679–80.

85. *Federal Register*, vol. 63, no. 241 (December 16, 1998), p. 69408.

86. Centers for Disease Control and Prevention, Division of Bacterial and Mycotic Diseases, "Bacterial Waterborne Diseases: Technical Information," March 9, 2001, http://www.cdc.gov/ncidod/dbmd/diseaseinfo/waterbornediseases_t.htm.

87. U.S. Environmental Protection Agency, Science Advisory Board, "Drinking Water Committee Commentary on Negotiated Regulation for Disinfection By-Products," (Washington, D.C.: USEPA, November 8, 1993), EPA-SAB-DWC-COM-94-002, 3.

88. Registries to track infectious diseases are of a different nature because the diseases are much more easily linked to the infectious agent and can help prevent the spread of infectious diseases.

89. James V. DeLong, *A Civil Action or A Civil Fiction: Hollywood Instructs America on Pollution and Greed* (Washington, D.C.: Competitive Enterprise Institute, January 1999), http://www.cei.org/MonoReader.asp?ID=568.

90. Marshall Eliot, "Woburn Case May Spark Explosion of Lawsuits: Drinking Water Pollution in Massachusetts," *Science*, vol. 234 (October 24, 1986), p. 418.

91. Agency for Toxic Substances and Disease Registry, "Trichloroethylene," *ToxFAQs* (fact sheet) (Washington, D.C.: ATSDR, 1997).

92. DeLong, *A Civil Action or A Civil Fiction*.

93. Eliot, "Woburn Case May Spark Explosion of Lawsuits," p. 418.

94. As quoted by Michael Fumento, "Disney Pollutes," *Forbes* (December 28, 1998).

95. U.S. Environmental Protection Agency, Integrated Risk Information System (IRIS), Chromium (VI) (Washington, D.C.: EPA, 1998), http://www.epa.gov/iris/subst/0144.htm.

96. Robert J. Scheuplein, "Pesticides and Infant Risk: Is There a Need for an Additional Safety Factor?" *Regulatory Toxicology and Pharmacology*, vol. 31 (2000), p. 275.

97. Scheuplein, "Pesticides and Infant Risk," p. 270.

98. For example, airborne lead has declined 94 percent between 1979 and 1990 and another 60 percent between 1990 and 1999; see U.S. Environmental Protection Agency, *Latest Findings on National Air Quality: 1999 Status and Trends* (Washington, D.C.: EPA, August 2000). The National Research Council notes that studies show that there has been a "progressive and substantial decline" of PCBs in the environment; see National Research Council, *Hormonally Active Agents in the Environment* (Washington, D.C.: National Academy Press, 1999), pp. 66–67.

99. *Carcinogens and Anticarcinogens in the Human Diet*, pp. 336–37.

100. International Food Information Council Foundation, *IFIC Review: On Pesticides and Food Safety* (Washington, D.C.: IFIC, January 1995), http://www.ific.org/relatives/17060.PDF.

101. Frank Cross, "Dangerous Compromises of the Food Quality Protection Act," *Washington Law Quarterly*, vol. 75, no. 1155 (1997), pp. 1163–66.

102. Sandra O. Archibald and Carl K. Winter, "Pesticides in Our Food," in Carl K. Winter, James N. Sieber, and Carole F. Nuckon, eds., *Chemicals in the Human Food Chain* (New York: Van Nostrand Reinhold, 1990), p. 39.

103. U.S. Food and Drug Administration Pesticide Program, *1999 Residue Reporting* (Washington, D.C.: USDA, 1999), http://www.cfsan.fda.gov/~acrobat/pes99 rep.pdf.

104. Theo Coburn, Dianne Dumanoski, and John Peterson Myers, *Our Stolen Future: Are We Threatening Our Fertility, Intelligence, and Survival—A Scientific Detective Story* (New York: Plume, 1997).

105. Stephen Safe, "Endocrine Disrupters: New Toxic Menace?" in Ronald Bailey, ed., *Earth Report 2000* (New York: McGraw-Hill, 2000), p. 192.

106. American Council on Science and Health, *Endocrine Disrupters: A Scientific Perspective* (New York: American Council on Science and Health, July 1999), pp. 14–15.

107. National Research Council, *Hormonally Active Agents in the Environment*.

108. Ibid., p. 4.

109. Ibid., p. 6.

110. Ibid., p. 272.

111. Ibid.

112. Ibid., p. 273.

113. Ibid., p. 184.

114. Jonathan Tolman, *Nature's Hormone Factory: Endocrine Disrupters in the Natural Environment* (Washington, D.C.: Competitive Enterprise Institute, March 1996), pp. 4–5.

115. Ibid., p. 5.

116. Ibid., p. 8; Tolman derived figures from research of Stephen Safe, "Environmental and Dietary Estrogens and Human Health: Is There a Problem?" *Environmental Health Perspectives*, vol. 103, no. 4 (April 1995), p. 349.

117. Keith S. Delaplane, "Pesticide Usage in the United States: History, Benefits, Risks, and Trends," research paper (Athens, Ga.: Cooperative Extension Service, University of Georgia College of Agricultural and Environmental Sciences, November 2000), http://www.ces.uga.edu/pubcd/B1121.htm.

118. Ibid.

119. Ibid.

120. Dennis Avery, "Saving the Planet with Pesticides," in Ronald Bailey, ed., *The True State of the Planet* (New York: Free Press, 1995), pp. 74–76.

121. Ibid., p. 71.

122. World Health Organization, "Malaria: Fact Sheet" (Geneva: WHO, 1998), http://www.who.int/inf-fs/en/fact094.html.

123. Amir Attaran and Rajendra Maharaj, "Doctoring Malaria, Badly: The Global Campaign to Ban DDT," *British Medical Journal*, no. 321 (December 2, 2000), pp. 1403–05, http://www.bmj.com/cgi/content/full/321/7273/1403#resp1.

124. Donald R. Roberts, Larry L. Laughlin, Paul Hsheih, and Llewellyn J. Legters, "DDT, Global Strategies, and a Malaria Control Crisis in South America," *Emerging Infectious Diseases*, vol. 13, no. 3 (July–September 1997), http://www.cdc.gov/ncidod/eid/vol3no3/roberts.htm. See also Amir Attaran et al., "Balancing Risks on the Backs of the Poor," *Nature Medicine*, vol. 6 (2000), pp. 729–31.

125. Richard Tren and Roger Bate, *When Politics Kills: Malaria and the DDT Story* (Washington, D.C.: Competitive Enterprise Institute, 2000), p. 26.

126. For example, public health officials have signed letters supporting use of DDT for malaria control; see the Malaria Foundation International letter and signatories, at http://www.malaria.org/DDT_open.html and http://www.malaria.org/DDT_signatures.html, respectively, as well as a petition hosted by the Save Children from Malaria Campaign at http://www.fightingmalaria.org/.

127. Roger Bate, "A Case of the DDTs: The War Against the War Against Malaria," *National Review* (May 14, 2001); and Amir Attaran, "DDT Saves Lives," *Globe and Mail* (December 5, 2000).

128. Institute of Medicine, Committee on Emerging Microbial Threats to Health, *Emerging Infections: Microbial Threats to Health in the United States*, ed. Joshua Lederberg, Robert E. Shope, and Stanley C. Oaks, Jr. (Washington, D.C.: National Academy Press, 1992), p. 161.

Chapter 7

1. William Claiborne, "A Biotech Food Fight: Two Sides Square Off at FDA Hearing," *Washington Post* (November 19, 1999), p. A3.

2. International Food Information Council, "U.S. Consumer Attitudes Toward Food Biotechnology," Results of an IFIC/Cogent Research Consumer Survey on Food Biotechnology (Washington, D.C.: International Food Information Council, September 2001).

3. Richard Caplan, *Raising Risk: Field Testing of Genetically Engineered Crops in the U.S.* (Washington, D.C.: U.S. Public Interest Research Groups, 2001).

4. Friends of the Earth, "GMOs: The Case for a Moratorium," Friends of the Earth Briefing (June 2001), http://www.foe.co.uk/resource/briefings/gmos_case_for_moratorium.html.

5. Quoted in Ron Bailey, "Dr. Strangelunch, Or: Why We Should Learn to Stop Worrying and Love Genetically Modified Food," *Reason* (January 2001), pp. 20–29.

6. Siobhan Gorman, "Future Pharmers of America," *National Journal* (February 6, 1999), p. 355.

7. Mae-Wan Ho quoted in "The Ecologist," quoted in Pat Murphy, "The Raging Debate over Biotech Foods," *Environmental News Network* (March 5, 2000), http://www.enn.com/enn-features-archive/2000/03/03052000/gefood_5991.asp.

8. Rachel Carson, *Silent Spring* (New York: Houghton Mifflin Company, 1962).

9. Chris Sommerville and John Briscoe, "Genetic Engineering and Water," *Science*, vol. 292, no. 5525 (June 22, 2001), p. 2217.

10. E. C. Oerke, A. Weber, H. W. Dehne, and F. Schönbeck, "Conclusion and Perspectives," in E. C. Oerke, H. W. Dehne, F. Schönbeck, and A. Weber, eds., *Crop*

Production and Crop Protection: Estimated Losses in Food and Cash Crops (Amsterdam: Elsevier, 1994), pp. 742–70.

11. Thomas R. Malthus, *An Essay on the Principle of Population*, P. James, ed. (London: Cambridge University Press, 1990) [original work published 1798].

12. The term *biotechnology* has been used for nearly 100 years to describe any process of applying scientific knowledge to the development of biological organisms. In that regard, biotechnology could be used to describe many traditional types of plant breeding. More recently, the term has come to represent in the vernacular only the most advanced techniques of genetic engineering and recombinant DNA techniques. In this chapter, we use biotechnology only in this latter, more specific meaning.

13. National Academy of Sciences, *Introduction of Recombinant DNA-Engineered Organisms into the Environment: Key Issues* (Washington, D.C.: Council of the U.S. Academy of Sciences/National Academy Press, 1987).

14. Royal Society of London, the U.S. National Academy of Sciences, the Brazilian Academy of Sciences, the Chinese Academy of Sciences, the Indian National Science Academy, the Mexican Academy of Sciences, and the Third World Academy of Sciences, *Transgenic Plants and World Agriculture* (Washington, D.C.: National Academy Press, 2000).

15. United Nations Development Programme, *Human Development Report 2001: Making New Technologies Work for Human Development* (New York: Oxford University Press, 2001).

16. Clive James, *Global Review of Commercialized Transgenic Crops: 2000*, ISAA Brief, no. 23 (Ithaca, N.Y.: International Service for the Acquisition of Agri-Biotech Applications, 2001).

17. Janet Carpenter and Leonard Gianessi, *Agricultural Biotechnology: Updated Benefit Estimates* (Washington, D.C.: National Center for Food and Agricultural Policy, January 2001).

18. Ibid.

19. USDA National Agricultural Statistics Service, *Acreage* (Washington, D.C.: National Agricultural Statistics Service, U.S. Department of Agriculture, June 29, 2001).

20. Royal Society of London, the U.S. National Academy of Sciences, the Brazilian Academy of Sciences, the Chinese Academy of Sciences, the Indian National Science Academy, the Mexican Academy of Sciences, and the Third World Academy of Sciences, *Transgenic Plants and World Agriculture* (Washington, D.C.: National Academy Press, 2000), p. 34.

21. Charles C. Mann, "Crop Scientists Seek a New Revolution," *Science*, vol. 283, no. 5400 (January 15, 1999), pp. 310–14.

22. Gordon Conway and Gary Toenniessen, "Feeding the World in the Twenty-First Century," *Nature*, vol. 402, no. 6761 (December 2, 1999), pp. C55–C58.

23. Ibid.

24. Indur M. Goklany, "Meeting Global Food Needs: The Environmental Trade-Offs Between Increasing Land Conversion and Land Productivity," *Technology*, vol. 6, nos. 2–3 (1999), pp. 107–30.

25. World Resources Institute, *World Resources 2000–2001*, CD-ROM database (Washington, D.C.: World Resources Institute, 2001).

26. Goklany, "Meeting Global Food Needs."

27. Norman Borlaug, "Ending World Hunger: The Promise of Biotechnology and the Threat of Antiscience Zealotry," *Plant Physiology*, vol. 124, no. 2 (October 2000), pp. 487–90.

28. United Nations Development Programme, *Human Development Report 2001*.

29. "Hunger Fighters See Biotech Hope for Poor Nations," Reuters (November 8, 2001).

30. Anthony J. Trewavas and Christopher J. Leaver, "Is Opposition to GM Crops Science or Politics?" *EMBO Reports*, vol. 21, no. 6 (June 2001), pp. 455–59.

31. Florence Wambugu, *Modifying Africa* (Nairobi, Kenya: Florence Wambugu, 2001), p. vii.

32. Donald G. McNeil, Jr., "New Genes and Seeds: Protesters in Europe Grow More Passionate," *New York Times* (March 14, 2000), http://www.nytimes.com/library/national/science/health/031400hth-gm-europe.html.

33. International Food Information Council, "U.S. Consumer Attitudes Toward Food Biotechnology," Results of an IFIC/Cogent Research Consumer Survey on Food Biotechnology (Washington, D.C.: International Food Information Council, September 2001).

34. Ibid.

35. Ibid.

36. The Mellman Group and Public Opinion Strategies, "Public Sentiment About Genetically Modified Food," report prepared for the Pew Initiative on Food and Biotechnology (Washington, D.C.: Pew Initiative on Food and Biotechnology, March 2001).

37. Ibid.

38. Ibid.

39. Jack Rodney Harlan, *Crops & Man* (Madison, Wis.: American Society of Agronomy and Crop Science Society of America, 1992).

40. Svante Pääbo, "Agriculture: Neolithic Genetic Engineering," *Nature*, vol. 398, no. 6724 (March 18, 1999), pp. 194–95.

41. Robert M. Goodman, Holly Hauptli, Anne Crossway, and Vic C. Knauf, "Gene Transfer in Crop Improvement," *Science*, vol. 236 (April 3, 1987), pp. 48–54.

42. Ibid.

43. Ibid.

44. International Atomic Energy Agency, *Officially Released Mutant Varieties: The FAO/IAEA Database* (Vienna, Austria: Joint FAO-IAEA Division, International Atomic Energy Agency, December 2000).

45. Goodman, Hauptli, Crossway, and Knauf, "Gene Transfer in Crop Improvement."

46. Adrianne Massey, "Crops, Genes, and Evolution," *Gastronomica* (summer 2001), pp. 21–29.

47. Goodman, Hauptli, Crossway, and Knauf, "Gene Transfer in Crop Improvement"; and Maarten Koornneef and Piet Stam, "Changing Paradigms in Plant Breeding," *Plant Physiology*, vol. 125, no. 1 (January 2001), pp. 156–59.

48. C. S. Prakash, "The Genetically Modified Crop Debate in the Context of Agricultural Evolution," *Plant Physiology*, vol. 126, no. 1 (May 2001), pp. 8–15.

49. National Corn Growers Association, "The World of Corn—2001," http://www.ncga.com/03world/main/index.html.

50. Trewavas and Leaver, "Is Opposition to GM Crops Science or Politics?"

51. Mann, "Crop Scientists Seek a New Revolution."

52. Prakash, "The Genetically Modified Crop Debate in the Context of Agricultural Evolution," and Eric S. Grace, *Biotechnology Unzipped: Promises & Realities* (Washington: Joseph Henry Press, 1997).

53. Trewavas and Leaver, "Is Opposition to GM Crops Science or Politics?" and Nina Federoff, "Transposons and Genome Evolution in Plants," *Proceedings of the National Academy of Sciences*, vol. 97, no. 13 (June 20, 2000), pp. 7002–7.

54. Institute of Food Technologists, *IFT Expert Report on Biotechnology and Foods* (Chicago: Institute of Food Technologists, 2000).

55. National Research Council, *Field Testing Genetically Modified Organisms: Framework for Decisions* (Washington, D.C.: National Academy Press, 1989), p. 13.

56. Nina Federoff, "Genetically Modified Plants: Monsters or Miracles?" AgBioWorld.org Web site (November 30, 1999), http://www.agbioworld.com/biotech_info/articles/miracles.html.

57. U.S. Food and Drug Administration, "List of Completed Consultations on Bioengineered Foods," http://www.cfsan.fda.gov/~lrd/biocon.html.

58. No varieties of bioengineered crops have been approved for commercial cultivation in Brazil. However, farmers there believe that they are put at a competitive disadvantage relative to their Argentine neighbors who may legally grow biotech varieties. Thus smuggling of bioengineered soybean seed from Argentina is rampant and, by one estimate, Brazil is now the fifth largest grower of bioengineered varieties. See, for example, European Commission Directorate General for Agriculture, "Economic Impacts of Genetically Modified Crops on the Agri-Food Sector: A First Review," Working Document, Revision 2 (Brussels: Commission of the European Communities, 2000), http://www.europa.eu.int/comm/agriculture/publi/gmo/full_en.pdf.

59. Clive James, *Global Status of Commercialized Transgenic Crops: 2000*, ISAAA Issue Brief, no. 21-2000 (Ithaca, N.Y.: International Service for the Acquisition of Agri-Biotech Applications, 2000).

60. Ibid.

61. U.S. Department of Agriculture, "Petitions of Nonregulated Status Granted by APHIS as of 2-8-2002," http://www.aphis.usda.gov/ppq/biotech/not_reg.html

62. Thomas R. DeGregori, *Agriculture and Modern Technology: A Defense* (Ames, Iowa: Iowa State University Press, 2001).

63. Jorge Fernandez-Cornejo and William D. McBride, *Genetically Engineered Crops for Pest Management in U.S. Agriculture: Farm-Level Effects*, Agricultural Economic Report, no. 786 (Washington, D.C.: USDA Economic Research Service, April 2000).

64. National Academy of Sciences, *Introduction of Recombinant DNA-Engineered Organisms into the Environment: Key Issues* (Washington, D.C.: Council of the U.S. Academy of Sciences/National Academy Press, 1987); National Research Council, *Field Testing Genetically Modified Organisms: Framework for Decisions;* and National Research Council, *Genetically Modified Pest-Protected Plants: Science and Regulation* (Washington, D.C.: National Academy Press, 2000).

65. American Medical Association, "Report 10 of the Council on Scientific Affairs (I-00): Genetically Modified Crops and Foods" (Chicago: American Medical Association, 2000), http://www.ama-assn.org/ama/pub/article/2036-3604.html.

66. Institute of Food Technologists, *IFT Expert Report on Biotechnology and Foods.*

67. World Health Organization, *Strategies for Assessing the Safety of Foods Produced by Biotechnology: Report of a Joint FAO/WHO Consultation* (Geneva, Switzerland: World Health Organization, 1991).

68. See, for example, National Research Council, *Field Testing Genetically Modified Organisms: Framework for Decisions;* and Institute of Food Technologists, *IFT Expert Report on Biotechnology and Foods.*

69. National Research Council, *Field Testing Genetically Modified Organisms: Framework for Decisions.*

70. Institute of Food Technologists, *IFT Expert Report on Biotechnology and Foods,* p. 23.

71. U.S. Food and Drug Administration, "Statement of Policy: Foods Derived from New Plant Varieties," *Federal Register,* vol. 57 (May 29, 1992), p. 22985.

72. Ibid., pp. 22984–23005.

73. Goodman, Hauptli, Crossway, and Knauf, "Gene Transfer in Crop Improvement"; Steve L. Taylor and Susan L. Hefle, "Seeking Clarity in the Debate over the Safety of GM Foods," *Nature,* vol. 402, no. 6762 (December 9, 1999), p. 575; and National Research Council, *Field Testing Genetically Modified Organisms: Framework for Decisions.*

74. U.S. Office of Science and Technology Policy, "Coordinated Framework for the Regulation of Biotechnology," *Federal Register,* vol. 51 (June 26, 1986), pp. 23302–50; and Donna Vogt and Mickey Parish, *Food Biotechnology in the United States: Science, Regulation, and Issues* (Washington, D.C.: Congressional Research Service, January 19, 2001).

75. Plant Quarantine Act, 7 U.S.C § 151; and Federal Plant Pest Act, 7 U.S.C § 150.

76. Federal Insecticide, Fungicide, and Rodenticide Act and Food Quality Protection Act, 7 U.S.C § 136.

77. Federal Food, Drug, and Cosmetics Act, 21 U.S.C § 321(s), 342, and 348.

78. Alan MacHughen, *Pandora's Picnic Basket: The Potential and Hazards of Genetically Modified Foods* (New York: Oxford University Press, 2000).

79. Prakash, "The Genetically Modified Crop Debate in the Context of Agricultural Evolution."

80. National Research Council, *Genetically Modified Pest-Protected Plants: Science and Regulation.*

81. Trewavas and Leaver, "Is Opposition to GM Crops Science or Politics?"; and Federoff, "Transposons and Genome Evolution in Plants."

82. Institute of Food Technologists, *IFT Expert Report on Biotechnology and Foods.*

83. Pew Initiative on Food and Biotechnology, *Harvest on the Horizon: Future Uses of Agricultural Biotechnology* (Washington, D.C.: Pew Initiative on Food and Biotechnology, September 2001).

84. J. H. Clark and I. R. Ipharraguerre, "Livestock Performance: Feeding Biotech Crops," *Journal of Dairy Science,* vol. 84, suppl. E (2001), pp. E9–E18.

85. Jeremy Rifkin, *The Biotech Century* (New York: Tarcher/Putnam, 1998), p. 105.

86. Steve Taylor, quoted in American Medical Association, "Genetic Enhancement Guards Against Food Allergies," AMA Media Advisory (October 4, 2001), http://www.ama-assn.org/ama/pub/article/4197-5330.html.

87. Ibid.

88. Cindy Lynn Richard and Dan Holman, "Ecological Impact Assessment" (Ames, Iowa: Council for Agricultural Science and Technology, October 12, 2000), http://www.cast-science.org/biotechnology/20001011.htm.

89. Trewavas and Leaver, "Is Opposition to GM Crops Science or Politics?"

90. David Quist and Ignacio H. Chapela, "Transgenic DNA Introgressed into Traditional Maize Landraces in Oaxaca, Mexico," *Nature*, vol. 414, no. 6863 (November 29, 2001), pp. 541–43.

91. Mark Stevenson, "Accidental Spread of Modified Corn Is Seen As Cultural Attack: Mexicans Are Angered About Contaminated Crops," *St. Louis Post-Dispatch* (January 1, 2002), p. C1.

92. AgBioWorld Foundation, "Scientists Say Mexican Biodiversity Is Safe: Concerns About Cross-Pollination Unfounded," AgBioWorld Foundation Press Release (December 19, 2001), http://www.agbioworld.org/biotech_info/pr/mexican _biodiversitysafe.html.

93. Rick Weiss, "Sowing Dependency or Uprooting Hunger?" *Washington Post* (February 8, 1999), p. A9.

94. Rural Advancement Foundation International, "Biotech Activists Oppose the 'Terminator Technology,'" *RAFI News Release* (March 13, 1998), URL: http://www.rafi.org/article.asp?newsid=141.

95. Quoted in Jeffrey Kluger, "The Suicide Seeds," *Time* (February 1, 1999), pp. 44–45.

96. Quoted in Rick Weiss, "Sowing Dependency or Uprooting Hunger?" *Washington Post* (February 8, 1999), p. A9.

97. Dennis T. Avery, "Fears About Biotech . . . Old Whine in New Bottles," *The Bridge News Forum* (April 9, 1999).

98. Jocelyn Kaiser, "USDA to Commercialize 'Terminator' Technology," *Science*, vol. 289, no. 5480 (August 4, 2000), pp. 709–10.

99. Charles B. Heiser, Jr., *Seed to Civilization: The Story of Food* (Cambridge, Mass.: Harvard University Press, 1990).

100. M. J. Crawley, S. L. Brown, R. S. Hails, D. D. Kohn, and M. Rees, "Transgenic Crops in Natural Habitats," *Nature*, vol. 409, no. 6821 (February 8, 2001), pp. 682–83.

101. Maarten J. Chrispeels and David E. Sadava, *Plants, Genes, and Agriculture* (Boston: Jones & Bartlett, 1994).

102. National Research Council, *Field Testing Genetically Modified Organisms: Framework for Decisions.*

103. Fernando Nuez, Juan José Ruiz, and Jaime Prohens, "Mejora genetica para mantenerla diversidad en los cultivos agricolas," Commission on Genetic Resources for Food and Agriculture Background Study Paper, no. 6 (Rome: Food and Agriculture Organization, May 1997).

104. Prakash, "The Genetically Modified Crop Debate in the Context of Agricultural Evolution."

105. Stanley W. B. Ewen and Arpad Pusztai, "Effect of Diets Containing Genetically Modified Potatoes Expressing *Galanthus nivalis* Lectin on Rat Small Intestine," *The Lancet*, vol. 354, no. 9187 (October 16, 1999), pp. 1353–55.

106. Harry A. Kuiper, Hub P. J. M. Noteborn, and Ad A. C. M. Peijnenburg, "Adequacy of Methods for Testing the Safety of Genetically Modified Foods," *The Lancet*, vol. 354, no. 9187 (October 16, 1999), pp. 1315–16.

107. Anthony J. Trewavas, "Substantial Equivalence," *Chemistry & Industry*, vol. 10 (May 22, 2000), p. 334; and Harry A. Kuiper, Hub P. J. M. Noteborn, Ad A. C. M. Peijnenburg, "Adequacy of Methods for Testing the Safety of Genetically Modified Foods."

108. The Royal Society, "Review of Data on Possible Toxicity of GM Potatoes," Review Ref: 11/99 (London: The Royal Society, June 1999), http://www.royalsoc.ac.uk /templates/statements/statementDetails.cfm?StatementID=29.

109. Zhang-Liang Chen, "Transgenic Food: Need and Safety" (presentation to the OECD Edinburgh Conference on the Scientific and Health Aspects of Genetically Modified Foods, February 28–March 1, 2000), http://www1.oecd.org/subject /biotech/chen.pdf.

110. Reiko Teshima et al., "Effects of GM and Non-GM Soybeans on the Immune System of BN Rats and B10A Mice," *Journal of the Food Hygiene Society of Japan*, vol. 41, no. 3 (June, 2000), p 3.

111. Clark and Ipharraguerre, "Livestock Performance: Feeding Biotech Crops."

112. See, for example, Jennifer Ferrara and Michael K. Dorsey, "Genetically Engineered Foods: A Minefield of Safety Hazards," in Brian Tokar, ed., *Redesigning Life? The Worldwide Challenge to Genetic Engineering* (New York: Zed Books, 2001), pp. 51–66.

113. John E. Losey, Linda S. Rayor, and Maureen E. Carter, "Transgenic Pollen Harms Monarch Larvae," *Nature*, vol. 399, no. 6733 (May 20, 1999), p. 214.

114. Kathleen Fackelmann, "Engineered Corn Kills Butterflies, Study Says," *USA Today* (May 20, 1999), p. 1A.

115. David Kinney, "Lab-Designed Corn May Harm Insects," Associated Press Newswires (May 19, 1999).

116. Associated Press, "Butterfly Deaths Linked to Altered Corn," *Boston Globe* (May 20, 1999), p. A24.

117. Anthony M. Shelton and Mark K. Sears, "The Monarch Butterfly Controversy: Scientific Interpretations of a Phenomenon," *The Plant Journal*, vol. 27, GM Special Issue (2001), pp. 483–88.

118. Laura C. Hansen Jesse and John J. Obrycki, "Field Deposition of Bt Transgenic Corn Pollen: Lethal Effects on the Monarch Butterfly," *Oceologia*, vol. 125 (2000), pp. 241–48.

119. Trewavas and Leaver, "Is Opposition to GM Crops Science or Politics?"

120. Ben J. Miflin, "Crop Biotechnology. Where Now?" *Plant Physiology*, vol. 123, no. 1 (May 2000), pp. 17–27; and David S. Pimentel and Peter H. Raven, "Bt Corn Pollen Impacts on Nontarget Lepidoptera: Assessment of Effects on Nature," *Proceedings of the National Academy of Sciences*, vol. 97, no. 15 (July 18, 2000), pp. 8198–8199.

121. Henry Daniell, "New Tools for Chloroplast Genetic Engineering," *Nature Biotechnology*, vol. 17, no. 9 (September 1999), pp. 855–56.

122. Susan E. Scott and Mike J. Wilkinson, "Low Probability of Chloroplast Movement from Oilseed Rape (*Brassica napus*) into Wild *Brassica rapa*," *Nature Biotechnology*, vol. 17, no. 4 (April 1999), pp. 390–92.

123. Mark K. Sears, Richard L. Hellmich, Diane E. Stanley-Horn, Karen S. Oberhauser, John M. Pleasants, Heather R. Mattila, Blair D. Siegfried, and Galen P. Dively, "Impact of Bt Corn Pollen on Monarch Butterfly Populations: A Risk Assessment," *Proceedings of the National Academy of Sciences*, vol. 98, no. 21 (October 8, 2001), pp. 11937–42; Diane E. Stanley-Horn, Galen P. Dively, Richard L. Hellmich, Heather R. Mattila, Mark K. Sears, Robyn Rose, Laura C. H. Jesse, John E. Losey, John J. Obrycki, and Les Lewis, "Assessing the Impact of Cry1Ab-Expressing Corn Pollen on Monarch Butterfly Larvae in Field Studies," *Proceedings of the National Academy of Sciences*, vol. 98, no. 21 (October 8, 2001), pp.

11931–36; Richard L. Hellmich, Blair D. Siegfried, Mark K. Sears, Diane E. Stanley-Horn, Michael J. Daniels, Heather R. Mattila, Terrence Spencer, Keith G. Bidne, and Leslie C. Lewis, "Monarch Larvae Sensitivity to *Bacillus thuringiensis*-Purified Proteins and Pollen," *Proceedings of the National Academy of Sciences,* vol. 98, no. 21 (October 8, 2001), pp. 11925–30; Karen S. Oberhauser, Michelle D. Prysby, Heather R. Mattila, Diane E. Stanley-Horn, Mark K. Sears, Galen Dively, Eric Olson, John M. Pleasants, Wai-Ki F. Lam, and Richard L. Hellmich, "Temporal and Spatial Overlap Between Monarch Larvae and Corn Pollen," *Proceedings of the National Academy of Sciences,* vol. 98, no. 21 (October 8, 2001), pp. 11913–18; John M. Pleasants, Richard L. Hellmich, Galen P. Dively, Mark K. Sears, Diane E. Stanley-Horn, Heather R. Mattila, John E. Foster, Thomas L. Clark, and Gretchen D. Jones, "Corn Pollen Deposition on Milkweeds in and near Corn-fields," *Proceedings of the National Academy of Sciences,* vol. 98, no. 21 (October 8, 2001), pp. 11919–24; and A. R. Zangerl, D. McKenna, C. L. Wraight, M. Carroll, P. Ficarello, R. Warner, and M. R. Berenbaum, "Effects of Exposure to Event 176 *Bacillus thuringiensis* Corn Pollen on Monarch and Black Swallowtail Caterpillars Under Field Conditions," *Proceedings of the National Academy of Sciences,* vol. 98, no. 21 (October 8, 2001), pp. 11908–12.

124. Tanja H. Schuler, Roel P. J. Potting, Ian Denholm, and Guy M. Poppy, "Parasitoid Behaviour and Bt Plants," *Nature,* vol. 400, no. 6747 (August 26, 1999), pp. 825–29; Ellin Doyle, "Environmental Benefits and Sustainable Agriculture Through Biotechnology," Executive Summary of the Ceres Forum, Georgetown University (November 10–11, 1999); Carl Pray, Danmeng Ma, Jikun Huang, and Fangbin Qiao, "Impact of Bt Cotton in China," *World Development,* vol. 29, no. 5 (forthcoming); and Deepak Saxena and Guenther Stotzky, "*Bacillus thuringiensis* (Bt) Toxin Released from Root Exudates and Biomass of Bt Corn Has No Apparent Effect on Earthworms, Nematodes, Protozoa, Bacteria, and Fungi in Soil," *Soil Biology & Biochemistry,* (2001), vol. 33 (9) p.1225-1230.

125. See, for example, http://www.ucsusa.org/index.html.

126. Ronald Smith and Roger Leonard, "Farmers and Public Benefit from Insect-Protected Cotton," Alabama Cooperative Extension System *Newsline* (July 9, 2001), http://www.aces.edu/dept/extcomm/newspaper/july9a01_op-ed.html.

127. Martin B. Main, Fritz M. Roka, and Reed F. Noss, "Evaluating Costs of Conservation," *Conservation Biology,* vol. 13, no. 6 (December 1999), pp. 1262–72; and Goklany, "Meeting Global Food Needs: The Environmental Trade-Offs Between Increasing Land Conversion and Land Productivity."

128. Swappan K. Datta, "A Promising Debut for Bt Hybrid Rice," *ISB News Report* (December 2000), pp. 1–3.

129. Jumin Tu, Guoan Zhang, Karabi Datta, Caiguo Xu, Yuqing He, Quifa Zhang, Gurdev Singh Khush, and Swapan Kumar Datta, "Field Performance of Transgenic Elite Commercial Hybrid Rice Expressing *Bacillus thuringiensis* d-endotoxin," *Nature Biotechnology,* vol. 18, no. 10 (October 2000), pp. 1101–04.

130. Parliamentary Office of Science and Technology, *The "Great GM Food Debate": A Survey of Media Coverage in the First Half of 1999* (London: U.K. Parliamentary Office of Science and Technology, May 2000).

131. Ibid., p. 46.

132. Ibid., p. 46.

133. George Gaskell, Nick Allum, Martin Bauer, John Durant, Agnes Allansdottir, Heinz Bonfadelli, Daniel Boy, Suzanne de Cheveigné, Björn Fjaestad, Jan M. Gut-

teling, Juergen Hampel, Erling Jelsøe, Jorge Correia Jesuino, Matthias Kohring, Nicole Kronberger, Cees Midden, Torben Hviid Nielsen, Andrzej Przestalski, Timo Rusanen, George Sakellaris, Helge Torgersen, Tomasz Twardowski, and Wolfgang Wagner, "Biotechnology and the European Public," *Nature Biotechnology*, vol. 18, no. 9 (September 2000), pp. 935–38.

134. See, for example, Parliamentary Office of Science and Technology, *The "Great GM Food Debate": A Survey of Media Coverage in the First Half of 1999.*

135. Parliamentary Office of Science and Technology, *Genetically Modified Foods: Benefits and Risks, Regulation and Public Acceptance* (London: U.K. Parliamentary Office of Science and Technology, May 1998).

136. House of Lords Select Committee on European Communities, *Second Report: EC Regulation of Genetic Modification in Agriculture* (London: House of Lords Publications, December 15, 1998).

137. However, for such products as corn oil or soy oil, where neither DNA nor proteins remain in the consumer product, biotechnology-derived foods can be commercialized if the producer can demonstrate that the products are "substantially equivalent" to the nonbiotech-derived counterpart in nutritional value, metabolism, intended use, and other characteristics. European Commission, "Questions and Answers on the Regulation of GMOs in the EU," Memo/00/277 (Brussels: Commission of the European Communities Directorate General for Health and Consumer Protection, July 24, 2001), http://www.europa.eu.int/comm/dgs/health_consumer/library/press/press171_en.pdf.

138. European Commission, "Questions and Answers on the regulation of GMOs in the EU."

139. Michael Mann, "Tough New EU Law Opens Way for GM Crops," *Financial Times* (February 15, 2001), p. 8.

140. European Commission, "Questions and Answers on the regulation of GMOs in the EU."

141. John Hodgson, "National Politicians Block GM Progress," *Nature Biotechnology*, vol. 18, no. 9 (September 2000), pp. 918–19.

142. Sabine Louët, "EU Court Overrules France's Bt Maize Ban," *Nature Biotechnology*, Vol. 18, No. 5 (May 2000), p. 487.

143. Parliamentary Office of Science and Technology, "GM Farm Trials," POST Note 146 (London: Parliamentary Office of Science and Technology, September 2000).

144. John Vidal, "GM Trials Face Delay as Crops Destroyed: Company Examines Damage to Six Test Sites," *The Guardian* (June 9, 2001), p. 20.

145. Agriculture and Environment Biotechnology Committee, *Crops on Trial: A Report by the AEBC* (London: Agriculture and Environment Biotechnology Committee, September 2001).

146. Michael Mann, "Tough New EU Law Opens Way for GM Crops."

147. Robert Paarlberg, "Shrinking International Markets for GM Crops?" (speech to the U.S. Department of Agriculture Agricultural Outlook Forum, Arlington, Virginia, February 22–23, 2001).

148. Cartagena Protocol on Biosafety to the Convention on Biological Diversity (Montreal: Secretariat of the Convention on Biological Diversity, 2000), http://www.biodiv.org/doc/legal/cartagena-protocol-en.pdf.

149. Cartagena Protocol on Biosafety, Article 3, Section 2.

150. Cartagena Protocol on Biosafety, Preamble; Article 1; Article 10, Section 6; Article 11, Section 8; and Annex III, Section 4.

151. Henry I. Miller and Gregory Conko, "The Science of Biotechnology Meets the Politics of Global Regulation," *Issues in Science and Technology,* vol. 17, no. 1 (fall 2000), pp. 47–54.

152. See, for example, World Trade Organization, "EC Measures Concerning Meat and Meat Products (Hormones)," Report of the Appellate Body WT/DS26/AB/R (January 16, 1998).

153. Miller and Conko, "The Science of Biotechnology Meets the Politics of Global Regulation."

154. Cartagena Protocol on Biosafety, Article 18.

155. European Commission Directorate General for Agriculture, "Economic Impacts of Genetically Modified Crops on the Agri-Food Sector: A First Review."

156. European Commission, "Proposal for a Regulation of the European Parliament and of the Council Concerning Traceability and Labelling of Genetically Modified Organisms and Traceability of Food and Feed Products Produced from Genetically Modified Organisms, and Amending Directive 2001/18/EC," COM(2001) 182 Final 2001/0180 (Brussels: Commission of the European Communities, July 25, 2001).

157. United Nations Development Programme, *Human Development Report 2001,* p. 69.

158. See, for example, The Campaign to Label Genetically Engineered Foods Web site, http://www.thecampaign.org/.

159. Henry I. Miller, "A Rational Approach to Labeling Biotech-Derived Foods," *Science,* vol. 284, no. 5419 (May 28, 1999), pp. 1471–72; and U.S. Congress Subcommittee on Basic Research of the Committee of Science, *Seeds of Opportunity: An Assessment of the Benefits, Safety, and Oversight of Plant Genomics and Agricultural Biotechnology* (Washington, D.C.: United States House of Representatives, April, 2000), pp. 53–55.

160. Karen A. Goldman, "Labeling of Genetically Modified Foods: Legal and Scientific Issues," *Georgetown International Environmental Law Review,* vol. 12, no. 3 (spring 2000), pp. 717–69; and Gregory Conko, "Labeling and Risk: The Case of Bioengineered Foods," in Jonathan H. Adler, ed., *Ecology, Liberty & Property* (Washington, D.C.: Competitive Enterprise Institute, 2000), pp. 227–37.

161. U.S. Food and Drug Administration, "Statement of Policy: Foods Derived from New Plant Varieties," pp. 22984–23005.

162. U.S. Food and Drug Administration, "Draft Guidance for Industry: Voluntary Labeling Indicating Whether Foods Have or Have Not Been Developed Using Bioengineering," *Federal Register,* vol. 66 (January 18, 2001), pp. 4839–42.

163. American Medical Association, "Report 10 of the Council on Scientific Affairs (I-00): Genetically Modified Crops and Foods" (Chicago: American Medical Association, 2000), http://www.ama-assn.org/ama/pub/article/2036-3604.html.

164. Institute of Food Technologists, *IFT Expert Report on Biotechnology and Foods.*

165. U.S. Food and Drug Administration, "Statement of Policy: Foods Derived from New Plant Varieties," pp. 22984–23005.

166. Karen K. Marshall, "What's in a Label?" *AgBioForum,* vol. 1, no. 1 (summer 1998), pp. 35–37.

167. U.S. Food and Drug Administration, "Statement of Policy: Foods Derived from New Plant Varieties," *Federal Register,* pp. 22984–23005.

168. Federal Food, Drug and Cosmetics Act, 21 U.S.C § 343(a)(1).

169. Institute of Food Technologists, *IFT Expert Report on Biotechnology and Foods,* p. 25.

170. *International Dairy Foods Association, et al. v. Amestoy,* 92 F.3d 67 (2nd Cir. 1996).
171. See, for example, C. Ford Runge and Lee Ann Jackson, "Negative Labeling of Genetically Modified Organisms (GMOs): The Experience of rBST," *AgBioForum,* vol. 3, no. 1 (winter 2000), pp. 310–14; and Michael I. Krauss, "Regulation vs. Markets in the Development of Standards," *Southern California Interdisciplinary Law Journal,* vol. 3, no. 3 (summer 1994), pp. 781–807.
172. C. Ford Runge and Lee Ann Jackson, "Negative Labeling of Genetically Modified Organisms (GMOs): The Experience of rBST."
173. U.S. Food and Drug Administration, "Draft Guidance for Industry: Voluntary Labeling Indicating Whether Foods Have or Have Not Been Developed Using Bioengineering."
174. U.S. Department of Agriculture, "National Organic Program: Final Rule with Request for Comments," 7 CFR § 205.
175. Population Division of the Department of Economic and Social Affairs of the United Nations Secretariat, *The World at Six Billion,* Working Paper ESA/P/WP 154 (New York: Population Division of the Department of Economic and Social Affairs of the United Nations Secretariat, 1999).
176. Bjørn Lomborg, *The Skeptical Environmentalist* (Cambridge, U.K.: Cambridge University Press, 2001), p. 100.
177. Amartya Sen, *Poverty and Famines: An Essay on Entitlement and Deprivation* (New York: Oxford University Press, 1981).
178. Conway and Toenniessen, "Feeding the World in the Twenty-First Century."
179. Jeffrey D. Sachs, "Tropical Underdevelopment," NBER Working Paper No. W8119 (February 2001).
180. Conway and Toenniessen, "Feeding the World in the Twenty-First Century."
181. Anne Simon Moffat, "Can Genetically Modified Crops Go 'Greener'?" *Science,* vol. 290, no. 5490 (October 13, 2000), pp. 253–54; and Urban Johanson, Joanne West, Clare Lister, Scott Michaels, Richard Amasino, and Caroline Dean, "Molecular Analysis of *FRIGIDA,* a Major Determinant of Natural Variation in *Arabidopsis* Flowering Time," *Science,* vol. 290, no. 5490 (October 13, 2000), pp. 344–47.
182. Fátima C. Alvim, Sônia M. B. Carolino, Júlio C. M. Cascardo, Cristiano C. Nunes, Carlos A. Martinez, Wagner C. Otoni, and Elizabeth P. B. Fontes, "Enhanced Accumulation of BiP in Transgenic Plants Confers Tolerance to Water Stress," *Plant Physiology,* vol. 126, no. 3 (July 2001), pp. 1042–54; and Mie Kasuga, Qiang Liu, Setsuko Miura, Kazuko Yamaguchi-Shinozaki, and Kazuo Shinozaki, "Improving Plant Drought, Salt, and Freezing Tolerance by Gene Transfer of a Single Stress-Inducible Transcription Factor," *Nature Biotechnology,* vol. 17, no. 3 (March 1999), pp. 287–91.
183. Hong-Xia Zhang and Eduardo Blumwald, "Transgenic Salt-Tolerant Tomato Plants Accumulate Salt in Foliage but Not in Fruit," *Nature Biotechnology,* vol. 19, no. 8 (August 2001), pp. 765–68; and Mie Kasuga, Qiang Liu, Setsuko Miura, Kazuko Yamaguchi-Shinozaki, and Kazuo Shinozaki, "Improving Plant Drought, Salt, and Freezing Tolerance by Gene Transfer of a Single Stress-Inducible Transcription Factor."
184. Kirsten R. Jaglo-Ottosen, Sarah J. Gilmour, Daniel G. Zarka, Oliver Schabenberger, and Michael F. Thomashow, "*Arabidopsis CBF1* Overexpression Induces *COR* Genes and Enhances Freezing Tolerance," *Science,* vol. 280, no. 5360 (April 3, 1998), pp. 104–06; Hayashi H. Alia, A. Sakamoto, and N. Murata, "Enhancement of the Tolerance of *Arabidopsis* to High Temperatures by Genetic Engineering of the

Synthesis of Glycinebetaine," *The Plant Journal,* vol. 16, no. 2 (October 1998), pp.155–61; and Mie Kasuga, Qiang Liu, Setsuko Miura, Kazuko Yamaguchi-Shinozaki, and Kazuo Shinozaki, "Improving Plant Drought, Salt, and Freezing Tolerance by Gene Transfer of a Single Stress-Inducible Transcription Factor."

185. José López-Bucio, Octavio Martínez de la Vega, Arturo Guevara-García, and Luis Herrera-Estrella, "Enhanced Phosphorus Uptake in Transgenic Tobacco Plants That Overproduce Citrate," *Nature Biotechnology,* vol. 18, no. 4 (April 2000), pp. 450–53; and Juan Manuel de la Fuente, Verenice Ramírez-Rodríguez, José Luis Cabrera-Ponce, and Luis Herrera-Estrella, "Aluminum Tolerance in Transgenic Plants by Alteration of Citrate Synthesis," *Science,* vol. 276, no. 5318 (June 6, 1997), pp. 1566–68.

186. Conway and Toenniessen, "Feeding the World in the Twenty-First Century."

187. Gary Toenniessen, "Biotechnology Breeding and Seed Systems for African Crop Improvement" (presentation to the 15th International Technical Conference of the International Society of African Scientists, Wilmington, Del., October 5, 2001).

188. See, for example, Miguel A. Altieri and Peter Rossett, "Ten Reasons Why Biotechnology Will Not Ensure Food Security, Protect the Environment and Reduce Poverty in the Developing World," *AgBioForum,* vol. 2, nos. 3–4 (summer/fall 1999), pp. 155–62.

189. Cyrus Ndiritu, quoted in Florence Wambugu, *Modifying Africa* (Nairobi, Kenya: Florence Wambugu, 2001), p. 5.

190. Dean DellaPenna, "Nutritional Genomics: Manipulating Plant Micronutrients to Improve Human Health," *Science,* vol. 285, no. 5426 (July 16, 1999), pp. 375–79.

191. Ibid.

192. Xudong Ye, Salim Al-Babili, Andreas Klöti, Jing Zhang, Paola Lucca, Peter Beyer, and Ingo Potrykus, "Engineering the Provitamin A (Beta-Carotene) Biosynthetic Pathway into (Carotenoid-Free) Rice Endosperm," *Science,* vol. 287, no. 5451 (January 14, 2000), pp. 303–8.

193. Ibid.

194. Michael Pollan, "The Great Yellow Hype," *New York Times Magazine* (March 4, 2001), pp. 15–16.

195. Rockefeller Foundation, "New Rices May Help Address Vitamin A and Iron Deficiency, Major Causes of Death in the Developing World," Rockefeller Foundation Press Release (New York: Rockefeller Foundation, August 3, 1999).

196. Quoted in Bailey, "Dr. Strangelunch, Or: Why We Should Learn to Stop Worrying and Love Genetically Modified Food."

197. Pew Initiative on Food and Biotechnology, *Harvest on the Horizon: Future Uses of Agricultural Biotechnology.*

198. Anne Simon Moffat, "Toting Up the Early Harvest of Transgenic Plants," *Science,* vol. 282, no. 5397 (December 18, 1998), pp. 2176–78.

199. Victor de Lorenzo, "Cleaning Up Behind Us: The Potential of Genetically Modified Bacteria to Break Down Toxic Pollutants in the Environment," *EMBO Reports,* vol. 2, no. 5 (May 2001), pp. 357–59; Scott P. Bizily, Clayton L. Rugh, and Richard B. Meagher, "Phytodetoxification of Hazardous Organomercurials by Genetically Engineered Plants," *Nature Biotechnology,* vol. 18, no. 2 (February 2000), pp. 213–17; and Doohyun Ryoo, Hojae Shim, Keith Canada, Paola Barbieri, and Thomas K. Wood, "Aerobic Degradation of Tetrachloroethylene by Toluene-o-

Xylene Monooxygenase of Pseudomonas Stutzeri OX1," *Nature Biotechnology*, vol. 18, no. 7 (July 2000), pp. 775–78.

Chapter 8

1. See, for example, Paul Simon, "In an Empty Cup, a Threat to Peace," *New York Times* (August 14, 2001), p. A17.

2. Steve Connor, "Stockholm Conference: Scientists Search for a Way to Avert World Water Crisis," the *Independent* (London) (August 14, 2001), p. 10; Maggie Farley, "Report Predicts Thirstier World," *Los Angeles Times* (August 14, 2001), part A, p. 3; and Vanessa Houlder, "Low Water: If Rivers and Lakes Are Drained Further, Many Parts of the World May Experience Increased Political Tension, Food Shortages and Environmental Damage," *Financial Times* (August 14, 2001), p. 14.

3. Connor, "Stockholm Conference," p. 10.

4. Janet N. Abramovitz, "Sustaining Freshwater Ecosystems," in *State of the World 1996* (New York: W. W. Norton & Company, 1996), p. 76.

5. United Nations Environment Programme, "Vital Global Water Project Inaugurated by Klaus Toepfer and Kjell Larson in Kalmar, Sweden," *UNEP News Release* (October 15, 1999).

6. See, for example, Danielle Knight, "Environment: Politics, Not Scarcity, Blamed for Water Wars," Inter Press Service (September 25, 2001).

7. For the original coverage of the water issue in this book series see, Terry L. Anderson, "Water Options for the Blue Planet," in Ronald Bailey, ed., *True State of the Planet* (New York: The Free Press, 1995), pp. 267–94.

8. World Resources Institute, United Nations Environment Programme, United Nations Development Programme, and World Bank, *World Resources 1998–99: A Guide to the Global Environment* (New York: Oxford University Press, 1998), p. 304.

9. Lake Superior is significantly larger than the other Great Lakes. It could contain all the other Great Lakes plus three more the size of Lake Erie. Great Lakes Information Network, "Lake Superior Facts and Figures," http://www.great-lakes.net /lakes/ref/supfact.html.

10. World Resources Institute et al., *World Resources 1998–99*, p. 304.

11. Igor A. Shiklomanov, "World Fresh Water Resources," in Peter H. Gleick, ed., *Water in Crisis: A Guide to the World's Fresh Water Resources* (Oxford: Oxford University Press, 1993), pp. 13–24.

12. *The World Almanac and Book of Facts 2001* (Mahwah, N.J.: World Almanac Books, 2001), p. 860.

13. Julian L. Simon, *The Ultimate Resource 2* (Princeton, N.J.: Princeton University Press, 1996), p. 99.

14. Problems with measuring water quality trends appear to have worsened in recent years. From 1975 to 1995, NASQAN attempted to provide long-term water quality trends. After 1995, however, a change in the network's focus has created a set of data not comparable to previous measurements. In 1996, NASQAN changed its focus from sampling a large representative geographic region to a more intensive sampling of just a few regions. Only 31 stations took samples in 1996, compared to the 1980 high of 513. Hence, from 1996 and forward, NASQAN data are not representative of long-term water quality trends.

15. Council on Environmental Quality, *25th Anniversary Report of the Council on Environmental Quality, 1994–1995* (Washington, D.C.: CEQ, 1996).

16. See, for example, David S. Broder, "A Skeptical Electorate in Search of Leadership," *Washington Post* (November 7, 1999), p. A1.

17. Riley E. Dunlap and Lydia Saad, "Only One in Four Americans Are Anxious About the Environment," *Gallup Poll News Service,* (Princeton, N.J.: The Gallup Organization, April 16, 2001).

18. Ibid.

19. United Nations Environment Programme, "Vital Global Water Project."

20. Sandra Postel, *Pillar of Sand: Can the Irrigation Miracle Last?* (New York: W. W. Norton & Company, 1999), p. 6.

21. Donella H. Meadows et al., *The Limits to Growth* (New York: Universe Books, 1972).

22. Donella H. Meadows, Dennis L. Meadows, and Jorgen Randers, *Beyond the Limits: Confronting Global Collapse, Envisioning a Sustainable Future* (White River Junction, Vt.: Chelsea Green Publishing Company, 1992), p. 56.

23. Paul Simon, "In an Empty Cup," p. A17.

24. World Resources Institute, *World Resources 1998–99,* p. 305.

25. Asit K. Biswas et al., *Core and Periphery: A Comprehensive Approach to Middle Eastern Water* (Delhi, India: Oxford University Press, 1997), discussed in Postel, Pillar of Sand, pp. 133–63.

26. Postel, *Pillar of Sand,* pp. 151–53.

27. U.S. Census Bureau, *Statistical Abstract of the United States: 2000* (Washington, D.C.: U.S. Department of Commerce, 2000), Table No. 1352, p. 822.

28. Peter H. Gleick, "Water in the 21st Century," in Peter H. Gleick, ed., *Water in Crisis: A Guide to the World's Fresh Water Resources* (Oxford: Oxford University Press, 1993), pp. 105–13.

29. Sandra L. Postel and Aaron T. Wolf, "Dehydrating Conflict," *Foreign Policy* (September/October 2001).

30. Ibid.

31. U.S. Census Bureau, *Statistical Abstract 2000,* Table No. 1352, p. 822.

32. For more on India's climate and rainfall, see http://www.worldtravelguide .net/data/ind/ind500.asp.

33. "Major Dams of India," http://www.216.167.16.32/overview/damsinindia.htm.

34. Reuters News Agency, "Indian State Suffering Bad Drought," *Globe and Mail* (April 20, 2000).

35. Postel, *Pillar of Sand,* pp. 46–47.

36. Postel, *Pillar of Sand,* p. 42.

37. U.S. Census Bureau, *Statistical Abstract 2000,* Table No. 1352, p. 822; and World Resources Institute et al., *World Resources 1998–99,* p. 305.

38. Lester R. Brown, *Who Will Feed China? Wake Up Call for a Small Planet* (New York: W. W. Norton & Company, 1995), p. 67.

39. "Trying to Stay Afloat: Forum Addresses Growing Concerns over Water Shortage," *China Online,* http://www.chinaonline.com (October 17, 2000).

40. "International China: Country Faces Large-Scale Water Shortage Problems," *Greenwire,* vol. 10, no. 9 (August 1, 2000).

41. U.S. Census Bureau, *Statistical Abstract 2000,* Table No. 1352, p. 822; and World Resources Institute et al., *World Resources 1998–99,* p. 305.

42. "Trying to Stay Afloat," *China Online.*

43. World Commission on Water for the 21st Century, "A Report of the World Commission on Water for the 21st Century," *Water International,* vol. 25, no. 2 (June 2000), p. 284.

44. Sandra Postel, "Dividing the Waters: Global Freshwater Supply," *Massachusetts Institute of Technology Alumni Association Technology Review*, vol. 100, no. 3 (April 1997), p. 54.

45. James Harding, "World Bank Warns of Global Water Crisis," *Financial Times* (August 7, 1995), p. 2.

46. A. Dan Tarlock, "Water Policy Adrift," *Forum for Applied Research and Public Policy*, vol. 16, no. 1 (March 22, 2001), p. 63.

47. Paul Holden and Mateen Thobani, "Tradable Water Rights: A Property Rights Approach to Improving Water Use and Improving Investment," *Cuadernos de economia*, vol. 97 (December 1995), pp. 263–89.

48. Garrett Hardin, "The Tragedy of the Commons," *Science*, vol. 162 (December 13, 1968), pp. 1243–48.

49. Mateen Thobani, "Formal Water Markets: Why, When, and How to Introduce Tradable Water Rights," *World Bank Research Observer*, vol. 12, no. 2 (August 1997), pp. 161–79.

50. Ibid.

51. Erin Schiller, "Oregon Water Trust" (Washington, D.C.: Center for Private Conservation, 1998), http://www.privateconservation.org/case_studies.php?article_id=2.

52. See Terry L. Anderson and Pamela Snyder, *Water Markets: Priming the Invisible Pump* (Washington, D.C.: Cato Institute, 1997).

53. See, for example, Gregory Palast, "Bolivia: TheHijacking of a Water System," *Toronto Star* (May 3, 2000); and Reuters, "Bolivian Water Plan Dropped After Protests Turn into Melees," *New York Times* (April 11, 2000), p. A12.

54. Sophie Tremolet, "Not a Drop to Spare: Why Privatization of Water Supplies Is a Global Growth Market," *The Guardian* (September 26, 2001).

55. Jennifer Hattam, "Who Owns Water?" *Sierra*, vol. 86, no. 5 (September/October 2001).

56. Thobani, "Formal Water Markets," pp. 161–79.

57. James L. Huffman, "A North American Water Marketing Federation," in Terry L. Anderson, ed., *Continental Water Marketing* (San Francisco, Calif.: Pacific Research Institute for Public Policy), p. 148.

58. Ibid., p. 151.

59. Ibid., p. 157.

60. Tony Perry, "Tensions Rise over Bill to Alter Water Delivery Policy," *Los Angeles Times* (May 6, 2001), Part 2, p. 8.

61. Vandana Shiva, letter to the editor, *Economic Times of India* (July 16, 1999).

62. Travis Engen, "Thirsty World Must Tap Market Forces," *Financial Times* (March 23, 1999), p. 14.

Chapter 9

1. Donnella H. Meadows et al., *The Limits to Growth* (New York: Universe Books, 1972), p. 66.

2. Kenneth S. Deffeyes, *Hubbert's Peak: The Impending World Oil Shortage* (Princeton University Press, 2001).

3. David M. Nemtzow, "More Power to You: On Bjorn Lomborg and Energy," *Grist Magazine* (December 12, 2001), taken from Web site http://www.gristmagazine.com/.

4. Sierra Club, "Global Warming Solutions: Clean Energy," http://www.sierraclub.org/globalwarming/cleanenergy/.

5. Energy Information Administration, *Annual Energy Outlook 2002*, Table A8, "Electricity Supply, Disposition, Prices, and Emissions."

6. Ibid., Table A1, "Total Energy Supply and Disposition Summary."

7. Scientists for a Sustainable Energy Future, "An Open Letter to the American People" (May 18, 2001), http://www.bu.edu/cees/openletter.html.

8. John P. Holdren, "Energy: Asking the Wrong Question," *Scientific American* (January 2002), pp. 65–67.

9. John P. Holdren, *Energy: A Crisis in Power* (New York: Sierra Club, 1971).

10. Paul R. Ehrlich, Anne H. Ehrlich, and John P. Holdren, *Ecoscience: Population, Resources, Environment* (San Francisco, Calif.: W. H. Freeman & Co., 1977), p. 403.

11. Amory B. Lovins, "Energy Strategy: The Road Not Taken?" *Foreign Affairs* (October 1976), p. 68.

12. Hazel Henderson, *The Politics of the Solar Age* (Garden City, N.Y.: Anchor Press/Doubleday, 1981), p. 136.

13. Ibid., p. 133.

14. Ibid., p. 132.

15. Energy Information Administration, *Annual Energy Review 2000*, Table 8.12 (Electricity End Use, 1949–2000).

16. Henderson, *The Politics of the Solar Age*, p. 138.

17. Energy Information Administration, *Annual Energy Review 2000*, Table 6.1 (Natural Gas Overview, 1949–2000).

18. James W. Schmoker and Thaddeus S. Dyman, "Changing Perceptions of United States Natural-Gas Resources as Shown by Successive U.S. Department of the Interior Assessments," U.S. Geological Survey Bulletin 2172-B, p. 7. Available only on the Web at http://greenwood.cr.usgs.gov/pub/bulletins/b2172-b/ (accessed August 21, 2001).

19. "Energy Resources Program of the U.S. Geological Survey," USGS Fact Sheet FS-032-01 (March 2001).

20. John H. Jennrich, "Potential Gas Committee Cites New Technology as Key to Increase in Natural Gas Resources," Beacon Energy *Spotlight on Energy Markets* (April 2001).

21. John B. Curtis, Potential Gas Agency, taken from http://www.mines.edu/research/pga/.

22. Energy Information Administration, *International Energy Annual 1999: World Energy Overview*, http://www.eia.doe.gov/emeu/iea/overview.html.

23. Ibid.

24. Energy Information Administration, *Annual Energy Outlook 2002*, Table A1, "Total Energy Supply and Disposition Summary."

25. Ibid., Table A17, "Renewable Energy Generating Capability and Generation."

26. International Energy Agency, "Benign Energy? The Environmental Implications of Renewables," published in 1998, accessed from the Web site http://www.iea.org/pubs/studies/files/benign.

27. Ibid.

28. Richard Rhodes and Dennis Beller, "The Need for Nuclear Power," *Foreign Affairs* (January/February 2000), pp. 34–35.

29. Glenn R. Schleede, *It's Time for a National Energy Policy Reality Check* (June 21, 2001), p. 7.

30. Ibid., "Executive Summary," pp. iii–iv.

31. Ibid., p. 7.

32. Jerry Taylor and Peter VanDoren, "Evaluating the Case for Renewable Energy: Is Government Support Warranted?" (Washington, D.C.: Cato Institute, January 10, 2002), p. 1.

33. Ibid., p. 3.

34. Ibid., p. 12.

35. Schleede, *It's Time for a National Energy Policy Reality Check*, p. 15.

36. The INGAA Foundation Inc., Exhibit ES-1, "U.S. Natural Gas Demand," *Pipeline and Storage Infrastructure for a 30 Tcf Market, An Updated Assessment* (January 2002), p. 2.

37. Schleede, *It's Time for a National Energy Policy Reality Check*, p. 13.

38. Glenn R. Schleede, president, Energy Market & Policy Analysis Inc., "Memorandum for Mr. Patrick McMahon, *USA Today,*" (August 22, 2001), p. 1.

39. Ibid., p. 1.

40. Ibid., p. 2.

41. Glenn R. Schleede, *California & Wind Energy*, electronic mail memorandum (July 23, 2001).

42. Joel Darmstadter, *The Role of Renewable Resources in U.S. Electricity Generation— Experience and Prospects,* Resources for the Future, Climate Change Issues Brief, no. 24 (September 2000), p. 9.

43. Ibid., p. 12.

44. Michael Economides and Ronald Oligney, *The Color of Oil* (Katy, Tex.: Round Oak Publishing Co., 2000), pp. 141–42.

45. Ibid., p. 142.

46. Ibid., p. 141.

47. Robert L. Bradley Jr. and Richard W. Fulmer, *Energy: The Master Resource* (Houston, Tex.: second draft of forthcoming book), p. 28.

48. Ibid., pp. 15–16.

49. Worldwatch Institute, "Hydrogen Rising in Energy Policy Debate," Worldwatch Institute Press Release (Washington, D.C., August 2, 2001).

50. Ibid.

51. David Ludlum, *New York Times* (December 23, 2001), Business section, p. 9.

52. Bradley and Fulmer, *Energy: The Master Resource,* p. 16.

53. Spencer Abraham, "Remarks by Spencer Abraham on Freedom CAR" (Detroit, Mich., January 9, 2002), accessed at URL: http://www.energy.gov/HQDocs /speeches/2002/janss/FreedomCar_v.html.

Chapter 10

1. Precautionary European regulation of biotechnology is summarized in Rod Hunter, "European Regulation of Genetically Modified Organisms," in Julian Morris and Roger Bate, eds., *Fearing Food: Risk, Health, & Environment* (Oxford: Butterworth & Heinemann, 1999), pp. 213–15; and Terrence P. Stewart and David S. Johanson, "Policy in Flux: The European Union's Laws on Agricultural Biotechnology and Their Effects on International Trade," *Drake Journal of Agricultural Law,* vol. 4 (1999), pp. 260–68.

2. See, generally, Bill Durodie, "Plastic Panics: European Risk Regulation in the Aftermath of BSE," in Julian Morris, ed., *Rethinking Risk and the Precautionary Principle* (Oxford, U.K.: Butterworth Heinemann, 2000), pp. 140–66.

3. Joel Tickner, Carolyn Raffensperger, and Nancy Myers, *The Precautionary Principle in Action: A Handbook* (Science and Environmental Health Network, 1999), p. 3.

4. The Wingspread Statement on the Precautionary Principle, reprinted in Appendix A, *Protecting Public Health & the Environment*, Carolyn Raffensperger and Joel Tickner, eds. (Washington, D.C.: Island Press, 1999), pp. 353–55.

5. Signatories of the statement included representatives of Greenpeace, Physicians for Social Responsibility, the W. Alton Jones Foundation, the Silicon Valley Toxics Coalition, and the Indigenous Environmental Network, among others.

6. The Wingspread Statement, reprinted in Appendix A, *Protecting Public Health & the Environment*, pp. 353–55.

7. Andrew Jordan and Timothy O'Riordan, "The Precautionary Principle in Contemporary Environmental Policy and Politics," in *Protecting Public Health and the Environment*, p. 23.

8. P. Horsman of Greenpeace quoted in Jordan and O'Riordan, p. 25.

9. The Wingspread Statement, reprinted in Appendix A, *Protecting Public Health & the Environment*, pp. 353–55.

10. Appendix A, p. 354.

11. Quoted in Julian Morris, "Defining the Precautionary Principle," in Julian Morris, ed., *Rethinking Risk and the Precautionary Principle* (Oxford, U.K.: Butterworth Heinemann, 2000), p. 4.

12. Joel A. Tickner, "A Map Toward Precautionary Decision Making," in *Protecting Public Health*.

13. Quoted in Ronald Bailey, "Precautionary Tale," *Reason* (April 1999), accessed online at URL: http://www.reason.com/9904/fe.rb.precautionary.shtml.

14. Morris, *Rethinking Risk and the Precautionary Principle*, p. 10.

15. Soren Holm and John Harris, "Precautionary Principle Stifles Discovery," *Nature*, vol. 400 (1999), p. 398.

16. Christopher D. Stone, "Is There a Precautionary Principle?" *Environmental Law Reporter*, vol. 31 (July 2001), p. 10790.

17. The Wingspread Statement, quoted in Appendix A, p. 354.

18. For a general overview of the antichlorine campaign, see Jonathan H. Adler, *Environmentalism at the Crossroads: Green Activism in America* (Washington, D.C.: Capital Research Center, 1995), pp. 40–42.

19. Ivan Amato, "The Crusade Against Chlorine," *Science* (July 9, 1993), p. 152.

20. Ivan Amato, "The Crusade to Ban Chlorine," *Garbage* (summer 1994), p. 36.

21. "Chemical Industry 'Outraged' by Chlorine Proposal; Proposed Regulations Would Seek to Reduce Use of Chlorine Compounds," *Chemical Marketing Reporter* (February 7, 1994), p. 3; and Russell Clemings, "Environmentalists Back Chlorine Limits," *Fresno Bee* (February 21, 1994), A4.

22. Peter Montague, "Modern Environmental Protection—Part 2," *Rachel's Environment & Health News*, no. 705 (August 3, 2000).

23. Ibid.

24. Quoted in Michael Fumento, "The War on Chlorine," *Reason* (June 1994).

25. Tickner, Raffensperger, and Myers, *The Precautionary Principle in Action*, p. 17.

26. Amato, "The Crusade Against Chlorine," p. 153.

27. Bette Hileman, "Debate Over Phaseout of Chlorine, Chlorinated Organics Continues," *Chemical & Engineering News* (December 6, 1993), p. 32.

28. Amato, "The Crusade Against Chlorine," p. 154.

29. Amato, "The Crusade to Ban Chlorine," p. 33.

30. Bette Hileman, "Concerns Broaden Over Chlorine and Chlorinated Hydrocarbons," *Chemical & Engineering News* (April 19, 1993), p. 11.

31. John D. Graham and George M. Gray, "Optimal Use of 'Toxic Chemicals,'" *Risk in Perspective* (May 1993).

32. Christopher Anderson, "Cholera Epidemic Traced to Risk Miscalculation," *Nature* (November 28, 1991), p. 255.

33. For an overview of the risk trade-offs involved with water chlorination, see Susan W. Putnam and Jonathan Baert Weiner, "Seeking Safe Drinking Water," in John D. Graham and Jonathan Baert Weiner, eds., *Risk versus Risk: Tradeoffs in Protecting Health and the Environment* (Cambridge: Harvard University Press, 1995), pp. 124–48.

34. World Health Organization, "Water and Sanitation," Fact Sheet No. 112 (November 1996), http://www.who.int/inf-fs/en/fact112.html.

35. World Health Organization, *Global Water Supply and Sanitation Assessment 2000 Report*, Box 1.2, http://www.who.int/water_sanitation_health/Globassessment/GlobalTOC.htm.

36. Quoted in Anderson, "Cholera Epidemic Traced to Risk Miscalculation."

37. Joe Thornton, "The Case for a Chlorine Phase-Out" (presentation at the American Public Health Association Annual Meeting, November 11, 1992).

38. Carolyn Raffensperger and Joel Tickner, "Introduction: To Foresee and Forestall," in *Protecting Public Health and the Environment: Implementing the Precautionary Principle* (Washington, D.C.: Island Press, 1999), p. 4.

39. Ibid.; and Jordan and O'Riordan, "The Precautionary Principle in Contemporary Environmental Policy and Politics," p. 19.

40. For an overview of the Delaney Clause, see Michael Fumento, *Science Under Siege: Balancing Technology and the Environment* (New York: William Morrow & Co., 1993), pp. 54–57.

41. Quoted in Raffensperger and Tickner, "Introduction," pp. 4–5.

42. Quoted in Appendix B in *Protecting Public Health and the Environment*, pp. 357–58. The Bergen Declaration was agreed to at a meeting of the United Nations Economic Commission for Europe.

43. Ibid., p. 359.

44. European Commission, *Communication from the Commission on the Precautionary Principle* (Brussels, Commission of the European Communities, 2000).

45. Rio Declaration on Environment and Development, Principle 15, U.N. Doc. A/CONF.151/5/Rev.1 (1992).

46. Convention on Biological Diversity, Preamble, 1992, accessed at URL: http://www.biodiv.org/convention/articles.asp?lg=0&a=cbd-00.

47. Quoted in Raffensperger and Tickner, "Introduction," p. 6.

48. See International Joint Commission, *Sixth Biennial Report on Great Lakes Water Quality* (Washington, D.C.: International Joint Commission, April 1992).

49. Quoted in David Appell, "The New Uncertainty Principle," *Scientific American* (January 2001).

50. For an assessment of the threat posed by climate change, see chapter 1 in this volume. For a discussion of precautionary measures and global climate change, see Jonathan Adler et al., *Greenhouse Policy Without Regrets* (Washington, D.C.: Competitive Enterprise Institute, July 2000).

51. Cartagena Protocol on Biosafety, Article 4.

52. Ibid., preamble.

53. Ibid., Articles 10 and 11.

54. General Agreement on Tariffs and Trade, Article XX (h), (b).

55. Ibid.
56. See, for example, James M. Sheehan, *The Greening of Trade Policy* (Washington, D.C.: Competitive Enterprise Institute, November 1994), p. 29 (discussing interpretation of GATT Article XX by dispute resolution panels).
57. Daniel C. Esty, *Greening the GATT: Trade, Environment, and the Future* (Washington, D.C.: Institute for International Economics, 1994), p. 103.
58. Frank B. Cross, "Paradoxical Perils of the Precautionary Principle," *Washington and Lee Law Review*, vol. 53, no. 3 (1996), p. 860.
59. See World Back Press Release, *Bioengineering of Crops Could Help Feed the World: Crop Increases of 10–25 Percent Possible* (October 9, 1997), http://www.worldbank.org/html/cgiar/press/biopress.html.
60. John H. Barton, "Biotechnology, the Environment, and International Agricultural Trade," *Georgetown International Environmental Law Review*, vol. 9 (1996), pp. 95, 99.
61. Laura Tangley, "Engineering the Harvest," *U.S. News & World Report* (March 13, 2000), p. 46 (quoting Calestous Juma, a Kenyan adviser to the Harvard University Center for International Development and former executive secretary of the Convention on Biological Diversity).
62. Sam Kazman, "Deadly Overcaution: FDA's Drug Approval Process," *Journal of Regulation and Social Costs* (September 1990), p. 35.
63. This discussion is based on the Kazman article; ibid., pp. 47–48.
64. George M. Gray and John D. Graham, "Regulating Pesticides," in John D. Graham and Jonathan Baert Weiner, eds., *Risk versus Risk: Tradeoffs in Protecting Health and the Environment* (Cambridge: Harvard University Press, 1995), pp. 186–87.
65. Cross, "Paradoxical Perils of the Precautionary Principle," pp. 875–76.
66. Richard Tren and Roger Bate, *Malaria and the DDT Story* (London: Institute of Economic Affairs, 2001), pp. 36–37.
67. Ibid., p. 37.
68. Some argue that the development of resistance to DDT by mosquitoes led to a reduction in DDT use in developing nations. DDT, however, remained effective at mosquito control even after some resistance was developed; ibid., pp. 46–47.
69. Quoted in ibid., p. 46.
70. Amir Attaran et al., "Balancing Risks on the Backs of the Poor," *Nature Medicine*, vol. 6, no. 7 (July 2000), pp. 729–31.
71. Quoted in Ronald Bailey, "Greens vs. the World's Poor," *Reason Online* (November 29, 2000), http://www.reason.com/hod/rb112900.html.
72. Attaran, "Balancing Risks on the Backs of the Poor," p. 729.
73. Tren and Bate, *Malaria and the DDT Story*, p. 60.
74. Appendix A, *Protecting Public Health & the Environment*, pp. 353–55.
75. Nicholas Eberstadt, this volume, chapter 3, page 13.
76. Ibid., p. 13
77. See, for example, Susan L. Ettner, "New Evidence on the Relationship Between Income and Health," *Journal of Health Economics*, vol. 15 (1996), p. 67; John D. Graham et al., "Poorer Is Riskier," *Risk Analysis*, vol. 12, no. 3 (1992), pp. 333–37; and Ralph L. Keeney, "Mortality Risks Induced by Economic Expenditures," *Risk Analysis*, vol. 10, no. 1 (1990), pp. 147–59.
78. This phrasing is attributed to the late Aaron Wildavsky.
79. Holly L. Howe et al., "Annual Report to the Nation on the Status of Cancer (1973 Through 1998), Featuring Cancers with Recent Increasing Trends," *Journal of the National Cancer Institute*, vol. 93, no. 11 (June 6, 2001).

80. Ibid.
81. Richard Peto et al., *Mortality from Smoking in Developed Countries, 1950–2000* (Oxford: Oxford University Press, 1994).
82. Ibid.
83. See Seth W. Norton, "Property Rights, the Environment and Economic Well-Being," in Peter J. Hill and Roger E. Meiners, eds., *Who Owns the Environment?* (Lanham, Md.: Rowman & Littlefield, 1998), pp. 37, 45.
84. Cited in Indur Goklany, "Richer Is Cleaner," in Ronald Bailey, ed., *The True State of the Planet* (New York: The Free Press, 1995), p. 347.
85. See, generally, ibid. See also Indur Goklany, *Clearing the Air: The Real Story of the War on Air Pollution* (Washington, D.C.: Cato Institute, 1999).
86. Goklany, "Richer Is Cleaner," pp. 339, 341.
87. Goklany observes that while the "environmental transition" for drinking water and sanitation occurs "almost immediately as the level of affluence increases above subsistence," the transition appears to occur at approximately $1,375 per capita for fecal coliform and $3,280 and $3670 per capita for urban particulate matter and sulfur dioxide concentrations, respectively. Ibid. at p. 342. For a fuller treatment of the correlation between affluence and air quality, see Goklany, *Clearing the Air.*
88. Aaron Wildavsky, *But Is It True?* (1995), p. 428.
89. Cross, "Paradoxical Perils of the Precautionary Principle," p. 924.

Chapter 11

1. The reader might note that resources that are integrated via property rights into our market economy are used sustainably. Indeed, the famous bet between Julian Simons and Paul Ehrlich addressed exactly this issue. The question was whether resources were becoming more or less available. Ehrlich picked a market basket of five metals (copper, nickel, chromium, tin, and titanium). Ten years later, all of these metals had become more available (lower in price).
2. Garrett Hardin, "The Tragedy of the Commons," *Science*, vol. 162 (December 13, 1968), pp. 1243–48.
3. Ibid.
4. An exception to this rule is when all involved in using the resource share strong cultural bonds. Church groups, small communities, clubs—all may create cultural norms that constrain use. Such culturally protected commons have been extensively studied by Elinor Ostrom. See Governing the Commons: The Evolution of Institutions for Collective Action (New York: Cambridge University Press, 1990). Unfortunately, shared cultural values are less likely in the modern community, nor at the scale that many environmental problems exist.
5. This section is taken from "The Tragedy of the Commons Revisited: Politics vs. Private Property," by Randy T. Simmons, Fred L. Smith, Jr., and Paul Georgia (Center for Private Conservation Publication, Competitive Enterprise Institute, October 1996).
6. Ronald Coase, "The Problem of Social Cost," *The Firm, the Market, and the Law* (Chicago: University of Chicago Press, 1988).
7. This case is discussed in Robert J. Smith, "Privatizing the Environment," *Policy Review*, (spring, 1982), pp.11-50; and Thomas DiLorenzo *"Does Capitalism Cause Pollution?"* (1990), St. Louis, Washington University: Center for the Study of American Business, Contemporary Issues Series 38.
8. Quoted by Jorge E. Amador, "Take Back the Environment," *The Freeman* (August 1987), pp. 309–15.

9. Cited in Coase, "The Problem of Social Cost," p. 131.

10. Pierre Desrochers, "Eco-Industrial Parks: The Case for Private Planning," *The Independent Review*, Vol. V, No. 3, (Winter 2001).

11. For a complete discussion of private alternatives to political management of the ocean, see Kent Jeffrey's *Who Should Own the Oceans?* (Washington, D.C.: Competitive Enterprise Institute, 1991).

12. Coase, "The Problem of Social Cost," p. 131.

13. The recent surge in support for federalism in the United States opens the door for some form of state ecological waiver in the next decade. How federalism might be made a meaningful tool in the environmental field is discussed in two recent papers: Jonathan Adler, "Let Fifty Flowers Bloom," *Environmental Law Reporter* (forthcoming); Michael Greve, "Friends of the Earth, Foes of Federalism," *Duke Environmental Law and Policy Forum*, Vol. 12 (Fall 2001).

14. That EPA was a poorly designed agency which would eventually fail has long been argued. See, for example, Landy, Marc K., Roberts, Marc J., and Thomas, Stephen R. *E.P.A.: Asking the Wrong Questions*. Oxford: University Press, revised paperback edition, 1994.

15. The technologies used to protect against shoplifting are suggestive of what is needed—that is, the ability to unobtrusively tag property (in this case, plants or wildlife) in ways that reduce the likelihood of that property being stolen (poached).

16. Note that some oil fields are so large that it becomes very difficult, and costly, to reach agreement on a single unit. Nevertheless, this obstacle has been overcome through the development of water-wall "fences" that subdivide the pool into separate units.

17. Robert Stavins, letter to *Policy Review* (Summer 1989): pp. 95–96.

18. This approach is discussed as an alternative to government subsidization of various gasoline-alternative vehicles and there is a general discussion of this approach in Fred L. Smith, "Environmental Policy: A Free Market Proposal," *The Tulanian*, (Summer 1989).

INDEX
